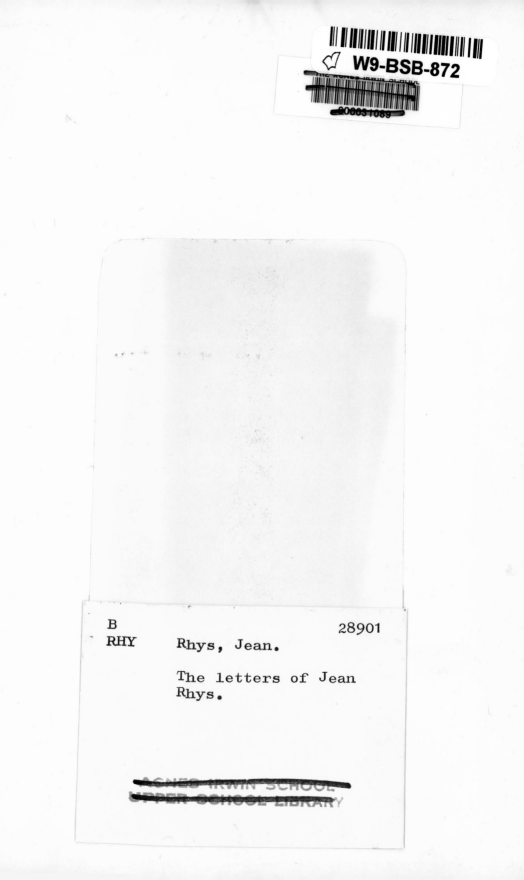

THE LETTERS OF

Jean Rhys

THE LETTERS OF

Jean Rhys

Selected and Edited by

Francis Wyndham and Diana Melly

Elisabeth Sifton Books

VIKING

ELISABETH SIFTON BOOKS • VIKING
Viking Penguin Inc.,
40 West 23rd Street,
New York, New York 10010, U.S.A.

Originally published in Great Britain
under the title *Jean Rhys Letters 1931–1966*

First American Edition
Published in 1984

LIBRARY OF CONGRESS CATALOGING IN PUBLICATION DATA
Rhys, Jean.
The letters of Jean Rhys.
Includes index.
1. Rhys, Jean—Correspondence.   2. Novelists, English—
20th century—Correspondence.   I. Wyndham, Francis.
II. Melly, Diana.   III. Title.
PR6035.H96Z48   1984   823'.912 [B]   83-40244
ISBN 0-670-42726-8

Printed in the United States of America
Set in Bembo

CONTENTS

ACKNOWLEDGMENTS

The editors owe an overwhelming debt of thanks to Madame Maryvonne Moerman, not only for making available her mother's letters to herself, her husband and her daughter, but also for her generous encouragement and diligent cooperation in every aspect of this book. They are also deeply grateful to McFarlin Library, The University of Tulsa, for allowing access to its Jean Rhys Collection, which includes letters to Selma Vaz Dias, Hans Egli, Phyllis Smyser, Morchard Bishop and Olwyn Hughes; to Diana Athill, for opening the Jean Rhys file at the office of André Deutsch containing letters to herself and Esther Whitby; to Dr R. Sauvan-Smith, for providing letters to Peggy Kirkaldy as well as a vivid memoir; to the Humanities Research Center, The University of Texas at Austin, for lending photo-copies of letters to Evelyn Scott, John Lehmann and Charles Osborne; to D. A. Callard (the biographer of Evelyn Scott), Mrs R. E. Smyser, Frances Linley and Eliot Bliss for useful information; to Mrs R. Kloegman, for deciphering and transcribing the original letters with the same flawless accuracy that she had shown when typing the manuscript of *Wide Sargasso Sea*; and to Susannah Clapp, for the invaluable help of her expert editorial advice.

INTRODUCTION
by Francis Wyndham

In her will Jean Rhys expressed the wish that no biography of her should be written unless authorised in her lifetime. I believe that her motive in imposing this posthumous ban (for none *had* been authorised before her death) was not so much a desire for secrecy as a dread of inaccuracy. It is true that she was a fiercely private person who took no pleasure in publicity; she had never wanted fame and did not particularly enjoy it when, late in life, a degree of it touched her. She firmly believed that an artist's work should be considered in separation from the facts of his or her life, even though the facts had provided the raw material for the work. But she was intelligent enough to know that having, as it were, entered the arena by allowing her books to be published, she could not expect altogether to avoid provoking some personal curiosity in the readers who admired them. What upset her – and increasingly so with age – was the falsity she detected in books written about people and places she had known, or set in periods she remembered. Her own life had been obscure; most of her contemporaries were dead; there would be little for a biographer to go on except for rumour and her novels. These, though based on her own experience, were essentially works of the imagination which transcended that experience, and to exaggerate the connection between her writing and her life would, she feared, confuse rather than enlighten an appreciation of the former. At the same time, the subject matter of her novels was sufficiently intriguing to attract an almost prurient interest in the source of their inspiration. To set the record straight she started an autobiography, but died before it was finished. *Smile, Please* covers her early life in Dominica up to the age of sixteen in vivid detail, but later the reminiscences become vaguer and they peter out altogether at about the year 1930.

After her death several authors approached her estate with requests for permission to write her "official" life. As her literary executor I felt bound by the terms of her will to discourage them as firmly as possible. I was often told: "It's no good – you will have to commission a biography in the end. If you don't, people will just go ahead anyhow, and without access to whatever genuine material there is they will have to rely on speculation and invention, and the result will be exactly what Jean hoped to avoid." Recognizing some truth in this, and alarmed by it, I felt trapped between two equally discouraging choices: to disobey Jean's instructions, or to follow them literally while running the risk of betraying their spirit. In search of a way out of the dilemma, I tentatively considered compiling a volume of her letters, which would be bound to provide a certain amount of biographical information and in which the information would be unassailably authentic – from Jean's point of view, at least – as it would be supplied by herself. Diana Melly, who had become a close friend of Jean's during the last years of her life, approved of my plan, and together we started to look for the necessary documents.

We expected the quest to be hard. People keep the letters of close friends and of famous people. Jean had few close friends, and some of those she had were dead; and her work was not widely known until the late 1960s, when she was nearly eighty. Her early books had been appreciated by a small, discriminating public, but with few exceptions the people among whom her life had been spent took no interest in that sort of writing. It was possible that none of her early letters had been kept. However, enough of them gradually accumulated for us to be able to form them first into a sequence and then a shape. I stopped worrying about "biographical information", which now seemed of incidental importance compared to the impressive self-portrait that the letters reveal and the insight they provide into the turbulent process of literary creation.

The self-portrait, though full and unsparing, is none the less incomplete: one thing that Jean could not know about herself is how she appeared to the outside world. What struck me most forcibly, when we finally met after a correspondence lasting nearly ten years, was her delicacy. Conversation with Jean was regulated by a sensitive tact which made clumsiness, embarrassment and misunderstanding out of the question, and cleared the way for confidence, honesty and fun. In my experience she was never exhausting and never a bore. An ill-educated neighbour in the remote Devon village where she lived had taken her for a witch, and it is true that the charm she exerted made one feel as though a spell had been cast over the occasion, lifting it out of the social sphere into another more disturbing and significant. Yet there was a cosy side to her personality which exorcised any suggestion of the sinister. She confessed to being an egotist, but she did not seem to me to be crudely self-centred. Her dislike of malice was so great, and her standard of loyalty so high, that she avoided speaking of mutual friends at any length for fear of provoking either unkindness or indiscretion in her interlocutor. On my visits she always tried to talk about my concerns, but that was not my reason for coming to see her, and if we spent most of our time together discussing her life and work it was because those were the subjects that interested me.

In old age Jean often said that, could the choice have been offered her, she would have preferred a life of only average happiness to the greatest literary triumphs. Yet these letters bear witness to the single-minded seriousness with which she approached the task of writing. They also illustrate the symptoms, if not the cause, of her chronic sadness and deep dissatisfaction. For most of her existence she was afflicted by two disabilities. She suffered from congenital physical fatigue which made many practical activities insurmountably difficult, and therefore had to be plaintively dependent on other people, whereas her true nature was proud, combative and individualistic. Friends, lovers and relations with sturdier constitutions were always distressed, often irritated and sometimes repelled by the air of helpless passivity with which she made her exigent demands: no doubt she was as distressed, irritated and repelled by this quality in herself as any of them.

More mysteriously, ever since the end of her first love affair she had also been cursed by a kind of spiritual sickness – a feeling of belonging nowhere, of being ill at ease and out of place in her surroundings wherever these happened to be, a stranger in an indifferent, even hostile, world. She may have wanted to think that this crippling sense of alienation was merely that of a native West Indian exiled in a cold foreign land, but in fact she believed that the whole earth had become inhospitable to her after the shock of that humdrum betrayal. All that had happened was that a kind, rather fatherly businessman, who had picked up a pretty chorus girl with a disconcertingly vague manner, decided after a year or so to pension her off. When speaking of it years later, Jean always said: "I was very stupid. I didn't understand. Nobody had warned me."

In one of her books she quotes the title of a popular song: "I'm Going to Lock My Heart and Throw Away the Key". The phrase adequately suggests the complex emotional amputation which Jean performed on herself to prevent any recurrence of the grief and hurt which had overwhelmed her then. Jean, who was a loving and generous person, made up her mind to be selfish and cold. But of course this willed transformation was never complete, and like a bungled sex-change operation it resulted in confusion of identity. The generosity and the capacity for love remained, but were denied complete freedom of expression; the ruthlessness, which should have sustained her throughout a career of happy hedonism and shrewd acquisitiveness, was too half-hearted to succeed. The tension set up by these conflicting impulses condemned her to a personal life made miserable by frustration, but also stimulated her to develop her gift for writing with a courageous and stubborn dedication until it achieved a rare artistic purity.

I should make it clear that this collection, far from being "complete", is purposely and unavoidably selective. The letters begin in 1931, taking up Jean's story roughly at the point where it was abandoned in *Smile, Please*. We have found only two written earlier, both tantalizingly torn from their contexts: one to her first husband Jean Lenglet, and one to Edward Garnett who helped her get her first novel published. Read in isolation, they make only partial sense, and there seemed little point in reproducing them. The letters are printed in chronological order, ending on March 9th, 1966, at the moment when she diffidently acknowledged that the long struggle to finish *Wide Sargasso Sea* was over at last. It was published seven months later, in October 1966 and had an outstanding critical success, winning two awards – the Royal Society of Literature and the W. H. Smith. Her four earlier novels and a portion of her first book of stories were reissued soon afterwards, and two new collections of stories appeared. Each publication further enhanced the reputation which had been re-established by *Wide Sargasso Sea*. Jean found herself a minor celebrity: in 1978 she went to Buckingham Palace to be given the CBE by the Queen. But little of the excitement of such events is conveyed in the letters she wrote at the time, and as her social circle grew larger, her correspondence became less revealing: either more formal (she made a point of answering every fan letter she received) or more allusive ("It was lovely seeing you last week. Do try to come again soon. All news when we meet"). To the correspondents who kindly made available to us a great many letters written after our closing date we convey both our gratitude and our regret. Of those letters in our possession which fall within the limits of our chosen time span, we have included a little over half.

Minor cuts have been made to avoid unnecessary repetitions (though many repetitions have been retained, when they seem to indicate a crucial obsession on the part of the writer), and the occasional irrelevance or banality. Cuts within a paragraph are indicated by [. . .], and when a whole paragraph has been omitted the same bracketted dots are placed alone to mark where the paragraph would have begun. When any part of a date at the head of a letter is given in square brackets, it has been supplied by the editors. Jean's punctuation and spelling have been followed exactly, except in rare instances when an absent-minded aberration has resulted in an obvious mistake which obscures the sense.

After the publication of *Wide Sargasso Sea* life became more pleasant for Jean in many ways: she made new friends whom she valued, had her cottage made warmer and more comfortable, and enjoyed yearly holidays in London as well as one in Venice, where she had never been before. But she often told people that she felt like a ghost.

She died on May 14th, 1979. For me the ghost of Jean Rhys is not the hunted, lonely woman who figures in her novels, nor the restless spirit so often near despair who wrote these brave, bitter letters, but the slant-eyed siren with whom one could enjoy the full intensity of a treat as with no one else – those sacred moments of frivolity (an old tune, a new scent, a perfect cocktail, a wonderful joke) which for her nearly made life worth living.

SUMMARY OF THE MAIN EVENTS IN JEAN RHYS'S
LIFE BEFORE THE LETTERS START

1890   She is born Ella Gwendoline Rees Williams on August 24th in Roseau,
        Dominica, West Indies. Her father, a Welsh doctor, had not been long
        on the island but her mother, whose maiden name was Lockhart,
        belonged to a family who had lived there many years. She had two
        brothers and a younger sister.

1907   She leaves Dominica in the summer, travelling to England with her
        father's sister. She goes to the Perse School for Girls in Cambridge,
        where she spends four terms.

1909   She spends two terms at the Academy of Dramatic Art. When her
        father dies in the summer she refuses to return to Dominica and joins a
        touring company of the musical comedy *Our Miss Gibbs* as a chorus
        girl, taking the stage name of Vivien Gray.

1910   She has her first love affair, with a much older man who leaves her after
        a year and pensions her off (as described in *Voyage in the Dark*).

1919   Anxious to break her financial dependence on her first lover, she leaves
        England for Holland to marry Jean Lenglet, a Dutch-French *chansonnier*
        and journalist whom she had met briefly in London in 1917. They move
        to Paris.

1920   Their son William dies at the age of three weeks. They go to Vienna
        where Lenglet works as secretary to a Japanese officer at the Inter-allied
        Disarmament Conference.

1922   They return to Paris via Budapest. Birth of their daughter Maryvonne.

1923   Mrs Adam (see page 65) introduces her to Ford Madox Ford who
        encourages her writing. Lenglet is arrested on a charge of illegal entry
        into France and of offending against current regulations in Vienna.
        After imprisonment in Fresnes he is extradited to Holland. Meanwhile,
        she has been befriended by Ford and Stella Bowen and (apparently
        encouraged by Stella) has become Ford's lover (as described in
        Postures/Quartet).

1924   Her first published story, "Vienne", appears in Ford's magazine *the
        transatlantic review* under the nom de plume Jean Rhys.

1927   *The Left Bank and other stories*, with an introduction by Ford Madox
        Ford, is published by Jonathan Cape. She comes to England to find a
        publisher for *Postures/Quartet* which Cape had rejected as he thought it
        libelled Ford. Edward Garnett (who had quarrelled with Ford over

Joseph Conrad) sends it to Chatto & Windus. She meets Leslie Tilden-Smith, who becomes her literary agent.

1928   Publication of *Postures/Quartet* by Chatto & Windus.

1930   *After Leaving Mr Mackenzie* is published by Jonathan Cape.

1931   She is living in London with Leslie Tilden-Smith.

A BRIEF
PUBLISHING HISTORY

The Left Bank and other stories,
with a preface by Ford Madox Ford
Jonathan Cape, London, 1927. Harper & Brothers, New York, 1927.

Postures (later known as *Quartet*)
Chatto & Windus, London, 1928 (as *Quartet*). Simon & Schuster, New York, 1929. Reissued (as *Quartet*) by André Deutsch, London, 1969, and Harper & Row, New York, 1971.

After Leaving Mr Mackenzie
Jonathan Cape, London, 1930. Alfred A. Knofp, New York, 1931. Reissued by André Deutsch, London, 1969, and Harper & Row, New York, 1972.

Voyage in the Dark
Constable, London, 1934. William Morrow, New York, 1935. Reissued by André Deutsch, London, 1967, and by W. W. Norton, New York, 1968.

Good Morning, Midnight
Constable, London, 1939. Harper & Row, New York, 1970. Reissued by André Deutsch, London, 1967.

Wide Sargasso Sea
André Deutsch, London, 1966. W. W. Norton, New York, 1967.

Tigers are Better Looking
(Containing "Till September Petronella", "The Day They Burned the Books", "Let Them Call it Jazz", "Tigers are Better Looking", "Outside the Machine", "The Lotus", "A Solid House", "The Sound of the River", and nine stories from *The Left Bank*.)
André Deutsch, London, 1968. Harper & Row, New York, 1974.

"I Spy a Stranger" and "Temps Perdi"
Penguin Modern Stories, London, 1969.

Sleep it Off, Lady
(Containing "Pioneers, Oh, Pioneers", "Goodbye Marcus, Goodbye Rose", "The Bishop's Feast", "Heat", "Fishy Waters", "Overture and Beginners Please", "Before the Deluge", "On Not Shooting Sitting Birds", 'Kikimora", "Night Out 1925", "The Chevalier of the Place Blanche", "The Insect

World", "Rapunzel, Rapunzel", "Who Knows What's Up in the Attic?", "Sleep it Off, Lady", and "I Used to Live Here Once".)

André Deutsch, London, 1976. Harper & Row, New York, 1976.

Smile, Please

André Deutsch, London, 1979. Harper & Row, New York, 1979.

PART ONE

Leslie

(1931–1945)

March 1st [1931]
94 Elgin Crescent
London w11

Dear Miss Kirkaldy,

I was most awfully pleased to have your letter and to know that you like my book[2]. It gives one a very nice feeling, you know, to get a letter like yours – and I can assure you that I don't get so many as all that!

I should be very pleased if we could meet. I shall be in London for the next few weeks at least, and shall be delighted if we could arrange something.

Yours sincerely
Jean Rhys

1. *Born Margaret Mansfield Jacks in 1891, she was educated at Bedales and married first to Lt Partridge of the Warwickshire Regiment, who died at the end of the First World War, and later to Tom Kirkaldy, from whom she was divorced in the early 1930s. She died in 1958. One of her closest friends has provided the following pen portrait: "Peggy's personality was highly complex. She could be overwhelmingly kind and compassionate or cuttingly cruel. Shifts of mood were as sudden as a summer storm. When she made wit she was like a rapier-blade flashing in the sun: when she made fun it was earthy and Rabelaisian. She could clown. She could make you laugh so it hurt. When she came into a crowded room the lights went up like obedient servants: a tinselly, glittering halo appeared. Had she lived in the eighteenth century she would almost certainly have had her salon. It must be admitted that she was a bit of a lion-hunter but she did it well and some of her captives roared to real purpose. Highly strung she certainly was and somewhat brittle. Her emotional reactions would be hair-triggered, particularly in the advance or defence of her very strongly held opinions. Fools she could not and would not suffer gladly. There were times perhaps when she made them smart a little too severely. She showed a sad tendency to drop her friends when so inclined, usually for no other reason than they failed to rise to her own intellectual level, or disappointed her with an unexpectedly poor talent. She was an intellectual snob and her repartee was devastating. Writers seemed to be her natural friends: Jean Rhys, Dorothy Richardson, Elizabeth Bowen, Osbert Sitwell, Jocelyn Brooke, Denton Welch and others. Her knowledge of literature was encyclopaedic and one wonders why with her many gifts she failed as a writer herself. She tried hard but abortively. Maybe some deeply cerebral instinct warned her of probable failure, and such a thing was just not to be borne."*

2. After Leaving Mr Mackenzie.

TO PEGGY KIRKALDY

Sunday [March 23rd, 1931]
Elgin Crescent

My dear Mrs Kirkaldy,

The cocktails did buoy me up – I should say so! I felt very joyous.

I've been thinking about the Broads – I should love to be able to manage it – and to visit you at your cottage.

I've been working pretty hard the last week. Perhaps I'll have some luck and make some money.

Meanwhile would you come and see me one day this week?

On Wednesday say about half past four?

I'm afraid I haven't got a telephone – but if I don't hear from you to the contrary I'll expect you. I do hope you'll be able to come.　　　Yours

Jean Rhys

P.S. Will you (if you do come) ring the middle bell? JR

TO PEGGY KIRKALDY　　　　　　　　　　　　　　　　*[May 4th, 1931]*
Elgin Crescent

My dear Peggy,

Don't forget that you're coming to see me tomorrow night – about seven?

Isn't this rain ghastly? Incredible and fantastic. Supposing that it went on for ever. Never stopped.

A slow cautious Deluge.

Yesterday Leslie[1] and I went to Cambridge. It poured. We walked around the Backs or backs[2] and said How lovely. We went into Kings College chapel for a bit.

The whole darned time it never stopped drizzling.

Leslie bought me a felt hat (the worst yet) and a powder bowl. I bought him a tie.

I'd entirely forgotten Cambridge except bits every now and again.

It's rather a darling place I think don't you.

À bientôt – as they say.　　　　　　　　　　　　　　　Yours

Jean

1. *Leslie Tilden-Smith, then aged forty-six, literary agent and publisher's reader (mainly for Hamish Hamilton). To some extent the model for Mr Horsfield in* After Leaving Mr Mackenzie, *Leslie became Jean's second husband in 1932 after her divorce from Jean Lenglet.*

2. *Grounds on the River Cam at the back of certain Cambridge colleges: the capital B is correct.*

TO EVELYN SCOTT　　　　　　　　　　　　　　　　*June 23rd [1931]*
(MRS JOHN METCALFE)[1]　　　　　　　　　c/o L. Tilden-Smith Esq
94 Elgin Crescent

My dear Mrs Metcalfe,

I had your letter about "After Leaving Mr Mackenzie" this morning.

Probably you can imagine what great pleasure it gave me. Thank you for writing. . . .

I like Mackenzie better than anything I have done yet, and I am hoping that it will have some luck in America where it is to be published by Knopf on the 26th of this month. Both the books I wrote before, "The Left Bank" and "Quartet", were published in America (the first by Harper's and the other by Simon & Schuster) but neither of them did much though they had some kind reviews.

I am always being told that until my work ceases being "sordid and depressing" I haven't much chance of selling.

I used to find this rather stupid but through much repetition I have come half to believe that it must be so. You can imagine therefore how much your letter pleased me and how grateful I am to you for writing it.

I am working on another novel now[2], but it is going rather slowly and it certainly is not likely to be published before next year.

Yours very sincerely

Jean Rhys

1. *Jean was replying to the following letter, written on board the* Aquitania *on June 9th, 1931: "On our way back from London to America, my husband and I are carrying with us, as our happiest recent impression, the pleasure we had in reading* After Leaving Mr Mackenzie. *Within the circumference chosen by the author, it seems to us a perfect book. The quiet irony kept us in perpetual chuckles. The beautiful and exact measure of character delighted us. The flawless ending, which so completely avoided the sentimentalization of a situation full of poignant suggestion, was a joy. We feel grateful for the pleasure given us by so fine an artist as the author is and cannot resist expressing this while the mood is fresh. I hope you will overlook the presumption of a stranger and, perhaps, be kind enough to let me know whether or not you are contemplating another book soon and whether this one has already been published in America. I feel so keenly that stumbling upon* After Leaving Mr Mackenzie *in a Salisbury Library (Smith's) was an important discovery that I should like to spread the good news. I want to talk about it, and I shall, and I wonder if you would be willing to give me more data about your work. I realize my previous lack of acquaintance with it may be shocking ignorance. On the other hand it may be that you have never essayed America. My husband and I are writers and at least have the acquaintance which should learn (if it does not already know) of the existence of such a rare, subtle and sensitive talent. I am afraid this is effusive; but that is the effect of your own beautiful restraint and the soundness and purity of every line in your book." Evelyn Scott had published a book of verse, an autobiography and six novels of which* The Wave: Narratives of the Civil War *had been highly acclaimed. Born Elsie Dunn in 1883, she was brought up in Tennessee among the Southern aristocracy. At the age of twenty she eloped to Brazil with Frederick Creighton Wellman, who was twenty-four years her senior and had been married twice before. They changed their names to Cyril Kay Scott and Evelyn Scott. With a vivid personality, she became a leading figure among the bohemian intelligentsia in Greenwich Village throughout the 1920s, interested in every "modern" movement in politics, literature and art. She left Scott for the painter Owen Merton, father of*

Thomas, later the Trappist monk and poet (whose jealous rages as an infant brought the love affair to an end). Since 1926 she had been living with John Metcalfe (they married in 1930). Metcalfe's best works are his brilliant "tales of unease" collected in The Smoking Leg *(1925) and* Judas *(1931). He was in poor health throughout the 1930s and his increasing depression culminated in a nervous breakdown.*

2. Voyage in the Dark, *which was not published till 1934.*

[1933]
197 Adelaide Road
London NW3

TO EVELYN SCOTT

My dear Evelyn,

I've been away from London for a month at a place called Rottingdean near Brighton. I'm still there but am leaving tomorrow or think so.

Rottingdean is a nice place, one street, beach, downs, foals playing about on downs, larks etc. I expect Jack[1] knows it. (The larks foals and downs are just outside).

I came down here crazy with depression my dear (Not Possible! you exclaim) and really feel better now.

Haven't touched a drop for a month. Won't it be fine when I do. It ought to give me a kick. A drop of drink I mean.

I have a little rather stuffy room over a teaplace. Hung with lace curtains it is but there's a feather bed and I've done a lot of sleeping.

Berlin fell through. Leslie's friend who is a Jew has packed up and gone to America or is going. There was so little money and I wanted to get away from London so badly that I chose a month here instead of a week in Holland.

So you see – I'm so horribly sorry things are rotten in America too. Sorry for myself too. For everybody. But it *can't* go on. It's impossible and incredible – Evelyn I wish I could get hold of Eva Gay[2] –

About my books. The thing I'm writing – It's a rum business. If I could make one more effort I could finish it I think. One more – You know – You do know don't you?

But I've gone so dead I don't know whether I'm mad or everybody else is. But one of us is – I will not go on with this gruesome conversation.

I've read today The Daily Mail, Evening News, Evening Standard, a novel by P. G. Wodehouse called Mulliners Night, bits of a thing called "Woman" by somebody Ludovici[3] (who is rather an old dear).

The reason being that I'm not so very well thank God and as usual on these occasions have to lie down, and have no books with me.

Well. I've lain there and eaten two huge meals and read – as above – so feel a bit shaken –

Never mind, I'm relying on the kick I'll get out of my first drink.

Leslie has been down at weekends. He'd send his love if he were here I know. And so do I.

And my best wishes from the bottom of me 'eart to you both for every sort of luck.

Jean

1. *John Metcalfe.*

2. *Novel by Evelyn Scott, published in America in 1933 and in England in early 1934.*

3. Woman: A Vindication, *by Anthony Mario Ludovici (1923).*

TO EVELYN SCOTT

Sunday, February 18th [1934]
23 Brunswick Square
London WC1

My dear Evelyn,

Thank you for your letter (letters) more than I can say. You don't know how dam pleased I am when you write. My dear about the book (still Voyage in the Dark because I can't get another title tho I wish I could) it is still being typed. Leslie had an awful rush of work at Harpers end of last month and beginning of this.

I, of course, couldn't resist fiddling about and making alterations.

However it is really in its last stages. Leslie reckons to be able to finish the typing in ten days to a fortnight.

I don't know what I feel about the blessed thing. I had the horrors about it and about everything for a bit. I mean the complete futility. Nightmarish. But I expect that was my liver and lights giving way under the strain of two bottles of wine per day. Also the weather – more like hell than anything you can imagine – a yellow fog very cold. Blasted people wailing hymns outside.

You feel as if you're being slowly suffocated. At least I do.

Here I may say we still are in two Bloomsbury bed sitting rooms. And I don't see us getting away in a hurry either. Never mind. This morning (it was rather funny) a huge coloured lady presented herself while I was still in bed and demanded her rent. Very chic she was, pearl earrings and everything (and I believe a compatriot). Leslie was in the bathroom.

She wanted to be paid on the nail "Can Mr Smith give me a cheque?" she said. "No" I said, "I shouldn't think so". "Why not?" she said.

There was no answer to that so I just looked vague.

"Perhaps", she said, "Mr Smith could let me have so much." "Well" I said, "it'll be a bit difficult today". "Why?" she said. A forthright creature. I said "Well you see today is Sunday". She said *Why* should Sunday be different from any other day" and I looked very shocked. So she retreated.

Isn't it funny me upholding the Sabbath?

This is a rum house. The West Indian lady is the late owner. She's just sold the house to two German Jewish ladies (born in Wales and very sympathique.) I suppose she wanted to collect before departing.

I don't know why I'm writing all this rot as I wanted to tell you about my book.

Well Evelyn I don't know if I've got away with it. I don't know. It's written almost entirely in words of one syllable. Like a kitten mewing perhaps. The big idea – well I'm blowed if I can be sure what it is. Something to do with time being an illusion I think. I mean that the past exists – side by side with the present, not behind it; that what was – is.

I tried to do it by making the past (the West Indies) very vivid – the present dreamlike (downward career of girl) – starting of course piano and ending fortissimo.

Perhaps I was simply trying to describe a girl going potty.

You see I don't even know myself and am really trying to argue it out with myself – anyway it isn't very important. I didn't want to use any stunts and haven't. But I have no self confidence – have cut too much and worried over things that were already done as well as I could do them with my one syllable mind. So there you are.

(I expect I've made it sound even pottier than it is).

I'm reading "Eva Gay" which Leslie got for me. I can't tell you how I admire it – Evan's story especially I like. Gould gave it a fine review in the Observer which of course you've seen and Leslie and I were as pleased as Punch to see that it had been recommended by the Book Guild. Evelyn – I hope you make some money out of it. My God what a fine writer you are.

Last week I spent most of my time in bed. Read "Hunger" by Knut Hamsun that gave me a great kick. Translated 1899 and might have been written yesterday. Also reread parts of Escapade[1] & Spring Darkness[2].

(Tell Jack for me how longing I am to see his new book).

That's all for now dearie –

Jean

Leslie sends love to you both. Lovat Dickson are advertising second large impression printing of Eva

1. *Memoirs by Evelyn Scott, first published 1923.*

2. *Novel by John Metcalfe (1928).*

Sunday, June 10th [1934]
Luxor, Pharaoh's Island
Shepperton, Middlesex

TO EVELYN SCOTT

My dear Evelyn,

Jack turned up to visit us just before we left Brunswick Square – that's about a fortnight ago. We were awfully glad to see him and find him looking better – when Leslie saw him in London last week he was going to the school of Tropical Medicine for a week. My Lord I *was* glad to see a friendly face – I'd been feeling as down as hell. The book is having decidedly stormy weather.

I minded more than I would have believed possible as I've always prided myself on being more or less indifferent to what most people thought about a book once it was finished. Self deception obviously – because after Cape had written and told me how grey I was, without light or shade, how much people would dislike it, that he couldn't hope to sell it even as well as Mackenzie etc and so on, then Hamish Hamilton wanted it cut so much that it would become meaningless.

Well etc and so on – 'nuf details. My dear I really began to feel as if I were crazy or wrong headed or something. Do you know the feeling.

Sadleir of Constable[1] likes it and has written very kindly about it but he also wants it cut. Not of course his own taste he explains but to please prospective readers.

Evelyn I don't know what to do. I suppose I shall have to give in and cut the book and I'm afraid it will make it meaningless. The worst is that it is precisely the last part which I am most certain of that will have to be mutilated.

My dear it is so mad – really it is not a disgusting book – or even a very grey book. And I *know* the ending is the only possible ending.

I know if I tinker around with it I'll spoil it, without helping myself a bit, from the being popular point of view. Oh Lordy Lord.

Well I won't bore you any more with my troubles. I wish you were here. I'd ask you to read it and tell me if I am mentally lopsided. I mean more so than is necessary.

The worst is that all objections will probably hold good for America and as they can't get at me to parleyvoo and I haven't got an agent who cares a tinkers D what happens to my books I fear the result there also.

Never mind.

The grass is green

The rose is red

God bless King George's

    Noble head

In the days of my youth all the young girls of Roseau Town had confession albums. Your favourite poem? That was a favourite verse. (Meaning George IV).

I expect you can imagine what Luxor looks like. Do you remember "Upway" on the Wye? Well, "Luxor" is the same sort of thing only a bit more comfortable. Pharoah's island this place is and we've got "Rameses" and "Ishta" on one side of us and "Assouan" on the other side and "Thebes" over the way.

There's even a what's the name a picture of Osiris on the lavatory door which I think disrespectful and going a bit far. Write soon.

Jean

---

1. Michael Sadleir, publisher and novelist, best known for Fanny by Gaslight (1940). Constable published Voyage in the Dark and Good Morning, Midnight (1939).

TO EVELYN SCOTT

17 Bury Street
London SW1

My dear Evelyn,

We were awfully glad to hear from you. Hope you're getting a bit more established now.

I've been feeling damnable lately what with my wrist and everything – too much at a full stop to write a letter even or I'd have answered before.

But Maryvonne[1] has turned up to visit me. She is so tall and gawky and sweet and sings so loudly all over the place that she's bringing me to life again. She is of a hopeful disposition I notice, spent hours yesterday making a contraption with chalk and cotton wool to clean white shoes with! Hopeful and practical. So unlike me thank God.

We're actually moving away at the end of the week too! That prospect also fills me with new life. We've bought a car for £12.10 (sharing it with someone else) but it does go all right and we're planning to hitch it on to a caravan and go to Wales.

Wish us luck and that it doesn't rain.

Thanks for the press cutting – it's kind of Mr Gregory[2] to read me to the assembled school. (But I had to laugh too Evelyn).

I can't write anything except an interminable short story which I will certainly never sell.

Perhaps I'll get to feel better and more courageous in a week or two.

Love from Leslie and myself.

Jean

1. *Maryvonne Lenglet (born 1922). Jean's daughter by her first marriage to Jean Lenglet. After the divorce it was agreed that Maryvonne should stay in Holland for her schooling and spend the holidays in England with her mother. This arrangement continued until the outbreak of the war when she chose to remain with her father in Holland.*

2. *The American poet, Horace Gregory (see postscript to letter written on March 7th, 1964, page 255).*

TO EVELYN SCOTT

[December 1935]
St James's Hotel
Torquay, Devonshire

My dear Evelyn,

I was so glad to hear from you. I wanted to write all about how glad and why.

But it's so cold in this dam place that I can't think of anything except how cold I am and cold in general and that cold is hell and hell cold etc etc.

There are radiators around but they don't work except on Sundays – then they all make a hell of a row and become lukewarm, but Monday it's all gone again.

I've only been here one Sunday and shan't be here next (touch wood cross my fingers and spit). The radio is playing "Give me my boots and saddle" and I think it's a fine song.

Torquay is pretty though in a curious Victorian way a bit smug. But the seagulls are not smug or the fishing boats or the one or two fishermen around.

All the same I'm not cracked over Devonshire or Cornwall either.

I thought Wales lovely in parts – really lovely and wild but perhaps that was only because I'd made up my mind it was going to be lovely.

No I don't think so. It is really lovely –

But Evelyn to go back to the start of my letter – I loved hearing from you. I wish you'd write and you were coming to London and to see us on any old day whatsoever – but I do understand that you mayn't be able to or mayn't feel like London. As for the drawbacks of trying to stop drinking – well I know a little about that too!!

But I've been rather at the end of myself lately – a terrible "three quarters dead" feeling – a very lonely feeling and believe me your letter was welcome.

I ought to be rather pleased really, Leslie has got hold of some money in the usual way I mean somebody else has died[1] (I always think that alone is enough to prove how rotten the whole system is. Never mind.) It's fine not to be so terribly poor for a bit – and we're supposed to be going away for a long holiday early next year. We'll go to the West Indies a long way round via Spain. That's the present idea – I suppose going back to Dominica is foolhardy but I want to so much – I can't help risking it. You can imagine the wild and fantastic plans and hopes. Well, it hasn't come off yet. So touch wood, cross my fingers etc.

Love from
Jean

It's good news about Jack's book[2] – I wish it luck.

1. *Leslie Tilden-Smith's father had died.*

2. *John Metcalfe's novel* Foster-Girl *was published in 1936.*

TO EVELYN SCOTT

February 16th 1936
17 Bury Street

My dear Evelyn,

I was so glad to get your letter and apologise for not having answered before, but Leslie and I are departing next Wednesday. Everything has been left to the last moment and we are in the most ghastly state of muddle and rush – especially as the fuse which lights the whole house has gone and we are having to pack by candle-light today. We are leaving the flat, and everything has to be put away, stored, and so on.

Leslie is sending the poem on tonight[1], with author's address enclosed. He is asking Grigson to return it to New York if not suitable.

I should have liked so much to have seen you. I am awfully sorry it was so hopeless.

We may be coming back via New York if the cash lasts out, so could you let us know your address. Hotel St Antoine, Castries, St Lucia, BWI, will find us (I believe it's the only big hotel in Lucia in case you lose this letter) until round about the middle of April.

We hope Jack is feeling better, and again wish the book the best of luck.

The first week we shall be in Paris and Holland, as I want to see Maryvonne. We actually sail from Southampton on the *Cuba* (French line) on February 25th. I am awfully happy about it really, but so damned tired at the present moment that I hardly know what I am saying or doing. (I wish you could see our illumination. We have numerous candles stuck in the top of a biscuit tin, wax is over-flowing all over the place, and the whole effect is slightly spectral.)

Our permanent address is care of Leslie's bank – National Provincial Bank, Ltd, 88 Cromwell Road, SW7.

With love and best of luck from us both.

Jean

1. *The poem was almost certainly by the Southern writer Lola Ridge, who had been encouraged by her great friend Evelyn Scott to submit her work to the magazine* New Verse, *edited by Geoffrey Grigson. It was not accepted.*

TO EVELYN SCOTT

[1936]
"Hampstead"
Dominica, British West Indies

My dear Evelyn,

This is the loveliest place you can imagine – everything about it OK and just as I'd hoped (except the name. I mean Hampstead – however am getting used to that). Also several (many) years steady drinking hasn't made me calm about cockroaches I notice. Never mind everything else is fine.

It's four and a half hours journey from Roseau (by sea in a vile little launch) so nobody can get at me.

We've got sea on one side and mountains on the other – a beach with white sand, a good pool in the river, a nice girl to look after us, Dora is her name, etc etc.

The place is the Portsmouth side of the island. I don't know if your son ever got down here – it's quite cut off from the other. There's no road from Roseau to Portsmouth as the two places detest each other and don't want one – that is so West Indian – everybody hates everybody else. But always for political reasons not moral. Such a lovely change.

The wonderful thing is to wake up and know that nobody can get at you – nobody.

You can walk all day and meet about four people – lovely lovely lovely. I'm getting almost sane again – though I felt awfully tired when I first got here –

28

could hardly move – a nice fatigue but a bit as if one were dying of opened veins in a hot bath. Such a beautiful place to die in – what the devil more could anybody want? However I feel brisker already and hope to be bouncing with energy soon.

The lady to the right (Calibishee)[1] has already asked us to lunch and done her war dance at me. (Tomahawk in hand, smile on face). The lady to the left (Melville Hall) has also asked us to lunch. (Both ladies complete with gentlemen right and left figurative.) She's much milder – but adores Beverley Nichols and talked about books till I wanted to scream – or say Merde or something. Instead I agreed with everything she said God help me – and was miserable all next day.

The Calibishee lady is by way of being literary. She wrote a book which was offered to Hamish Hamilton and declined. The readers report (signed) was sent to her – so can you wonder that she had us to lunch double quick. I could see that she thought it was all my fault, because she was nice to Leslie and has already sent him a long novel to report on. ("I know it is *unpardonable* to bother a man on holiday but I should be so grateful if etc etc").

I hear Leslie clacking away on the typewriter like anything so all is well. She's going to England next week thank God.

We met Liam O'Flaherty[2] in Martinique also typing away for dear life and delighted with the West Indies, the only place left not written up he said. Also Somerset Maugham has been here[3] and (rather funny) the port officials tried to stop him from landing because he was rather shabby and came on a sloop. Enormous scandal with ramifications and frills. Roseau is still talking about it. Then there's a "lady writer" staying at Lady Nichols boarding house so whoops dearie now we shan't be long –

I'm awfully jealous of this place (as you gather no doubt) I can't imagine anybody writing about it, daring to, without loving it – or living here twenty years, or being born here. And anyway I don't want strangers to love it except very few whom I'd choose – most sentimental. (But they *are* a bit patronising you know.) However I've an idea that what with rain, cockroaches, and bad roads etc Dominica will protect itself from vulgar loves.

There's a man called Thaly[4] who has written some poems that aren't bad. Some lines aren't bad. But he's French – and coloured –

Forgive this long letter Evelyn. I never write long letters to anybody else or write at all if I can help it.

I hope we'll come to New York. I want to awfully.

We'll decide for certain within the next week or so.

But I don't want to think about going away yet –

Jean

1. *Presumably Calibishee and Melville Hall were the names of the houses to the right and left of Hampstead.*

2. *Irish novelist and short story writer, author of* The Informer *(filmed in 1935) and* Famine *(1937).*

3. In December 1935 Maugham had travelled with Gerald Haxton from New York via Haiti to the penal colony of St Laurent du Maroni in French Guiana, researching the background for his novel Christmas Holiday.

4. Daniel Thaly, author of Nostalgies Francaises *(1913),* L'Ile et le Voyage: petite odyssée d'un poète lointain *(1923),* Chants de l'Atlantique *and* Sous le Ciel des Antilles *(1928) and* Héliotrope *or* Les Amants Inconnus *(1932).*

TO EVELYN SCOTT

August 10th [1936]
7 Knaresborough Place
London sw5

My dear Evelyn,

I should have answered your letter long ago. I was waiting for a spot of peace and quiet. We've been looking for a flat furniture etc ever since we got back.

I've certainly got the peace and quiet now. Am anchored in a nursing home off the Cromwell Road of all terrible streets. Do you know it? Earl's Court way – very strong very respectable.

My foot is really behaving very badly indeed. If they cut it off it would save a lot of trouble – and am sure it would add to my chic –

I'm afraid I didn't wire any apologies my dear. I was feeling wretchedly ill the morning we left and not at all apologetic.

But I asked Leslie to wire my love and thanks to you and he added the apologies.

As they were necessary I can only send them all over again.

It was stupid of me to go off the deep end. (I should have waited till I got home like all nice people do!) But honestly I was feeling damned awful that evening – and I still think that there was a lot of antagonism flying around – (I mean Reactions weren't being entirely Satisfactory). However if one made a scene every time that happened, life would be one shambles after another I admit –

I haven't got your letter here – also this place isn't good for thinking – everything within sight so grim, clean, hard, cheerless, smug, smirking etc, but just in case you'd like to know my point of view – here it is.

I agree that my defence apparatus (is that right) is very groggy, in a bad state. It wants a stiff tot of rum. If a psychoanalyst can help I ought to rush to one. For as a well trained social animal I'm certainly not the goods.

But

I do not agree that there's nothing to defend myself against – I do not agree that my way of looking at life and human beings is distorted. I think that the desire to be cruel and to hurt (with words because any other way might be dangerous to ourself) is part of human nature. Parties are battles (most parties), a conversation is a duel (often). Everybody's trying to hurt first, to get in the dig that will make him or her feel superior, feel triumph.

I admit that the properly adapted human being enjoys the battle, I even admit that it can all be done charmingly wittily and with an air (though I don't think anglo saxons shine at that). It can also be without significance.

But I do not admit that because I am badly adapted to these encounters I'm therefore a mental deformity – I could fight in a big battle – or accept a great cruelty – or be cruel myself – but the little petty day by day snips and snaps – why should I be crazy if I say that I don't think it's worth it – that it takes something from one that is necessary to me – a certain how shall I say single mindedness –

Well lady there you are – you'll have to imagine the rest. I'm getting tired. The I in above paragraph was impersonal – will now return to the personal, the all important I. Me. I.I.I.

Except that – as regards persecution maniacs (this is one of my pet subjects) persecution maniacs (so called) always have been and usually still are, the victims of persecution.

Of course they're called maniacs. It's part of the game Society plays – Let's Pretend that there is no such thing as this petty, leering, unsplendid cruelty, this damnable dropping of water on the same place for years. This mean bloody awful hatred of everything that isn't exactly like your mean self (now she's well off –) Here comes the nurse with tea one piece of bread and butter and a bit of cake yellow trimmed red cherry and black currant. I'll read a detective story while I eat because I like things to fit – Tea and detective stories – My dear that's a fine thing for making you serene.

Listen. I liked Jig[1] most awfully I assure you. I thought him sympathique and guessed how fond of him you must be and he of you. I liked Manly[2] too. In fact it was just because of that that the antagonism bewildered me. It seemed so unnecessary. Excuse me and hand my excuses round if you like. I didn't notice Manly's hand. I hardly ever notice things like that.

I spent most of the voyage over in the cabin. My foot the size of a house – then it got better but last week (we were spending the weekend in Wales with Maryvonne) suddenly worse again and very painful.

I had to go to the local cottage hospital, most alarming experience, and when I came up to London be bundled in here.

It's better now and I feel better. When I can leave will go to the new flat in Chelsea. The address is 22 Paulton's House, Paulton's Square.

I loved New York Evelyn it was so alive (I'd expected that) and it was beautiful which I hadn't expected. At least Manhattan was beautiful. I liked so many of the people I met and enjoyed it all so much before I began to feel dicky – will often think of those three weeks you bet.

Isn't this affair in Spain terrible? It gives me the blues and the English papers holding forth make me *sick*

Love from
Jean

PS. I've just re-read this and find a rather disagreeable tendency to "hold forth" about it, also Horrors! can my one sixteenth particle of English blood be showing up or is it the Welsh desire to preach? Don't be fed up. I'd write another but am not energetic enough so forgive all shortcomings. And as I've got so much off my chest, I'll get this too.

I think that the anglo-saxon idea that you can be rude with impunity to any female who has written a book is utterly *damnable*. You come and have a look out of curiosity and then allow the freak to see what you think of her. It's only done of course to the more or less unsuccessful and only by anglo saxons.

Well my dear if it were my last breath I'd say HELL TO IT and – to the people who do it –

1. *Jig (real name Creighton Scott) was Evelyn's only son, born in Brazil in 1914 after she had eloped with Dr Frederick Creighton Wellman, who had assumed the name of Cyril Kay Scott on the journey. In 1936 Jig was living with his father in the Mid-West. Scott and Evelyn were divorced in 1928.*

2. *Manly Wade Wellman was Evelyn's ex-stepson, being a son of Wellman/Scott by his first marriage. He and his brothers and sisters had long been estranged from their father, until recognizing a fictional portrait of him in* Eva Gay *they wrote to Evelyn via her publishers and she brought about a reconciliation.*

[1936]
22 Paulton's House
Paulton's Square, Chelsea
London SW3

TO EVELYN SCOTT

My dear Evelyn,

My foot is getting better thank you – but slowly. I can't walk much yet which is an awful nuisance.

I agree that an argument by letter is unsatisfactory. One's always two and a half points out.

So I'm not going on with it when I beg you please please *please* to get well into your head (enforcez vous *bien* dans la tête as that nice advert for Poudres Cock says. Picture a man driving a wedge into another man's head) please please *please* get it into your head that I don't think your friends were rude to me and didn't say so. On the contrary I enjoyed two of the parties you (and they) gave for me more than I've enjoyed anything for years. I was happier the first time, at the little restaurant, but I wasn't miserable or shy at the other – Mr Studin's[1]. Even if I had been his perfectly charming manner to me would have put me at my ease.

You *didn't* cause me any misery at all by asking your friends to be kind to me. On the contrary I was enormously pleased and flattered.

I'd mind dreadfully if there was any misunderstanding on that point, for I liked some of the people I met so very much. When I said at the end of my last letter that anglo saxons were often rudely curious and then curiously rude, or something to that effect, I was really thinking of one or two experiences I've had in London. My letter had stopped being an argument and become a

32

rambling monologue – I daresay you'd skipped a connecting page or two and God knows I don't blame you.

As for the last evening, that unfortunate last evening – and for the last time accept my apologies –

I was really ill the last few days before we left New York – and I was drinking a hell of a lot to keep me going. Also I was screwed up because it was my last night. In that abnormal condition you seemed to me – unfriendly – is that a better word – even very unfriendly. So I blew up. It didn't mean a thing except – see above. Of course once I got going old griefs and grievances overwhelmed me. I got that nightmare feeling of a scene which with slight variations had often happened – as it has, and I mixed it up with all the other scenes.

I don't suppose I'm making things any clearer. Besides these long letters are becoming a bad habit.

But believe me or believe me not – it is true that all the worst messes I've ever been in in my life (and the Lord knows I've been in bad ones) all the worst mistakes have started because out of a weak futile conceited gutless desire to please I've done *something I didn't want to do*. That won't make it any clearer either.

If you all were to come walking into this room at this moment (which God forbid I hear you say) I would soon show you how completely I've forgotten my "explosion" and I'd try to make you forget it too[2].

For after all they do clear the air – explosions – also as you so justly say, they are very funny (other people's emotions always are). So that's two points in their favour.

The flat is at last finished – I've even got a little room with a desk in it to write my next "masterpiece" on. All I've got to do is start it go on with it and then finish it – Nothing!

Yours ever

Jean

1. *Frances Linley, of the publishing firm Harper and Row, remembers Mr Studin and describes him in the following terms: "Charles Studin was a wonderfully pleasant and gentle man who gave parties – often "publication day parties" – for friends, and friends of friends, who had recently published a book. He lived somewhere just off Fifth Avenue between 12th Street and the Washington Square arch. I don't know if the entire house was his or if he simply had the spacious parlour floor and garden to himself. He had been either a business-man or a lawyer at some unspecified earlier time. When I was first taken to one of his parties circa 1935 he was a large, sweet-faced man in fragile health (although he did not appear fragile) who, as I understood it, rarely went out, rested most of the day, and gave one party a week in that Jamesian space – large, high-ceilinged. It was obvious that he was not a lion-hunter; his guests were often known to each other (in part because a guest brought along other guests), but they were assuredly not famous or even successful. It always seemed to me that he gave parties as a means of leavening his isolation and in order to give people pleasure. There was never any sense of there being anything in it for him. . . . In other words, he was a dear, good man."*

2. But it seems likely that their friendship never recovered as no letters from Evelyn or Jean survive later than this. Evelyn wrote to Emma Goldman on May 25th, 1937: "During the last year . . . life has, so to speak, gotten out of hand, and between the near-tragedies in personal affairs, the intensive labour and pressure about livelihood, I have simply dropped interchanges of correspondence with even my dearest friends." In 1937 she published an anti-Stalinist novel called Bread and a Sword *and a book of memoirs,* Background in Tennessee. *After this her career collapsed and although she worked on several novels only one was published, with little success, in 1941. To quote from her biographer, D. A. Callard (London Magazine, October 1981): "The remainder of her life makes depressing reading. During the early 1940s she suffered a mental breakdown and she and her husband endured poverty and neglect in London for a decade until a fund was set up to allow them to return to America in 1952. When the boat docked in California, Evelyn Scott was toothless and the couple lacked the money to land their baggage. Eventually they made their way to New York and took up residence in a cheap hotel which was to be their final home together. Evelyn Scott died of complications following a cancer operation in 1963; John Metcalfe returned to England where he was to die some eighteen months later." The Metcalfes were perhaps the most enthusiastic and generous of all Jean's early admirers and Evelyn was tireless in her attempts to promote Jean's work in America. A letter survives from Evelyn to the novelist Thomas Wolfe, then at the height of his fame and success, inviting him to one of the parties she gave to introduce Jean to New York which had so disastrous and unforeseen an effect on their relationship.*

TO MORCHARD BISHOP[1]

June 1st [1939]
11 River Court, Taplow
Maidenhead, Berkshire

My dear Mr Bishop,

I've just got back from Wales to find your letter. Thank you for writing it and I really mean that.

I expect you know the horrible empty feeling one gets after a book is finished (it's much worse than usual this time too!) and the pleasure that a letter like yours can give.

I'm sorry Good Morning Midnight depressed you. No I didn't mean it to be hopeless – and anyway –

Well I won't start on that argument.

Taplow is a dreadful place to get at I always think, along the Great West Road, but if you are ever in London and care to come and have tea or a cocktail I'd be delighted.

I'm sorry your first letter got lost and thank you again for writing and for the kind things you say.

Sincerely yours
Jean Rhys

1. Novelist and biographer, born 1903, real name Oliver Stoner. His publications include Two for Joy *(1938),* Aunt Betty *(1939),* The Green Tree and the Dry

(1939), The Star Called Wormwood *(1941),* The Song and the Silence *(1947)*
and Valerie *(1949).*

TO PEGGY KIRKALDY

[March 21st 1941]
Norwich, Norfolk[1]

My dear Peggy,

I must write this quickly while I can and while it's in my heart.

I'm so deeply deeply sad. Please believe it. Please believe too that I admire you and have cared for you and always will.

I'll often think of your warm cool rooms and your profile, the one I like, and the many times you've been charming and human to me. And warm – cool and kind too.

I understand perfectly that you dislike women or only like them superficially, you are right. For that's your character. I mean I *realised* perfectly that my talk of myself, Ford, Paris, "Perversité"[2], myself, gramophone records, myself was irritating you. But I couldn't stop. For I've been alone so much and so long that talking went to my head. A bloody flux as it were.

I've tried to train myself to bear complete loneliness, tried hard. But the night before I left Colchester I lay awake horrified at the thought of it. Revolted – longing to come down to you and implore you to help me out of my solitary confinement. And what it's made of me.

I didn't come of course for I'm now too deeply suspicious of human beings and I'm glad I didn't. For it would have been useless.

Still that accounts for my quite unforgiveable reaction next day.

Dear Peggy – I meant for once to write about you and not about myself. You see – it's "stronger than I" – Nevertheless.

Please think of me kindly. I need it badly. Badly.

Also *please* don't think that I contemplated hanging on to you – mentally or otherwise.

No it was just – I wanted to be sure you were my friend and –

How stupid all this is. Pompous and meaningless. Impossible –

You must fill in the gaps yourself. To avoid sentimentality and end on the astringent note so beloved of the Angliche.

You *were* rude to me and it's silly to say that Elliott Bliss smells[3]. She was probably pulling your leg if she did, trying to shock you.

Anyhow – darn it all – what's it matter. What else?

I didn't mean to be rude last Wednesday – didn't – I just was off my guard. Not suspicious.

Oh Peggy. I can't bear much more of my hideous life. It revolts me quite simply –

Happy days to your many pals. Be a little gentle with females sometimes. Irritating ones.

So original it would be.

Jean R.

1. *Leslie Tilden-Smith, who had flown for the RFS in World War One, was now too old for active duty but served in various para-military capacities. He was stationed in Norwich and Wales (accompanied by Jean) before returning to London in 1944.*

2. *In 1927 Ford Madox Ford got Jean the job of translating a French novel,* Perversité *by Francis Carco. Her version, entitled* Perversity *(plus a Carco story called "The Knife"), was published in 1928 by Pascal Covici, of Chicago, with the translation wrongly attributed to Ford. At first Jean thought that Ford had deliberately exploited her, and Leslie wrote him an angry letter, but Ford maintained that Covici had used his name without permission and omitted hers by mistake.*

3. *Eliot (real name Eileen) Bliss was born in 1903 in Kingston, Jamaica, and educated at a Highgate convent and University College, London. She published two novels:* Saraband *(1931) and* Luminous Isle *(1934). She got to know Jean in 1937, through an introduction from Horace Gregory, and used to visit the Tilden-Smiths at Paulton's Square where Jean would cook her "delicious West Indian meals". They lost touch with each other at the beginning of the war. In 1941 she stayed with Peggy Kirkaldy (this time with an introduction from Dorothy Richardson) and remembers that Peggy did not like her – but the reference to her in this letter remains mysterious, and seems only to make sense if the existence of a fourth woman is assumed, who made the silly remark about Eliot Bliss in order (as Jean suggests) to shock Peggy. Eliot Bliss wrote to Jean in 1956 and they continued to correspond (though did not meet again) until just before Jean's death in 1979. In May, 1970, Jean wrote to her agent, Olwyn Hughes, about an unpublished novel by Eliot Bliss: "If she sends her MSS to you will you please have a look at it. It might be good and you never know. She's not well I gather and hasn't been having a very good time." Eliot Bliss never sent the MSS to Olwyn Hughes, but twelve years later she sent* Luminous Isle *to Virago Press who offered to republish it.*

October 10th [1945]
c/o Colonel Rees Williams[2]
Knottsfield
Budleigh Salterton, Devonshire

TO MRS R. E. SMYSER[1]

Dear Phyllis,
   I'll try to tell you exactly what happened but I'm so utterly bewildered and miserable that it may be incoherent and lengthy.
   Leslie seemed quite well when he woke that morning. We had breakfast and talked over our plans. While I was dressing he came into the bedroom. He said that he had a terrible pain in his arm and chest. "I've had it before" he said "but never for long". He lay down and I brought him a hot water bottle and a hot drink.
   The cottage was isolated you know, and the hostel where Mr Barker lived was a little distance away. He (Leslie) said – "I can't bear this pain Jean I must have a doctor. Barker will be out now. Write him a note and ask him to 'phone". Something like that. He said "It can't be angina can it? it's my arm". I

36

said no it must be sciatica. I saw he was in great pain, so as I had some medinol tablets I gave him one with some orange juice and wrote the note to Barker. As I went out of the door he said something like "Oh Jean what a terrible strain for you". I took the note marked urgent and left it where Barker could see it. The hostel was empty and the office where the telephone was, locked. When I got back to the cottage I sat on a sofa thing for a moment for I'd had 'flu and felt giddy. I heard a strange groaning noise but it was a few seconds before I connected it with Leslie. Then I rushed into the bedroom. I saw at once that he was terribly ill – I believe unconscious then. He didn't speak or make any sign. I called out of the window but there was no one. Then I ran back to the hostel and managed to break the door and crawl through to the phone. The operator put me on to a doctor but it was all slow and slow as a nightmare. Then I ran back to the cottage and as I took Leslie's hands in mine he died. I couldn't believe it. I couldn't. Then some people passed outside. I waved and called to them and they came back to me. They said they didn't know if he was dead so I kept on hoping it might be a faint. Then the doctor came at last. He (the doctor) asked if Leslie had been seeing any doctor. I said "not to my knowledge". He said there would have to be an inquest and post mortem. About four – I think – they came and took Leslie away. I don't remember the time or anything much about that afternoon or night. These people, two men and a woman, were wonderfully kind to me. I thought all people were so cruel but these three were kind. It was the man who got through to Muriel[3] – I remembered Netherlands Publishing Co – and later to my brother who has been living here since he left India.

Next morning my brother came over. Mr Barker's bill for our stay has already been paid – please do not worry about that. It was paid in full. All was paid in full.

There isn't any more to say that will interest you. It seems that Leslie's heart must have been in a bad state for a long time. It may even have been bad when he was passed for the RAF. – It cannot always be detected by an ordinary medical examination. The death certificate has been forwarded by my brother to the lawyers.

Leslie talked very often to me of his mother's death. He spoke again of it the day before he died and said he was glad she died quickly. He too died quickly and his face looked peaceful when he was dead.

I went to see him at the place they took him. I took flowers there. Yesterday (for there are endless delays and formalities) he was cremated at Plymouth. I went with my brother, for I wanted to be there to the last. It was a fine and clear day and I had all the time the feeling that Leslie had *escaped* – from me, from everyone and was free at last.

I tell you this because I cannot come to any service you may hold. I'm smashed up. But I was there so far as I could be to the end.

There's just one thing more I must say. I loved Leslie too and I think he knew it. In spite of all the worry and all the strain which I cracked under so badly (and I won't ever forgive myself for that) still he was sometimes a little happy with me.

37

These last months or even two years were unhappy because I grew *frightened* of my own loneliness, the not knowing. I did not *know* anything you see.

During the last months especially I had a dreadful foreboding – also apart from vague things like forebodings and dreams I saw that Leslie was ill and I was ill myself. But there was no one I could speak to.

If I had known your aunt's address I would have written to her. But I did not – and couldn't bring myself to ask. I did suggest that he spend a while with her [*his sister*] but he seemed very anxious to go to Devonshire. I was against it, but as I've already written dreams and forebodings are vague things. No one will take them seriously. I know Leslie's sister will be sad – please tell her that he died quickly – I cannot imagine him really old or broken down and he never was. Will you thank her for helping with the flat. I will go there and settle up everything as soon as I'm well enough, at the end of this week I hope. I wondered if there was anything of his she'd like to have – or whether she would care to go through his papers – I do not know.

My brother whom I scarcely knew, for I haven't seen him since I was a very small girl, has been wonderfully good to me. I don't think I could have gone through things alone.

That is quite all now Phyllis. I felt I must say it once and for all. I loved Leslie. I shall not ever forgive myself that I didn't stand up to things better – not ever.

But at the end I was ill and the strain smashed me up sometimes. Especially as I was trying to write.

I did love him though and knew all his generosity and gentleness – very well.

> Yours
> *Jean Rhys*

There was a snapshot of yourself and your son in the pocket book he always carried. Would you like it?

1. *Born Phyllis Tilden-Smith, Leslie's daughter by his first marriage.*

2. *Jean's brother, Edward.*

3. *Mrs Anthony Tilden-Smith, the wife of Leslie's son by his first marriage. Phyllis Smyser writes: "It was Muriel who telephoned the news to me of Leslie's death. I was a WAAF officer at the time, working in RAF Welfare in Curzon Street. It was a shock. He was only sixty, and had gone down to Dartmoor for a brief holiday with Jean. I wrote to her immediately and this letter was the reply. I am afraid none of my family had been close to Jean, mainly because she could be rather a frightening person at times, and she and my father often had terrible rows, and naturally we, his family, sided with him! So I had not seen very much of her during the war. He had tremendous faith in her writing and considered her a "genius". He worked endlessly, editing, typing, and walking around trying to get her novels published. I wish he could have lived to know of her later-life success."*

[*October 1945*]
c/o Colonel Rees Williams
Budleigh Salterton

My dear Peggy,

This is written on an impulse – I don't even know if it will reach you or what your reactions will be when you read it.

A few days ago – I don't know how many it's such a nightmare – Leslie died very suddenly. We were staying at an isolated cottage on the edge of Dartmoor. I was alone when it happened. It was heart trouble and over before the doctor could reach us.

He died really while I was trying to telephone for help from the nearest house, so we didn't even say goodbye.

My brother who's back from India came over and helped me through all the horrors of the inquest post mortem and so on. I should have – well I couldn't have gone through it alone.

I did all I could – now I am resting for a few days at his house.

What, you will say, does she want of me a stranger?

Well I'll tell you – I have a flat in London at 3 Steeles Rd Hampstead NW3 where I can live till Dec 1st, some furniture and enough money to exist for a while. Also I have a novel half finished[1]. I should like to finish it – partly because Leslie liked it, partly because I think it might be the one book I've written that's much use – mostly for Leslie.

But I've a *horror* of London. I will go to pieces there alone.

Do you know of a flat rooms or a cottage where I could live quietly and try to finish my book? I say *try* for I don't know yet if I'll be able to find the courage.

Please believe my dear that I know the enormous request this is – must seem to your – sceptical mind.

I know our last meeting wasn't too happy, that you have your own life and troubles, that I know you only slightly after all.

But I know too that you are one of those few women I've met or liked in England, that you are generous enough to believe that I am *not* casting myself on you at all.

But I think of you as such a – wise person in your way and I am *so* at a loss.

I cannot stay with my brother kind as he is. His wife is not well and you know how difficult everything is. Also I must be alone to write. They are terrified poor dears that I will sit down on them for good – well I'm leaving on Wednesday for 3 Steeles Road.

This is one of those very strong impulses which one doesn't resist – writing to you.

Dear Peggy, even if you don't know of any room flat or cottage write me a line to cheer me I'm horribly alone.

I can't speak of Leslie – he was a very gentle and generous man and oh Peggy I'd give all my idiotic life for an hour to say goodbye to him.

Do you remember Maryvonne? She is married. She was a member of the Dutch Underground and had incredible adventures. Then she married a man on Prince Bernhard's staff. She came over to me and is here now but she must return to Holland soon in about ten days. She is charming in a strange way, quite beautiful sometimes – sometimes not caring a damn.

Her husband's name is Moerman – well I will not hang round *their* two young necks you may be sure. She has none of my fear of life and people thank God – she's a gay creature like her father.

I don't indeed want to hang round anyone's neck only I've an utter horror of London and I've just given into an overwhelming impulse.

Well bless you my dear and don't answer at all if you don't feel kindly to me. Then I'll just think the letter didn't reach you.

I've a book of short stories² finished but no faith in them. Too bitter – also who wants short stories?

Still I suppose I'll try with Constable – I suppose –

The novel might be some good if it's ever finished.

My love
Jean Rhys

1. *This was an early version of* Wide Sargasso Sea.

2. The Sound of the River, *which included the title story,* "Till September Petronella", "Tigers are Better Looking", "Outside the Machine", "The Lotus", "A Solid House", "I Spy a Stranger" *and* "Temps Perdi", *never found a publisher. These stories, with the exception of* "I Spy a Stranger" *and* "Temps Perdi" *and with the addition of* "Let Them Call it Jazz" *and* "The Day They Burnt The Books" *finally appeared in book form in 1968, together with a selection from her first book,* The Left Bank, *under the title* Tigers Are Better Looking, *published by André Deutsch.*

PART TWO

Max

(1946–1950)

February 11th [1946]
3 Steeles Road
London NW3

My dear Peggy –

When you send back "Tropic of Cancer" (I'm glad you liked it) will you address it to

> Lt. Comr. G. V. M. Hamer.
> H.M.S. Aeolius,
> Tring,
> Herts.

This is because I may be away for some days, also I assure you that living on the top floor of a tall house has its disadvantages. Over and over again I've dashed down – usually out of the bath – to find the postman or milkman or whoever it is gone with the wind.

I don't want to lose Henry Miller, and I know that this man Max Hamer[1] will bring it along when he comes to see me. Hope you don't think me fussy – and as I know that I've already enlarged on the knock, ring, or kick difficulty here that's assez.

Of course I remember Sarah Salt's books[2]. She sounds interesting. Didn't she write "Joy is my name"? Log fires and old oak and lovely lovely food sound fine too.

It would be charming to meet her – I live on such a desert island Peggy. You wouldn't believe. Am getting used to it too – not a good sign. It isn't a bad desert island – you must be brave and have a brief look at it sometime.

I hope to send my book to Constable this week[3] – it's been the hardest thing I've ever done in my life – the only advantage of that being that I don't much care what happens to it. Yes I do care, but only because Leslie liked the stories. I plan a holiday now for a week. I will buy some new books, gramophone records, see Françoise Rosay[4] etc – At least so I plan.

Are you well again – I trust so. But, my dear, why do you think that I do not understand the hatred of small uglinesses – not ugliness, annoyances, like chair covers and clothes one's sick of and so on. I'm quite incompetent to deal with them, but don't you see, that makes me hate them *more*, not less.

In fact I can see now that my great mistake was resenting ugliness so much – I wasted so much energy in my futile fight with it. Yes. If I could have shut my eyes to what seemed to me the dreadful and not to be escaped ugliness of life in England without money – well, I might have escaped – by other methods – other weapons which I can use.

Very complicated. This flat isn't bad – "I've learnt to do without mountains, seas (*blue* sea), bright colours, everything I love." Though I still obstinately hope that I will get away to die.

Bury me under the ole flamboyant tree every time. Now I'm being like a morgue am I not? Talking of blue seas I have such a comic picture near my bed – Patrick Trench did it for me – and I think he was pulling my leg as so many English people do. I asked him to paint me something to remind me of my native land and my God, he's got *everything* into that picture – from a whale to a

43

butterfly. Also, four human figures, *very* rum – I call them my dumb friends –
very original.

But the sea is nice and purple.   love
                                                                   Jean

1. *Then aged sixty-three, Max Hamer was Leslie Tilden-Smith's cousin and became
Jean's third husband the following year.*

2. *Novelist (real name Mrs Coralie Hobson), author of* A Tiny Seed of Love *(1928),*
Sense and Sensuality *(1929),* Joy is my Name *(1929),* Strange Combat *(1930)*
and Change Partners *(1934).*

3. The Sound of the River *was rejected by Constable.*

4. *A distinguished French actress (1881–1974): her film* A Woman Disappeared *was
showing at the Academy Cinema.*

TO PEGGY KRIKALDY   *July 3rd [1946]*
                                                         3 Steeles Road

My dear Peggy,

Tomorrow – God willing – I'll post you Prater Violet[1]. Thank you. My dear
this is the *third* day of sunlight and warmth – it's not to be believed. I'm almost
half alive again though not alive enough to make any plans.

Have never felt so completely indifferent to everything and everybody
before. It's a *lovely* feeling and may it last.

Anyway it's all very fine to say Face Facts and so on but what's the use? I call
my present existence very sensible. Hopping from day to day like Eliza
crossing the river in Uncle Tom's Cabin – do you remember?

Peggy – about my book – the trouble is – it is not good. Three stories are all
right. The others are competent. That's all – I can't try to sell it with passion for
I know its faults. I tried too hard for one thing, and was so afraid of offending
that I wrote and rewrote the life out of the things. It's all right of course – if
anyone believed the truth, that the novel I have half finished is a very different
matter, they'd publish the Sound of the River to give me a helping hand. Sad to
say the facts are otherwise. No one does believe in me. That was all sound and
fury or rather froth and bubble.

I debate the ethics of the thing very seriously. *Must* I finish the novel? "not
for fear of hell or hope of heaven but for love" as the Catholics say.

Yes – obviously. Also *must* I try to sell the three good stories? Again *yes*. I'll
try some tomorrow or other –

Meanwhile I cannot feel or want anything much.

And after all when it comes to Facing Facts, I *have* worked hard for a long
long time and it's been no good at all – None.

My dear I do not wish to write a woeful letter for I am not woeful. Are you
liking the sun and having a good time? You always seem to be having a fine
time.

Peggy you are pure 18th century and you are wasted in this disgusting age. I do like your gaiety and courage so much and have forgotten our fight which was another aspect of the 18th century dance (hasty judgement, barbed remarks etc, a *faint* touch of Lady Sneerwell[2] – don't be vexed.)

I expect I seemed the worst 19th to you – very debased – tears, weeping willows, gloom etc, "The carp eye!" I *am* too, a bit – tho' not always. About Shelley – all this ghastly winter I've only been able to read poetry (I don't even read that now. Who-done-it's my line now).

But it was the only thing that kept me from cracking up utterly. I like Keats better than Shelley – Shakespeare the best and to my surprise Milton next best – all the seventeenth century lot too – I have many anthologies and spent days in bed browsing over them and then going to the fountain head. I couldn't *look* at Rimbaud whom I thought so great or Mallarmé or Baudelaire (I haven't got Verlaine) without a horrible pain – I don't know why – also I couldn't *bear* music. That will gradually come back. I turned on the radio last night and a *glorious* German voice, male, burst through the atmospherics. As to music dearie I really am 19th century. French school. Also I do like the moderns. Yes – some of them anyway – I never know their names – is it Clifford Bax? And I got a Soviet man once whom I loved. (*Loved*! What a word) But most Russian and Spanish music says something to me. You see I like emotion, I approve of it – in fact am capable of *wallowing* in it. Adore negro music for instance. It's life according to my gospel – and in some strange way discord or an ice cold feeling can be emotional don't you think?

What (amateur) rot I'm writing but it doesn't matter. I'm *ashamed* to say that the Germans are too serene for me – well some of them. Serene or tinkling or something. I can feel Beethoven though (Bravo for ME!) *However*. What a silly letter – the flat looks so nice. Clean and peaceful. I work hard at it and Max Hamer who still hangs around has done a lot of painting – the lopped trees have covered themselves up thank God. I've had several offers – could let this flat and so solve my money problems but the landlord won't allow it. As I don't play cards I figure the balloon will go up in about six months. That's to say I'll have nix NIX and who cares? Not me. It isn't long enough to finish my novel anyway –

"As *I* don't play cards" sounds so pinched mouth – not meant a bit. On the contrary lots more luck of all kinds.

Saw the Javanese Dancers, a bit disappointing didn't you think?

There's a thing by Martha Gellhorn at the Embassy this week[3] I want to see it – I like her book "Liana". Have you ever read it? I'll send it to you if you'd like it.

She's divorced Hemingway or he, she – Now I must get up and get my rations from the loathly grocer and all the other chores.

If you know of a nice cottage (no rats) will you tell me?

That's like saying if you know of any marble halls for sale –

I'd like to spend my last months in the country.

Jean

P.S. The play is by Martha Gellhorn and Virginia Cowles[3]. Let's be exact for *heaven's* sake.

1. *Christopher Isherwood's novel had recently been published.*

2. *Character in Sheridan's play* The School For Scandal.

3. Love Goes to Press, *a light-hearted comedy about two American women war correspondents, presumably based on the authors.*

TO PEGGY KIRKALDY

[July 8th 1948]
35 Southend Road
Beckenham, Kent. Beckenham 6922

My dear Peggy,

It was such a pleasant surprise – your letter. No I haven't seen Caribbean Rhapsody[1] yet but I will do as soon as possible. God knows I could do with an hour or so of oblivion – or even longer – not to say longest.

I had a fall a few weeks ago and hurt my back. Nothing serious but it mended slowly so I've had a boring time – one nice book about Africa cheered me a bit. If only I could transport myself to Timbuctoo – but unfortunately I'd be still myself.

Maryvonne came to see me with her baby. She is going to Java where her husband's got a job.

Dear Peggy. I don't know what else to say except Salut which is a cliché (I hear) –

I shall be here till about August but I can't face another winter in this darned House of Usher, besides it's turned out too expensive so am already starting slow preparation to depart. Heaven knows where. Valiant Max is still around. He always has some music hall act or other which he imagines will get rid of all the sea of troubles. But they (the acts) sound a bit dud to me – for instance a robot car which is driven by a little robot man who opens and shuts his mouth while a gramophone "roars" comic songs. Sounds the last word in weariness and dreariness doesn't it?

But maybe it's just what the great heart of the people is yearning for and so on.

I must tell you that he (Max) is an ardent socialist with leanings leftward and ever leftward, despises everything but majorities – large ones too.

He insists that I'm a high Tory and tries to convert me by the hour – only result I've grown to dislike and despise the great heart etc – and *how*!

However as robots are obviously on the way, if not already here, he may be right. It would be lovely if he were – and we got rich quite sudden like.

Dear Peggy please write again soon – it helps me to imagine I'm still alive.

What a gloomy letter – "and some of it is dreariness
                                    And most of it is weariness"
Edwardian poem about – what do you think – Life dearie but it sounds like my letters.

The real trouble is I'm obstinately sure that given six months of decent food and a little encouragement I'd come alive again. Unfortunately I don't see how it's to be managed. Perhaps God will provide but I have my doubts.

I can't send off this moan without one grace note.

Well Maryvonne's baby is a darling – she has slanting eyes and red brown hair – I fell in love with her and pray that they'll get safely to Java.

Sun to sun in one generation. It's true there's a war over there.

Still even a war would be better than this ghastly hopelessness and treachery in Europe and my son-in-law is – I think – a good sort.

Here's a snapshot of these only hopes of mine – but send it back for it's precious.

She Maryvonne thinks I'm a donkey though she doesn't say so – I think I only wear the disguise of a donkey and that most unwillingly.

End of moan in minor.

Love
Jean

1. Katherine Dunham's troupe of dancers was having a great success in London.

TO MARYVONNE MOERMAN *January 11th [1949]*
Beckenham

My dear Maryvonne,

I had your telegram yesterday and very nearly wired back asking you to come if you could – for I haven't been well for some time and "things are getting on top of me" as they say. Then I realised how impossible it would be and how selfish. Also it will be more helpful later on, that is if you can manage it and wish to come for I'm *longing* to see you.

But I'll tell you all about it and that will be a great relief for I'm rather lonely.

The chief difficulty is of course, money – This house is horribly expensive. There is always *something* to be paid. Then when that is paid, something else. When we first came Max wanted to repair the place and lost a good deal over trying, so we've really been in difficulties from the start. He has also of course other expenses, his first wife's alimony and so on – (you see I'm telling you everything). All this was not so bad so long as I had something, some money of my own, but that has of course been getting less and less.

When I realised how events were going I wanted to leave, selling or storing my furniture. But it is not easy to find anywhere else that wouldn't be quite horrible – or even more expensive – for Max has to live in or near London as his job is there.

Several times I made up my mind to pull out *no matter what* but something always happened to stop me. Max is a very optimistic man, a little money would come in soon. So we stayed on – with much argument, and I worried and worried.

Then the darned winter came. This place is terribly cold and I got 'flu. Then I got all right but I found a great indifference taking hold of me. All I wanted was to be warm. That has gone on since week before Xmas.

It's a curious feeling and will doubtless pass – but there it is – I can't feel that anything matters at all – except not thinking, for I've thought a lot and tried hard and à quoi bon? Also I haven't been eating much, for I like being warm better than going out or even into the kitchen. That's quite unheated and like a *wolf* (or the South Pole).

Only you and Ruthie[1] mattered to me (especially thank you for the photographs) but as you know I do not feel I have the right to bore you with my troubles. I think very very strongly that your baby and Job[2] and life in general – well that's enough for you to cope with, though you are very brave and very sensible (which I'm not).

In fact the worst part of all this has been the feeling that I've let you down and not helped you enough or been the right sort of person for you.

However when I tried to write you a conventional Xmas letter – well I *could not* – and that's that –

The words looked so silly. My dear I hope you'll try to understand this collapse and why I tell you of it.

It's in answer to your telegram.

There is nothing wrong with me but the rest of my 'flu, and the worrying about what to do for the best and the bitter cold. All that will pass. I am nearly sure that I'll pull myself together, sell my furniture and we will find rooms or a room near or in London.

I hope you'll understand my dear why I write this, don't worry a bit about me but try to believe I've done my best – and will be all right when this ghastly feeling of weakness has passed.

I can't of course say all that's happened it would take too long. But one thing more to show you why I'm depressed. That horrid neighbour of mine – d'you remember the pompous one – has a horrid dog. First poor Gaby was killed, then the black cat Mister Wu. He was a darling. I wrote a song about him.

My black cat is a gentleman
A gentleman proud and true
He has teeth and he has claws
But he'd never use them on me.

Great Writing I don't think!!

Well I had a fearful row about it and she's gossiped about us like jimmy oh ever since.

Now the cellar (*oh God that cellar*) is full of rats. Mr Wu was a great hunter and kept them down.

The third one the only one left MI-KAT (Mycat) does his best but he has the dreadful habit of bringing them upstairs to show me – Or else they are invading the house. For I went out to get the milk just now and nearly had a fit. There lay an enormous dead rat the size of a kitten.

That settles it. I must go. The slippers I bought for you are here waiting for the gloves and a toy for Ruthie to join them. I hope to drag myself to London by the end of the week, buy the other things and post the lot.

48

I've seen a charm I want to buy for Ruth's bracelet a little gold key. I thought we might buy that together when you come for a short time as you said you might.

I will write to Job as soon as I'm well enough to manage a decent and coherent letter. Don't fear that it will be a melancholy one.

I think a lot of him mixed up in that wretched business out there.

I will write another and more sensible letter in a day or two.

Meanwhile a happy New Year to you my dear, hugs and kisses an especial hug for Ruthie. Her photographs were much the nicest thing that happened to me this Xmas.

Jean

1. *Ellen Ruth Moerman, Maryvonne's baby daughter.*

2. *Job Moerman, Maryvonne's husband.*

TO PEGGY KIRKALDY

March 9th [1949]
Beckenham

My dear Peggy,

I wrote a very long screed to you *weeks* ago and put it in an envelope formidable – so imagined it was posted.

But I've been ill and the darned thing got behind a photograph on my desk, and Max didn't see it. I'm sending it all the same as there are one or two things I won't ever have the energy to say again, and nothing I wish unsaid – so one day read it when you've nothing better to do.

My dear I don't know what's the matter but I ache and ache all over and am so tired. Sleep is so *lovely* better than food or thinking or writing or anything. The walls of this blasted house are trickling with damp, so maybe it's that – and when they dry off and the wind calms down I'll emerge fresh as paint can make me.

Meanwhile I am fast turning into a vegetable – non edible I'll bet.

I can't get hold of any decent books so make do with old ones. I read Borrow's "Lavengro" the other day. Do you know it? There's a very attractive honesty and freshness about the man – missing out the "wicked Papacy" bits I liked it. It's difficult not to think that something's died out in the world – zest perhaps? Or just honesty. Besides the hero what's his name gets the horrors like I do, only worse, and the gipsy girl says "Go to the nearest house (pub) and drink three or four pints of good strong ale". Which he does and is much cheered. I call that sense don't you?

Also I came across Scott Fitzgerald's "Tender is the Night". I used to hate S.F. and not even see he was good. I still dislike him but realize he could write – So Work in Progress.

This morning I tried to write an article about English Harbour, Antigua as your bugbear the Daily Mail (which I take because I like the strip cartoon) has a chap there nosing round about Oliver Baldwin and his doings[1]. He's struck English Harbour (that is the place where Nelson hung out) and hasn't heard about the ghost. Antigua is *not* a beautiful island. Except for the inevitable blues and purples (hibiscus etc) it's a flat and dull place to look at. But there is a very romantic "ghost of English Harbour" and a very romantic story tacked on. The story anyhow is true – I don't know about the ghost. I thought once of making a film and trying my luck with this story (I cannot see it as a book, or a play, only as a novel). However with the slump in films and what not I gave up the idea. Découragé!

Well this morning I wrote two lines of the article then went to sleep. What *is* to be done? If I could earn some shekels I'd fly from damp and bloody Beckenham and finish my book. Oh *God* if I could finish it before I peg out or really turn into some fungus or other!

I think of calling it *"The first Mrs Rochester"* with profound apologies to Charlotte Brontë and a deep curtsey too.

But I suppose that won't do (I'm supposing you've studied Jane Eyre like a good girl).

It really haunts me that I can't finish it though. Love from
                                                                                        Jean
Do write soon.

1. *The second Earl Baldwin of Bewdley had been a Labour MP before inheriting from his father, the former Conservative Prime Minister. He was Governor and Commander-in-Chief of the Leeward Islands from 1948 to 1950.*

TO MARYVONNE MOERMAN   *Sunday, July 10th [1949]*
                                                                                    Beckenham
Darling Maryvonne,

I had both your letters and I'm sorry not to have answered before. I've been ill and in hospital. I asked Max to write you but he thought it would worry you he tells me now. Well here I am all right again, a bit "rocky" perhaps but quite all right. My dear I'm sorry you find it hot and cramped. I can imagine that and hope you are just drifting along not worrying, sure that things will soon get better.

Please my dear do that. I was awfully interested in your letter about Singapore and envied you. I've grown to hate Beckenham. It's not town and it's not country – it's nothing except a lot of housework which I do badly.

Yes I can imagine Singapore but Batavia not so well. I hope you'll hear from the friends you made on the boat and make lots of others or as many as you want. But darling please don't say you've lost your illusions because, after all, life is dull without them and who's to know what is illusion and what truth?

I don't think you're a bit in danger of being reckless silly or obstinate about illusions as I've been. Reckless perhaps yes but not silly.

However all this will bore you. I hope you'll write again soon. We may be leaving Beckenham. In that case I'll wire you. The bank address will always find me.

National Provincial
St Giles Circus
London

Max's address

c/o Cohen & Cohen
112 Salisbury House
EC2

We are trying for a bungalow at Shepperton (do you remember Shepperton?) but even if that doesn't come off I hope to leave this place and not spend another winter here. My illness has quite determined me.

Please hug and kiss Ruthie for me. She won't be always tiresome you know.

I'm afraid this isn't a good letter and certainly not what I wanted to write but I still find it difficult to think and can't imagine Batavia as I told you. I associate heat with big dark rooms, iced drinks, ices and above all bathing. (Besides Batavia is perhaps much hotter than the West Indies.)

Well my dear I hope to do better in my next letter and forgive a certain wooliness.

Remember us both to Job. It must be fine being together again.

All love hugs and kisses

Ella

TO MARYVONNE MOERMAN

Friday [1949]
Beckenham

My dear,

How are you getting on? It's a great thrill getting your letters – so write soon.

We're still at Beckenham as you see – Max keeps making plans to go to Shepperton but something always happens to stop it.

As for me, I'm fifty-fifty about leaving. I've got rather fond of this funny old house, and spend hours pottering about doing this and that. The garden is quite wild now, and though the apple and pear trees have lots of fruit it's difficult to get at them because blackberry bushes have spread like the devil all over the place.

So I have to dress up in trousers and thick coat and gloves before I pick the fruit and even so get badly scratched if I don't watch out.

The real enemy is the damp. Really apples and pears in the garden are very nice, but toadstools on the kitchen wall – well that's a bit too much!

How is Ruthie? Is it getting any cooler and did you enjoy your party?

Nothing very much happens. We went to London for a week in search of a flat but it was so hot, and the search was hopeless. I think I told you that in last letter.

I heard from Peggy this morning. She has been staying with friends who breed horses. A fine way to make a living! Staying in Ireland.

She says it's so lovely there. D'you remember when we went from Dublin to Galway?

It's getting dark so I must stop. Am writing this on the famous balcony. I put the sofa there and meant to sleep out – and *of course* it at once started to rain.

I want to send you some books and hope I'll pick the right ones. If there is anything else I can send do let me know my dear and I'll try.

All my love to you a special hug and kiss for Ruthie and you. Max sends his love too. He has discovered *another* friend who is promising heaven and earth but I have grown so cautious!   Love again

                                                                                        Jean

TO MARYVONNE MOERMAN   *August 16th [1949]*
                                                                                  Beckenham

                                        [. . . . . .]

My dear,

I feel so bad about not answering your letter before, especially as I was so pleased to get it. I made three attempts to write, but I'm very much at sixes and sevens now trying to pack, find a new place, somewhere to store the furniture and so on. So always I tore up the page till another day when I'd more time.

There's so much to say that I don't know where to start. Perhaps it's not a very wise plan to leave here. It's quite impossible to get an unfurnished flat or rooms in or near London – and we are going to a service flatlet (one room) not far from Holland Park for the time being. But I felt I couldn't endure another winter here – the damp cold and loneliness get me down too much. Then I slipped and hurt my arm (or wrist) the hurt runs up and down! The right one too, and it's getting better very slowly. So that was the last straw. I'm so useless left handed.

I'm going to try and relax, get my hair cut, buy a cheap dress and generally pull myself together. Please wish me luck. Then I must find a flat or rooms before the winter. I want to try the river or Guildford perhaps. Letters here will be forwarded – you have Max's office address and the bank. If we stay longer than a fortnight in Holland Park I'll send you that address too. But in any case I must return here to see my furniture and books stored properly.

That's all about me. *I am all right dear.* Now, about you.

My dear I'm glad you are slowly getting used to the heat and that the nights are cool – a mercy. The only thing in heat is to drift, relax I think: but I'm so horribly lazy naturally and that's easy for me – so I can't talk.

I can guess there must be all sorts of annoyances – and I'm afraid life is usually only half happy. But there are the things like lovely colours to hang on to. Have you lovely flowers there? I read a book about Burma called "The Jacaranda Tree"[1]. Have you that in Batavia? Flowering trees, I mean. I've read several novels about Java and Batavia – but always before the war. It must have been very exciting then. Or so they say. I'm glad you have the piano. It will come back if you stick to it. Wouldn't it be lovely if you could one day have a shack for week ends on that island and paint there. I *know* you can paint. Or visit Bali one day – Or Singapore?

Forgive all these fumbling efforts to imagine your life and possible pleasures. You seem so far away and I can only do my best.

Anyway, there is one thing you are spared a bit. The endless soul destroying domestic slavery here. Sweep, dust. Oh God how I *hate* it all. (And how badly I do it!)

You know I find it strange you should envy me or my generation. Personally I've always thought the Lost Generation a good name for us.

To start with – eight nearly nine years of war is a lot out of a life. The 1914–1918 war spoilt our youth, the other one smashed anything one had achieved between. And how!

You see I have not been often happy. I haven't a happy nature to start with. But really few of my lot have come through, and those not the best it seems to me.

Still there are always moments, or weeks – or months perhaps. And you will have them too be sure. I won't bore you with mine, except to say that they always happen when one least expects them. In between there are the little happy minutes or sensations. Perhaps with a calm happy nature it is not so bad. And some work some ambition that's perhaps the best.

I can't say at all what I mean – the gift of expression seems to have left me, so you must guess.

I'm awfully glad Ruthie is so sweet. You were a darling at that age. I have an angelic photograph of you at two – my favourite. But I have only one and don't want to part with it.

Don't let her burn her poor hand again. Are you letting her get brown in the sun or keeping her out of it? And you? To tan or not to tan?

When I was little my mother always kept me away from the sun, hats parasols umbrellas, God knows what. But when I went back with Leslie I noticed all the girls and children were without hats and very few clothes. I mean the white children.

They were all brown and most astonishingly pretty I thought with lovely hair.

But then it's not such a fierce sun – so I can't judge –

Dear I must have something to eat now, dust sweep and pack. We leave here this evening.

I eat lots of quantities of bread because it's no trouble. Besides the electric stove has conked out –

However will be very glad to change my diet in London.

Love kisses and hugs. Remember me to Job.

Jean

---

1. *H. E. Bates's novel had recently been published.*

53

My dear,

Thank you so much for your letter. It reached me not long after my birthday (which wasn't much of a birthday anyhow). Max gave me some beads and I gave myself a swell manicure, that was about all.

Your news and Ruthie's photograph were much the nicest part of it. She seems so jolly and a darling.

We went to London – the idea being to find another flat or rooms – but here we still are! And may have to stay too for a bit. It's almost hopeless looking for an unfurnished flat and the furnished places are drab and horrible or fearfully expensive. I cannot imagine where the mobs of people come from and can't get used to standing in a long queue for a cup of coffee or an ice. Especially as there is always some military looking bloke yelling out "Keep to the left there" or "Move to the right" and everybody is so darned meek – shuffling along inch by weary inch.

Well something *may* turn up!

I had one nice afternoon when after some dull shopping I got on a bus going down Bond Street. You know it's been a perfect summer. Day after day is fine and warm, often hot. I don't ever remember such weather. Perhaps the climate is changing. What a delicious thought!

Well on this particular afternoon I saw two women who looked nice. One young and one not young. But it was so wonderful to look at people, not hot and sticky and dressed anyhow, that I cheered up at once. They were both in black with black and grey scarves round their hair and very pretty shoes and came I suppose from one of the dress shops.

Anyhow they were very nice and cool and pleasant to see. I thought of the little black frock you have and hoped you wore it and am glad you do. I expect it suits you and I thought of you at once when I saw these two – especially the young one looking so charming in black in the sun and everybody else in blue or brown or eternal nondescript and hot and bothered and cross.

I expect it *is* much hotter in your part of the world than it ever was in the West Indies because for one thing the breeze from the sea and the breeze from the hills are as regular as clockwork, one in the morning and the other after sunset. Then we could go into the hills when the bad time (July and August) came.

Third I guess it isn't so hot anyway.

I'm glad you like oleander because I loved it almost the best – that and cloves.

Frangipanni is a lovely scent too, but heavier and I don't know how long the trees take to grow. For it is a tree. When it isn't flowering it's quite bare and black. Then it flowers and looks and smells like heaven.

I read all the news from Indonesia I can find but it's very contradictory depending a bit on the politics of the editor.

I've a horrid task in front of me. Last evening Max and I demolished all the red and blue glass on the little balcony – then so much of the rusty pipes and framework snapped that Max demolished them too – and threw them gaily outside. So now the balcony is fine and windy and looks like a debased Greek temple (*very* debased). But outside looks like a battlefield and I feel I must go and pick up some of the bits.

However the more I think of doing it the more weary and lazy I get. My laziness is awful.

My dear I hope you liked the party and that the cooler weather will come soon. I send you love and hugs and kisses galore for Ruthie and you and love to Job and Max sends his love too.

It looks as though we may be staying on here faute de mieux. However if we *do* move letters will be forwarded [. . . .]

Ella

P.S. I'm longing for a swim instead I must collect bits of old iron and glass. *What* a life –

TO PEGGY KIRKALDY

October 4th [1949]
Beckenham

Thank you for your warm and generous letter – I need a bit of that badly. Some days of course more than others.

My dear about my writing. I know very well that I ought to start again – for many reasons, practical reasons too.

Unfortunately there it is – I don't want to – so can't. The desire has gone – for the present at any rate. It's the first time in my life (my life since I can remember) that it's happened, and is a bit like losing one's arms or even eyes, but it's not my fault and I can't do anything about it.

I couldn't in any case write much about Holloway because I wasn't there long enough[1] (perhaps that may be remedied!) It's such a vast monster of a place and I only saw a small part of it for a short time. I saw enough to be quite sure that it's an evil and useless place – it does nothing but harm to everybody – but that's not enough to write a true book. My dear I don't know anything about the doctor (who by the way was young, or youngish, not old) – except that she terrified me. She had large glittering spectacles and long sharp teeth and she smiled and smiled and yet was a villain – For instance she always broke promises, which a doctor ought *not* to do, what do you think? This promising and not performing is part of the prison system.

They promise *everything* – from an extra blanket to a sleeping pill but it never comes off.

It takes a few days to tumble to this and meanwhile they've had some fun.

Soon after I left there was a riot, but I noticed that the newspapers faded it out pretty damn quick. The *rot* they talked! For instance this bread and water business. Well the food is mostly bread and tea anyway – I suppose they could keep down tea. Otherwise you cannot take zero from zero, though you may want to.

Also the blasted newspaper talked about the "humane" governor.

She's not humane. She's a fat woman like a Pekinese. She talks in a pseudo genteel voice about "my" prison. Very self satisfied. "My prison" – *My* prison – that ship of misery!

Her second in command *does* look intelligent and sad and may be humane too and some of the prison officers aren't quite stone yet.

But oh Lord why wasn't the place bombed? If you could see the unfortunate prisoners crawling about like half dead flies you'd understand how I feel. I did think about the Suffragettes. Result of all their sacrifices? The woman doctor!!! Really human effort is futile.

'Nuff said about charming Holloway except that it's an old castle. I thought it was imitation – but it seems not, it's old and wicked. I often think of my bold gipsy who was tough as old boots. Of course I knew people called London the Smoke but never heard anyone do it "so natural". I couldn't understand some of the girls at all. My dear quite young girls with no teeth and hardly any hair. They ought to be in a hospital surely, or a lethal chamber not a jail.

You see I'm seething to write an article tho' I couldn't manage a book – but it would not be published.

Firstly because I fear that a good deal of gossip has got around (with knobs on) and done me no good. Secondly because the whole business is on the hush hush list like much else.

I know Peggy that you don't care for Americans but they have one great virtue, they don't stifle criticism. You can write about the Chain Gang or a canned meat factory or a loony bin and what have you and there's a chance of an audience. But not here! The English clamp down on unpleasant facts and some of the facts they clamp down on are very unpleasant indeed, believe me.

My dear I hope I may write again some day. I have a novel half done and the rest safely in my head. It's about the West Indies about 1780 something.

But this horrible creeping *indifference* stops me – I can't find anything worth while.

Do you know a picture called "L'Indifférent"? Watteau (of course!). Not that sort of indifference, alas –

I think it would be best for me to leave here. The people have me in very holy horror, and might easily make trouble.

Shepperton is still hanging fire and your idea of Greenwich is a good one.

It's quite close so I could look round without getting too tired.

I haven't seen my dear cat this morning, and get so nervous when he doesn't leap in to say Howdy because they could so easily kill him as they did the others and I could prove nowt.

He's a dear cat but a bit lethargic or perhaps indifferent – like me.

My black cat *was* my real love. I have James Agate's Anthology here, and Sonnet to a Monkey reminds me of him. "He was a buck, he was a beau", something like that.

My dear I get rotten books from Miss Puss in Boots. Always *always* The Crime Club or a fragrant love story. That sweetie pie Henry VIII the hero, and Anne Boleyn and Katherine Howard walking to the block.

How I dislike that man! Didn't like Edith Sitwell's book on the period because she called him the Lion King. Lion!! With those pig eyes. No siree. No. Not my kind anyway.

Write soon dear Peggy and don't get bored with 1 2 3 4 5 6 from me.

Love
Jean

Did you have a good time at the races?

1. *Jean had been found guilty of assault at Bromley Magistrate's Court on May 6th, 1949. Sentence was deferred until June 27th, when she was remanded in custody pending a medical report. After five days in the hospital at Holloway Prison she was put on probation for two years. For her account of the incident, see page 78.*

TO MARYVONNE MOERMAN

Monday, October 24th *[1949]*
Beckenham

My dear –

It seems such a long time since I heard from you. How is everything? Here we still are as you see, vegetating away in Beckenham and still planning to leave – (As a matter of fact it is not too easy to find anywhere else these days.)

I'd miss the Venetian blinds and the trees. Otherwise I feel a change is about due.

We're both all right, and Max is very optimistic about making some money soon. I'm keeping my fingers crossed (for luck). If it does come off the nicest thing will be that I'll be able to help you and Job. You don't know how I long to do that. And Ruthie. I didn't forget her. She was included.

Otherwise there is no news. I saw a good film "The Third Man" about Vienna. My God how long ago Vienna seems – at least a couple of hundred years.

But this movie was of course about Vienna 1949, full of international police and the black market – though *that's* nothing new.

My dear I often read news about Java that worries me – one paper says one thing one another – so send me anything – a post card even to say you're all OK.

This week I hope to get into London and do some shopping mostly books for you, a toy for Ruthie and so on.

I wish I knew what she'd like and you – but haven't a clue. Hope I guess right.

Now I must wrestle with the darned house work.

That blot was a violent ring at the bell – and your letter.

Isn't it odd?

I was so delighted. But darling please don't get sad and lonely. Please make a great try not to be. I know how easy that is to say and how difficult to do, but please try. Remember I am here – tougher than you know – and all for you.

So is Max – He shows your photograph to everyone and they say How lovely!

I do think there is a chance that we may not be so poor then we can really help perhaps. Meanwhile one reason I cling to this house is because there is a room for you if you want a holiday. If we move it will be to a place where there is a room for you too. There's nothing I would not do and will start by sending some books pronto which may amuse you.

Just think of Java as an experience. It will pass and other things and places come along. You are so young with all life ahead. Then Java will fall into place as an experience – perhaps a useful one. Even the heat!

I feel you're too creative and restless to be a hausfrau (is that right?)

Is painting no use?

Or writing? Every day a little. Don't laugh at these suggestions. Writing can be (among other things), a safety valve.

My dear you are so right about the Nazi for that she *certainly* is "with knobs on". So is her husband. I guess they converted him in Germany. In fact there's a little nest of Nazis down here. Sometimes they frighten me as much as your silent footed people frighten you – and in the same way.

However I've managed up till now to hold my own and will go on doing so dam them!

All my love to you all and Max joins me though he's at the office now of course so it's a figure of speech. Still he does and freely.

Special hugs and kisses for yourself and Ruthie. I promise to post off some books this week.

Jean

P.S. Do you remember Moira Shearer the dancer you saw. Well she's having a great success in New York. So is Margot Fonteyn and all the Sadlers Wells ballet.

November 5th [1949]
Beckenham

TO HANS EGLI

Dear Dr Egli,

I have just seen your advertisement in the New Statesman[1]. This is my address – and I'd be pleased and interested to hear from you.

I married again some time ago – my name is now Hamer – Mrs Max Hamer. The Beckenham postman wouldn't recognise anything else I fear!

Yours sincerely
Jean Rhys

1. *The* New Statesman and Nation, *November 5th, 1949, contained the following*

58

insertion in the Personal Column: 'Jean Rhys (Mrs Tilden Smith) author of Voyage
in the Dark, After Leaving Mr Mackenzie, Good Morning, Midnight, *etc. Will
anyone knowing her whereabouts kindly communicate with Dr H. W. Egli, 3
Chesterfield Gardens, N.W.3.' Hans Egli was the husband of Selma Vaz Dias, who
had made an adaptation of* Good Morning, Midnight. *She needed Jean's permission,
and had no idea of her whereabouts.*

TO SELMA VAZ DIAS (MRS EGLI)[1]

Monday, November 7th [1949]
Beckenham

Dear Miss Vaz Dias,

I had your letter and MSS this morning. You can imagine how excited and
pleased I am, indeed it all seems a bit like a dream. Probably my usual
November 'flu helps this dreamlike feeling.

I expect it was a troublesome search. I don't belong to the PEN club and I left
all business contacts to Leslie Tilden-Smith. Anyway – it's easy to disappear.

I will send tickets[2] to John Lehman[3]. (I know he liked the book for he tried to
get a French translator for it), to Cyril Connolly[4] and to Mr Sadleir the
publisher also to a couple of personal friends and I'll try my hardest to come
you may be sure and I wish you and Good Morning Midnight all the luck in the
world.

I feel I should be flying about stirring up everything and everybody possible.

It's stupid being ill and in Beckenham which is a God forsaken place – and
cold.

Now I must get down to reading the MSS and sending off the tickets.

I'll write or telephone tomorrow. I hope we can meet before the 10th. I'm so
much looking forward to that.

Yours sincerely
Jean Rhys

1. *Born in Amsterdam in 1911, Selma Vaz Dias was educated at Highgate in London
and Versailles, studied at RADA and made her theatrical debut in 1929. With a forceful
personality and a striking if somewhat bizarre appearance, she was usually cast in
rather macabre roles, often in distinguished plays (by Ibsen, Cocteau, Genet) produced
at comparatively obscure theatres. She was also a professional painter. Her nature was
dominating, possessive and touchy. As her friendship with Jean progressed these
qualities became increasingly obtrusive and were eventually to verge on paranoia. She
died in 1977.*

2. *The tickets announced:* "Good Morning, Midnight *from the novel by Jean Rhys
adapted and read by Selma Vaz Dias. Thursday, November 10th, at 8 p.m. at the
Anglo French Art Centre, 29 Elm Tree Road, St John's Wood. St John's Wood
Station, Buses 13, 113 and 2 along Finchley Road, 59 and 159 along Abbey Road.
What the Press said of the book. . . . 'Miss Rhys engages the reader's concern for the
desperate small personal agonies over which the heroine treads her frantic way . . . .
The whole effect is femininely acute and the end is very pitiful and bitter': Kate
O'Brien. 'An uncomfortable and even rather terrible book, oddly impressive': Ralph*

Straus. 'A triumph of precision and honesty for an English novelist': Wynyard Browne. Admission 2/–."

3. Poet, publisher, editor of New Writing, *Lehmann had been an early admirer of Jean's work, as had his sister, the novelist Rosamond Lehmann.*

4. Writer, critic, editor of Horizon, *Connolly had briefly praised* Voyage in the Dark *in his essay "The Novel-Addict's Cupboard", reprinted in* The Condemned Playground *(1945).*

TO SELMA VAZ DIAS
Tuesday, November 9th [1949]
Beckenham

Dear Miss Vaz Dias,

I went through your script carefully yesterday afternoon. You've adapted my novel very sensitively, and seen Sasha almost as I saw her. Thank you.

I made two or three suggestions – all very slight – all cuts. I meant to send them with the script. However, I find that my husband has taken it to the post with the rough notes. He leaves very early in the morning when I'm still half asleep, and believes in speed!

I don't want any mistakes so am relying on my memory and sending this.

I know it seems stupid to fuss over a few lines or words, but I've never got over my longing for clarity, and a smooth firm foundation underneath the sound and the fury. I've learnt one generally gets this by cutting, or by very slight shifts and changes –

First and most important is the start. Sasha says "Anything can be brought up on a trolley but alas the waiter has a louse on his collar". Well in that sort of shabby Montparnasse hotel breakfast is (or was) brought up by the chambermaid. Drinks perhaps if you tip her. Anything else is out of character. There aren't any luxuries. That sentence comes later on when she's remembering a "swing high" period – a suite in a hotel in Vienna and a very different matter. I know that yesterday today and tomorrow are all mixed in her mind. But don't you think it is a good thing to anchor your character and her background firmly *at first*. Then the confusion can be led up to smoothly and more convincingly. That one sentence is the only snag. The rest goes.

On page 6 – "He called it the Pig and Lily". Oughtn't *he* to be *we*? As I read it "he" seemed to mean Pecanneli and makes him too important and his role a bit confusing. He's only the boss of a place where Sasha and her friend, or friends used to eat. I liked your calling him Pea. That's fine, and so like the man I had in mind that I had to smile.

Couldn't you cut "It wasn't far from the place I usually eat at" – same page I think. Not necessary. Better without. You'll see what I mean when you look at it.

That's all I can remember and it's only from my point of view. You as an actress, may have some special effect in mind. I don't know.

I hope you won't find all this fussy and longwinded and I won't bother you with anything more. I'll do my very best to turn up. (Talking about character, I assure you that being down with 'flu in a cold flat and no telephone just at this moment is *exactly* me. It would happen just that way and no other.)

I wish you again the best of luck. You've already lifted the numb hopeless feeling that stopped me writing for so long. I hope we'll meet soon but I won't bother you now with any plans or details about myself. I expect you want to concentrate on your own ideas and work. If I cannot be there my husband will go and tell me all about it. I'm trying to round up everybody I can but it's short notice. Given time I might be able to pull a few strings.

Yours sincerely & hopefully

Jean Rhys

TO MARYVONNE MOERMAN   *November 9th [1949]*
Beckenham

Dearest Maryvonne,

I'm sending you a book called "Jenny Villiers"¹ which I like and one of nursery rhymes for Ruthie. I will also send her a toy and something for you that I can get into a letter. I hope that some of these things will reach you safely if not by Xmas then for the New Year. Max wants to write to Job and will you give him my love and all good wishes.

My dear your last letter disturbed me, though it was very interesting. I don't like much what I read about the situation in some newspapers – others are optimistic, it's so difficult to judge.

But I can't *bear* to think of you being bored or unhappy.

I have had some news which may cheer you up. The enclosed advertisement was in the New Statesman on Friday. I answered it at once – very puzzled.

It turned out to be from a BBC actress called Selma Vaz Dias who wants to broadcast my work. She says she has been looking for me for "years" as the BBC like my stuff.

The preliminary reading is tomorrow.

I am very astonished that the BBC like my work (especially Good Morning) but it seems they thought I was dead – which of course would make a great difference. In fact they were going to follow it up with a broadcast "Quest for Jean Rhys" and I feel rather tactless being still alive!

However I'm cheered up too for if they can make a fuss of me dead surely they can make a *little fuss* though I'm not.

I can't write a long letter for I must send some of these leaflets to various people. Goodness knows I'm hopeless at the publicity stuff. Besides they've given me hardly any time –

However I will do my best for I'm jogged on by the determination to get some money for you and Ruthie. Then you'll feel very different. I will write soon again and tell you how it goes.

Meanwhile all my love darling and *cheer up Sam.*

Kisses & hugs
Jean

P.S. If only you were here to represent me. Max is frightfully busy. He too has visions of money money beautiful money.

1. *Novel by J. B. Priestley (1947).*

TO SELMA VAZ DIAS

November 12th [1949]
Beckenham

Dear Miss Vaz Dias,

You must think me a very odd fish. I wasn't able to come on the 10th and even telephone by proxy!

But I really have been ill and can do nothing else but cough and sneeze. Things always happen in twos and threes, and my husband is very busy just now. He has to go to Courts and suchlike outside London and on the 10th he'd been at Aylesbury. However he managed to get to the Anglo French place in time and told me all about it. He said you were splendid and that everything went off all right. I'm so glad and congratulate you.

Even this 'flu cannot last for ever and I hope that we may be able to meet soon. In about a week's time? You must imagine me in a dark road, in a dilapidated house (once very nice I should say) a neglected garden, and the nearest phone box a long cold walk away. Well, long when one's feeling ill.

I liked the place at first. It has space and trees but in the winter – really one's got to stiffen the sinews indeed.

I'm writing because though Max (my husband) promised to ring you up, he's very forgetful and also very busy. I wish I could have sent more people to the show but I hadn't much time to drum them up and as I told you most of those I've kept up with live in the country.

I cannot see "Good Morning Midnight" as a play – though last night I did have a flash about how it *might* be done with a big twist. However I did write one of my novels as a four act play[1] and have the MSS somewhere. I mean I saw it first as a play.

I am really very grateful to you – for I was convinced that I never wished to write again, and now I do – even rather badly.

It was really a chance my seeing your advertisement – but then – I don't believe in chance do you?

Yours sincerely
Jean Rhys

1. *This was* Postures/Quartet.

November 22nd [1949]
                                                        Beckenham
My Dear Selma Vaz Dias,

   I'll be delighted to see you on Thursday, and am so sorry to drag you all the
way here.

   You can't think how vexed I am with myself for cracking up just now – but
if you do see this place you'll understand that 'flu might hang on a long time –
(Don't be afraid for I'll manage to have one room heated anyway). Cold just
shrivels me up and I become incapable of all but shivers and shakes.

   I know I shall like you and hope you'll like me.

   But if you don't – that doesn't matter – for a writer is only a telephone
anyway, no not a telephone I can't think of the word. Besides I've been told I
grow on people which *isn't* a compliment!

   The play I wrote is very ancient you know – it dates from Paris and the late
twenties – But I have some other stuff which might interest you – and I've a
copy of Mackenzie too – though only one.

   If you change your mind or cannot manage Thursday you can always phone
my husband MON 5432 and we'll arrange something. I'm simply longing to be
well and clear headed again.

   I wish you luck for your broadcast and we'll certainly listen in.

                                                        Sincerely yours
                                                        Jean Rhys

November 22 [1949]
                                                        Beckenham
My dear,

   I hope you are better, but why oh *why* do you give pints of blood? There are
so many fat, beefy people about, *gorged* on Black Market food. Why can't they
blood let a bit? Because it would be so good for them. Please don't do it again.

   My BBC acquaintance is coming probably day after tomorrow. I'm utterly
drained of all ideas. All that's left of my excitement is a frightful longing to get
away from this dreary place at all costs.

   I could bear it as long as there was no hope at all – but one glimmer and I'm
like a darned greyhound at or on the leash.

   Oh Peggy I've been such a monumental fool (though on the other hand I
don't see *what* I could have done otherwise). But surely the last three years has
paid for that. My dear – this vast, grim, unheated kitchen, walls streaming
with damp, is worth a day in Purgatory – to say nowt of everything else.

   Well I have some stuff for her and hope the glimmer won't fade, for then I
fear I'll have to jump under a bus and that's not my fancy at all of an exit line.

   I'm pretty sure that with a few months peace and rest I could produce
something. So pray for me.

   I have sent Maryvonne and her baby some silly Xmas presents which will
probably be stolen by bandits en route – So what?

This is a thoroughly cheery letter isn't it?

But I've one laugh at the end. My bitter enemy next door is now telling everybody very loud and clear that I'm an imposter "impersonating a dead writer called Jean Rhys". She's accused me of every crime in the calender from adultery through dog poisoning to whatever Z stands for. Zenophobia? What's that? From adultery to Zenophobia, and Max has kept quite calm. But he's up in arms about this and has written her a stiff letter. However I've had to ask him to rewrite it for he named (of all people) Hamish Hamilton and yourself as witnesses to my identity. Well Hamish would find it a bore, and I would not dream of implicating you. But I've letters and contracts enough, and I'm pretty sure that Sadleir would step along and identify me if necessary. He doesn't like old girls like that old girl who's the wife of a retired shoemaker, and uncrowned queen of Beckenham. She's a long distance enemy. I bet I couldn't identify *her* in a crowded street but she's tough. She's the one who killed Gaby and the Black Cat and she's of the bulldog breed herself.

I bet they manage to spoil things somehow. Well, I've always got Holloway up my sleeve. And so, I bet again, has she! Love

Jean

It's a weird feeling being told you are impersonating yourself. Rather nightmarish. You think: perhaps I am!

TO PEGGY KIRKALDY

December 6th [1949]
Beckenham

I am so sorry Peggy my dear but I mislaid your letter, however suppose you're back in Colchester again.

I hope your indigestion is better. It's a damnable thing – so worrying and *carping* and always there. But I guess it's gone now. No there'll be no need for you to identify me. I could have done that myself. Anyway it's a bit comic that charge – unlike some others which do real and lasting harm.

However! It all fizzled out with the couple wishing me luck (I *don't* think) I do *not*!

Well I saw Miss Selma Vaz Dias and liked her. She's sensitive and as generous as a woman can be in these hard times.

But she's also very ambitious, I should say easily influenced by adverse comment and adverse advice, gossip etc.

I told her that the BBC wouldn't touch the book however much it was adapted and altered. And they won't I'm sure. Or anything else I've yet written.

The whole point is that I could write something else given a little peace, a little sympathy and all those other elusive things. "Elusive" is good!

It's a thousand to one chance I know. Nevertheless I will try. First because it's woken up my desire to write. Second because I'm seeing red at the lies that have got around and I want to hit back.

After all, I asked no one to help me, and complained only to myself. I gave up a hopeless struggle and walked into a worse but that's my own business – I didn't mix up anyone else except unfortunate Max.

So I'm bowled over when I find out that my being dead is about the kindest thing she heard. The unkindest – well let's not go into that.

My dear I had lots of letters, some fulsome, written when I was supposed to be on the up and up.

I wrote to nobody except yourself.

That wasn't because I imagined you liked me personally – I think you see me as a ridiculous human being – ridiculous and slightly (?) mad – also alien.

But I thought you liked my books and could sometimes forget the writer – that was a lot to hang on to. Because my loneliness has been terrible – (so now you know!)

Now I'm really hanging on to my belief in fate – I never wanted to write. I wished to be happy and peaceful and obscure. I was *dragged* into writing by a series of coincidences – Mrs Adam, Ford, Paris[1] – need for money.

I tried to stop – again I've been dragged back.

So I must go on now failure or not – lies or no lies.

Please forgive this exalted letter, I know that's a great fault of mine. I get exalted and make people hate me and wish to avoid me. And as I have no money background or friends – well off they are with a juicy morsel to laugh at and lie about.

Well that's the first fault.

The second danger is that my fierce boiling hatred of this dirty mob is going to sink me because I do silly things when I'm enraged.

Well well. Do wish me luck Peggy as I wish you all luck for the New Year and for always.

Jean

P.S. I can't resist quoting something Miss Vaz Dias said: "Dear Miss Rhys – You're so *gentle* and *quiet* – Not at all what I expected!" – I gathered afterwards that she expected a raving and not too clean maniac with straws in gruesome unwashed hair. Maybe I should have played it that way.

Never disappoint your audience.

---

1. *Mrs George Adam was the wife of* The Times *correspondent in Paris during the early 1920s. Jean, who had met her briefly in London during the war, approached her for help in placing three articles by Jean Lenglet which she had translated from the French. Instead Mrs Adam asked to see work of her own, and Jean showed her a diary she had kept between 1910 and 1919. Mrs Adam rewrote parts of it in the form of a novel called* Susie Tells *and sent the typescript to Ford Madox Ford. He changed the book's title to* Triple Sec *and the author's name (then Ella Lenglet) to Jean Rhys. The book was not published, but Ford encouraged her to go on writing and eventually printed her story "Vienne" in the last issue of* the transatlantic review *(December, 1924). By then, Lenglet had been extradited to Holland and Jean and Ford had become lovers. Jean jettisoned* Triple Sec *but later used the original diaries as a basis for* Voyage in the Dark.

December 9th [1949]
Beckenham

Dear Selma Vaz Dias,

I'm sorry you've been depressed. Please don't be. I don't know what to say to cheer you up – except that your coming here was the nicest thing that's happened to me for a long time. You did not stay too long – not long enough.

I'll not be surprised if the BBC turns down Good Morning Midnight, for I've had many brickbats hurled at it, so have grown a thick skin, then anyhow, some people do dislike my work intensely you know, and though others feel differently they are less vocal and perhaps less sure of themselves – and of me.

I was warned about all this ages ago, but I was fairly young then and self confident and imagined I could stand any number of brickbats.

All this is not interesting – you've done a very big thing for me, you've made me want to write again. It's not your fault, so don't be frightened! I am a bit, for I'm rather lazy and dread the effort and drudgery, and sometimes torment.

However I've one or two ideas which won't mean much of all that. I've got the title for one – "Black Castle"[1] which sounds like a boys book or Kafka but is neither.

I don't know whether it will be suitable for broadcasting and should like to consult you about that, for I'll use it as a short story or novel if you think the subject dubious. It's not Sex (strange Anglo Saxon word) or Insanity.

I'm afraid I seemed awfully all of a twitter and moony when you saw me (I *hate* to remember that coffee[2]) but things always happen at once and we were in the midst of a "crise" money mostly, and everything seemed to fall on me at once.

That's now safely over and there's a real chance of a few months peace and even a short holiday which would be heaven. If it comes off I'll eat a lot and get lots of fresh air then come back all poised and smooth ("Tomorrow, Tomorrow, Tomorrow"). Then I'll telephone you if I may – First there's a ghastly Social Occasion to be got through, a week end at Bournemouth and I can *feel* my face taking on its corrugated iron expression of fright already. So awful for other people but worse for me.

I'll listen in on the 13th you bet. If you do talk about my short stories will you remember that they were all written during the war and in London. Except one[3]. That explains a lot. One couldn't imagine any end to that time, and indeed if I'd known what the end was going to be for me, I'd have walked into the street instead of hiding under the table saying Hail Marys which I'm ashamed to say I did several times. (At least I hope I would.)

Till tomorrow then, and even if you don't think Black Castle the goods I hope to write something for your lovely voice one day.

Sincerely yours
Jean Rhys

1. *This was completed over ten years later and published under the title "Let Them Call It Jazz".*

2. *At their first meeting Jean offered to make coffee for Selma Vaz Dias, but forgot to put any coffee in the pot and poured her a cup of boiling water.*

3. *"Till September Petronella", which was written during the 1930s and set in 1914.*

TO MARYVONNE MOERMAN   *December 15th [1949]*
                                            Beckenham
My dear,

I was so very pleased and relieved to hear from you because I'd been worrying rather. In fact I nearly wired but didn't want to make a fuss. I was pleased I mean to hear at all but sorry you've been so ill poor darling.

Perhaps now you will get well and strong soon now. Gosh I do hope so and am sure too.

[. . . . . .]

My dear about the writing – I will do my best but it's hard to get back after so long. Selma broadcast on the Third Programme on Tuesday last and wrote me she was going to talk of my stories, but just as I was going to listen in the radio and all the lights went out. A strike. So I couldn't listen in and on top of that had to sit in the dark for about three hours. For now it's dark soon after four of course. Well I hope to God this dispute will soon be settled, for sitting in the dark is not my favourite amusement and of course everyone has rushed and bought up all the candles. The lights are working again but dimly. Life is like that now. I'd give anything for a few hours of warmth just as you like coolness. Again – life is like that.

Selma broadcasts again on Saturday and I may catch it this time. Unfortunately at the end it all depends on me. Can I or can't I be clear minded and ready to work again.

I'm going to try to have a holiday and forget the dark cold and damp of this house. You simply don't know how I hate cold and Beckenham is on top of a hill drat it.

I've had my fur coat shortened but am not sure if it is nice or silly if you were here you'd tell me.

Also I think of all the "material" "stuff" you have to write about. I have some but it's different. Yours would have more the spirit of now – the Zeit-gheist? – mine is not.

But do you know I think you could write. Only don't speak of it to anyone – just *do* it if you wish. A diary. Anything –

This is a silly letter but it's so cold and I don't know what to say. Was your hospital all right? I wish I knew the flowers Ruthie brought you.

Get very well and strong soon for you have all my love.

                                                    Jean

[. . . . . .]

Thursday [1949]
Beckenham

My dear Peggy,

Thank you my dear for the scent, and I'm sorry my thanks didn't get to you before. And my love and best wishes for the New Year. I've been ill and worried and didn't want to spoil your pleasant time with moaning at the Bar. I just couldn't write an ordinary letter.

Things aren't so good. Max has got into an awful jam at his office, has left and set up with a new partner. The less said about *him* the better. Maybe I'm wrong for I am so often – Here's hoping – Altogether I feel like Katherine Mansfield's fly after it was drowned the sixth time or was it the seventh[1]? I haven't written to Selma the BBC woman for my head is dazed with thinking.

I got this idioitic handshake before the smash.

The 'phones been cut off for ages.

1. *"The Fly", a story in Mansfield's* The Dove's Nest.

January 27th [1950]
Beckenham

Dear Peggy,

Your letter cheered me on a horrible morning and thank you.

I've seen this smash coming for three months but didn't know how to stop it – *What* to do *what* to do.

Get away from this frozen hell of a house for one thing. But where to go? Don't know.

Max isn't a bad chap but he's used to practical women, I guess – and despises my woolliness tho' really he's wool too.

Different colour though.

I will write again when things are better but write to me about cats and books – Please.

I've read nothing I like lately. Got Anthony West's On a Dark Night. Now a horrible and sinister thing called Harriet[1]. It has a certain power but is awful awful awful – a shocking book and true.

My cat is sweet and stays with me because it's so cold. I love him very much. Toi aussi – I mean my love to you.

Jean

What to do *what* to do and getting no answer at all – There *is* no answer so far as I can see.

Never mind, I'm a grotesque creature in this lovely day and age. So what? It's horribly cold in this awful house perhaps my brain's frozen and will thaw out.

One nice thing is that Maryvonne who has been very ill is better. She seems carefree about the bandits at the gate.

1. *Elizabeth Jenkins' novel* Harriet (1934) *is indeed a "horrible and sinister" story, based on a true Victorian scandal, about a family who keep their rich relation locked up, half starved, in an attic. Harriet's fate has obvious affinities with that of "the first Mrs Rochester" in* Jane Eyre *and* Wide Sargasso Sea.

TO SELMA VAZ DIAS

Monday [1950]
Beckenham

Dear Selma Vaz Dias,

Thank you for writing. I'm afraid it is a pretty bad smash and I do not see what is to be done about it. I've known of course, for a long time, that things weren't right but I didn't think they were so bad.

I'm trying now to sell my furniture and books tho' not with much success.

We are leaving this place in a day or two. When I have any address I'll write to you about the short stories – it might be a good thing to have them.

I'm afraid this is a very inadequate letter but I've been horribly worried for a long time, and this darned shock on top of it. Well! The worst is that the whole business is incredible and no one can be expected to believe it.

I'm not surprised the BBC didn't like "Good Morning Midnight". I knew they wouldn't. But the script I had in mind was different. It's a pity – I wanted so much to write again.

I will not forget, whatever happens, your warm and generous letter[1].

Yours
Jean Rhys

1. *Selma Vaz Dias attached to this letter the following newspaper cutting, dated February 15th 1950: "A charge of stealing seven cheque forms, valued at 1s 2d, was made at Guildhall yesterday against George [Max] Hamer, 67, solicitor, of Southend Road, Beckenham, Kent and Michael Donn, 35, solicitor's managing clerk, of Ellingford Road, Hackney. They were charged as servants to Cohen and Cohen, solicitors, of Salisbury House, London Wall. The hearing was adjourned until next Wednesday. Hamer was allowed bail in £500 and Donn in £1,000. Donn was ordered to report daily to the City Police. Det. Insp. Prothero, of the City Police, said that more serious charges would be preferred at a later stage, when the case was taken up by the Director of Public Prosecutions. He had reasons for believing that Donn had made arrangements to fly to the Continent. His passport had been taken from him. Det.-Sgt. Scott said that when arrested Donn said, 'I will tell you all about it. I have been a fool'."*

My dear Peggy,

Thank you for writing. I don't know if you've heard or have guessed that I'm pretty well sunk without trace – I say "have heard" because the news of Max's arrest about a fortnight? (am not sure) ago was in most of the evening papers.

The ghastly thing about it is that I guessed that a smash was coming as long ago as last October, and knew it was *certain* by Xmas. What I did not know was quite how bad the smash would be.

It's an incredible business and I suppose it's only natural that no one believes it. I hardly do myself. Keep hoping I'll wake up.

However it does seem to be a fact that most of the fairly large sums of money have gone into the pocket of this famous "partner" – I think I wrote you at the time how much I disliked and distrusted him. However my saying so did no good it only led to bitter arguments. If I'd had *one* person, I mean one of Max's relatives who would have believed me, and acted, the worst might have been staved off. But, unfortunately, my appearance or manner or something is *dead* against me and no one takes me seriously till it's too late. It's a pity for I'm not without a modicum of horse sense really.

The trouble is snubs and ridicule discourage me so I just sit tight and wait – and this time the resulting crash has been much worse than I feared in my most pessimistic mood.

Poor little Max he is so smashed up and I cannot comfort him at all. He is on bail at present and with me.

As for me – you know how frightened of life and of people I've been for a long time, so you can imagine my state of panic. Sometimes it's pure panic – other times my mind goes blank which is a mercy.

I restrained myself from writing to you because I didn't see what good it would be. I don't see what good anything is. I've made arrangements to sell all my furniture and stuff by auction. That may give me a few pounds. I couldn't wait to try to sell it privately because this place is mortgaged, and they foreclosed at once! We cannot stay here longer than a fortnight at the most. Foyle's are coming down about my books on Tuesday. It's about all I can do – for my own personal things are junk. I had a couple of decent rings but lost them (of course). Even the dressing case Leslie gave me isn't worth much, for some of the fittings are gone. I suppose I'll have to auction that. Some linen and blankets and that's the lot.

My dear I don't see what's the good of going on with this tale of woe.

I'm a hell of a misfit really and I don't know how I've survived so far – though in fairness to myself I do feel that I'm more sensible and adaptable than a casual glance etc – finish that sentence yourself for I'm tied up in it.

Peggy I *don't know what to do*. I really want of course to vanish for *good and all*, but I haven't the means of doing it quickly, and am a coward about the more obvious methods.

So I must get a job.

But *what* job – I can't type, am too slow and lethargic for a servant. So *what*? I'll try if possible to go to Christina Foyle and ask her for work. I believe I could pick up anything about books fairly quickly. I could answer the telephone and so on somewhere, but am a bit ancient aren't I? The same applies to a servant's job – I'd like that best if I could be just waiting at table and answering doors – I could do that. On the other hand I can't sew – in fact I'm completely useless really. At first sight anyway.

The really sad thing is that I wanted to write again so badly the first time for years. But that doesn't cut much ice now. All is strictly utilitarian. I believe I can get £1 a week from the state and a small sum for rent, so if I could find a very cheap unfurnished room I might just exist and scribble. Again that's all if if if – I've gone over everyone in my head and it's all quite useless.

I belong to a past age really or a future one. Not now.

Peggy forgive this dithering, it's the only relief I've allowed myself for a long time. That and reading Esther Waters[1] – why Esther Waters? I don't know. It's beautifully done and doesn't date a bit. I suppose reading about someone strong quiet and simple helps me.

I liked your letter about your lovely dress and worldly clerics. (I *mean* that.) It came on one of my "trance" days and somehow added to the unreal feeling which is I suppose kindly Nature's way when complete catastrophe arrives. Anodyne has always been my favourite word.

Well my dear write to me, for it helps. I'll try to save a book so that you can remember me –

Yours ever

Jean

P.S. You know I was really sunk when Leslie died. I was left with hardly any money – and his (Leslie's) sister dropped me like a hot brick tho' she oughtn't to have done that – not justly.

Max's sister is doing the same thing (with more excuse). But I wish she wouldn't try to persuade herself that I'm responsible for this last fiasco. When I think of how I begged, prayed, stormed and fought about this wretched creature (the partner) in fact I broke with Max outright over him – Well – it's a bit tough! Even now he's only to send a telegram and poor Max chases off after yet another damned will o' the wisp. He must be a hypnotist or something for I notice it works with other people as well. It damn well didn't work with me. *And* he knows it.

I've heard of a Catholic place I can go to – if I can manage that I will. I'm so tired –

I could read to people. Do you think that would be possible? I know a woman in New York who used to earn a sort of living that way. But this is not New York – or 1936.

1. *Novel by George Moore.*

TO SELMA VAZ DIAS

[1950]
42 Stanhope Gardens
London SW7
Fre 2393

Dear Selma Vaz Dias,

At last I've a moment to write to you. Things have been tumbling on my head like a shower bath (and not a pleasant one either) for some time. So I feel a bit dazed.

Max's affair will come off some time next week or fortnight. I hope so much, so terribly much, that he'll be all right.

In any case I can manage for a bit, and I want to go into the country and write. That is, I'll try.

I'd like to see you if you're not too busy. Can you ring me up here any morning before eleven or evening after nine – and we could arrange something. Don't be afraid I won't cry on your shoulder! You know I've seen this coming for a long time, and could not think how to stop it. That was one reason I was so nervous and so on when I saw you. But I've got over that now. Besides, I find that this perpetual moving round in a mass of people, acts like a drug. I dislike it intensely – all the same it is a drug.

Opium of the people etc. I do hope we can meet in some more or less cheerful place and have tea or a drink or something. There are some not so bad rather empty pubs round here, with comfortable chairs and I should like to see you so much.

I didn't get any letters from you before I left Beckenham except the one of the 16th March. But I believe some letters did go astray after we left – I did get a Xmas card. Thank you. I would have written long ago but have been so distracted.   Yours
                                                                                           Jean Rhys

If you ring here could you ask for Mrs Hamer room 12.

TO PEGGY KIRKALDY

April 12th [1950]
Stanhope Gardens

Peggy my dear,

I left Beckenham some time ago but when I went back yesterday to sell my books found your letter. Am sending this to Colchester and hope you'll get it.

I'm sorry you feel ill – and know so well that inertia which it's impossible to fight against. It runs its course and then something happens and it vanishes. My dear I hope hope *hope* you'll be quite well and yourself again soon.

I cannot write very sensibly for my own affairs are in such a complete and hopeless muddle that there is nothing at all to be done.

I feel like a baited bull and look a wreck, and as for my unfortunate brain well I saw it neatly described yesterday on an automatic thing in the tube

72

This machine is
EMPTY till further notice

The ghastly part of it is that I foresaw the whole crash. I've guessed that Max was riding for a fall ever since we were at Beckenham, *known* it since last October. If *one* person would have listened to me – Max's relations, his former partner, anybody – it might have been averted. I wouldn't have cared what they'd thought or said of me if only they'd given me a break and heard me out. But no. I just had to watch it happen, growing more hysterical every day. And so what. The almighty smash has come. Yet still in some new and twisted way they all blame me. It's more comfortable I guess.

Well all this wailing is no good and very undignified and not even convincing perhaps.

I'm still with Max, for I felt I couldn't leave him stranded. His affair comes off in a week or so. It's pretty bad, but I don't know the truth of it yet. He still hangs on to this ghastly person, this glib and sinister creature. So there you are – I'm not a worm and would have pulled out long ago, but I hadn't any money. I managed (at last) to sell my furniture tho' not for much. That's what we're living on now. I suppose I ought to have broken away at once when we left Beckenham. But I couldn't. He's so smashed up and I'm so alone and such a helpless person really. Like a jelly fish without the sting. At least that's what it must seem like to the candid onlooker.

But then he "don't know everythink".

I know I oughtn't to ramble on in this confused way but it helps me a bit.

Well we're in this ghastly place for a fortnight. It's ghastly because it's up seven flights of stairs and every morning at 8 o'clock they toll a gong and one has to leap out of bed and eat porridge.

Porridge makes me sick so I'm going to skip it in future. It's very expensive, so I eat at those automatic places – and my God there's something wrong with a world where one has to eat like that and everybody looks so darned miserable.

Yesterday the man in front of us smelt everything before he chose and fingered the cakes, but nobody cares – they eat the stuff looking miserable and dirty and so I daresay do I because all my clothes are at Beckenham. So who am I to carp. But still wire netting might be an idea don't you think? I mean over the horrible cakes. I can't be a cook Peggy because what between the porridge and the help yourself ABC I never wish to see food again. Besides I can only cook when I'm a bit tight and no sensible person could bear me for a week – as well you know so must be tongue in cheek.

I could pull myself together in a month or six weeks but it would need an angel's tact and delicacy and so on. So what –

My dear this is such an idiotic epistle but I can't write another. I'm so tired – Max met his sister today and she was horrified. She says it's too expensive round here. The dear lady doesn't know that everywhere is expensive. It's astounding and all landladies must be *very* wealthy.

I don't know what I shall do or what will happen and don't care. Am awfully weary and I minded selling my books, I feel so strange and defenceless with no books, no furniture, above all no cat.

I let one of the horrible women at Beckenham have him and it was the hardest of all. She's *such* a swine and smirked so triumphantly. She is a very fat young woman with a squeaky voice and so one day I called her the mountain who brought forth a mouse or some such idiocy, and she's been my sworn enemy ever since. But she likes cats and I could not kill him. Peggy am so ashamed of this letter but so tired and it's a relief. So excuse –

I know how complicated and senseless it sounds but I did my best for a long time and it is complicated.

Well now I'm going to have a lovely bath and go to my hard bed.

Today we went to Les Parents Terribles at Studio One. First rate acting, but I cannot lose myself in Jean Cocteau. I liked his "La Belle et la Bête" though – except the end which was absurd I thought. I mean I do not think Beauty and the Beast should be wafted to Heaven at the end, do you? I like just "lived happily ever after".

I must be a bit hysterical to run on like this. A bit? Very!

Do write soon and I'll answer more sensibly. Am here for a few days or so.

Yours
Jean

Get well soon dear Peggy.

Monday [1950]
                                                                Stanhope Gardens

Peggy my dear,

Max's case comes on tomorrow, he's with his lawyer now, and as I'm too weary to tramp about the stony streets I'll talk to you instead and risk boring you. My dear if I'm confusing about what has happened – well I'm pretty confused too. But I'll tell you all I know and make it as short as possible – thank you for listening.

To start at the start as Ford would say – You remember don't you that when you came to see me at Beckenham I was full of plans for fixing up the poor old house. That was the start (at any rate so far as I know). A very plausible man who called himself a "builder" had agreed to repair the water pipes, make the basement habitable and all the rest. I was very enthusiastic about this, I was simply delighted when I thought of settling in that house and just flopping for the rest of my life. I'm awfully tired, tired to my soul, and I am not brave at all now but an almighty coward. I hadn't the slightest reason to distrust Max. He was Leslie's cousin, he knew I had no money when he asked me to marry him, none better, for he was the trustee (Leslie's will). He'd been very kind to me. Also I am perfectly certain even now that Max is not a bad hat. He's potty. I *look* potty, he *is* potty. There's no other explanation. Listen. This builder (so called) got a hundred quid from me and *three* hundred from Max (to start off with). He sent some workmen along and they made a hell of a row for a week.

The second week they sat around and smoked, the third week they vanished. So did the builder, Wilson. So did the £400. Well, I was a bit shaken but not suspicious. Max repaid me my £100. When I asked why he didn't go to the police he said it would be useless as the whole affair was black market. All *accident*, you see, that might happen to anyone!!

However Wilson was followed by "Wells". His stunt was something to do with night clubs. He got £300 from Max. Then I began to get jittery – especially when Wells rang up and told me that Max was getting in with the worst gang of crooks in London.

I didn't know what to do. Wells told me that Max was always drunk, that his new partner Yale was just out of jail and was always drunk aussi. (That was true for Yale was generally so tight by lunch time that I couldn't understand him when he telephoned.) (When I met Max he was partner in a firm of Lincolns Inn solicitors but they quarrelled. That I think was the *real* start but I don't know the details or indeed anything about the affair). Wells shortly after this useful information vanished too. So did the £300. Then Max's association with Yale came to an end and they had an awful row.

Then my dear I went all of a doodah and of course I started to drink again –

You see I am weak and a coward and it wasn't a pleasant situation. The house was a bit ghostly and *lonely* oh Lord! and my small money was melting away, gas, electricity, phone, hairdos and housecoats to woo back the straying Max. God what a fool I am! Clinging vines aren't in it.

But remember that I was also deadly deadly tired – cannot explain how tired.

When Wells departed Roberts appeared. He was the worst. He didn't borrow a wallop and go. He borrowed small sums but constantly – and he stayed. I mean he hung round.

About Christmas I'd worked myself into a frenzy. I told Max that our marriage was a failure, and that I wanted to give it up. I asked him to repay me about £50 and let me depart. He said he was broke: I said What about Roberts? He said Roberts was a great inventor and would make his and our fortune. I swore. Then we started to quarrel – constantly. Everyone blamed me – ça va sans dire – I was a harridan, a drunkard, Heaven knows what. And bats of course.

The more they abused me, the more bitter I became, and the worse I handled the whole affair – in fact I couldn't have behaved worse or with less tact.

I don't know if I've given you the feeling that Max is a pansy. Au contraire. He is a very male creature and in a heart-rending way he is naive. He hates my writing for instance, I'm sure of that. Perhaps I might have managed him – perhaps.

No he's no pansy, but a gambler and as he's grown older he's become a crazy gambler. He clutched at any chance of making money. He talked of money constantly. That bored me to tears and I said so. Then we'd fight.

Of course there were long weeks of peace. Max got a job with Cohen & Cohen – and sometimes I pretended I was happy. Well Happy! What a word! Time marched on anyway. I didn't drink so much but I didn't eat much either and was desperate inside. One day the man in the flat upstairs was rude to me. I slapped his face. He had me up for assault[1]. I had no witnesses. He had his wife and umpteen others. I began to cry in the witness box and the magistrate sent me to Holloway to find out if I was crazy. I told you about that – the Holloway people said I wasn't crazy and sent me back to the magistrate who told me not to be violent any more plus fines of course. After that I sank into apathy as they say.

It was just then or not so long afterwards that the BBC girl Selma advertised for me. I saw her and liked her. It meant a lot to me and I began to wake up and make plans and come alive again.

I wanted to do a thing about Holloway to be called Black Castle –

And it was exactly at this time that this archfiend came into the picture. This Donne or Dunn person.

I saw at once that he was up a different street – unlike the others. Very intelligent, very sensitive, and a bit mad. It also stuck out five miles that he was a crook. Max asked me what I thought of him. I was very cautious because I know Max's mulish obstinacy, so I only said that I liked him but would he be wary about money. Max said "Oh I'm going to get him a job at Cohen's". Well I was fairly easy in my mind – I thought they'll see what I saw. Here my dear is the incredible part. *They didn't.*

M. Cohen père is over seventy and has been a solicitor for fifty years or something. He lives at Grosvenor House so hasn't done badly. Cohen fils hangs about night clubs and chases theatrical ladies. You'd think wouldn't you that those two would be cautious – not a bit of it. Inside of a week, Donne was installed at Cohen's office – chief cook and bottle washer. I didn't know one instant's peace afterwards. Every night Max would send me a wire "Detained" – I thought "Donne has produced some ghastly smart girl". Perhaps he did – but surely if he had Max would have cut his hair and bought shirts and socks and things. Vain and obstinate as he is, surely he'd have run to a new tie!

But no. Every day he'd say "Tonight Donne's getting me two hundred or five hundred" or a thousand and always he'd get more haggard and shabby and disappointed. I couldn't bear it any longer, and asked him if he'd lend me enough money to go away for a week. I meant to pull myself together and do something. Well the Saturday I was to go he disappeared for five days. That was when I cracked up – physically I mean and I do not think I'll ever be well again – not really. On Thursday I determined to sell my furniture for what it would fetch and depart. On Thursday night Max turned up again dramatically. He climbed through the window and said "C'est moi". I could only say "Tiens!" It was like a farce or a dream or both. I asked him why they'd gone to Paris. He said to borrow money because *He* has friends there. Apparently the celebrated charm didn't work because they'd come back empty handed. Max told me that they'd left Cohen's and were starting on their own in Bell Yard. He said they'd make all the money in the world because Donne knew all the crooks in London. (That part I believed). I went to their office once, it was packed with counsel clients and all the set up. Everybody hung on Donne's Come in Go out. Aitch (that's what he calls Max – H. fetch me this).

76

The clerk a nice young man told me "Mr Donne is a wonderful man. I'm proud to be working for him I'd do anything for him I've never met anyone like him." I could only stare.

Well what could I think or do or say against all this? I don't know how long it was before Max vanished again and after a few days I heard through the Law Society that Max and Donne had been arrested.

Then it all came out. Thousands were missing. Cohen, money-lenders and some clients'.

Max swears Donne had it all, I don't know what Donne says but can guess. Still they meet, still he can hypnotise Max or so it seems.

I thought when I began this that I'd clarify the situation but I've only made it more confused. I don't know any more. I can see that Donne is clever as hell, sensitive, heartless. But all that clever? No, I don't see it. You'll say How could I stick it? Why didn't I go? I really had so little money and I got so weary. You don't know. I got so that I slept all the time and the only thing I wanted was sweets. Yes my dear SWEETS.

I cannot explain how this anxiety can smash one up.

Well you'll say Max is a rogue. No he isn't. He's mad for money and Donne hypnotised him. He says he wanted it for me. That isn't all true but it may be a bit true. He just wanted it. He may have spent some on women or a woman but not much. He doesn't give me that feeling – besides he is too cynical. I simply can see nothing clearly at all. It's *crazy*. I can't think how Donne got rid of it all or why they keep on seeing each other.

My dear have you read all this? I may as well bring it up to date. Yesterday I had a letter from a solicitor in Lincolns Inn Fields. A friend who wishes to remain anonymous will supply me with money to live on for the present. I don't know who it is. Certainly not my relatives. Max says Lord Listowel who's a friend or relative or something – or a combination of his sister and Listowel I don't know and hardly care. It's all very uncertain – I don't know whether to stay in London and see people or go away and rest.

I must rest a bit, I must or I'll crash utterly. But I must be careful where I go for they'll only pay my hotel bill and there's not any margin for mistakes. I want somewhere to rest where they'll just let me rest.

Perhaps I'll find something in the New Statesman. I thought of your place in Monmouth, but it's a long way off.

I don't know why I'm not more grateful to this very very generous person. I will be when I'm better.

I do know Eric Ambler's books and I'd like to meet him and his wife. But I must be better first. I cry so easily and fly into a rage so easily that I'm not fit for human society.

I haven't written to anybody tho' Selma heard the dire news and wrote me a very nice letter. She's a good sort. I must write and try to see her.

Peggy I'd like a job in a shop but alas I am not chic or elegant. I'm grotesque except somebody else dresses me and advises me. I was all right sometimes in Paris because Jean bought all my clothes. Funny – he was odd about money too.

And Peggy to show how hopeless I am, *I cannot type*. Can you beat it? You see I didn't revise so much my two first books. Then Leslie used to say he liked typing tho' I bet he didn't really.

I'm lazy and hopeless Peggy but honestly I do have a rum time.

Love
Jean

Max has just come in. His thing has been adjourned. Donne's mother wants to meet us. Well with what human curiosity I've left I like to hear about Mr Donne's mother.

1. *See footnote, page 57.*

TO PEGGY KIRKALDY   *[April 21st 1950]*
Stanhope Gardens

I will post this and the other which is all I know at the same time. Thank goodness I've told somebody.

My dear Peggy,

I said I'd write you a sensible letter and you will get a long incoherent screed and perhaps you'll be worried when you get it or tired and you'll think for goodness sake *what* is it to do with me.

Well, if you feel like that, just tell yourself that I had no one to talk to for nearly two years – with all that on my mind! I couldn't give Max away, and if I had, no one would have believed me. Max looks so sane and sensible you see and I don't.

When I had proof (a money lender's letter which I opened) it was already too late.

I hope that Max's sister brothers and former partner will all reflect that if they'd given me a chance to talk a year ago they could have saved him – and it wouldn't have cost them much. Tea and a smile – or just tea would have done it.

However it's no use. I know them. They won't reflect anything of the sort.

The case is adjourned or supposed to be for three weeks.

Peggy, I'm rather finished and am desperately anxious to rest.

This is what I want. A quiet place, a quiet room where they'll let me have some tea and bread and butter in the morning. Then I'll get up and go out and be no trouble at all. And a bed that isn't hard where I can sleep and sleep and sleep. I can pay about four and a half guineas or so and the dough is quite all right for they'll get it from the anonymous pal – and if he, or they, suddenly stop then I've enough to settle up and go.

Unless I can rest I'm going to crack up utterly. The spring is broken as they say en français. If it could be a place near trees that would be heaven. Trees plus a river is too much to ask.

I'm writing to a place I saw in the New Statesman but if you know of anywhere it will be a good deed – really it will and enough said.

I have lost the Monmouth address do you think that would be good? But I dread any sort of hotel or boarding house. I don't want to have to see people much. I don't want to bore anybody.

You see my dear if I have that to look forward to it may pull me together.

The situation is as rum as ever. The case is supposed to be adjourned but even that seems doubtful. Everyone has warned Max to keep clear of Dunne but he lives in Dunne's pocket. The latest idea is that I should go and live with Ma Dunne. In what capacity I wonder? Personally I don't believe that Mrs Dunne exists. Dunne thinks it sounds good to talk about her – that's all.

She's made several dates but never turns up. Besides why does Max not leave him alone? His lawyer, the police, all warn him – it's no use. A clear case of hypnotism or madness. Or there's lots more to this that I still don't know.

I saw Detective Inspector Protheroe – was the name I think. He calls D "The Bright Boy" or "The Fiddler" – he said "I told him 'Well Dunne, my lad you say you're a musician, if you fiddle in heaven one half as well as you've fiddled on earth the heavenly choir'll stop to listen.'" I had to laugh. Indeed I often stop crying to laugh, or both at once which is a bad sign.

Last night I was thinking "If I could jump out of the window one bang and I'd be out of it." For this is the sixth floor.

Then I thought of Max's story of the old lady who went to church with her ear trumpet. And so the stern Scotch sexton or verger or something, eyed her a bit. Then he said "Madam one toot and you're oot". Perhaps that's what it would be like, One toot and you're oot –

I don't know what you must be thinking of this hysteria. But really this is an odd situation. Max and I wander about to all sorts of places when he's not telephoning to D – being telephoned to, or waiting for D who never turns up. We've been to Westminster Cathedral, Westminster Abbey, and the Tate.

The Tate was on Sunday. We wandered about and I found a lovely Modigliani, and a lovely flower piece, Gauguin – and a still more lovely one, Chagall?? Don't know the spelling of anything now. Very mysterious and moonlighty and Max liked Stanley Spencer and Epstein and I liked Renoir and Courbet very much, very romantic and gloomy woods. Oh God if I could be there. And I liked a man called Tissot? whom one isn't supposed to like. Who cares? Nobody's going to tell me what to like. Very gay ladies with fans and bustles and the light was right, I don't care what anybody says. I know that light on a ship's deck with the sun striking up from the water, and it was right, and who cares if the ladies are too jolie jolie and have yellow bows on their bustles. It was gay.

Well I thought all was well but as soon as we got outside Max had a violent fit of rage, really violent, and started to abuse Winston Churchill so it all ended badly as usual.

Dear Peggy I won't write any more nonsense. I shall be here for another week for I don't want to leave Max (Mrs Micawber) and I've lots of rubbish to collect at Beckenham, and I must see this solicitor about the anonymous benefactor. I don't feel awfully happy about it.

So you see. I'm good and busy. But if you can think of a place tell me please.

I won't write any more letters but I want to tell you about Max.

Well he looks like an elderly reliable lawyer when he's at his worst, and like an elderly naval type when he's relaxed, at his best he does not look elderly at all, for he's astonishingly quick and vital and all that. He runs very fast. He's shortish and bald but what hair there is is dark. He has a strong face, aquiline, good bones. No sign of weakness, only of bitterness. He has very dark blue eyes and sensitive good hands.

I could understand him doing reckless things – but this business. No I cannot understand it. I cannot understand a man like Max trailing after a man like Mr Dunne or Donne to prison. I haven't a clue either.

I could understand Max getting deadly sick of me for I'm not his type (or anybody's) but I cannot understand his casting me into stony London and not realising that I feel like a homeless cat with a tin can tied to it too. He just doesn't realise *why* I'm so unhappy tho he knows I'm unhappy. He doesn't know how I like trees, shadows, a shaded light. Well, all the things I like. He doesn't realise anything and neither do I. So there we are. Miles and miles away.

Love

Jean

TO MARYVONNE MOERMAN *May 1st [1950]*
Stanhope Gardens

Dearest Maryvonne,

I don't know what you must think of me for not writing for so long, but a great deal has been happening, and I ended by being ill. I thought it would only worry you. I'm a lot better now and am soon going into the country for a long rest (I hope).

We've left Beckenham for good. I'm half glad and half sorry because the summer is nice there. But the place was getting too much really, so damp and cold and a drag up to London. On the whole it's better.

We're living now in a Kensington hotel very pleasant but too expensive for long. We spend Sundays wandering about picture galleries and museums. *How* I used to hate them long ago! But now I'm awfully interested. There are some lovely things – I saw some Persian vases and carpets yesterday oh so lovely – a glorious blue the vases – very consoling. Also some fourteenth century Madonnas – I loved. It sounds a funny mixture.

Well my dear you'll be wondering what it really is all about. Max, as I told you, got into money difficulties but I think all will be well now. But it's been an anxious time. I feel it's all my fault – that I should have looked after him better – but really I'm so bad at finding out things and short of following him like a detective I don't see what I could have done.

I'd like to be one of those detectives who solve things by *brain*work in a comfortable armchair, for I cannot see myself as the other kind at all. Well I try not to worry too much and here we still are looking at Persian vases so all is well.

80

We are both here and nothing is wrong between us. It's only dam dam money. Things are bad for a lot of people now you know. Taxes are terrific and everything goes up and up.

We'll be here for another week or ten days.

After that the bank address will find me.

Or better still Peggy's address.

> c/o Mrs Kirkaldy
> 8 Beverley Road
> Colchester
> Essex

Perhaps Peggy would be better. Do you remember her? We're still friends and write each other long letters.

Now my dear what is much more important. How are you? How is Job? How is Ruthie? [. . . . .] I long to know all this so do write soon and tell me.

I haven't forgotten your birthday [. . . . .] and will send a hanky or something. I wish it could be more. Anyway there's many happy returns from both of us, hugs and kisses galore to you and Ruthie and love to all.

> Yrs as ever
> *Ella*

I hate signing myself Ella to you really.

[. . . . . .]

TO PEGGY KIRKALDY   *[May 1950]*
                                                  Stanhope Gardens
Peggy my dear,

Thank you for your letter. It means a lot, a friendly word just now. Max's case comes off on Monday[1]. It is still a muddle so far as I can see. The waiting's pretty bad so I'm trying to live from day to day or from minute to minute, and so get by.

I can understand nothing. It's a crazy affair. It's not benefited anybody. Nobody's even had a good time except Donne Dunn? and that not for long. I've seen Mrs Donne, the mother though that can't be her name as she hardly speaks English at all. Middle Europe somewhere. She seems a very simple, kind soul and says this is killing her. She certainly looks ill enough and very frail.

Max's sister says it's killing her. Though she just implies it. She also thinks I am to blame, though God knows how. I am, of course, to blame for as soon as I suspected anything I should have gone to the sister, the brothers or the ex-partner and *forced* them to listen.

True, I would have risked the loony bin, as I had no proof at all, but that would have been a small risk compared with this crash.

My dear I am awfully grateful to the unknown donor, but I can see it's all very tentative and insecure. Still I am determined to have a rest for a week or two or three and have written to the Welsh place[2], I hope she can have me, for I don't want to crack up. People are so merciless. It's terrifying. Also they are stupid. I'm sorry if that sounds arrogant but it is true.

They *always* believe a lie. They *never* believe the truth – Never! I carry round letters to prove everything I say now. They bulge out of my bag and are a great nuisance, but I find it better just to plonk the evidence down and say nothing.

Max and I wander about odd pubs near Victoria, and cheap cinemas and museums. We went to the Victoria & Albert last Sunday and saw some lovely things. Persian vases, such a consoling blue quite glorious and perfect. And XIV century Madonnas which I always like and so on. Have just spoken to Donne on the 'phone. *Very* chirpy. He's a rum creature. It's a pity. He must have something, yet jail is all this blasted world can find for that bird of fire (bird of prey too though).

I'll write soon again Peggy less jerkily.

I've done something which I hope you won't mind. I've given your address to Maryvonne. She is, as you know, in Java and not well. Sentiment apart, it won't be good for her if I just *vanish*, and as she knows your name I thought it would be a good plan.

Continuity you see. So important. I know how ghastly it is to be stranded when you're young, without even a name to hang on to.

One thinks it doesn't matter, but it is definitely bad. I also gave her the solicitors, so she may not write to you. I mean write to me c/o you.

I hope I've explained properly. It's only that I have no fixed address and I don't want her to guess anything's wrong so I wrote "Do you remember Peggy? She still writes to me and if you write etc the letter will be forwarded –" I also gave her the solicitor so won't have vanished. Must stop, maid wants to do room.

Love

Jean

I hope you will not mind about Java. She only writes once in a blue moon. I should have asked you first but so – distracted.

1. *The trial began at the Central Criminal Court, Old Bailey, on May 9th, 1950. On May 22nd George Victor Max Hamer was convicted on two charges of obtaining with intent to defraud a cheque for £1,400 and £100 in cash from one person, and a cheque for £1,500 from another person, in each case by false pretences. Two days later he was sentenced to three years' imprisonment. Michael Donn (who admitted to two previous sentences of three years and three and a half years respectively) was convicted on six charges and sentenced to four years imprisonment.*

2. *Peggy Kirkaldy had sent a long, worried, affectionate letter dated April 22nd in which she said: "The address is Half Moon Inn, Llanthony, near Abergavenny . . . . If the house is full, try Llanthony Abbey, or the 'Monastery' Capel y fin near. But ask Edith Colley at the Half Moon to put you up. Tell her you are my friend." It is not known whether Jean got to Wales: her next surviving letter, written to her daughter nearly a year later, is from an address in Maidstone where she was staying (although she does not give the reason) to be near Max while he was serving his sentence in Maidstone Prison.*

PART THREE

Maryvonne

(1951–1956)

TO MARYVONNE MOERMAN

My Dear Maryvonne,

I was so glad to get your letter and Ruthie looks a sweetheart. You know quite apart from anything else it is wonderful to hear of someone wearing gay clothes (your outfit sounded *very* nice) or to think of the sun. This morning there was a weather map in the paper. I meant to send it as a joke – but someone has pinched it.

Well it is like this: North Snow. East Rain and Snow. West Rain. South Rain and Sleet. That is correct – except that a few hailstones are usually thrown in for good measure. Also there is a nice lovely strong wind straight from Siberia. This has been going on for seven months or so – I simply don't remember what the sun looks like. Sometimes there is a glare in the sky, but as the wind is always at its worst on those days I do not like this glare. Well that is enough about the weather. They say that it is the only topic of conversation here, but it is certainly very strange weather.

Of course I remember the red shoes. Do you remember that other time one Xmas when we shopped at Harrods? We bought pyjamas for Leslie, a very good mouth organ as you wanted one and some other things. Then we or rather I lost the whole lot. Left it in the Ladies room.

But you got another mouth organ somehow because I remember you playing it.

Nobody wears red shoes here. The girls wear a mackintosh of a drab colour, snow boots and a draggled head scarf. Underneath a check skirt and a jumper brown or beige. The older women are either very fat or very thin, and nearly always wear glasses. They stare without moving their eyes at all.

Well more or less. They talk about rheumatism because most people have it, which is not surprising.

And that's enough about Maidstone too.

There's so much else I want to talk about. First (as it comes into my mind) about your hair. I am simply delighted that you are letting it wave naturally. It is much prettier and besides it is a horrible bore to depend on a hairdresser – really awful to know that you must scrape up the money or else look a savage. I have to and it is about my biggest small worry. Especially as hairdressers put their prices up and up.

Your hair is naturally curly so you will not have this beastly choice and I'm so glad.

Now about smiling – I'm all for it – it is a good plan and worth an effort. I find people who show their teeth letting their eyes remain quite blank – or even hostile – a bit alarming, but I honestly don't think that is the majority verdict. They don't notice.

Besides you have a real smile and "les belles dents rendent gai." (Is that right?)

Do you know this business of looking cheerful whatever happens has always cropped up. I suppose it's a sort of habit in fact I know it is and I'm sure it's a good habit and very *very* useful I can assure you.

There is so much I want to say and I'm so afraid of saying it badly and being heavy handed about it. You must forgive me if I am.

I am very glad about your shorthand and typing.

Don't you think that at the back of everything when one gets down is that awful *anxious* feeling. The insecure feeling, that prevents you from being happy and living from day to day?

Well this or that may cause it. But I'm certain one cure (half anyhow) is to feel that a job, perhaps a good job, is a possibility.

I cannot say what I want to, so you must imagine it, and I think you can.

I spend a lot of time imagining you and what you are doing. Now I can do it a bit better. Short hair, face okay, smile.

I also spend time thinking about Ruthie. I have a very special feeling for her. It is so damnable that I cannot send her all sorts of things as I'm so hard up. But that will be better in a few months. Also I want to send you things especially books.

I will manage some for your birthday. If they aren't all new excuse – I'll send ones you may like.

The people I see most of now don't like books at all.

They speak, as it were, another language. Of course I don't for one moment alter my own opinions but it is rather like facing a blank wall all the time.

However I am, perhaps fortunately, very stubborn. So that is that. Besides I can always (obstinately) go back into myself as it were, but too much of that isn't good.

I will write Ruthie a letter soon and send her some stories.

Will you give her my best and dearest love and the same for you and many hugs.

Also my love to Job and *be nice to him*. But I'm sure you are. He is nice I think. I liked him very much (said the famous judge of character!).

Max sends his love and good wishes.

I will send the letter to Ruthie to you in a few days and I will send something more exciting than a letter soon I hope.   Your loving

                                                                                                        Jean

PS. Have you got one of these brushes that brush scent into the hair – "Kent" brushes?

They are good.

June 5th [1951]
TO MARYVONNE MOERMAN   2 Lower Faut Road
                                                                                                Maidstone, Kent

My dear Maryvonne,

Another address! It's rather confusing to move around like this and I wish it wasn't necessary. However . . . these rooms are much nicer.

First my dear I must wish you very many happy returns of the day – of May 22nd.

I meant to send you a greetings telegram but I wasn't able to manage it. Money!! This made me rather sad. That's why I didn't write – a stupid reason really.

Still I thought of you all day if that is any good and I hope this won't seem too belated.

I got a pair of gloves for you and I will send them along as soon as I've recovered from the latest move. I haven't been awfully well but am quite okay again now. I do not know why I have to move so much for I'm an awful packer and a worse manager as you know.

[. . . . . .]

I haven't forgotten about the books. But do you know I feel that everything I send to you goes to a void. I mean I'm never *quite* sure if it reaches you. I wrote a long letter to Ruthie and you. Did it ever arrive?

It was very heavy over weight perhaps.

Well there is one thing if you have written to 5 Hever Gardens it'll get to me all right.

But to make things quite certain here is an address which will certainly find me in Maidstone:

c/o Messrs Bracker Son & Miskin, Solicitors
Star House
Maidstone

(Don't think I'm getting divorced for I'm not!! Only that is a safe address.)

Well what else can I say. I've been reading even more than usual since I haven't been well.

I've struck some good books. I wish I could send you dozens – all the ones I like. People say that books and writing and writers are finished. Well I do not agree do you? The form may perhaps change – in some way one cannot foresee – But the thing itself not. Well the books that impressed me

The Age of Longing by Arthur Koestler – that most I should say. Not at all cheerful but very very good.

He is a good writer though pessimistic.

Now I've got Jean-Paul Sartre's plays very well translated – I like them better than his novels. I am not quite sure how I feel about Jean-Paul Sartre – He has something. But not perhaps enough. ??? WHO HAS?

I never get with him that knock on the heart which means

That is truth, that is final. That came from au delà.

I expect one only gets that from the greatest.

This is such a restless and anxious time so nobody can quite give that feeling of certainty any more.

I don't know why I am saying all this. But you said you liked books. Anyway it is quite impossible for me to talk about writers and writing.

I become at once very banal and out come all the clichés, "knocks on the heart" – the au delà and all the rest – (As I daresay you have noticed!).

87

Anyway to finish up the catalogue I have an English book by H. E. Bates about Burma. That is of course more or less an adventure story and a bit of a relief after Jean Paul Sartre. (Besides I imagine perhaps quite wrongly that Burma and Java are alike.)

At any rate I hope it is not quite so hot as Mr Bates says it is. Really if you cannot move a step without your clothes being soaked in sweat it must be bad. The Purple Plain this thing is called.

Anyway the girls are always cool it seems, and they wear green blouses, red skirts and frangipanni flowers in their hair. Well *that's* okay.

All my love hugs and kisses and a big hug for Ruth a bigger for you.

I wish you would send me a line for I am starting to feel like Old Faithful the big hearted dog who *wouldn't* get lost!

Jean

TO MARYVONNE MOERMAN   *Monday, October 22nd [1951]*
                                                      Maidstone

My dear Maryvonne,

When I see a letter of yours lying on the mat I'm simply as pleased as – I cannot think of a simile. Well I am *pleased*.

You asked me how I live and why we moved. I manage somehow though not easily. As to why I would rather tell you about that when it is all over.

That will be soon with any luck – in a few months. So every day I say to myself, Excelsior and Onward it's *nearly* over and soon will be finished. For frankly I do not like Maidstone.

I am well and quite OK and don't ever worry about me. I am the cat with nine lives.

Talking about cats you don't know how I miss mine. Luckily we found a good home for him. But if you can believe it – I still dream of him. As soon as I can I will have another kitten, Persian if possible. But now I have to be satisfied with talking to every cat I see in the street, or on doorsteps or in restaurants.

Dogs I detest – more and more. But they don't seem to know it – they always come close to have a look. Last night I went out to post a letter and a huge animal jumped up at me and almost knocked me over. The owner said "'E won't 'urt you. 'E's playful." I didn't answer but of course thought of the most crushing and witty remarks five minutes afterwards (as one always does).

One nice thing about my life is that this is a pub, a small one. But still a pub. The rooms are small and dark but not without a certain something attractive – for it's an old house.

In this place where I'm writing now there is a row of black elephants on the mantelpiece, a table with a plate of red apples and some flowers (a present from the landlady this morning), a lot of books and an electric fire. So you see what more can I want? She (the landlady) is a real dear and so is her husband. Jesus

88

Christ was quite right about publicans (and about sinners too in my opinion). They are nicer than other people – I sincerely hope that they will walk first into Heaven leaving the holy righteous and respectable outside looking very puzzled.

This pub has the funny name of "The Ropemaker's Arms", but don't put that on any letter (*if* you write some time again) or it will go to the front of the house, the bar.

I never go there and don't drink. Can you credit that? Really *never* to drink that is not me at all!

However I'm saving up for a real debauch some time, probably at Xmas.

I am well, and I don't think I've changed awfully, except that I blue my hair when I can, and don't wear black any more for it doesn't suit me now but blue or grey. When I can get anything new. I still adore clothes. It is ridiculous. Now that's all about me, let's come to you which is what matters.

I do know how one longs for company, companions I mean, or a friend. Oh *don't* I know! I'm afraid I've solved that by burying myself in books.

The result is I do go about in a sort of dream I suppose.

But after all it is one solution. But I think yours will be a better one.

It is quite true that wealthy people especially if they've had money for some time, even some generations are the most broadminded and sometimes the gentlest too. (Though that brings in the aristocrat heredity and so on). They get more tolerant – that is the word I want. Also simple people can be grand if they aren't too brutal.

But oh dear the middle way respectable ones – they *can* be the devil – I do think gossip can be such a cruel thing and they gossip so much. *Everyone must be exactly alike*. Or woe to them. It is a horrible idea. Talk about "the soul destroying middle". That is right. I expect there are a lot about everywhere and the East can be bad they say. I don't know what to say about escaping them. Books, music, you can escape that way.

I ran right away you know like "la chèvre de M. Seguin"¹. Do you know that – Daudet I think. "Et le lendemain les loups l'ont mangé".

However I had some good times first and now still books, and the hope of writing again and Max.

But I must say the wolves certainly had a meal off me! I've gone back to myself again. How selfish I am. Really! Don't let them eat you. But you won't, I know.

Now I must "stop my interesting narrative" and go to bed. Max says that – "Pray continue your most interesting narrative."

It's a quotation from "Sherlock Holmes". I read Adventures of Sherlock Holmes again the other day and really it is still rather fun. It has *atmosphere*. Gas–light, fog, hansom cabs, Baker Street, and so on. Do you know one of the things I hate most about being so hard up? I can't send you and Ruthie the books I'd like. I've made a list though and one day I hope you'll get a big package.

Next day

It's lovely to think of your holiday coming so close. I expect you have fun

89

planning it. I haven't seen the Thames since that week in 1939 when war broke out. Do you remember?

I think often of our punting and camping – it was grand. All our holidays were. I read that the Thames is spoilt a bit now because so many people use motor launches as they can't punt or even paddle.

Of course the river is too small for that. The wash makes it impossible for other boats.

However I expect that's near London and that beyond Oxford is still all right.

Things are changed a bit here you know, there is something rather robot-like about a lot of people.

There is an election going on but nobody seems to care much, not in this town anyway. Perhaps they are too *exhausted*.

I think that is all my news except that the winter has started oh dear. Icy winds are blowing.

I am sad about John[2]. I wish he could be better. His wife sounds nice. He has much charm don't you think? So somebody will always care.

What can I say to Ruthie except that I'd love to see her dance. I adore ballet – real escapism – but can only go to the films of it these days. Red Shoes and Tales of Hoffman, the last unmercifully "cut" in Maidstone.

You saw Moira Shearer with Max didn't you? He sends his love and so do I and all of it. Also hugs and kisses galore.
Your loving
Jean

or Ella as you like it.
Salutations to the cats.

1. From Lettres de mon Moulin *by Alphonse Daudet.*
2. *This refers to Maryvonne's father, Jean Lenglet, whose health had been shattered by his experiences in a concentration camp during the war. After his divorce from Jean he had married Henriette van Eyk, but that too had ended in divorce and he was now very happily married to a young Polish woman.*

November 25th [1951]
Maidstone

My dear Maryvonne,

This is a letter I am going to like writing very much and I hope you'll like getting it.

Remember I told you that things were going to be better for me soon? They're a bit better already so I think I can send you and Ruthie a present if not for Xmas for the New Year. But I am very anxious that it should be something you'd like.

I've thought and thought of various things.

For Ruthie a book. But as she is only four poor darling what book would amuse her?

I wanted to send her some "classic" she'd like later on. Or do you ever read aloud to her? The Green Fairy Book is still lovely if I can get it. Or the Blue or the Red? Or "The Wind in the Willows" or any of E. Nesbit's like "Five Children and It". Is there anything you can think of? I will send too a gay one for somebody who is still a baby.

For you. A book too? Or is that dull. I have not belonged to a decent library for some time.

But here are some advertised –

The New Yorker 25th Anniversary Album (drawings)

Short Stories from the New Yorker.

"A year of Grace" Anthology

I hear that is good.

Anything you think you'd like?

But perhaps you'd like something else. Here are some things I thought of. A jumper – (anyway *that* is good in England –) Short Sleeved I suppose.

But what is your size. And what colour. Black? Very smart. Red? Blue? Yellow? Pink? Would you like a woolly one for the hills. Or cotton? Or a nylon and wool mixture. Just a jumper or a twin set. The little coat useful for after tennis perhaps.

Or

Camiknickers or a nightgown

Or

Stuff to make underclothes. Nylon? What colour?

Green, Sky? White?

Or

A pair of slippers trimmed with fur. I saw an emerald green pair that looked like you.

Or a box with soap powder or any cosmetics. You don't like scent or usen't to. But lavender water Yardleys?

Don't laugh. I'm just floundering about. Do tell me.

I don't really know if there is a huge duty on all these things so that it isn't worth sending them.

I don't know what you can buy easily yourself and what is difficult for you to get.

Or would you like me to try to send the money to you. It will be so little honey. But perhaps you could get some little thing you want.

I'll wait for an answer to this. But not too long. I expect I'll fall back on books as usual if I don't hear.

Well my dear I'm in a hurry to post this so for now – All my love, hugs and kisses. A happy New Year to you all.

It's real winter now cold and dark. How I hate it.

Love again *a very great deal of that.*

Ella

PS. Remember I don't know your exact size for a jumper. Or indeed any *other* useful information.

I think about your holiday too. Wouldn't it be lovely if you could spend some time in Italy as you've always wanted to.

A subscription to Vogue. Does that attract you?

TO MARYVONNE MOERMAN   *April 29th [1952]*
                                                        Maidstone

My dear Maryvonne,

Max and I will be leaving Maidstone on the 9th of next month[1], a bit sooner than we expected.

I think we're going to London, but as soon as I know for certain I'll write the new address.

Meanwhile this place is still all right for letters. I'll keep in touch with the landlady. My dear I feel that I'm an awfully unsatisfactory sort of parent, skipping around like this when I ought to be settled peacefully somewhere learning how to knit.

You can't think how much I long for it – and the only excuse I have for not doing better is that a lot of people are unsettled these days.

Did you ever get the Penguins I wonder?

I still have the other books I bought for Xmas. The Blue Fairy Book, Fierce Bad Rabbit, Hemingway and so on. I could take them back I suppose but I don't want to do that – will try and hang on to them till that very nice day when I can give them to you. As there are one or two other things I want to present to you I hope that day will roll along quickly.

I thought of registering the books to John – is that a good idea? But if you think so let me know his address.

It will be nearly your birthday when you get this, so I send you all my love and hugs and kisses of the largest size.

Many happy returns. One of the things I hate most about my present situation is that I can't afford telegrams or anything nice.

But it will not last believe me.

I don't know what else to say except (sentimentally) that I love you. Always have, always will.

But I expect you know that really.

And that I do hope you didn't think that because I told you I was in money difficulties I expected a lot of sympathy or anything at all.

I simply didn't. I know you need all your money and all your energy for yourself and Ellen[2] – I'm only wretched because I can't help for the present.

As a matter of fact I get rather furious over this money question.

You remember Peggy?

Well we'd stayed friends for so long and wrote enormous letters.

But as soon as she heard I was in difficulties she wrote like this:

Dear Jean, I can't let you have any money because I had a bad week at the races and am heavily in debt to the bookies. Yrs Peggy
(She had become a great racegoer and betted a lot)
I wrote back
Dear Peggy,
I never asked you for money. Yrs Jean.
And that was that[3]. I was sorry because I liked her and had known her so long. But really!
I've been an awful fool over money and I'm sorry now because of you.
For myself I don't care any more. Except that I still adore clothes and pretty things.
Again all my love hugs and kisses to all. And a special birthday hug for you my dear.

Jean

1. *Exactly two years since the start of Max Hamer's trial: earning full remission, he served only two thirds of his sentence.*

2. *Maryvonne's daughter came to prefer her first name.*

3. *Fortunately, this letter marked only a temporary break in Jean and Peggy's friendship. On May 4th, 1957, Peggy wrote to Selma Vaz Dias: "You probably won't remember but I wrote you some time ago to see if you had Jean Rhys's address and it could not be found. I used to know her well and was fond of her and much regret I lost touch. All efforts to find her failed and I felt perhaps she wanted to live in retirement. She is a very difficult person and it is quite impossible to live with her in any ordinary way, for she has a strong character and I used to find that she took offence at most unsuspected things and used to imagine mankind was 'agin her'. I do so admire her work and have for years wondered what had become of her. I feel I have failed her but that could not be helped as I have been very ill. If you will send me her address I shall be so glad. If not, I enclose a letter to her which I would be so glad if you would forward to her. Her life was tragic, her courage quite indomitable. . . ." This prompted a revival of the friendship and an affectionate correspondence during the last year of Peggy's life. "My dear, I was so glad to get your letter," she wrote in February 1958, three months before her death, "found it very vital and a flashing bit of Jean. You comfort me; I am so scared. . . . Do write again soon. Love, as ever, Peggy". Jean's letters of this period have not survived.*

June 22nd [1952]

TO MARYVONNE MOERMAN
29 Milestone Road, Upper Norwood
London SE19

My dear Maryvonne,
I had your letter all right. I am awfully glad you have a job. Everyone seems to have one now and the money must come in handy – lovely now.
Here we are back in London at last *thank God!* Really Maidstone is a horrid place though it was no use saying so while I was there.
When I say "London" it is about as far off as Beckenham, but pleasanter –

93

and we found an awfully nice flatlet – after the usual agony of searching. There is a kitchen and bathroom for us and as the people who share the house (a Pole and a Czech) are always out we have the place to ourselves – almost. I love that of course being a hermit.

It's a bit expensive but I do trust we'll be able to stay. The house is on a hill and the roofs go up and down not straight.

Also the Polish monsieur is a great gardener and has some lovely roses. Two are now near me and make me rather joyful.

Max is a lot better so our troubles are not so bad you see.

I have to keep going up to Maples to sort out the debris of my things there – on these days I become very bad tempered because of sadness and general King-Kongishness.

Do you remember when you used to call me King Kong? That was really a bit naughty of you – and hurt my feelings very much. . . .

[. . . . . .]

I think it's a very good idea to bring up Ellen with no inhibitions. Still, don't let her put out her tongue too much. Everybody is so rude now that it is very original to be polite.

Some of the kids here are *awful* especially in the cinema. The noise they make is terrific. Three kids make enough row for twenty. Also they get bored when there is no shooting going on, and clatter about buying ices while I am in floods of tears over the pathos and tragedy.

I was always an easy weeper as you know.

As I told Max today M.G.M. ought to keep me to try out their starlets. The one who couldn't make me cry would be indeed a bad actress!

I like so much not being alone. Hugs and kisses and for Ellen a big hug.

Jean

I'll write soon again

TO MARYVONNE MOERMAN   *August 31st [1952]*
                                                          Milestone Road

My dear Maryvonne,

How are you and how is Ellen whom I always think of as Ruthie? And Job?

I meant to write to you on my birthday, but as a great treat I spent the day in bed and went to sleep! When I woke up it was too late to write. . . .

[. . . . . .]

We are still undecided whether to stay here or not.

I don't like this part of London much, and it's quite an affair getting up to anywhere but Croydon, which is dull and so crowded. Also it's a bit expensive. But the little flat we have is rather pleasant and there's a pretty garden complete with pond and goldfish. So here we still are. Hesitating! . . .

[. . . . . .]

How goes the job? Are you still pleased with it? Would you like any fashion papers? If so which?

Your books and Ellen's are still here waiting. I often think "I must get such and such a book for Maryvonne." If I always did there'd be a trunkful.

So my dear write soon for life is going on muted strings for us at present. Not a bad thing either perhaps. But not thrilling to hear about. . . .

[. . . . . .]

Max is OK. So am I and I always like September. The old Crystal Palace which was burnt down was near here and there are huge grounds. Almost empty, and nice to walk in. Not melancholy, but rather open with magnificent trees. Near here was also The Convent of the Faithful Virgin to which I took you because that was the order my West Indian Convent belonged to.

Do you remember? You simply *hated* it tho' you didn't tell me why and your stay was short.

Write soon my dear.

Max sends his best respects and much love.

Ella

TO MARYVONNE MOERMAN   *Thursday October 16th [1952]*
                                                                Milestone Road

Take care of yourself.
Glad about the job.

My dear Maryvonne,

I was awfully glad to have your letter written on Ruthie's birthday. But it was not dated and I couldn't distinguish the postmark so I'm still doubtful about exact day. September anyhow. I have now become a great numerologist – at least I do think it odd the way certain numbers turn up over and over again in people's lives. Two is your number I know, six is mine. All nonsense I daresay.

She sounds a great darling and I am sure you are awfully good with her. Perhaps you can guess how much I'm longing to see you both so I'll say no more about *that* except that I hope you'll have a grand time and it must be fun planning for it. They say Spain is the cheapest country in Europe now and the best. And Portugal? Here there will be the Coronation, God knows what that will be like. The most hideous "Coronation souvenirs" mugs, boxes of sweets, cups and plates are already sprouting all over the place. They also propose putting a gilded cage around Eros in Piccadilly (you remember that statue). Everybody tries to climb on it when they're tight and it's usually protected by an awful wooden hutch. The other idea is to let Charles I in Whitehall wear a scarlet cloak. *That* will have to be guarded or it will be stolen at once.

About Ruthie. Don't think I'm getting all grandmotherly if I remind you that *Calcium* is awfully good for teeth – It certainly worked with you. It isn't nasty only a bit dry.

I've been going to the dentist lately and having front teeth stopped. Oh Lord teeth can be so important. And *can* they hurt.

I have some of my things from Maples a few books pictures and so on now.

Among them are some sketches you did when you were about twelve. I like them most awfully. One of a tree and some little beings (fairies I suppose) dancing is so good, and Max is very fond of it – I have found a frame for it and will get it glazed. It is so light and simple and full of movement. Beaucoup du talent. They are making a great fuss about children's pictures now. Quite right too. None I have seen can touch yours though.

Do you mind Ruthie looking like a doll? Sometimes I think it is rather sweet and after all it is easy to change that by the way you dress her when she grows older.

I am of course awfully clever about everything. In theory. And too late.

Now I will tell you why I didn't answer at once.

A couple of weeks ago or so there was an advertisement of a caravan to let in Cornwall. Near Penzance. I was crazy to go. We, you Leslie and I, never went to Cornwall but parts of it especially near Penzance are lovely. The sea is quite blue and the whole feeling is different. Like it is in Wales.

Well I wanted to chuck up everything and just go. Perhaps you can imagine the storm of sarcasm and opposition I ran into.

I have now given way, but only for the present.

I intend to find somewhere like that whatever they say. We will get a little fishing boat and call it the "Je m'en fous". That was the name of one I saw on the Riviera.

I really gave in because it is true that it rains a lot in the winter and Max's chest isn't too good and a caravan could be tough.

However he knows all about boats and sooner or later I *will* go. Je m'en fous.

I hate this suburb and all the mean little streets around. One can't breathe. However this house and street are fairly pleasant. It is a bright October but very cold. This is being written in bed to keep warm.

Now I must get up so all my love and kisses and a belated birthday hug and kiss to Ruthie from her loving Grannie.

January 1st [1953]
Milestone Road
Tel LIV 1631

TO SELMA VAZ DIAS

Dear Selma Vaz Dias,

Do you remember meeting me about three years ago and adapting Good Morning Midnight and our talk about a play?

Well I'm in London for a while – if you can call this God forsaken spot London – and I'd like to see you.

I expect you are very busy and three years is a long time. Still, it's a long time to simmer too – and I'm nearly on the boil if you understand.

I don't know how you'll react to all this and I'll understand if you don't react at all.

I won't talk about the banished three years. They've been *awful*, except for one peaceful period when I got rooms in a nice pub in the country called "The Ropemakers Arms" and was able to work. But that could not last long.

However I have survived and I think I've discovered a place in Cornwall where I (we) will be able to settle down and write.

I've a play in my mind and a part you might like. But I don't know if the subject and the treatment would get by. That's what I'd like to talk about.

This place is a long way off it would be a bore coming here. Somewhere near Victoria Station?

I'm free for the next two or three weeks. I prefer afternoons – am nearly always in mornings – have given you my telephone number. Any time any place which is a large order. I leave the initiative to you as I am not sure how you'll feel about the proposition. It must sound a bit nebulous.

If you do meet me remember that I always *sound* vague. I hate talking about something that is not finished and am sure that as a rule it is a bad thing to do. For me.

But I don't think so in this case.

I wonder if you'll get this letter. I hope so.

Anyhow I do wish you a happy and lucky New Year.

Yrs sincerely
Jean Rhys

TO MORCHARD BISHOP

January 11th [1953]
Milestone Road

Dear Morchard Bishop,
Thank you for your letter to my husband. I am so glad that you still remember my books and wish me well.

I've been quite out of touch with everything and everybody for a long time, or it seems a long time. (Meaning of course that so many people I've come across have been indifferent to books, and quite a few hate books *any* books). So I needed cheering up. I *don't* mean this literally, of course, and in any case it's an enormous and delicate subject don't you think?

I did write another novel "Good Morning, Midnight"[1]. It was published not long before the war, so the title was apt anyway. It was abused a good deal but for such contradictory reasons that I didn't mind much.

It did have repercussions not so long ago and what with one thing and another I want very much to try again.

Believe me, I don't under-estimate the difficulties.

The chief is a place to write in. Any peaceful place. But what a lot to ask!

My husband read something of yours and liked it very much. I told him that you had written to me sympathetically years ago and that you lived then in Devonshire.

Hence his letter[2].

Thank you for the list of papers. We will try.

We've heard of a caravan in Cornwall, but the winter has been so long and so horrible that one hesitates about a caravan. A nice warm cave now. That would be splendid. If you hear of one do not forget us.

I have not yet read your last book. Indeed I read few new books these days.

However I did find Denton Welch at one God forsaken library and Sartre at another. Not sure about Sartre. I do think his plays are good and that "Nausea" is a fine title.

I'm now reading "The Turn of the Screw" for the 6th time. It fits this deserted suburb and the fog.   Yours sincerely
Jean Rhys

1. *Jean must have forgotten for the moment that Morchard Bishop had written to congratulate her on this book when it was published in 1939.*

2. *Max Hamer had written to Morchard Bishop on December 29th, 1952: "Dear Morchard Bishop, My wife Jean Rhys tells me that that is the proper way to address you. It is about her I want to write, as at one time you corresponded with her. She has had a very difficult time since her husband died and now is most anxious to resume what she feels is the only career she is fit for i.e. Writing. My own bumbling efforts have proved quite fruitless so I thought of writing to you to ask if you have any suggestions to make. Our present difficulty is accommodation and I thought that possibly you might know of somewhere in the West Country where it would be possible to rent a cottage. I am quite sure that the place we are now in is quite unsuitable for her purpose though otherwise she is most anxious to recommence. Incidentally she has a book planned out. Yours sincerely, G.V.M. Hamer. P.S. She is mentioned in Alec Waugh's 'The Clock Strikes Twice' so she can't be absolutely forgotten."*

TO MORCHARD BISHOP   *January 27th [1953]*
Milestone Road

My dear Morchard Bishop,

I liked getting your letter. It is such a relief to hear from someone who understands one's difficulties.

A kind of stiffness is one of them yes, another is an unwillingness which goes deeper than laziness – as if something is *flatly refusing* to jump through the hoop once more.

The worst of the lot though is the mood when the unfortunate – Me in this case – starts off full of self confidence, bursting with ideas – too many, rather incoherent and words come so fast that they can't be caught and an interruption drives one into a frenzy of rage, and it all ends in a horrible cafard because the whale is only a sprat.

I expect you know all these moods. They aren't important, except perhaps the unwillingness, which wearies me. I've never had it before and it is very strong so I tell myself Softly softly catchee monkey and hope it will depart.

The really important difficulty is the place, room, cave, cabin to write in. I cannot see how I can manage without that – Or how anybody can. Our flatlet place in SE19 has some advantages but there is no vestige of space outside or in and not much privacy. The walls are so thin. It faces a row of low-ceilinged houses like rabbit hutches. One feels so shut in.

The street had a curious feeling in the fog – not so much sinister as empty. "The Deserted Suburb"? I suppose that's because the inhabitants work in London or Croydon and just trickle back at night to sleep.

The Crystal Palace is not far off. That is rather fascinating. Don't you like ruins? There are so many in the West Indies. I grew up with them. No I do not idealise the West Country. It has always rained when I've been there. But I thought the caravan would be a jumping off ground.

However the winter has been so awful and everybody disapproves. So it's become slightly remote.

I *must* leave SE19 and Max feels the same. Meanwhile I am trying rather half heartedly to rewrite an early novel as a play. It could be done. The play is there. But – well But –

All this does not sound very lively or courageous. But if I can manage to make one more effort and finish something I'll feel I've done my job and be at peace. I don't much care what happens to the thing *when* it is finished. Not my business I feel. That is very impractical but so it is.

I was living in Chelsea when the war broke out, then Leslie my husband joined up – the RAF. We wandered about the country a bit, but were back in London for the fly bombs and those other horrible affairs the V2s. Leslie died suddenly in 1945 and I rather smashed up after that for some time.

But I do hope my seven years bad luck is over now or nearly over –

I finished a book of short stories but didn't make any great effort to sell it. Rather lifeless though I tried hard enough. Too hard.

Everyone does seem very pessimistic about the future of writing and art in general. But hasn't it always been a fight? I remember how very bitter most of the English in Paris were about that very subject ages ago.

And – please don't think me impertinent – but I do find that so many people here are not phoney but *unreal*.

I read a letter in the Observer last Sunday from some editor – Peter Green – promising to accept any story up to (of) the standard of "Boule de Suif"[1]. Well I should damned well think he would! And Hemingway's last thing[2]. Why not add Prosper Merimée's "Carmen" for good measure.

Poor Boule de Suif. They won't let her rest –

The thing is I very much doubt whether any story seriously glorifying the prostitute and showing up not one but several British housewives to say nothing of two nuns! – their meannesses and cant and spite – would be accepted by the average editor or any editor.

And "La Maison Tellier"[3]? – Well imagine –

Of course I may be quite wrong. I don't know much about it these days. But I do read a lot and have a very definite impression that "thought control" is on the way and ought to be resisted. But will it be resisted?

Why say as Mr Green does "I demand a positive and creative view of life?"

What is that? And why *demand* a view of life. Not his business surely.

It's all very well to talk about The Old Man and the Sea but what about "Hills like White Elephants" or "A Way You'll Never Be"[4]. . . .

[. . . . . .]

Would those be up to his "positive and creative" standard?

As I am getting excited and you are getting bored that is enough. It has done me a great deal of good to write this so forgive me.

I do know something about the way a reviewer feels.

Like a publisher's reader only more so I expect – And this is growing into a young MS. right here and now!

But I do feel rather deeply about the thought control matter. So insidious. And suddenly it's there – Not to be resisted any more.

Yours sincerely

Jean Rhys

I have seen two or three people. They tell me I am generally supposed to be dead. Also that my last book was cribbed from Henry Miller's Tropic of Cancer.

That makes me fierce, though it is also rather comic. It would take too long to tell you why. *J.R.*

1. Story by Guy de Maupassant.

2. Hemingway's novel The Old Man and the Sea.

3. Story by Maupassant.

4. "Hills Like White Elephants", "A Way You'll Never Be": stories by Hemingway.

TO SELMA VAZ DIAS *Tuesday February 17th [1953]*
Milestone Road

Here is the book. It was called "Quartet" in America.

I'll write tomorrow all I can remember of how I saw it as a play. It won't be much, but sometimes there is a useful hint or two to be got from the original idea don't you think?

It was a literary play meant to be read not acted. Three Acts two scenes each act.

The first Act was in Lefranco's Restaurant Boulevard Montparnasse. The first words

"Here's hoping" – Heidler speaking, page 48.

I had such a cafard when you telephoned. [. . . . . .] I feel better now but still very shaky.

I will write to Mr Lehmann if you wish when I'm better – or leave it to you.

I have some short stories and poems which you have not seen. The poems – I don't know. One short story "Fort comme la mort"[1] might be something.

I won't be depressed if "Quartet" proves impossible as a play. Am horribly indifferent to a finished job – or what anyone thinks of it.

Yet I tried very hard over the damned thing for over a year. It was written in Paris in a rather horrid little rue.

I hope your little girl's cold will be better soon and that this truly awful winter will end. A bientôt!

Yrs
Jean R

1. *This story was later published as "The Day They Burned The Books".*

TO SELMA VAZ DIAS   *March 3rd [1953]*
                                                     Milestone Road

This is a pompous letter. Sorry.

Dear Selma Vaz Dias,

Did you get the book? It was posted the same day you rang me up Feb 17th.

I know that one waits for the right mood before reading anything and making up one's mind and I'm perfectly sure that this is as it ought to be. It isn't delay but watching out for a "No" "Yes" "Now" "Never" which is generally dead right.

So this isn't to say Have you read it? but Did you get it?

My God how portentous all this sounds!!

I'm still in bed but not ill any longer, tired and horribly lazy and sleeping a lot and reading all (some) books that are magic to me without wondering how the wheels go round or how it's done – which invariably spoils everything.

I've had some worries lately but they've withdrawn for a bit.

Well about Postures. When I say I don't care what anyone thinks about my books I don't mean of course that I don't care what you think about that particular one. Of course I do. For I'm depending on you to tell me some time whether there's a play in it. Or not. At least to a great extent I am depending on you.

What I meant was that when a book is finished I'm not vulnerable about it. It is off and away, not mine any longer, but on its own. So why should I care what's said about it? It can't be altered now. It can only be rewritten and made into something else. Perhaps.

I'm awfully thick skinned about my past work. Really that is true. But I'm thin skinned (also receptive) to any hints about future work.

So when you told me that somebody (I forgot who) thought everything I'd done dated a bit, I considered the matter – especially as I've had lots of time to do it in.

I see what he means, but also doubt whether it is valid criticism.

After all books and plays are written some time, some place, by some person affected by that time, that place, the clothes he sees and wears, other books, the air and the room and every damned thing. It *must* be so, and how can it be otherwise except his book is a copy?

Well this is an interminable subject. (Fashion of course is a different matter but surely an out of date fashion creeping in is covered by one word – Delete.)

I expect you are bored but I do think a lot don't I?

Good thing or bad? Don't know.

Write to me some time – remember that I am not sensitive about criticism. It's all on the surface if I seem so.

I may ring up to know if the book reached you.   Yours
                                                          Jean

"Don't judge a book by its cover". Do you know that ancient song? I haven't written to John Lehmann yet, I will. I hope this is legible. Max says he can't read a word I write in pencil.

March 4th

I had your letter this morning. Will ring you this evening or tomorrow. Glad you liked poor old "Postures". How is the play (rehearsals) going?[1] I hope well.

Best of luck.

1. *Selma Vaz Dias was about to appear at the Embassy Theatre in a play called* The Herald Angels.

TO MORCHARD BISHOP   *March 5th [1953]*
                                                       Milestone Road

My dear Morchard Bishop,

I have been so long answering your letter forgive me. I've been ill – 'flu of course, and it hung on grimly and hasn't quite departed yet.

So I can still lie in bed all day and write all letters in pencil. Very nice too – Provided you can read it.

Now about this age business – I do not agree with you – not quite.

Don't you think that age is often *forced* on people? The overwhelming opinion is that everyone (especially women) must be first elderly (when they've lived so long) then old, then very old – then, God help them.

Anyone who resists is ridiculous, then tragic, finally bumped off – or as good as – (if one can imagine anyone resisting fiercely enough to need that drastic treatment).

Well I am sure this is all wrong.

Everyone must die – but old age in many cases could be dispensed with. It will be one day.

It varies. It is not always a matter of years. It varies even from one country to another, time to another, one income to another. *Certainly that –* So you see – Anyway you are a man and the pressure is not so fierce then. You have fifteen long years probably to be still at your best. As a writer longer. As yourself at least ten. . . . [. . . . . .]

Well I've a way of starting these subjects which cannot be dealt with and then I have to drop them, and that is all.

But weariness and discouragement and dullness and so much else in this horrible world is enough – and perhaps that nothing is new any more. (Or only rarely) Yes, all the sympathy and kindness is needed desparately – And generally isn't there – But if it is then indeed it helps.

I don't believe in the individual Writer so much as in Writing. It uses you and throws you away when you are not useful any longer. But it does not do this until you are useless and quite useless too. Meanwhile there is nothing to do but plod along line upon line. Then there's a drink of course which is awfully handy. Or drinks. "*When* I've done that I'll have a drink . . ." I *do* wish you luck and am keeping my fingers crossed and thank you for being so kind.

I know a bit about reading MSS and how melancholy that can be – Leslie who was my last husband was a publisher's reader, and he would often be horribly bored. Horribly. And he was not a writer which makes things so much worse.

This I'm afraid is getting very much like a MS! So hurry, hurry. I have not even *started* on that fascinating subject – myself and I could write pages about that.

Or told you how old I am.

Well day before yesterday I read "Esther Waters" for the 60th time. It is a book I keep for very bad days, and it never fails me. It was published in 1894 and that's near enough to the date of my birth – I'm older a bit. So very old.

I don't know why "Esther Waters" has this magic effect on me – because I do not like horses particularly or care about racing [. . . . . .] or servants (White. Black ones are nice). Or religion – Still there it is. Magic for me. Every time. There are a few other books of course.

I do think there is something very mysterious about books don't you?

That's the only luck I have. I usually dislike my books, sometimes don't want to touch them. But the Next One will be a bit better. I am always excited and forget all the failures and all else.

Perhaps that's luck enough (If it doesn't fail me). I sold nearly all the books I owned except the Penguins. I had "Valerie"[1] I was so indignant about her. Why should that lovely girl have no fun at all? Not one day? Or night? Just a dreadful loathsome husband and a love affair too late.

But I expect you know Bournemouth and were indignant too. And hoped to stop other Valeries happening. Anyway –

Yours
Jean Rhys

P.S. I know that this is now a MS. It's the paper does it. And the clip.

So I must tell you – When Esther Waters was finished I began on "Journal d'un curé de campagne" Georges Bernanos. I expect you know it. Just as I was deciding I wasn't in the mood for it, I read this:

"*Il faudrait parler de soi avec une rigeur inflexible.* Et au premier effort pour se saisir, d'où viennent cette pitié, ce relâchement de toutes les fibres de l'âme et cette envie de pleurer?"

So one is caught, nothing to do but read on. I know that "parler de soi" is not supposed to be the proper thing to do. Not in England. And not now in 1953.

I feel so fiercely about that. No one knows anything but himself or herself. And that badly.

Don't you think so? Other people are seen and heard and felt. Known? Not on your life.

JR

1. *Novel by Morchard Bishop (1949).*

TO SELMA VAZ DIAS *March 27th [1953]*
Milestone Road

Dear Selma,

[. . . . .] If I can possibly crawl along to Great Cumberland Place on Sunday we'll come. My horrible 'flu hangs on and I ache all over like nobody's business (It'll be all right soon I expect.)

[. . . . .]

Anyhow I'll send you "The Sound of the River" also a short story called "Houdia". You might be able to use it, a bit melodramatic. It was written in Paris ages ago.

Max read it last night and at once asked it if had actually happened! No it didn't.

I did know a studio in Mont Rouge like the one in the story but all the goings on there are fiction and I assure you that I've never been arrested by bicycle cops either! Or tried to shoot anybody.

It was from this story "Houdia" that the book Quartet started. The idea, that's to say. It needs cutting (Houdia I mean). I can easily do that – It's a bit battered looking but readable.

About the play I have a sort of first act, and lying in bed does not stop me writing.

I'll try and get a synopsis characters and one act done. We'll see.

Max who I can't help quoting because I think his reactions are helpful says that Lois (the wife) must be built up into the chief part as she is more subtle, complicated and interesting.

I don't feel it that way.

The unfortunate Mado is too spiritless he thinks.

Of course one never knows how a character will strike other people. It might work out that way but I don't think so.

Please forgive this abominable handwriting. I am sitting on the floor with the pad on my knee very uncomfortable. Besides I've just made a risotto, not bad.

I will ring up some time next week. Even if I can't manage Sunday would like to apply for membership.   Yours

Jean

PS The man in "Houdia" is also called Max – funnily enough.

TO SELMA VAZ DIAS   *April 6th [1953]*
                                                                    29 Milestone Road

Dear Selma,

Here are the stories, sorry I couldn't send them along before. The River you know, and "Houdia" I've spoken about. Enclosed a note about the last.

The other two are a try-out. "The Story of Susan and Suzanne" was a very early effort and I'm not proud of it. But Hughes Massie thought it a business proposition ages ago when he was my agent.

I was supposed to change the end, not moral enough for the British Public, and I never got around to doing so. However I did start working at it, hence its battered look.

"The Day they burned the books" is fairly recent. I think however that one would have to explain that it is about the West Indies a good while ago when the colour bar was more or less rigid. More or less.

Also I don't think I've got over what I meant when I called the book "Fort comme la mort"[1] – However it could be done if you like it. I don't suppose you will for most people find it dull. I like it of course because it's about what used to be my home. I've never had another anyway.

So before I go all pathetic Happy Easter and forgive the wish coming so late.

Yrs

Jean

PS Will ring up towards the end of the week and find out your reactions

"Houdia"

This was written a long time ago. I suggest that you should insert the words "in the nineteen-twenties" or "before the war" after Montparnasse in

"This story is about . . . . Montparnasse"

I've tried to cut it – passages marked "delete" (mostly very necessary these cuts)

I've not tried to sell it, it's not been hawked about and you might like the atmosphere.

The name Max ought to be changed. I can't think of anything else. Bad at names – at any rate not too English.

It ought to be German I think and of one syllable. "Jon", JAN, Paul? Peter might do.

Not Jo or Jack, Bill or Philip or Charles or Giles, Rudi, Reg, Tom or even Guy. No, *Guy* might be possible also *Paul*. Name rather important. JAN best or JON.

Jean

[. . . . . .]
P.S. Max says, "Keep Max I don't care."

1. *"The Day They Burned the Books"* ends with a reference to Maupassant's novel of that name.

TO MORCHARD BISHOP   *April 7th [1953]*
                                                              Milestone Road

My dear Morchard Bishop,

I was so pleased to get your letter of the 18th March. I wrote a bit pompously didn't I, it was nice of you to overlook that – lying in bed reading, one does get dreary, full of quotations and apt to lay down the law don't you think?

I wanted to answer ages ago but one of those waves of worry came along, also my 'flu hung on grimly. However it's on its way out today – I hope.

Yes we both want to escape to the country. More than ever now. The Cornish thing fell through did I tell you?

I really would give my left hand, or an eye say, for a year of peace. (Painlessness part of the bargain) But no takers.

Yes, I would like to have a drink or a meal with you very much. But I find it easier to write than to talk. I'm a bit afraid of people now. (*Afraid!* Well you know what I mean.) "My personal relationships seem to go wrong" as somebody said.

Max says I alarm people because I'm so serious but that is only because I'm self conscious.

When slightly tight I can relax – also there are the red letter days when I feel that after all I'm as much fun as the next woman really. However this doesn't happen often and always when I least expect it!

That's all about myself now and not so very attractive. Sorry.

I'm trying to write a play or rather make one of my books "Quartet" into a play. So after all I'm an optimist. Not? Then I've spent much time lately trying to persuade a cousin of mine[1], also a West Indian, that she can write Creole songs and calypsos better than anyone I've ever struck.

She produces these things with the greatest of ease and rapidity – one line perfect the next terrible. Slap, bang, dash! Take it or leave it.

I'm sure she is a natural born money maker 1953– I feel it in my bones.

But she will not believe me – only says with a meaning look, "I want to be *safe* Jean" which is after all a 1953 outlook – I've tried to persuade her that our cases aren't a bit alike but it's no good.

So I have retired exhausted to private life in Penge or whatever this place is for I haven't found out yet. Some streets say Borough of Penge, others Camberwell. But the postal address Upper Norwood is very respectable after all – if scarcely chic! My God how it all gets on my nerves. As a matter of fact it ought not to be so bad, because it's hilly. The houses go up and down not straight along (If you call them houses for they are terribly like rabbit hutches)

But the trees have all been lopped so that they look like badly done poodles. A bit ashamed.

It is *terrible* what they do to trees. Why? Can you tell me? I've an idea (another of my ideas) that some men are jealous of trees and love making them look ridiculous.

Yes I thought literary people were alarming when I met many years ago. *Very* cut throat, behind back. I remember I was warned against the PEN club so never joined it. They cut throats very happily in New York too. However there are a few exceptions – I suppose. Did you ever hear about "Yaddo"²? the place left to writers by a millionaire in California (I think).

Each writer had a chalet, food brought to them and the swimming pool was grand. The only rule was that all must attend a communal meal every evening. Well the fights started at once. By the third night all the men had black eyes and none of the women spoke to each other. At the end of the week everybody left, a protest against the others being there.

This is more or less true. The country must be lovely today. Have you read Quartet? Postures in England. Dreadful title. Do you think there's a play in it?

Yours sincerely
Jean Rhys

[. . . . .]

1. *Lily Lockhart, whom Jean was to describe many years later in a story, "The Whistling Bird"* (The New Yorker, September 11, 1978). *Jean was trying to interest Selma (whose hobby was collecting folk songs and ballads) in Lily's work (see two following letters).*

2. *Yaddo is in fact near Saratoga Springs, New York. Jean's account of it (which she repeated delightedly in letters to other correspondents) presumably derives from the scandal in 1949 when the four writers in residence (Robert Lowell, Edward Maisel, Elizabeth Hardwick and Flannery O'Connor) discovered that a former guest, Agnes Smedley, was being investigated by the FBI as a Communist Party member. They complained to the board of directors, and found themselves the target of an injurious counter-attack: the episode developed into a tragi-comic cause célèbre of cold war hysteria among the intelligentsia. . . . This letter is the last from Jean to Morchard Bishop (Oliver Stoner) written at that time, but there were to be many more at a later date. Their friendship was resumed in the 1960s, when Stoner and his wife were living not far from Jean in Devon, and continued on increasingly intimate terms until Jean's death in 1979.*

TO SELMA VAZ DIAS

April 27th [1953]
Milestone Road

Dear Selma,

I may be leaving this address now, so I'd be very glad if you could let me have the stories back within the next week or so. I cannot imagine the BBC liking anything I write, past present or future (if any) and I think it was heroic of you to try. Thanks a lot. I wouldn't bother you but have no other copies.

I tried to listen in to your Lady Macbeth but the set jammed or something. It is a complicated affair downstairs. Sure you were splendid, but I don't see you as Lady Macbeth. Viola in Twelfth Night perhaps? Yes –

I enclose the ballads (songs) I spoke about. [. . . . . .] Please have a look at them and consider them and *please* believe me that they have an authentic ring about them which isn't too easy to get hold of, though the ersatz are cheap at four a penny. Surely *somebody* will see the difference.

There is a sort of charm about the French and half French West Indies, and indeed the West Indies as a whole and no other has got hold of it yet. It would be new.

It isn't Noel Coward's Jamaica or Katherine Dunham's Martinique – It just has not been done or even attempted.

I do think Lily might come very near it for it's in her blood. Her family have been in the West Indies for something like three hundred years. (All Creoles are not negroes. *On the contrary*)

Well I expect I'm talking double Dutch or Chinese but I do feel she might be very good indeed if encouraged though God knows I have been rather cursing myself for interfering.

But isn't there *anybody* who'll give a chance to something good? Or "will be good".

I'm a bit depressed today so forgive scrawl. It always takes me that way. (I'm only half Creole and haven't any lightness or gaiety to pull me through the black days. Or not much.)

Never mind.

Will send her address if you want it.

Yours
Jean Rhys

TO SELMA VAZ DIAS

June 8th [1953]
Milestone Road
LIV 1631

[. . . . . .]

My Dear Selma,

Thanks for sending the stories back. I guessed some time ago that they hadn't found favour, but I thought we were leaving Upper Norwood so postponed writing. Really I am not worried about the BBC. It would have been a miracle if they'd approved of anything I write or wrote and I do think you were a *heroine* to try. Thank you.

What *does* worry me is the impossibility of finding any cave or corner where I'd be able to work. I wish to God I were one of those lucky people who can work anywhere – or say they can.

Unfortunately not. I'm one of those no goods who need a room of my own (warm). Nothing else would matter – that I must have.

And, so far as I can see it, it doesn't exist – except at a rent I can't pay. So voilà! As I need Max too I want two rooms, which makes things utterly impossible – I've tried and tried and started out full of high hopes. But no good.

Never mind perhaps it will turn up when I least expect it. Do you remember the Beckenham place? That was quite good in a way. Quite a good atmosphere of decay, damp and so on. *Just* my place. But unfortunately I was so worried about other things – (*Always* some excuse you see). Here we must stay for the present. It's so damned small. But there is the telephone. Ring me up if ever you feel like it.

I'm awfully sorry to hear you have 'flu. Please cheer up. I wish I could send you some flowers. Consider them sent. Stefanotis? Too waxy. Carnations?

If you can use the ballads I'll be awfully pleased.

Lily's address is Miss Emily Lockhart, 48 Charlwood Street S.W.1.

I believe she thinks I've fraudulently run off with them and am passing them off as mine. She's so wary. But with reason. She's not had *such* a good time poor darling.

For God's sake don't tell her I said so. It'll be round the family grape vine in no time. My family are completely horrible. They all say I have written feelthy books and deserve my present lot, and much much more. Quite detestable people. I've *one* nice brother but he is poor. *What* luck don't you think?

Yrs ever
Jean

TO MARYVONNE MOERMAN

June 8th [1953]
Milestone Road

My dear Maryvonne,

I was so awfully glad to get your letter my dear, and await the second eagerly. I am sending this to Rotterdam to await arrival. I hope you will find John better when you arrive. Will you tell him I think of him a lot, and send my best love. Or rather tell him that if you think he wishes to hear it. I hope you've rested during the voyage and just relaxed and thought of nothing. The sea is good for that. *Wrap up well* as you come to Europe, *and wrap up Ruthie too*. It is a bitterly cold summer in England and I hear in Europe as well. But perhaps it will have changed when you arrive.

It poured with rain all day on Coronation Day. Such a shame for some of the people had waited all night and others for hours to see and they were soaked. So were the decorations which are good in parts I hear. We got as far as the Abbey on the day before then the icy wind was too much. I gave up. However we will see it like all the other faint hearts – on the cinema. The Queen is pretty and smiles much.

I think we will be here for another two months. I'd hoped to find somewhere else less cramped and not so far out but it was useless. London is packed in spite of the beastly weather.

Remember that the

                    National Provincial Bank
                    40 Oxford Street

will always find me.

No more for now. I hope to get one more letter from you.

I was getting worried for I understood you to say that you leave Java in March so your letter delighted me except for the news about John.

My love to all and my best kisses and hugs. A special one for you and for Ruthie. I will write again as soon as I hear.

Ella

TO MARYVONNE MOERMAN

August 29th [1953]
Milestone Road
LIV 1631

I telephoned Selma Vaz Diaz when you
left. She's on holiday in Austria

My very dear Maryvonne,

It was lovely seeing you, and I think Ruthie is a sweet child – sweet is not the word, a darling. I have become very grandmotherly about her and meditate about both of you (more than you'd wish, perhaps)

I expect you start off early in the morning, so thought I'd write instead of telephoning. Do try and visit Cambridge. I think you would like it and be glad you went. Some of the colleges are beautiful and the "Backs" are enchanting. It *can't* have changed all that much. The town is of course bigger and more "towny" than Oxford but Ely Cathedral which isn't far away is the most beautiful in England I think. Whether it is covered in scaffolding for repairs I do not know. So many of these beautiful places are tumbling down because no one has cared for them.

Have got to arrange the "Iron maiden" (the bed) for the night I mean day. One day that dam thing will smash my hands. I know and "serve her right" everyone'll say. Not?

Sorry for the harum-scarum reception you got but I was very excited so could not be the gracious hostess. I'm not much good at that role – as you know. But I was bursting with pleasure my darling, if for once I may be sentimental.

Have a lovely time. It's a bit cloudy today still I don't think it will rain much.

Will you lend me or rather Max and myself Ruthie for one day or afternoon?

She will be met any place any time and taken great care of, I promise. I should love it so much.

With all my love to all of you. We are absolutely free except for Monday for Ruthie or any minute you can spare.

Jean

PS Max was awfully pleased because he said you "looked at him

110

affectionately". So you see! You are all *much* appreciated to put it mildly and with restraint.

I wish my information was more up to date but you can easily check up and find out. So can only tell you the places I loved –

Brockenhurst is the place to make for if you wish to see the New Forest. Savernake Forest is not so far from *Marlborough* – Max says Herefordshire is a lovely county to wander about just peacefully and lazily. Somerset too and of course Devonshire if you are going so far. Do you remember Exmoor? I stayed once at Burford near Oxford and thought it the calmest and most soothing village I'd ever struck. Maybe they've got a steelworks there now. Who knows?

If one fine day you feel like the river, why not go to Taplow or Maidenhead and start from there. Did you like Windsor? But the best part of the Thames starts above Oxford.

Well this is an awful attempt at a guidebook, so that's enough. The best places are the ones you find yourself. Do try the Portsmouth Road out of London one day. Nice places to eat used to abound. Also it is or was the best *looking* way out.

TO MARYVONNE MOERMAN
September 16th [1953]
Milestone Road

Maryvonne my dear –

I'm afraid this won't reach you before you leave Amsterdam. If it does I wish you a lovely time and the same if it follows you.

I would have written before but I have been feeling a bit down and a bit tired out (I don't know why: packing I guess. I'm so hopeless at it) and I wanted to wait till I was my usual gay self. I miss you so much – it's absurd – and long for the week or two weeks all over again, to hug Ellen tighter and talk to you *not* about the weather.

However –

It was grand seeing you and I thought you looked well and I'd forgotten how *blue* blue your eyes were. You looked very young and a dear.

Ruthie I mean Ellen, was a joy. I hoped she liked me a bit. If only I could have seen a little more of you all – but what I did see was very very comforting. I loved it.

Job looked splendid "Handsome men are slightly sunburnt" –

I remember our last tea with *shame* those *awful* cucumber sandwiches. Really I couldn't help it.

We leave for the "yacht" by a fairly early train on Monday 21st. When I arrive I will sleep and sleep and sleep. I simply don't and do not care what anybody says or thinks.

> "All I want is sleep sleep sleep
> And all I ask is sleep – O!"

I forgot to give you a book of Hemingway's stories I'd bought for you. It'll be sent pronto, and I'll send Ellen a series of postcards so that she shouldn't forget her funny granny – Not quite.

Tell Job I have no longer my golden locks (*quite* natural!) because I've discovered a rinse called "silver ash". It is very nice and suitable and really not bad. I'm sure I'll be very popular now. Don't you think?

Darling I did so love seeing you all – but you most – for I am a horribly *faithful* type. So dull, but there it is –

Ellen is already "somebody" and will be more so. (She was sweet).

Wait – and see I am right. I don't know the part of Italy you are in because when I went to Florence I came back by the lakes which were very lovely – but I expect it's pretty nice.

I must stop now and do some cooking – poor me.

Never mind! When we get to S. Wales I will refuse to cook as I hope to start writing again.

There's much I want to say God knows.

Max sends his love he was very struck with Ellen and says she has loads of charm.

I send hugs and kisses as many as you want, and my best and deepest love.

Jean

October 15th [1953]
TO MARYVONNE MOERMAN
Yacht Atlast, Haverford West
Pembrokeshire

My dear Maryvonne,

I had your letter from Rome, also the p.c. from Avignon and was so glad to hear that you did take the fine weather with you.

It all sounds so lovely and I can imagine how you're enjoying it. I got as far as Florence once, and stayed there three weeks then l'argent (dough) gave out and I had to go home. Fell in love with Fiesole. Did you go there at all? A perfect place it seemed especially in the evening. I will always put France the first though. It is my best love and heaven knows why.

When you were very little (as Ruthie – I mean Ellen – is now) you always wanted to go to Italy. You talked and talked about it and imagined you had been there. Indeed you were certain you were born there, and got horribly angry with me when I said not. I think you called me King Kong you were so vexed – You wouldn't remember – But the really strange thing is that you *were* nearly born in Italy!

However that is another story.

I'm awfully happy about the good time, and being shown round is such a help.

Now I must tell you about the yacht and I hope I'll explain why I have been so long writing.

Well the yacht Atlast was once a gunboat, and the owner Captain Marshall

and his wife bought her from the Admiralty and fitted her up for a cruise round
the world which never came off. Something to do with a film I believe. Now
here they are anchored. They are both nice. He was very badly wounded in the
war poor man and is not well.

Our "flat" is two cabins knocked into one (large cabins) and a "cooking
galley" – the two cabins are divided by a red curtain which can be drawn across
or left open. It is all very nicely arranged.

It is however way way down below the deck and when I first saw the steep
ladder I'd have to climb, clinging to a rope getting down and up, I thought
"God help me now I am lost!"

However, I clamber up and down now without fear but very cautiously –
You would laugh. Step by Step –

It is nice to wake up, to see portholes instead of windows and to be out of
that detestable place in Upper Norwood.

But. The real snag is that everything in the entire place is a "*gadget*" – and I
cannot work gadgets. Neither (it turned out) can Max.

There is electricity, but we were asked not to use too much as it's their own
plant. So we have to light a thing *called* a lamp. But it is not so simple as an oil
lamp. Simple! My God, it is the most complicated thing I've ever seen. It has
two piston pumps, two screws and a special lighter to clamp on and take off.

Each of these affairs must be handled just right or the lamp either (a) flares to
the ceiling or (b) hisses and goes out. I don't know which is more alarming.

The heater is just as complicated.

So the result was that we both spent all the morning lighting the heater and
all the afternoon lighting the lamp with arguments about which pump or
screw to twist and when.

So in the end I got awfully tired and simply went to bed and slept –

Now it goes better. Captain Marshall has fixed us a chimney, and we can use
the stove for heating instead of the horrible gadget thing.

I bought a lot of candles at Woolworths and now the lamp only takes half an
hour or so to light. It's just a matter of the right screw at the right time.

Like everything.

I have not been much into the little town. It seems so shut in and rather dark.
Max likes it and maybe I'll get to. But South Wales towns are not nice as a rule.

Do you remember at all?

The people are though. It's astonishing how different they are from the
English. They speak mostly Welsh here and their voices are very soft and
gentle in English – I do like that. Also the men are very polite to women, make
way for them and will do little things to help with the shopping.

In short – a different race.

Everybody says "it's only on the surface". But damn it all the surface is what
you see most.

I looked for a shop with postcards for Ellen. But haven't found one yet.

I am only just getting my bearings as it were so forgive me for not writing
before (I wrote once to the address you gave. John's.)

I am longing to know all your plans and where you are.

I asked Max what message he wanted sent. He said "My love".

Mine also to all. Handshake as well to Job. Hugs and kisses for you. A special kiss for Ellen from her granny. Did she like me? Or has she forgotten me already? Never mind.

I have a very good memory – And there she is quite fixed. Please remember me to John and wish him luck.

Your loving

Jean

PS. I did not want to talk about the weather at all you know. But I did not want to bore you either.

PPS. There is a glass wheel house on deck where one can sit if it's sunny. Ellen would like it here I think.

January 31st [1954]

after Haverford (Atlast)

2 Craven Hill Gardens

London w2

TO MARYVONNE MOERMAN

My very dear Maryvonne,

I had your letter sent to the Atlast.

My dear I could not answer at once for I've been ill in hospital. I had a tumble down the ladder and banged my head rather badly and was pretty rocky for days.

However all is better now. I am in London with Max at these rooms which are not so far from Elgin Crescent do you remember it. Near Paddington Station.

To tell you the truth – I was not sorry to leave the yacht – That is putting it mildly.

It was awfully gloomy. We couldn't use the electric light often, the oil lamps went wrong, the washplace didn't function.

As a final touch I found that there were mice in large numbers. *Large* mice in large numbers.

Our two cabins were below the deck – the run shallow.

When a mouse ran over my foot I nearly expired. Personally I do not think it was a mouse it was too big. However –

I don't altogether regret going for after my fall I met some people who were wonderfully kind to me – One little girl called Christine and I talked a lot about Ruthie. She was a sweet child. I wish they could have met and been friends. She was very interested. Only about four or five.

I am worried that you had to go back to Indonesia – and worried that this letter may not get to you in time.

This address will find me. So will the bank. For it is rather expensive here and we must find somewhere else I suppose.

When the doctor saw me he said

Well. Did a horse step on your face?!

However it has got along all right and only one eye is still a bit rum looking and is healing up.

I had my hair washed and set yesterday and am still a nice and loving granny for Ruthie. And you.

I wish you could have stayed longer and I could have seen you more.

We hardly talked at all and there was so much to say.

Was it my fault?

[. . . . .]

As you guessed we have not much money. Rather cramping.

For that reason leaving the yacht was a pity as it was cheap.

But my gosh it was a dark place –

I'll be longing to hear from you again. Love from us both to all.

Jean

[. . . . .]

TO MARYVONNE MOERMAN

April 4th [1954]
Hotel Elizabeth, Leinster Terrace
London w2

My dear Maryvonne,

[. . . . .]

The Celebes! It sounds a *long* way off, and I don't know a thing about them. I'll try and get hold of some travel books while I'm waiting to know if you like them or not. There is one good thing. You will have a house. That seems to me a dream of delight for I have been moving so rapidly from one damned room to another – that I have longed for a nice warm cave just so that I could settle down.

This place where we have settled for a bit I *hope* – is rather gaunt and bare but I think that can be improved and I like the neighbourhood. It's not far from the Craven Hill place and near Whiteleys. Anyway it seems very civilized after Upper Norwood. Oh how I detested that place, and the rows of peering women opposite. Always some face peeping out at you from behind the curtains. I wish we hadn't been there when you came.

I am nearly well again from my wretched accident. You know the doctor who made the remark about my face was quite nice really. I *did* look as if a horse had been running races over me. But all is well now except a tiny scar on my forehead. I can hide it easily with powder – I still go to the hospital about a pain in my back but it is getting better and they are awfully kind to me.

That's all about wretched me – except that the Atlast was a mistake, and that I'm a bit disappointed not to go to Wales.

I like those people Mrs Bell, her mother, and little Christine most awfully. They were so human.

But Max changed his mind and definitely preferred this.

Now about you. I don't know what happened about the money but I'm most awfully sorry.

My dear, do please be careful because you see there is a reckless strain *on both sides*. I am *hopeless* about cash, and have been all my life, though sometimes with the best of intentions – John a bit too though in a different way – So you see, be careful. Though "nothing venture, nothing have" is true too. Money is, unfortunately, a damned necessity.

I nearly bet on a horse called "Sweet Ruth" the other day because I liked his name. I would have won £20 if I had not lost courage at the last moment.

Then there was "Jean's Dream" who ran when I was writing Voyage in the Dark years ago. I wanted to back him and if I had I would have got £20 for every £1 staked. He was an "outsider" – 20 to 1.

Max is lucky but cautious and I don't think I'm lucky, so hesitate – Now!

My dear I am longing to know if you like your new place. . . .

All my love hugs and kisses from Max and from myself.

Your loving
Jean

TO MARYVONNE MOERMAN

May 9th [1954]
Hotel Elizabeth

My dear Maryvonne,

I hope this will reach you in time to wish you many happy returns of the day my dear. I am longing to hear from you. The Celebes sounds so very far away somehow even farther than Djakarta and that was distant enough!

[. . . . . .]

We've been in this new room for about two months. I've been busy in my usual way trying to build up my own special retreat from the world, with a few books and pictures, my two glass fish and so on.

I feel a bit like an ant sometimes. They do that. If you knock their nest to pieces they just scuttle away and start somewhere else. Quite useless, but it passes the time and maybe isn't useless after all.

I must say that my nest when you saw me had *not* been a success.

Penge was a *horrible* place and the yacht was not too good either.

This place is again quite different. It has two advantages. It is right in London, near the Park. Also there is Constant Hot Water.

This last I do appreciate. A hot bath can be most comforting. As for the Park, I don't care – But it's nice not to have to take a long train journey every time you want to get away from a dismal suburb.

Also another big advantage we are almost on the top floor and away from everybody.

The disadvantage is that it is all too small and looks on to blitzed houses. Sometimes there are workmen there moving about in an aimless way, but more often only their scaffolding and ladders. I find that so odd. Surely the houses are being repaired. Or not. But no, it is still a mystery. . . .

[. . . . . .]

I wish I could send you a lovely birthday present instead of only my love and hugs and kisses. I would send flowers (lilac and roses) a bottle of champagne or two or three, one of Scotch whisky for Job. I would also send a bracelet (sapphires) and about a dozen books – very beautiful covers.

[. . . . .]

I hope all this rather idiotic day dreaming does not irritate you. If so – well say it amuses me.

I think things may get better for Max and myself for I am a stubborn person and I am still fighting.

I take a lot of pills to cure this darned rheumatism got on the yacht and maybe they'll work. It really isn't so bad.

I am so glad the summer is coming. Again all my love and many happy returns. Stay as pretty as you can and are. It works better than the staid people pretend.

Feel like writing soon. Love and respects to Job.

Your very loving
Jean

[. . . . .]

TO MARYVONNE MOERMAN

September 5th [1954]
Hotel Elizabeth

[. . . . .]

My dear Maryvonne,

I was so pleased to get your letter – you know I had started to wonder what had happened.

It was lovely to hear about a beautiful place because this summer (so-called) has been the worst I've ever known. [. . . . .] You see I am, as usual, discussing the weather, but really it has been something to discuss – not only buckets of rain, but thunder, lightning, gales. [. . . . .] However it has been much the same all over northern Europe and anyway it's a dull subject.

It is more exciting to talk about Makassar and your new job which sounds so interesting. If I could (repeat could) get hold of any books would that help? [. . . . .] You know I've been always sad I couldn't send Ruthie all the books I loved as a child. Perhaps she wouldn't like them but I wanted to send them. [. . . . .] I'd be awfully pleased to have the photograph of the tutu complete with little girl. And you know some sort of sketch or painting of this wild and beautiful place would simply delight me.

I found an old sketch book of my Aunt Clarice's, my father's sister – water colours done when she visited the West Indies years and years ago long before I was born – in 1881 I think, and they still have something. I've put them up here and some sketches you did when you were about twelve. I still have my black and white parrot and the trees and the one of Amsterdam. But the one of the girl in the green sweater, the sad girl, has been stolen. (Pictures I'm talking about). Well I've contrived yellow silk phoney but nice curtains and we look out at London rooftops, a battered house which is being very very slowly rebuilt and painted white [. . . . .] We can also see the trees in Hyde Park by craning our necks a bit.

Has Ruthie still got her doll Honey? She seemed so attractive and sensitive, so of course naturally will appear not easy to handle sometimes.

But you seemed just right with her. And so did Job.

It sounds very exciting at Makassar but *don't get kidnapped!* [. . . . .]

Get all the sleep you can my dear. Do you ever strike some stuff called "Horlicks". It's like Ovaltine but much better and really does make one *sleep* calmly and wake up rested.

Love again, hugs and kisses. Write again soon – when you have a moment and feel like it. Don't forget the photo.

Jean

I went to see a revival of La Dame aux Camelias with Greta Garbo. She is so lovely, really she haunts one. She makes everyone else meaningless and rather vulgar.

December 12th [1954]
Hotel Elizabeth

TO MARYVONNE MOERMAN

My dear Maryvonne,

This is to wish you a happy New Year – best of luck and to send you my love. Max also.

I hope you will like the cards. You'll know that I'd love to send other things, much nicer, much more exciting – That may happen too one of these days. The card "Here's hoping" is for you – I thought it might make you smile – I mean it too. [. . . . .]

Max and myself set out yesterday for the Victoria and Albert to buy the cards for they had some lovely ones some time ago.

We walked across the cold and very wintry park and a long way round and there we were. All was well except that Max kept asking for the Queen Alexandra exhibition instead of the Queen Mary scandalising the attendants (I am never sure whether he does this on purpose or not).

There is an exhibition of Queen Mary's personal jewellery and treasures, rather good. However we passed that by, passed the Chinese, Arabic, Gothic, Italian and so on rooms and finally came (rather weary) to the stand where they sold the cards. The best seem to be out of print and I couldn't find a dancer for Ruthie. However I will send one. This is just the first batch.

Well we went out by the wrong door and walked and walked and walked finally realising that we were hopelessly lost and I'd left my proper "rich" purse at home.

There was a bit of a fog and really it began to be rather like one of those dreams – you know –

At last we emerged by Harrods and I knew where we were.

The windows looked lovely but I was too tired to appreciate them. Do you remember shopping there one Xmas and losing our purchases in the ladies? I did – most vividly.

When we finally got home I was too tired to grumble even – I just tore my clothes off and flopped into bed.

That is the Adventure of the Christmas Cards.

Please let me know your news some time.

We're all right. A friend produced a chicken for Xmas. Tough but well meant. I am determined to have some Yo ho ho and a bottle or half a bottle of rum – for the New Year.

I wish you such a lot of luck my dear, hugs and kisses galore and it goes without saying all my love.

Best of luck to Job. Be a good gal and write to me sometime.

Jean

Somehow I'll find a dancer for Ruthie – this week.

TO MARYVONNE MOERMAN

Boxing Day [1954]
Hotel Elizabeth

My dear Maryvonne,

I was so glad to get your letter card. It seemed so long since I heard, and when Max went downstairs for the post and shouted "Letter from Maryvonne!" was as pleased as anything. [. . . . . .]

My dear, as I told you in the Xmas card epistle I want to send you books very badly. I'll be able to send a parcel very shortly – for only *Demon Money* has been stopping me and now I have a bit saved up for that.

If the books are mostly Penguins you'll understand won't you? After all they are quite well printed and covered with red or yellow paper, or better still, wall paper they look quite gay and make a splash of colour in a room – or a quietness whichever you prefer.

I have discovered that colours are very important – Red is energetic but quarrelsome, blue, silver, or best of all flowered paper restful. White is clean and gay. And so on.

I have experimented a lot with this room, which was very dismal. Now it is possible. I have yellow curtains to fight the darkness and blue bits and pieces to fight the lack of space, also glass lightens it. *Any* glass however cheap.

Well you have different things to fight and before I say anything else I will talk about *cockroaches*.

My dear you cannot *hate* them more than I did. So did my mother.

We have a rainy season too in the West Indies (though not so bad as yours I expect) and these dam things zoom about just the same there.

Well when I was home in 1936 – you remember? – I hated them as much as ever. I was complaining bitterly to an Englishwoman who had lived in Tahiti a long time. She gave me a tip to get rid of them.

Mix *boracic powder* and sugar together, slightly more sugar, spread it near all cracks and crevices. They cannot resist the sugar and the boracic kills them. She said she had cleared her place of them.

I was rather sceptical, still I tried it, and true enough every morning there were four or five or more slain cockroaches. Dead as doornails. I should suppose the best time for this is before the rainy season starts. Before they fly. Still it would be effective any time. Some people use screens over the windows – of fine wire, but even Venetian blinds might stave them off a bit – and with the slats open the air comes in all right.

I like Venetian blinds very much but I know everyone doesn't. I like the noise of crickets and frogs at night too. But again everybody's taste isn't alike.

The other day we went to a very silly film and they provided this noise for local colour. It was about the jungle – the film I mean.

I was simply entranced and wanted to sit through the whole thing twice with my eyes shut to hear this homesick making noise.

Max, however, thought it nerve racking. So you see!!

My dear do not let the rains get you down. They will stop and everything be fresh again. *Sleep* all you can.

I think that one can't really compare the West Indies and your present home. The West Indies are softer, and it is so easy to get up into the hills where the air is fresh and delicious.

But oh boy I *can't* believe that your cockroaches are worse than ours!!

I have read about how strung up Europeans get in China and Malay and Java. It's easy to say "Relax" but hard to do. Still "Softly softly catchee monkey" as Max would say.

Well talking of jungles we did not have a bad Xmas. I was dreading it.

A friend sent us a chicken and another a box of sweets.

Also we got asked to a party yesterday, Xmas day, and ate a lot of turkey and plum pudding. I got this little book out of a cracker. I hope Ruth Ellen won't think it too babyish. Give her my best love and a big huge hug from a not very satisfactory granny –

Today, of course, everyone is a bit lethargic sleeping off yesterday's huge meals.

There is not much more news. I told you about our visit to the Victoria and Albert in my last letter.

You see life is not a whirl of pleasure.

Still it will be all right when this dark winter lightens up.

I hate the darkness like you hate the rains.

My dear please take care of yourself. All my love hugs and kisses. A hug from Max and best wishes to you all from us both. Till next letter and the books.

Jean

PS. If you have pets, a dog or a cat perhaps better find out if the boracic would be harmful to them.

I *know* it kills cockroaches. I must wake Max up and have our evening meal.

I'm not a bit hungry. I think yesterday's turkey will last me a week.
But I could do with a "Yo ho ho and a bottle of rum" – like the lady on the
Xmas card. I do hope you get it.
Happy New Year – Here's hoping! –

Jean

P.S. I forgot to say how I envied you the garden.
If you knew how dismal the outlook was here you would not wonder I talk
so much about colours!
Max says: Why not a DDT spray for the cockroaches.

TO MARYVONNE MOERMAN

March 6th [1955]
Hotel Elizabeth

My dear Maryvonne,

It is so long since I've written and I feel so bad about it. For though I hear
very seldom from you I know I ought to tell you my news always – besides I
want to, I want to write pages.

Well we've been having flatlet trouble – that's the reason.

It's too long to explain and it's over for the present. This hotel got sold and
the new owner stuck the prices up enormously. Nearly everyone has left, but
we came to an uneasy agreement and here we still are. For the present.

It's not a very attractive place and I'd like to blow up the houses opposite,
but it is *somewhere*.

This winter has been dreadful – snow and east winds every day. The one fine
day makes one hope, and next morning snow and whistling wind again. Do
you remember your poem to the wind?

[. . . . . .]

When the weather is bad and the snow has turned to slush or ice – well I'm a
bit shut in for I have no proper snow boots.

My great distraction is planning a new dress. Well there it is – awful I know.
Absurd.

Still that distracts me. Shall I save for a navy with white collar and cuffs, or
brazenly wear shocking pink? Or tan? Or what have you.

That and my hope that we'll find a place with *two* rooms or a cottage with a
garden keeps me going. More or less.

I did hear of a cottage in Wales the other day and nearly went.

But it is very small and dark and the traffic passed the door.

So on the whole after a lot of talk we said no.

The *great* thing I find is to hope and I am a very hopeful person really.

So do wish me luck, my blue dress, my cottage and all. And *do* write even a
card.

How is Ruthie? And Job? Above all how are you? All my love and thoughts
and everything good for you.

Especially hugs and kisses.

Jean

Max sends love.

I've been reading this over and *what* a dull letter. But today the sun shone – the first time for weeks and weeks that it hasn't been cold.

Life has been a bit like Mark Twain's famous diary –

Monday. Got up, washed, went to bed

Tuesday. Got up, washed, went to bed

Wednesday   "   "   "   "

And so on. Surely now the ice may break up a bit in all directions.

But really that's about all I've been doing – washing stockings of course and all those chores which I hate included.

[. . . . . .]

I'm sorry I've been so long posting this. It couldn't be helped. Soon things will be better. Do write quickly a line. Meanwhile my best love and hugs and kisses.

Jean

Do you remember the time I bought you a hand bag from Paris – for one of your birthdays? I thought it lovely – but you were not pleased because it was a *little girl's* bag you said and you were at least fourteen or fifteen – I forget. "*Can't* you understand that I am grown up" you said very indignantly.

Well do you know I still don't – quite. It is my private and particular belief that very few people change after well say seven or seventeen. Not really.

They get *more* this or *more* that and of course look a bit different. But inside they are the same.

May 30th [1955]
Hotel Elizabeth

TO MARYVONNE MOERMAN

My dear Maryvonne,

I got the books off, at last, on the 24th – two days after your birthday.

It was difficult to get the ones I wanted hence the delay. They were on order for a long time.

I couldn't send them by air mail – but they are registered and ought to take about a month I'm told. The parcel is from the Quest Bookshop and the books are

Kingfishers catch fire[1]

Short Stories Hemingway

Margot Fonteyn

(mostly photographs rather nice) for Ruthie, and a National Costume book (inexpensive) for fun.

I have not been able to get the one I really wanted for you yet. It's a great favourite of mine and I think you'd like it too, *Novel on Yellow Paper*[2]. It's on order and I hope will follow.

If the parcel does not arrive will you let me know? I might be able to enquire about as it's registered.

I nearly bought "The Wind in the Willows" for Ruthie but hesitated because if she finds English difficult it might bore her.

There is not much news – except a rather uncertain feeling. We may be leaving here about the end of the month. I am determined to find two rooms somewhere. Do wish me luck. Today is quite warm, the first warm day this year, a bit muggy. Oh I have been so cold and do welcome the sun. I must get tea. My best love and another big hug. Love from us both to you all.

Jean

1. *Novel by Rumer Godden (1953).*

2. *By Stevie Smith (1936).*

TO MARYVONNE MOERMAN

October 24th [1955]
Bellair, Widemouth Bay
Bude, Cornwall

[. . . . . .]

My dear Maryvonne,

It's my turn now to be sorry I was so long writing.

We left the Hotel Elizabeth some time ago. I got your letter all right but delayed answering till I could give some address.

My dear I am so tired of wandering and every time I pack something is left behind.

So my belongings will soon be very few!

We saw this place advertised and took it on the chance. Here we are for six months.

It is not badly furnished and I was quite delighted with it at first. It is so lovely waking up to sea and sky instead of a view of horrible houses. There are *three* spare bedrooms (if only you could come and stay!) – and a splendid kitchen really a dream kitchen.

However I found out the drawbacks *gradually* and the reason why it is so cheap.

It is *very* cold tho' Cornwall is supposed to be so warm – I can't stop shivering. It's a summer house.

Also the boiler – on which depends hot water and heat is a demon.

If you could see me wrestling with it in the morning you'd laugh, dressed in ancient slacks and an ancient jumper. *Swearing!*

Even now I haven't quite got the hang of it and never quite know what it will do.

About tea time Max lights a big coal fire in the sitting room and for the first time I get warm.

Bude is some way off and we depend mostly on tradesmen calling – the baker and the milkman are faithful, the others – one never knows!

Most of the other bungalows round here are empty at this time of year, and I prefer it that way. We've had four perfect days – this is one – the sea is actually blue, but a lot of rain the rest of the time and this cold wind that's going through one like a knife.

Cornwall is not so soft as Devonshire – rather bare and rocky and few trees – which I miss, but when the tide is out there are splendid sands. Ruth would love them I think and so would you.

I will write again soon but please let me hear from you before my next birthday for God knows where I shall be then!

How are you all? I loved your last letter – your voyage must have been great fun.

I am well except for the pain the chilling and killing wind gives me – and it blows up over the sea just like in Annabel Lee.

Max is well too and sends his love to you all.

[. . . . . .]

A big hug and so many kisses as usual –

All my love
Jean

My dear little Ruth,

Thank you for writing. I am in a bungalow in Cornwall near the sea and I wish you were here too.

This is a rocky coast and up to about fifty years ago it was the wreckers and smugglers coast. I sympathise with the smugglers but the wreckers were bad hombres. They used to put a light on the rocks (pretending it was a lighthouse) then when the poor ships smashed up, they'd all swarm out and grab the cargo. (*Not* the people!)

However they are not so enterprising now. Though different I think from the English.

I will send you some post cards soon. Now I send my best love to you.

Your loving Grandmère

TO MARYVONNE MOERMAN
January 2nd [1956]
Bellair

I did leave my address at the hotel.
It was stupid of them not to forward
your letter. A new management.

My dear Maryvonne,

I was so awfully glad to have your letter. It cheered me up like anything. I wasn't feeling so very optimistic for (you are quite right), Cornwall is not a place for the winter.

However after news from you and a chicken for Xmas from Edward life was more cheerful.

I should have written at once to wish you all, but especially you, a happy

New Year – and there's no excuse for waiting till now except that I felt tired, and had a sort of cold – you know a half cold, half headache which made me stupid and lazy.

Well here at last are my best wishes for 1956 to everybody and to you hugs and kisses and all my love.

This is the rummest place I've ever lived in.

I don't know where *ultima Thule* was but it looks like it. Lands End too sometimes – other times too many bungalows. It is not even real country for there are all these empty bungalows and only one muddy rough road to the sea and the bus stop. The bus goes in to our metropolis Bude three or four times a day, but I never go. I asked Max to get some Xmas and New Year cards but he said there were no nice ones and indeed the shops are few and not good.

Everyone seems to have a car or anyhow a bicycle. There's no library – W H Smith is a railway bookstall presided over by the *silliest* girl you can imagine. She stares as if one was a dragon if asked to order a book. I tried once but gave it up feeling as baffled as she looked. Now Max changes the books and brings me mystery stories which I've read before. So all in all I began to feel a bit moony and lost.

However I have determined to wake up and force myself to be active and all the rest for the New Year.

Sometimes there are lovely days – today was one – the usual gale of wind and rain stops and it is beautiful on the sands.

There are wide lonely sands – and sunsets with fantastic clouds.

Two flights of birds went just over my head. I suppose on their way to Africa is it? I don't know. They flew straight out to sea.

So at moments I feel ashamed of disliking it here, only a little more and I would like it. More what? Well books I suppose and fur clothes to keep out the cold and gum boots to keep out the wet and someone to do the horrible chores. Also a few trees.

Well that's enough about me. I am delighted you are going to Sourabaya as you seem pleased.

Of course I remember the diary (Dairy!) I've often wondered if you still had it and am glad you have.

Well it is getting late and I must have a bath and go to bed. There is hot water – one good thing.

All the books in the house are very ancient. I read them all when I was a little girl. It gave me quite a strange feeling to see them turning up again. However as there is nothing else I must find one to put me to sleep – if I can. Will finish this tomorrow.

3rd. Here is tomorrow very dark and dull. There isn't much more to say except to wish you all the luck in the world again.

I am sorry that John is ill – I wish he could be better.

As for me don't worry my dear the pain in my back is nothing much. It *is* dull here but that will pass and when I write again – that will be soon – I'll tell you all my plans.

I want terribly a place of my own – it's my greatest wish.

Happy New Year again. Max too wishes you a lot of joy and good luck.
[. . . . . .]

Your loving

Jean

April 5th [1956]

The Garden Bungalow,

Whins Upton

nr. Bude, Cornwall

TO MARYVONNE MOERMAN

My dear Maryvonne,

I was so glad to get your letter my dear just before we left "Bellair".- If I haven't answered before blame this eternal packing and moving. As you know I'm not good at it and it seems to get worse every time! If I try to leave any tired old rubbish behind Max is sure to pick it up, pack it carefully and produce it at the new place, "I thought you forgot this". Sometimes I don't know whether to laugh or cry when some terrible old hat or scarf or what not turns up for the ninth time and stares at me. "You thought you'd got rid of me HA HA!!"

On the other hand spoons, pillowcases, writing paper and sometimes shillings or good ash trays get left behind and are never seen again.

I don't choose to live like this. I want to settle somewhere more and more but it is difficult to find anywhere possible. If the rent is cheap everything else is not and the other way round. However I have now reached a stage of grim determination, so it may be near. I did miss one very possible place because I wasn't quick enough. That won't happen again.

Meanwhile we are here till *June 15th*. My great worry is to miss a letter from you so remember that the bank address will find me. At least as long as I have any money there, and perhaps afterwards for a bit, and this till June 15th.

The cold was awful this winter and as these optimistic bungalows are hardly heated at all I thought I would expire. There was a long verandah and a quite good view of the frozen sea but after a while I just turned my back on it and huddled near the kitchen stove.

I don't really like Cornwall much. It is so bare, with hardly any trees, and I don't like all these whimsical bungalows, "Journey's End" and "At Last" (bis). "The Garden Bungalow" has no garden needless to say. There is a bit of earth around meant for vegetables I think.

However there is an old house down the road which is quite lovely. Long and low with a thatched roof and several trees. It is a pale yellow colour. I must say *why* are the old things so beautiful and the new ones so ugly and shoddy. Something is wrong. The only nice piece of furniture here is a Chippendale table. It is so simple and beautiful and all the joint bits work so easily. It makes everything else look very vulgar and badly made.

Well that's enough about Cornwall and me. Today the west wind is blowing – very strong and noisy but much softer – There are lovely sunsets and clouds and a feeling of space. As they haven't (yet) found a way to build red and green bungalows on the sea (called perhaps "Chez nous" or "Want-a-cot?") that is still there too and very grim it looks sometimes.

I believe it'll be there still when "Chez nous" and "Garden Bungalow" are not. Just between you and me.

Well with all this nonsense I am forgetting to tell you how it bothers me that you are not so well and that the new place isn't too attractive. Please take care of yourself and Ruthie and Job. It is so difficult to think of heat except with longing. But it can be bad too, I know. Can you get showers and lots of water?

I am glad you are teaching Ruthie English because it will make it easier to send books which I *will* do as soon as I can. There is no bookshop in Bude. I have not forgotten your birthday (you bet) and will write again. Meanwhile all my love to you all kisses and hugs as usual. I've been writing this in bed. Now I must get up and face the cold and putting things straight – oh *God!*

Jean

[. . . . . .]

TO MARYVONNE MOERMAN

May 16th [1956]
The Garden Bungalow

[. . . . . .]

My dear Maryvonne,

I am so sorry my dear that my best love and wishes for your birthday will reach you a bit late – Or I fear so. My only excuse is that it has gone on being very cold and damp – Max has a pain in his back and me too – So everyday I said tomorrow when it's fine.

Here at last is a fine warm day and not too soon! Well my dear I am utterly sick of the country. Also this place has a glass sitting room. Or nearly so. All windows and no curtains. The owner and his wife garden all day just outside and have a good look at us. Sometimes I feel I shall jump out of my skin with nerves. I sit in the bathroom-lavatory or the bedroom just to get away from this terrible staring. Perhaps some people don't mind but oh Lord I do – I feel like a fish in a tank and am consumed with a great wish to make faces at them. Well I *hope* I shall get used to it. So no more of that – I don't know what we shall do after June 15th when we leave. There was some idea of returning here for a year from next September but I don't know. It's not as cheap as it's supposed to be – Meanwhile everything waits – books for you and for Ruthie and one dress for me. There are no shops at all in Bude – or such odd ones. They sell hideous wool underclothes and jumpers and shoes – and all the dullest books ever written have ended their lives here. You wouldn't believe. All about cotton manufacturers in Lancashire. Five generations. Great granny, granny, mother, daughter – that's only four. Well the print is very small and the book goes on and on. Nothing ever happens and nobody ever leaves Manchester and it rains always.

Max loves these things. I long to tear them up. Because I *know* (as he doesn't) why they are written. To make money without any effort. So much per thousand words. Oh well now I'll tell you the nice things – There is a lovely walk along the cliffs – a sheer drop to the sea in some places – and another lovely walk inland – green meadows, gates cows and sheep. Even a few trees. The lanes are narrow with lots of little gay bright flowers.

I picked some and pressed them in a book to send to you with this letter. But they haven't turned out so well so perhaps I won't. A primrose, some violets and Ragged Robin because I like the name –

If I don't send them please imagine them.

As soon as I know where we are going I'll let you know – and be sure that I won't forget those long due presents.

I do hope you are well and nice things happen sometimes.

I feel awfully inadequate. I long to send you all sorts of things and all that can be sent for now is love and hugs and kisses.

Very genuine anyway –

Again many happy returns

Jean

[. . . . .]
Are you well? Here is one primrose as the Ragged Robin and violets are kaput.

July 5th [1956]
4 Carteret Road
Bude, Cornwall

TO MARYVONNE MOERMAN

> P.S. I have discovered a book shop at
> last and I'll get something out of the
> proud lady there and send it along.
> Not much choice.

My dear Maryvonne,

Another address as you see! But still in Bude where it rains and rains steadily – also there is a lovely cold bracing wind. However it does not brace me. I shrivel up, I wish all my clothes were lined with fur or I wish I were a cat and could curl up to sleep and sleep.

Well – we are here because one day Max came in from the Garden Bungalow to shop, saw these rooms and liked them. Then he persuaded me.

I like them too – in a way. Anyhow there is space, a big bedroom, a sitting room and a rather cheerful kitchen with a red tiled floor.

As I think I told you there is a lot of dark furniture carved into knobs and sharp points. During the last week I have pulled and hauled it about at the risk of my valuable life.

I actually moved a heavy wardrobe across the bedroom *alone*. I do think I'm a Strong Woman and no mistake. But it was so hideous and despair gave me strength. So now the bedroom is quite pleasant, one sees only trees and grey roofs of houses. It is very peaceful and I like it. The sitting room is a bit impossible, so I've bought some roses for it, they are cheap here, and taken down the pictures of stags and doggies and Roundheads and Cavaliers which festooned the walls and that's all I can do.

As you can imagine the landlady thinks I am more than a bit cracked (Don't you *like* the doggie? Well now. Well I never! Fancy that!!!) She is very nice really (I think and hope) about eighty and quite gay. She tells me she is real Cornish and knows a few words of the language. It was a language like Welsh but it has died out now – *unlike* Welsh.

She is, as I say, very nice and adores money and she's always trying to sell me things. She succeeds too. I've bought – well promised to buy – a screen to hide the wash stand and a rum sort of box which collapses into a writing table affair. It is very old and made of cedar. I like it. However when I try to sell her something in my turn, such as a green cardigan with gold buttons (which I wanted to get rid of because I don't like green) she takes it away and show it to all her pals and tries it on with all her dresses and (I firmly believe) wears it to a whist drive or two then she brings it back and says "no it doesn't go with my red".

So you see there's never a dull moment in Cornwall. I do miss the lovely walks round the Garden Bungalow. I loved the cliffs and there was never anybody around so heavenly but Max hated the owner (so did I) and he found it too much coming in to Bude to shop. So here we are, and it's all very green and damp and "the Western wind doth certainly blow and the small rain down doth rain." Did I ever send you that book of poems. That is a nice one. Cavaliers song 17th century. It ends "and in my bed again".

Please answer all this nonsense some time and tell me that you're well and doing fine which is what I long to hear. All my love hugs and kisses. Love from Max

Jean

My dear. I feel I must apologise for starting a letter on the 5th and posting it on the 14th. But I get interrupted all the time. To start with I leave things in the bedroom and have to search. Max also. There seems an awful lot to do – I'm not properly unpacked yet. We went to the cinema this afternoon – the first time for months.

It all felt quite strange. This is my last sheet of paper. Forgive blots.
It was used as a blotter by mistake.
Do write soon.

Love and hugs and kisses
Jean

PART FOUR

Selma

(1956–1960)

TO SELMA VAZ DIAS

> I have after all spoken about your
> adaptation in my letter to the BBC.
> Also about your interest and my regret
> that I never saw you act –

My dear Selma Vaz Dias,

I've just had a letter from a friend telling me that Sasha Moorsom of the BBC Features Department wanted my address and tried to get it through the New Statesman.

I have not mentioned you in my reply to him (or her) but as I feel sure that I have to thank you for any interest the BBC takes in my book, I'm writing directly by the same post.

About a year ago Max and I took a bungalow on the coast near Bude. We used the last scrapings of the barrel to do so.

Unfortunately the cold was quite awful and I was ill most of the time. I'm afraid that lost hope was the real trouble but the cold finished me off good and proper. *Never* let anyone tell you that North Cornwall is warm – It is not. [. . . . .]

We moved to Bude a few months ago but I still felt moribund. Till this morning. Now I am trying to stop hope growing again like the beanstalk.

I still work but write mostly about the vanished West Indies of my childhood. Seems to me that wants doing badly – for never was anything more vanished and forgotten. Or lovely –

Still –

(Don't worry I'm keeping a firm hand on the beanstalk). This is the first time I've felt half alive for months – all the same – Now that's the lot for the present – But one last thing. How's this for telepathy?

About two weeks ago Max came in with an air mail envelope. He said he was going to send you "Postures" published as "Quartet" in America and ask you to reread it. He thinks it my best book. I stopped this, telling him you'd already seen it. However he obstinately repeated that he wished to give you my address. I thought you'd be too busy and I'm afraid the whole question got lost in an argument about the merits of "Postures". [. . . . . .]

Well except to wish you much good fortune this is the lot. "Here's hoping" as the wicked Mr Heidler said to desolate Marya in this first book of mine – so long ago.
Yrs
Jean Rhys

TO MARYVONNE MOERMAN   *October 16th [1956]*
                                                        Carteret Road

> P.S. There are some trees of course round
> the older houses. But as the "new rich"
> lot buy them they chop the trees and plant
> potatoes! *They* don't like trees

My Dear Maryvonne,

I don't know what to say about my long delay in answering your lovely long letter – the Bali letter which I've read often.

Well first of all I was ill. Bude is a horribly cold, bleak place and it has rained and hailed all this so called summer. There are no trees and Cornish people don't seem to care for hedges or vines. So the wind comes straight across the Atlantic at 90 miles an hour, blows off a few roofs on the way then hits you in the chest. First, of course, blowing off any hat or scarf or what not. (Imagine me chasing my poor old hat, swearing all the time). Well, first I got a bad cold, then my back and legs began to hurt. Then I collapsed. I got all right but so tired – I only wished to sleep and sleep.

I tried to write to you but found my letter so gloomy that it was better not to send it. Well before I continue abusing Bude let me tell you two nice things. The first that Max has been so wonderful. He has a beard like an Old Testament prophet and his same old beret and he charges about, hardly ever loses his temper, brings me ices to cheer me up always with hot water bottles to counteract the ice.

He is really "all wool and a yard wide" as they say and I envy him and feel very wanting in character and courage. As you know! In a way!

Till this morning – when I had a letter telling me that the BBC were after my address with view to "feature production". I know quite well this may mean nothing. Still I am feeling so different – almost alive again – honestly I thought I was finished for good and for keeps.

But hope grows up like the Bo tree (was it the Bo tree?) and at once I write to you – Well lest you should think that I'm too feeble to *know* let me tell you about Bude.

At Widemouth and the Garden Bungalow it was cold – but there was the sea, and the view. Here there is dam all. No view no sea. All the furniture is black or brown and there's lots of housework to do. There are no walks and most of the few shops are shut because the "summer" is over.

The books are few and silly beyond words. When I found I was reading pages and pages of this awful stuff all about people knocking each other's teeth out and "arm locks" and "swell dames". Not good thrillers – just rubbish. Then I despaired and thought "I'm really done for now".

Well this is a selfish letter. My landlady is still quite kind, and I'll tell you a funny story about her. Remember that Bali post card you sent?

Well I showed it to her and she kept shaking her head and saying "Poor soul, poor soul!" So at last a bit irritated, I said, "*What* poor soul?" She said "That poor animal creature standing by the little girl." I told her it was a dancer

134

disguised as an animal. *And she didn't believe me!* She kept shaking her head and muttering "Poor poor soul with an 'ead like that. *How* does he eat?"

That's of course part of the Bude feeling. Nothing exists but money. Certainly not Bali.

But she's nice really. I think I must stop now and cook eggs and bacon for it's getting late. I'll write again soon for I'm all right now, or almost. Meanwhile my best love my biggest hug and a special hug for Ruth.

Max sends all his love too and he says "Tell Job that it's not only in Bali that a smile costs a penny or shilling in the slot. In Cornwall also."

Don't give me up, or stop writing me lovely long letters for I get a lot of cheer from them. Your loving

Jean

22nd. PPS. It *has* come off! The BBC are going to do Good Morning. Just in time! I was nearly done.

TO SELMA VAZ DIAS   *October 22nd [1956]*
                                                    Carteret Road

My dear Selma Vaz Dias,

Your letter arrived this morning. Of course I feel a bit dizzy with joy so I won't say much now except to thank you, to thank you again, and assure you that I know you will bring Sasha to life.

Your advertisement only got to me through one of those chances. The friend who told me heard about it by telephone so though the BBC got through and the name "Sasha Moorsom", the title of the book and my own name were so garbled that I wasn't at all sure if I was meant.

I don't know why everybody thinks I am dead – but I was feeling a bit that way myself at the end! – I did not mean to disappear, but besides hearing once or twice that I was a ghost – there were such *rum* stories tacked on by people I've never met in my life that I felt it was damaging me I mean me as a person – god that does sound pompous. You know it was getting me down. Anyway we gathered up our last sous and fled to Cornwall (hail, snow, wind 90 miles an hour and all).

I imagined I'd given you a bank address (account £3.3 as a rule) – It was so stupid of me not to. Forgive.

[. . . . . .]

Yes I have seen some notices[1] in the Sunday Times and Observer about you – was so glad. But I still think it was strange – Max's wish to write to you a couple of weeks ago. He'd even started the letter.

There are one or two things I'm bursting to say but they must wait. Anyway Bonsoir tristesse let's hope – Yrs with Love

Jean

I got some flowers to celebrate – or Max did.

1. *Selma Vaz Dias had appeared as Solange in Jean Genet's* The Maids *at the New Lindsey Theatre in June, 1956.*

October 27th [1956]
Carteret Road
c/o National Provincial Bank
40 Oxford Street, London W1

TO SELMA VAZ DIAS

My dear Selma,

You can't think what a relief it is to be writing to you. It's been scribble, scribble scribble for the last few days – not quite sure if I was saying the right thing.

I have written to Miss Moorsom and to Michael Sadleir and or Martha Smith at Constable's about copyright. Also something else cropped up which had to be attended to. *It would*. Then I have lost or mislaid my contract wandering about as I do – can you wonder?

I don't know why Miss Smith & Co thought I was dead. It does seem more fitting I know, but life is never neat and tidy. I feel a bit like poor old Rasputin, who was poisoned, stabbed in the front and shot in the back but was still alive kicking and crowing when flung out into the snow.

He apparently couldn't or wouldn't die! Never mind.

My dear you'll understand what outer darkness I live in when I tell you that I haven't got a radio. There was one at the Widemouth bungalow, our first attempt at a Cornish home home home. But it didn't work. We had it fixed up. Then the gales started. Oh Lord – that wind – 90 miles an hour chilling and killing and straight from the sea. The radio conked out at once, except for Hilversum, groans and strange noises, you never heard the like. I nearly conked out (period slang) too, but had (as usual), a very ancient fur coat which saved my precious life.

Max wore an Esquimaux affair with a hood. We spent all our time getting coke and coal for the Rayburn and waiting for the roof to blow off. However though the whole place shivered and shook the roof stayed on. Then, of course, the pipes burst and I went to bed ill. The dust piled up in the six empty rooms "with loggia dining room", but I just stayed put. Poor Max grimly kept the show going. *Then* our six months let was over and the sun came out the day we left.

Forgive all this nonsense. Am writing this on my knee in front of the fire which accounts for much. And I'm excited too.

Now it's time to be serious. I took and take the Observer and Sunday Times and was rejoiced at your notices. I nearly wrote when "The Maids" was on, but had this idea that you were very busy. That seems to be so. I'm glad,. I'd given up "Good Morning Midnight" – but as you say there is a right time for everything and you knew it. Get very well and keep well in this tough world. Salut!

136

I told Miss Moorsom and Mr Sadleir about our first meeting, that I had consented with joy to your idea of adaptation for broadcasting but did not hear the reading. I also told them that at our second meeting you asked me to keep in touch no matter what. I meant to. But so much happened and I lost hope. I feel now that "Good Morning Midnight" is yours as well as mine and I bet you feel that too. It must have been awful cutting something so stark for I cut cut cut also.

I want to tell you something about the writing of it in the first place. But that is better typewritten. It was the end I couldn't get. I wanted fireworks but couldn't manage a damp squib. Nothing. For weeks.

Then I got tight in desperation and you know the result. Have you cut the Man in the Dressing Gown? Don't – he is right.

But I won't interfere now.

Please don't think me starry eyed if I tell you that a book has a life of its own when it's finished and can fight for existence.

For it's true. G.M.M. had a strong one. Now I feel it's out of my hands and over to you Selma. You can do it beautifully (I have not forgotten the short story you read me. I burst into tears and you were rather taken aback.)

I'll get a radio now by hook or by crook. Probably crook – but the Cornish are a difficult lot. So suspicious.

My landlady is very nice, but her eyes flash when she talks about money – and she grows years younger. Just the word charms her and it does me too. Now – I wasn't always like that.

On the contrary – and do you know I *still* believe in other things much more. Much.

This letter is getting quite out of hand so I'll now lay down this awful pen which is a real sugar.

I will send a neat typed one, letter I mean, and some notices of G.M.M.

I do hope Michael Sadleir is still at Constables. Miss Martha Smith is an unknown quantity.

I had an awful time of despair when I tore up the picture. There was one. Man with Banjo[1]. Also the book and my contract, I think.

One is never brave enough.
Yours with love
Jean R.

I've said I'll come to London. Not looking like Ma Rasputin, I hope!

1. *In* Good Morning, Midnight *the heroine, Sasha, buys a picture of "an old Jew with a red nose, playing the banjo" from a painter, "Serge", whose work makes a deep impression on her. When Jean was visiting Paris in November, 1937, she bought a similar painting from Simon Segal. After she had returned with it to England, Segal wrote to her: "J'espère que vous aimerez mon petit bonhomme jouant du banjo. Il est misérable, digne et résigné comme le sont les sages, les artistes et les fous. Peut-être vous donnera-t-il du courage. Ne désespérez pas. Je sais que la douleur 'est la noblesse unique' a dit Baudelaire. Et c'est du fond de notre détresse terrible que jaillit enfin l'étincelle et le torrent créateur. Moi aussi je souffre souvent – toujours, beaucoup –*

croyez-moi. Mais je l'aime, cette souffrance, car elle seule ne me trahit jamais, me donne courage et la belle colère. . . ."

November 4th [1956]
                                                                    Carteret Road

> I have deluged you after all! Never
> mind. Look at anything promising.
> May I have them back some time

My dear Selma,

This is letter No. 3. The first, enthusiastic and grateful, may have been addressed wrongly. [. . . . .] I hope it reached you.

Here are some press cuttings about G.M.M. They may help. If not, it doesn't matter. The Revue Nouvelle Litteraire[1] did its best, but when John Lehmann took the book to Paris the translator was anti. I don't think I answered his letter about this, which was idiotic, for I admire him very much.

But I was downhearted at the time and quite at sea and not a clue.

The Times chose G.M.M. and then tore it to pieces. I still think a bit spitefully. I am *not* like Becky Sharp – wish I were, and wasn't poverty haunted as Mr Clever[2] hints. Not then. A bit of a stabber in the back and a smiler with the knife.

As for the others, macabre was the usual adjective[3]. Here are some anyway. You'll understand how comforting the Nouvelle's was to me.

"Voyage in the Dark" was translated into Dutch, very well[4], title "Melodie en Mineur". Victor Van Vriesland wrote a preface and reviewed it (enclosed). He also wrote very understandingly about G.M.M. but I can't find the cutting or translations.

I was going to deluge you with these things, but when I was looking for my contract found so many old letters. Talk about a *sinking feeling*! I won't inflict it on anyone else.

The American critics were penetrating and helpful sometimes, but the best are lost or read to pieces. Here's one of "Quartet" English "Postures", *what* a title! Can't think why Chatto insisted on changing a harmless title like "Quartet". I must have been very "Don't care a dam. Take it or leave it" in those days.

Well that's the lot.

About G.M.M. I was never a bit satisfied with the last chapters. I wanted Sasha to enter the No time region there. "Everything is on the same plane". I tried and rewrote and rewrote but no use.

So as the book had to be finished I drank a bottle of wine. The gigolo, René became very important, the Man in the Dressing gown appeared from Heaven knows where to supply the inevitable end.

It got done somehow – but I was worried about it.

Much the nicest letter I discovered in my old trunk was v. short and ended

"Dam you Jean you know what I am trying to say", so I'll end too:
"You know what I'm trying to say" yours affectionately

Jean

I've heard from Constable's about my contract. Great relief for mine vanished.

1. Les Nouvelles Littéraires *printed an article called "Jean Rhys: Romancière Inconnue" on 26 August, 1939, by E. de Nève (a pseudonym of Jean Lenglet, Jean's first husband).*

2. *An anonymous reviewer in* The Times Literary Supplement, *22 April, 1939.*

3. *"Yes, 'macabre' is the word": Hilton Brown, reviewing* Good Morning, Midnight *in* The Nineteenth Century, *July, 1939.*

4. *Again, by E. de Nève (Jean Lenglet).*

TO SELMA VAZ DIAS   *November 12th [1956]*
                                                    Carteret Road

> My guess is that you didn't read the
> press cuttings and you are *quite right*.
> Mostly guff.

My dear Selma,
   I hope the press cuttings didn't deluge you and were some good. One never knows.
   This is about the ending of G.M.M. – I haven't got the book with me, so have to trust to memory.
   It's fine – except that one cannot *feel* a rustle. One *hears* a rustle – and I don't think rustle is the right word for a man's dressing gown. I must have slipped up. Haven't got the MS either. Taffeta rustles and so do stiff silks I suppose, but wouldn't a man's dressing gown be a heavy silk? Please don't think me pernickety but every word must be exact. Like "The Daring young man on the Flying Trapeze", by Saroyan. Have you ever read it?
   It's like this – isn't it? Sasha, who is hoping that she has "willed" René to come back to her, puts on the light and leaves her door open, or the key outside. I forget. She thinks she heard him but *before the door opens* or as soon as she sees it moving (again I forget) she knows that the man approaching is not the gigolo René, but someone else – She knows.
   This I think is what she would do (being Sasha). She would lie quite still and shut her eyes, even perhaps put her arm over her eyes. Then when the man is close to her she would touch his sleeve or shoulder and *feel* the silk instead of the coat or overcoat René would be wearing.
   So the end must be, would be:
   "I don't need to look I know. I can feel (or I am touching – feel better) the silk of the dressing gown – the white dressing gown."

139

If you like "rustle" better keep it of course but she must *hear* it and it isn't quite right for a man's dressing gown somehow. Do you think?

It is so cold here and real November. Sometimes my landlady bakes bread or cakes or scones and there is such a *comforting* smell in the house. Very much needed for I'm terrified to look at the newspapers.

The only ideas I have about production are very banal and not too original.

(1) That the thing should start by the patronne (a hard metallic voice) saying "Bon soir madame, le numero 24 (or 72) n'est ce pas?" Something like that and music of course.

The other: Theme tunes – this is because the "man in the dressing gown" theme has been in my head for days. But, as I can't write music, or whistle, and would be self conscious if I sang, *how* can I get it over to anybody?

I have no ideas about Sasha's theme or the gigolo's except vague ideas. And anyway I've made up my mind to trust you and Miss Moorsom completely for I don't know a thing about broadcasting. Still, this "theme" is persistent.

[. . . . . .]

                                              Yours affectionately
                                                        Jean

TO SELMA VAZ DIAS   *February 21st [1957]*
                                                     Carteret Road

                          [. . . . . .]

My dear Selma,

I've heard from Miss Moorsom, and will be in London early next week – all being well.

I was in the midst of packing to move into the new flat. (Not house my dear but a minute flat by the sea).

However I'll chuck everything into storage and am in the middle of packing (bis!) which God knows, I hate.

I am awfully excited, of course, and longing to hear the adaptation.

[. . . . . .]

I wish I *had* a house – then I would reserve a room for you when the "driven" feeling gets acute. In the summer, for the winter is bitter.

You'd see nothing but the clouds and hear nothing but the sea. No one would come near you, except to bring trays of food (and drink) and there'd be lots of books, ancient and modern.

As this is my idea of Paradise I will offer it to you – if ever I have a house.

And if that doesn't seem likely, now, who knows?

                                                   Yours affecty
                                                        Jean

February 21st [1957]
Carteret Road

> This is a hurried letter as the packing
> and confusion is a bother.
> Tell Ruthie I'm taking her elephant to
> London for luck.

My dear Maryvonne,

I had your letter and am a bit worried about your being in hospital my dear. A bit very! I would have answered at once but have been in a great flurry.

We have at last found a very small flat where we hope to have some peace for a year anyway. It is a real flat (instead of rooms) and will be nice in summer, though it is so close to the sea that when the winter comes – and the gales – well I wonder if the whole house won't be blown away! However let's not think of that yet. With any luck we will stay put, and be fixed when you arrive in October.

As (of course) *everything* has to be packed and moved I've been rushing about in a great confusion. Then the B.B.C. wrote that the "read through" is to be next week instead of in March. So more confusion as I must be in London on Monday.

However I'm doing my best to cope and Max is being valiant as usual and I hope all will be well. It'll mean a lot if it goes down and is liked of course.

I do not know the broadcast date yet – as soon as I know I'll tell you.

The Third Programme is advertised (VHF 91.3 M.C./S) does that mean anything to you?

It's difficult to get – even here, because of the wind which never stops. The actress is Selma Vaz Dias.

I'll ask about broadcasting to Indonesia. It would be lovely if you could listen in. [. . . . . .]

The landlady here has a good set, but it is used exclusively for church services and the Queen's broadcast at Xmas!

Indeed she (the landlady) gets more religious every day. Sunday is eating day and everything else is forbidden even washing a pair of stockings. And wine is taboo. Shocking! I asked her what about Jesus Christ the wine-bibber providing drink for a wedding.

She said, "Oh but He drank *ginger* wine (sic) temperance stuff. He wouldn't drink *alcohol*."

As you see she can be amusing, but it gets a little trying and I'll be awfully glad to get into our own place, shut the door and think This is mine – ours. I'm touching wood and crossing fingers all the time.

The new address is

> Rocket House
> Breakwater Road, Bude

and after a week in London we'll go there – all being well.

This address will always find me, so at a pinch will Edward's. Knottsfield, Budleigh Salterton, Devon. Yes this has been rather a grim winter.

I'm glad it's nearly over. That's all about me.

Now about you. *Keep well.* Don't worry about your English, your letters are fine and I keep them all in a special case.

I hope Ruthie looked lovely in her tutu.

Give her my best and dearest love and say I'm sorry I'm such a movable granny. My greatest ambition is a pair of horn rimmed specs and then I'll look the part very well.

My best and dearest love to you too and a big hug and Max sends greetings to everyone. He is very pleased to be going to London for a few days and so am I.
Yours always
Jean

March 7th [1957]
Rocket House, Breakwater Rd
Bude, Cornwall

TO SELMA VAZ DIAS

[. . . . . .]

My dear Selma,

Forgive pencil. Ink vanished when we moved, and it's early closing day in peaceful, treeless Bude.

My dear, here we are after an all night journey and an early morning unpacking which went on and on. I am a bit weary, and I bet Max is too. They forgot to provide a wardrobe and our clothes are lying about – tied up in heaps as Max says.

But there is a rum cupboard place and he is knocking nails into that and soon all will be clean and tidy.

I felt I must write at once and tell you again how pleased and excited I am.

You cut the book beautifully, and as you know your reading moved me to tears. (I bet you understand how I feel about that) – So I'll only tell you how much I enjoyed the evening at your house, and your delicious cooking. Your family were quite charming and it's the nicest thing that's happened to me, for years and weary years.

I am slightly dazed at the moment – have reached the stage when I can't stop looking for a T. S. Eliot book about cats. That too has vanished – and it must be somewhere.

We can see the sea from one window and the cliffs. It's peaceful and secluded. If all goes well I can work here (Touch wood and fingers crossed.)

It's a little damp and the geyser is v. odd. I feel it may blow up at any moment.

Also I want a few *trees* around. What a lot I want!! –

142

It's nice really and Max says the nails are in and will I hang the lovely clothes up. With love

Jean

About the name –

Tania or Tanya might do. Do you think?

I don't want to change Sasha, but feel Miss Moorsom might like it – I do feel that Tania is near enough and anyway doesn't come in much.

The character is Sasha to me but no one else would notice –

M. sends salutations.

J.R.

I had your letter this morning. It was quite OK tho' a bit wearying (the journey I mean). The worst of course was moving into a new place at the crack of dawn so to speak. We're still not quite straight but it'll be fine when we are. Quiet. Max dashes round and gets things done in an amazing way.

J.R.

TO SELMA VAZ DIAS   *March 18th [1957]*
Rocket House

> P.S. If and when I can know approximate
> date of broadcast v. helpful. BBC don't
> seem fixed.
> If I can't come to London I'll certainly
> get a radio – somehow I will next week.

My dear Selma,

You are having a read through of G.M.M. with music on the 21st aren't you? This is to wish you luck and to wish I were in London.

I came back brimful of ideas and enthusiastic – felt I could have spoken the whole of Mrs Rochester (very provisional title) into one of those recording machines you know. After all it has been simmering in my head for a long long time.

For years –

However getting into this place was quite a thing.

It's going to be nice I trust, but it was awfully damp and all sorts of articles were (that was Max tapping on the window to get in) were missing. A tea pot a mop etc etc – felt something would burst, trying to cope and so absent-minded.

Well everything is getting fixed up except that it goes on raining and as we're entirely surrounded by water – the sea at high tide, the Bude river, an affair like a weir, and the Bude canal, I'm a bit apprehensive.

It will be all right when it's fine, you'd like it for a few days. The weir makes a very pleasant noise and there's no one around but sea gulls and dim men in raincoats staring at the water.

I could not work properly it was getting me frantic, so I did a nonsense called *English Harbour* to calm myself. It's not quite a nonsense as it is based on an old story about English Harbour in Antigua (partly true certainly). Nelson's headquarters where he was stationed in the West Indies. It's (English Harbour) supposed to be haunted and the whole affair was dramatic – romantic and so on. When it's finished I'll send it to you. I've written it as a film script because that's the way I see it – it ought to be ready in a day or two – dialogue only indicated, as I was told the script writers would do that – well I wonder.

I don't believe anybody has the "feel" of the West Indies as they were in the 17th 18th and part of 19th century at all. Should say perhaps the 18th, 19th and part of twentieth. Anyway I'll send it because I could work it up into something, ghost story, play.

Also I don't want it to steal any of the Mrs Rochester stuff. I don't think it does, it's nearly a century earlier – say 1740 instead of 1840 where I want Mrs Rochester and quite a different subject.

Well that's enough of that and I must go and join Max, he is so good and patient. Love and best wishes

from *Jean R.*

P.S. Are you sure there's nothing in the "Times" idea? It wouldn't be an anthology exactly. More an escape from time and place as we know them – or think we do.

Here is St Teresa (of Aquila)

"O Conquistadores! Conquerors of the Americas! Mine is a journey more difficult and dangerous than yours. At the cost of a thousand sufferings, at the cost of a long death before the fact I will find that country which is ever new and ever young. *Come with me and you will see.*" (Religious ecstasy of course but there are other ways.)

Many like that – so lovely. Accuracy not vouched for as quoting from memory.

J.R.

TO MARYVONNE MOERMAN   *April 14th [1957]*
                                                        Rocket House

[. . . . . .]

My dear Maryvonne,

I've been wanting to write to you for ages my dear, but I've been very excited and busy. So much has happened. At the end of Feb I had a letter from the B.B.C. asking me to come up to London to hear the read-through of "Good Morning Midnight" so we managed to squeeze together the money and I'm so glad we did. It was lovely to see London again, and somehow I got a cheap dress and *A HAT* and had a make up and rushed off to hear Selma Vaz Dias. She was very good and of course I wept with excitement and my make up came off but everyone was kind so it did not matter. *Much*.

Then we went to lunch at Verrey's and it was a fine day. Everything was fine and I felt happier than for years and years.

We had to come back rather soon for the hotel was pretty expensive. I have not heard the music yet.

Well, it is very nice of course and a slight chance. It will be broadcast on May 10th, 9.55 to 10.55 p.m. and Saturday May 11th, 6.45 to 7.45. The Third wave length is VHF 91.3 metres. As for time lag I just don't know. Are you twelve hours earlier or later than Greenwich time? I do so hope it'll be possible to get something. [. . . . . .] The indefatigable Max has found someone with a Hi-Fi and I'm going to their house for the occasion.

The B.B.C. wanted me to come up to London again but it just couldn't be done though I longed to go. Well I've sent off the life story they asked for (publicity – only dry facts) and some press cuttings. So can only wait. Please wish me luck, very hard. Selma is awfully good, she is a fine actress and I have a new idea I've been working on if this goes well.

Now about this place which is quite important too. It is at the other end of the town, and very near the sea. There is also a river, a canal, *and* a weir – so no lack of water. It is one big room divided by a curtain and the furniture is quite pleasant. There's a tiny kitchen and tiny bathroom. We both like it so much – it's *heaven* having no landlady.

There is only one drawback, the cold. It is a stone house and the Bude wind is a terror (from Siberia I should say). We are at the limit of the houses – just behind us a hill which is so beautiful on fine days – covered with tiny violets and the birds sing very loud and happily. I think I heard a nightingale yesterday. But when the wind gets up and the sky is grey you can see what a cruel coast this is. No Birds sing. Huge black rocks and a stormy sea. But lovely sands. Max remembers a big man of war being lost near by. (Still even then it is not ordinary but wild and savage.) All the same I long and long for warmth. I could soak up sun like a sponge I think and still want more. People say cold is bracing and healthy. Well hum – ha. Maybe! But not for me.

I am longing to hear from you, how you are and how Ruth is. When are you coming to Europe? [. . . . . .] My dear I can't write more as my letter will be overweight and we are so stony till I'm paid. Please forgive this being all about myself but I'm excited of course. Max is much better here and sends you (all of you) love.

I do too with hugs and kisses added. Please write soon –

Jean

May 8th [1957]
                                                        Rocket House
My dear Selma,

Perhaps you had a letter from me this morning and thought it odd and ungrateful that I didn't mention your article in the Radio times[1].

My dear I have not seen it, and heard about it from Mr Francis Wyndham of Andre Deutsch for the first time by the post this morning.

If I told you what Bude was like I'd use up six sheets. There is one small newsagent who said he'd sold out when asked for a copy, and hedged about ordering another, *no* bookshop and a library with a nice girl presiding over *what* a collection! – However she did get me Jane Eyre (after some delay) so mustn't nag.

Mr Wyndham wrote very kindly about my books and the next one, and of course I'm feeling fine and hopeful.

The book is there in my head like an egg in its shell, but it's fragile as an egg too, till safely on paper.

When we arrived here we discovered that the damned agent hadn't done anything he'd promised. I've had to scrub the floors, find a wardrobe and must buy curtains somehow for there are huge windows and people peer through them on their way to the cliffs. Can't *bear* that! Well, all my nails are broken so I hope I can now stop chores after that sacrifice.

Max has just come in with the Radio Times of May 3rd. He got it at the station. It's a West of England edition and can't find article. I would like to see it and will get hold of the London edition somehow.

Lot of luck and thanks   affecly
                                                                Jean

[. . . . . .]

1. *"In Quest of a Missing Author"* by *Selma Vaz Dias*, Radio Times, *3 May 1957*.

May 9th [1957]
                                                        Rocket House
Dear Mr Wyndham,

Thank you so much for your letter, and the generous things you say about my books.

I was in London at the end of February to hear the read through of "Good Morning Midnight" and was much impressed by Selma Vaz Dias' performance. No one could be better, and she has cut the book very skilfully.

I hope you'll like the broadcast. I'm excited about it of course.

Yes I am working on a new novel. I'm not under contract to any publisher, so far as I'm aware, and will certainly submit the MS to you[1] when it is finished.

I've wanted to write it for a very long time, and I ought to be quicker – well not so slow – in this peaceful place.   Yours sincerely
Jean Rhys

1. *Francis Wyndham was then working as an editor for the publishing firm of André Deutsch, Ltd.*

TO SELMA VAZ DIAS   *May 15th [1957]*
                                                           Rocket House

My dear Selma,
     Well at last I can say thank you not for the first time.
     We went by taxi (which was late) to a kind acquaintance and there we were left with family portraits and radio. I haven't one. (Yet.) However you soon triumphed over that little sitting room – very alien at first.
     Hope the B.B.C. were satisfied and others pleased too. I'm nicely tucked away, and know nothing about the general reaction bad good or what. Good – I do pray. Some very heartening letters have reached me all praising your performance to the skies. Also two offers from publishers for option on next book.
     [. . . . .] Several letters have suggested your doing Voyage in the Dark. One from an excellent judge. Would you consider it at all? I know the idea didn't appeal to you but think about it, for it could be quickly done and might be effective. That is of course if the BBC were satisfied repeat satisfied with me and criticism not hostile.
     I'm getting along with Jane Eyre but am still held up with tackling business letters and money oh dear.

> Oh how happy I will be.
> When my tired eyes do see
> That beautiful joyful lovely *Fee*

     Thank you again anyway and love

                                                           from *Jean*

I have written to Miss Moorsom.

TO DIANA ATHILL[1]   *June 1st, 1957*
                                                           Rocket House

Dear Miss Athill,
     Thank you for your letter which gave me great pleasure, and for the cheque[2]. That helps a good deal.
     I hope to be able to submit the MSS of my new novel to André Deutsch by

the end of this year – in six to nine months time – as a large part of it is already written.

I enclose a signed copy of your letter.   Yours sincerely
                                                            Jean Rhys

1. A director of André Deutsch Ltd, Diana Athill is the author of an autobiography, Instead of a Letter *(1963) and a novel,* Don't Look at Me Like That *(1967).*

2. For twenty-five pounds, as an option on the new novel.

TO MARYVONNE MOERMAN   *July 24th [1957]*
                                                    Rocket House
My dear Maryvonne,

I was so pleased to get your letter posted at Colombo, and am answering at once so that you will find this waiting for you when you arrive – to say welcome and my love.

As I have told John I'd meant to suggest that Bude would be nicer in September than August, but on second thoughts come when it fits in best with your plans. Now I'll tell you a bit about Bude that you may know what to expect.

It is North Cornwall of course, so very windy and rather cold. No trees but high steep cliffs and a rocky shore. A small very provincial town.

There is a bathing pool (you can see it from Rocket House) but few people seem to bathe in the sea, perhaps because there are notices up saying "Bathing at Low Tide is Dangerous", whereas Bathing at High Tide certainly *looks* dangerous, for the sea is usually rough and the rocks very black and sharp.

(It would be perfect for sailing Max says. To me it looks "Choppy". But he ought to know.) It is a wreckers coast, and when it is not raining has a sort of splendour, but as it has been raining for six weeks on end, it's a bit difficult to imagine fine weather.

[. . . . . .]

It is strange that your ship is called Rees Williams or nearly, for it was my name. A good omen – it must be so!

[. . . . . .]

I am so longing to see you all. The broadcast was a bit confused I thought (I didn't write the script). There were some rum letters (one woman said that she didn't believe there *was* any novel or novelist either so why make one up!) But there were some nice letters too which cheered me a lot. Also the vague faint hope of another try is good too. I want to post this tonight if I can but our stupid clock is always wrong.

So more in a day or two. Salutations from Max, all my love hugs and kisses to you especially; to all – love

                                                            from *Jean*

Dearest Ruthie, Welcome to Europe. The sea here is a lovely blue green colour (when it's fine) and I bet you'll enjoy swimming. Love and millions of kisses from your affectionate and in a hurry but very loving Grandmother

TO SELMA VAZ DIAS

[. . . . . .]

My dear Selma,

I was delighted to hear from you – have had 'flu – not badly but badly enough, so news and letter very welcome.

Your house was warm and attractive I thought – you probably hate even the possibility of leaving it, the fuss and chaos. But all will be well – you will see – and lots of dough will materialise from flats. Please let me know if you do change address – Important.

"So much to say and how to say it" – to tell the truth – I feel a bit bewildered, what between 'flu and sputniks. Max, who has been very kind and dear to me, does not like the Russian surprises one bit. And Rocket House, Bude is *not* the place to fight a malaise. [. . . . . .]

However I expect you want to hear about work in progress not journey into fear.

Well I got down here bursting with optimism. Then this that and the other *had* to be dealt with. Finally I got Jane Eyre to read and reread and hook on *my* Mrs Rochester to Charlotte Brontë's. I was a bit taken aback when I discovered what a fat (and improbable) monster she was. However I think I have seen how to do it though not without pain struggle curses and lamentation.

(Whether I have any *right* to do it is a question which I'll face later. One thing at a time). I have written about half (in longhand) the rest is safely in my head. In a week or two, I'll have a typewriter from Exeter, then will be able to judge better both quantity and quality for it all will look different – I'm prepared for that –

I hope (clutching wood) that early next year I will come to London and report progress. I wish I were more slap dash and here you are, but alas I'm not.

I wish also that I could see you and be cheered up for really Bude is *hellish*. No radio, only black sea and rocks and fog. It feels isolated but is not peaceful, for in the summer swarms of tourists, now upstairs a man who stamps about.

You see – *Lamentations*. Never mind.

Now about V in D. Do you see it as a play? Its original title was "Two Tunes". That's what I meant. Past and Present. Then Past got altered and cut to an echo, and though it had been advertised as "Two Tunes" I altered the title to V in D. Of course a "happy" ending could be contrived but that time seems so long ago. Much longer ago than 1840! (If you see what I mean) "Quartet", though tiresome to read – too many dots, too much emotion, was written as a play, and I think situation and dialogue would still stand up. I'm so sure of this that I considered trying to do it myself. But Mrs Rochester (to say nothing of mister R) takes all I have, and I hope I'll have enough.

I shouldn't think the B.B.C. would like The Left Bank now. I have a story unpublished and untried but again very "period", 1890 this time. I will send it if you think any good. I simply don't *know* what they'd like, though had a feeling that if I were *there* I could do it off the cuff. Probably not. I just think so and what an optimist.

Was so interested to hear about Maclaren Ross[1] and glad he liked G.M.M. I do hope he's heard you in it.

Do you know Selma I feel it's very *tactless* of me to be alive. No savoir faire. (Dam little savoir vivre either)

Never mind. I am alive I *think*. Not at all sure sometimes, and waving not drowning. Have you read Stevie Smith's last poems? I want to. Title *"Drowning Not Waving."*   Love
                                                                                                                    Jean
P.S. The drink here is terrible. Day before yesterday M bought some Spanish Red and my dear it tasted so filthy that I couldn't swallow it. Six lovely bobs down the sink.

1. *Julian Maclaren-Ross, the novelist and short-story writer, was an admirer of Jean Rhys's books. In 1950 he told Francis Wyndham that she had recently died in a sanatorium.*

TO SELMA VAZ DIAS   *December 21st [1957]*
                                                                                              Rocket House

[. . . . . .]

My dear Selma,
    Thank you for card – We are at sixes and sevens my dear, because I've stupidly hurt my back. So all chores fall on unfortunate Max. He is very sweet, but swears a lot, and I hear clatter bang crash from kitchen and know another plate cup or saucer has gone west.
    This is such a rum place. Geyser bursts, lights go out, fish knives and forks disappear (last relics of former comfort). Makes me sad and what a thing to be sad about.
    Maryvonne my daughter paid me a short visit. She is nice and not a bit like me – *thank God*.
    She got away from Indonesia with husband and baby before trouble, but is of course very worried and unsettled.
    So am I – especially as I cannot make out what is actually going on. English papers useless.

Well here's hoping for 1958. Best of luck to you all and love from

Jean

I will produce goods in 1958 *if it's the last thing I do.*

TO MARYVONNE MOERMAN   *January 14th [1958]*
                                                    Rocket House

Max sends love to all.

My dear Maryvonne,

So delighted to get postcards. They are now on that old screen – look fine.

I'm longing to hear your news and all about new flat, so *don't* forget promised letter. Please –

I'm in the middle of my flu, so will only send love to you all and many many hugs and kisses for Ruth Ellen and for you.

This is an awful place – so like a public lavatory in spite of all efforts. Max is smashing away in the kitchen. He says it's only an egg-cup but it sounded like that dreadful tea thing – I'd better heave myself up and look.

Again love from   Your most faithful yet useless
                                                    Mother

Forgive pencil safer in bed.

It *is* the egg cup and can be stuck together again. So that's one mercy.

TO MARYVONNE MOERMAN   *Sunday February 16th [1958]*
                                                    Rocket House

[. . . . . .]

My Dear Maryvonne,

I was so glad to have your letter. Edward wrote and asked for news of you. I said that you were in the midst of moving. Well anyway your place sounds rather nice my dear, and I'm delighted because this question of where to live can be formidable. Our year in this cold place is up next month. So far as I can see we must stay on for another year.

They will not let it for another summer only. That is the time when rents go up. Would you believe that people will pay about £15 to £20 a week for a bungalow in Bude – and £6 for a place like this?

But they *do*. I imagine they expect it will be warm – It is crazy. Warm!!! I was very dubious about it. I don't really care for Cornwall and never will. Then I saw that there was a place to let in Wales – a cottage on a lake. "Absolute privacy". Doesn't it sound attractive? The trouble is that we'd have to take it without seeing it – a great risk. Too great Max thought. He wants to keep this on and I suppose we will. It is the "safe" thing.

151

I do not think it's always wise to do the "safe" thing. However it is not too bad in the summer and there is a month or so before the tourists come.

I will get over all this dull talk of myself, and then go on to you and Ruthie – much more important.

I am worried about this book. I do know how much depends on it – just everything for me, and even perhaps it might make a difference for you.

The idea is possible I am sure, and a great deal that I have written can be used. But somehow after a few months here I got stuck, like in a bog. If this goes on I have determined to go up to London to wake myself up even if it's by myself and for a short time and with my last sous.

It is very strange the exact reason why one place makes you excited and alive, and another lethargic and indifferent.

I don't know why – if I did I might be able to do something. But it remains a mystery. Cornwall is supposed to be good – but NOT FOR ME! This darned sand and black rock, oh Lord! Well we will see.

I can be obstinate and I am determined not to let Methodist, black rock, Bude defeat me. Feb. is the worst month. It rains all the time. Thank you about the typing and I will take you at your word when ready.

Do you know what would cheer me up a lot? A gay poster for that damp wall. Or even black and white. But I've been thinking perhaps a big poster would be expensive and difficult to pack. But two or three smaller ones? I would stick them on proofed paper and so cover the damp patch on wall. Wouldn't shades or blinds be dear? I'd love them to blot out tourists, but don't want you to spend a lot on me. If they are really cheap will send measurements. Now that's enough about Bude – beastly Bude to me. Never mind – when the sun shines it will be better – and posters would simply delight me. Trees, flowers anything. Or a map perhaps. You will know. Things you bought big success.

I read all the news about Indonesia. It seems a muddle and I expect it is awfully trying for yourself and Job. I wish you so much luck my dear, and have a feeling things will turn out better than you think. Here's hoping.

About Ruthie. Her room sounds fine. I found one page of a Mitsou San[1] story but not the end. It is not bad, but can't imagine how it ended. It's about shadows. You know I lost a lot of MS moving from place to place.

I am wearing your white cardigan. It is lovely and warm. Did Job like the black skirt? It ought to suit you. Now I must stop and go to bed. It's raining as usual. Max has cut his beard very short. Also moustache (after much nagging from me). He looks much better.

Do write soon again and I will too – My love and hugs and kisses.

Jean

1. The heroine of a series of children's stories that Jean had written to amuse Maryvonne. Page One of "The Shadows" reads:

Sometimes Mitsou San used to watch her shadow. It was a long thin shadow or a short fat shadow. But there is was, tied to her heels. When she walked across the grass the shadow followed her – sad and obedient. And then there were the shadows of trees on the grass.

So one day she said to her nurse: "Tell me about shadows." Because she knew that her nurse knew everything.

First of all the nurse said: "Go away and don't bother me."

But Mitsou San said: "No, tell me, because I want to know."

Her nurse said: "The shadow is yourself that follows you, watching."

Mitsou San said: "I want to know where shadows are made, and you're a witch and can tell me. Take me on your back and show me where they are made."

So, as the nurse was a witch, she took Mitsou on her back and flew with her to the place where shadows are made.

And there were three old women, sitting under a tree, cutting the shadows out of brown paper. Long thin shadows and short fat shadows, and shadows of cows and goats and houses. . . .

They worked so quickly you could not see their hands moving, and when they had finished a shadow they threw it down into the world.

TO FRANCIS WYNDHAM   *March 29th [1958]*
                                               Rocket House
Dear Mr Wyndham,

This is to tell you something about the novel I am trying to write – provisional title "The First Mrs Rochester". I mean, of course, the mad woman in "Jane Eyre".

It's difficult for me to explain an unfinished book, this one particularly, and I hope I won't be tedious – or disappointing.

For some time I've been getting down all I remembered about the West Indies as the West Indies used to be. (Also all I was told, which is more important). I called this "Creole" but it had no shape or plan – it wasn't a book at all and I didn't try to force it.

Then when I was in London last year it "clicked in my head" that I had material for the story of Mr Rochester's first wife. The real story – as it might have been. I don't know why this happened. I was thinking of something else and had a title for it, hadn't read "Jane Eyre" for years and nearly forgotten Creole.

However (suddenly) I was very excited about "The First Mrs Rochester" and imagined it could be done quickly.

When I got back to Cornwall I read then re-read "Jane Eyre" and was rather taken aback. Still, I was all the more determined to write my book –

It has no connection with any play film or adaptation of "Jane Eyre" who does not appear at all – once perhaps. Mr Rochester does, of course, but only as a very young man.

It might be possible to unhitch the whole thing from Charlotte Brontë's novel, but I don't want to do that. It is that particular mad Creole I want to write about, not any of the other mad Creoles. There were quite a number it seems, and large dowries did not help them. On the contrary. It wasn't as easy as I'd thought, of course, and unfortunately I had to stop working twice.

But I have got a plausible story and a plausible way of telling it I hope.

I see it in three parts, in each part a different character speaks – but I am trying to make the whole smooth and inevitable naturally. Parts I and II the West Indies in the 1840s. Part III England. Grace Poole, the nurse or keeper speaking.

I am not satisfied with Part III, or really with any of it yet, but if you can have patience with this slow approach I believe I can do it. I do think it has possibilities if it's done as it ought to be.

It goes without saying that if I cannot let you have the MSS within a reasonable time – can you give me this year? I will return the part of my advance you so kindly sent me on behalf of Andre Deutsch.

It helped a lot. So did your very welcome letters. I lose confidence sometimes and long to be reassured. But so does everyone perhaps.

Rocket House is very bleak and cold. Also it seems to need constant repairs and proppings up – so not so peaceful.

However with any luck at all there ought to be some quiet months ahead. I don't think the book will be as remote or as gloomy as it sounds.

Please forgive a personal letter but as this is hardly business like and not typed, I thought it better that way.

I have no title yet. "The First Mrs Rochester" is not right. Nor, of course is "Creole". That has a different meaning now. I hope I'll get one soon, for titles mean a lot to me. Almost half the battle. I thought of "Sargasso Sea" or "Wide Sargasso Sea" but nobody knew what I meant.   Yours sincerely

Jean Rhys

TO MARYVONNE MOERMAN

April [1958]
Rocket House

[. . . . . .]

My dear Maryvonne,

I was so very glad to get your letter my dear, and I should have answered at once, but worries have piled up and I wished to write when I was calm (more or less).

First, my very dear child, do not let thoughts of me bother you. I *have* been ill, for it has been most bitterly cold and this is a concrete house. It was like being frozen to the heart – day after day.

Then when I was better I became very depressed, and it shows you in what a weak and silly mood I was that I let little things make me despair. For instance they have dug up all the grass and flowers round here. I don't know why. It's now a concrete desert outside as well as in. Then there was this and that. Never mind – I will get over it I guess.

I am glad that you are settled in your new flat and anyhow there are trees. I worry about you a lot, it is a rotten business – Indonesia but I am sure of one thing. That if you can stick the bad times the good ones come back. It is as sure as the swing of a pendulum. *Never* lose heart. You are young and better things will happen and soon too I feel –

About Ruthie, she's there in my head all the time and I am so delighted she has some pals. Yes I think groups of children can be horrible. So can all groups. I hate them and fear them like I hated termites nests at home – Everyone used to laugh at me for this. They don't sting like ants. They are only *vile* somehow – After all, ants do walk along in the sun. But these things build *huge* nests and little roads going from one nest to the other – very nicely made and they have Soldiers, Workers, and Nurses (I believe) and a few Drones or something – and *hell* to them. Well that is a Group to me.

Now you used often to tell me ages ago that I didn't realise you were grown up. I remember once that you were very angry because I brought you a little handbag from Paris and you said "that is something for a *Child* of 11 and I am 15 and Grown up and oh what a ridiculous person you are."

But I do realise you are grown up and yourself now (I always did really) so I am going to tell you my greatest worry.

You know don't you that I have an idea for a book. *It is good if I can do it.* Selma Vaz Dias liked it. So did my publisher André Deutsch.

Well I was working on it as a *book*. I saw how it must be done. Book first, Selma's dramatic monologue taken from it. The other day to my despair I had a letter from Selma, a very sweet letter but she firmly expects a script. And soon. Not on any account a book as BBC policy is changed. Almost at once a letter from the publisher – When is book coming along?

I've been quite frantic as you can imagine. I see it as a *book* – I cannot do it straight away as a BBC script. I could do it – but it would be false and bad – On the other hand I would do anything to please Selma who has a good deal of influence at the BBC. Also for what it's worth broadcasting pays better. Much better.

There is nobody to talk to and advise me or tell me I am right to stick to what I feel for that is what I hope to do after much worry.

But for some time I've been a bit frantic.

So now I'm telling you to relieve my mind. But do not talk of it much because I think Selma is known in Holland. It is better not.

She has been so nice to me and written me letters that cheered me up. I'm glad to say she had a great success in an Ibsen play[1]. Well there it is.

If I had proper conditions I could sort it out in three months.

But conditions are bad. Such a nasty place and no privacy. Not even a table or a desk.

Max who isn't very well thinks it all a bore and a fuss about nothing.

He doesn't understand about books. Very few people do. They are *mysterious* not mechanical. And always will be. I do think writers have a tough time and nobody likes them either! Till they are dead. Then they become quite respectable and useful.

With love to you all and many hugs from   Your unworthy
Mother

[. . . . . .]

1. *As The Rat Wife in* Little Eyolf *at the Lyric, Hammersmith.*

TO SELMA VAZ DIAS   *April 9th [1958]*
                                                  Rocket House
My dear Selma,

This letter is overdue. Please forgive. The last week has been difficult but better now. Well to start with – of course I saw your notices. Max and I read some and were delighted. I began to write to you and do you know what happened? *They started painting this house.* Suddenly. Just like that. (Why I wonder??) It has been bitterly cold and nowhere to go so I've sat miserably listening to clashes – bangs and watching faces at window – felt like a wet, sad cat.

Bank holiday was a break and today too. But they'll be back. My dear – Bude can be so stony – nothing but concrete and rocks and sand. I got tight and then felt ill because whatever that wine was – no juice of grape.

That's enough about my woes. I am so glad you had a success and wish I could have seen you. As to Mrs Rochester – yes I have been working at her and here is the story.

When I came back from London I tore along at great speed, full of self confidence.

Then arrived some very disturbing news from Holland which slowed me up a lot. In November my daughter Maryvonne came to see me – that was a joy, but her visit left me full of doubts and fears and self reproach because I feel so helpless. This Indonesia thing – and why have I no money and so on.

Eventually I got back to being a Creole lunatic in the 1840's. Quite an effort. Sometimes am almost there, sometimes I think I'll stay there!! –

Now this is not serious or business like enough. Must try – though still quivering and shivering with cold, men on ladders and bad wine.

I've read and re-read "Jane Eyre" of course, and I am sure that the character must be "built up". I wrote you about that. The Creole in Charlotte Brontë's novel is a lay figure – repulsive which does not matter, and not once alive which does. She's necessary to the plot, but always she shrieks, howls, laughs horribly, attacks all and sundry – *off stage*. For me (and for you I hope) she must be right *on stage*. She must be at least plausible with a past, the *reason* why Mr Rochester treats her so abominably and feels justified, the *reason* why he thinks she is mad and why of course she goes mad, even the *reason* why she tries to set everything on fire, and eventually succeeds. (Personally, I think *that* one is

156

simple. She is cold – and fire is the only warmth she knows in England.)

I do not see how Charlotte Brontë's madwoman could possibly convey all this. It *might* be done but it would not be convincing. At least I doubt it. Another "I" must talk, two others perhaps. Then the Creole's "I" will come to life.

I tried this way and that, even putting her into modern dress. No good.

At last I decided on a possible way showing the start and the Creole speaking. Lastly: Her end – I want it in a way triumphant!

The Creole is of course the important one, the others explain her. I see it and can do it – as a book. About half is done.

So your last letter disturbed me. I want so much that you should like this idea of mine and agree. I do realise that Voyage in Dark etc is no use now. But this, if I can manage it, will be something different. I'd meant to send you my version of "the Creole" for BBC and MS of book so that you could judge if I'd done a good job and add or subtract.

Now feel a bit uncertain and worried – I see it that way and no other, but am so very anxious not to let you down.

This letter is too long and I can't say what I mean properly.

I know very well that I have not all that time – not much perhaps and I know about being forgotten. That must not matter at all.

If it is done as truthfully as I can – Only that must matter. I do sound all of a doodah and am a bit. But can you trust me? Not for too long. Say six to nine months. Remember that I have only written novels, and see things in that form. Or as plays. Remember too that I'm writing under difficulties, many of them.

After all this it will sound ridiculous to say that I have another idea – an ambitious one. This time radio or TV. Last flare up???

If I had time to work at both – sometimes that rests one. But no time.

Everything must be for the "reactionary 19th century romance".

I read that in a progressive novel and was much shaken, till the writer started about the West Indies. So *utterly* false that the rest was water off duck's back.

Max who is nearly always wonderfully patient with me sends his love. He says he is certain you will see what I mean and agree. Please do.

Am a bit tired. Lots of luck on T.V. Will you please remember me to Sasha Moorsom.

Much love and again best of luck.   *Jean*

PS Bude is a bloody place. You have to *buy* everything. But soon I'll have a few necessities I hope. (Typewriter!)

I will not disappoint you. Come with me and you will see. Take a look at Jane Eyre. That unfortunate death of a Creole! I'm fighting mad to write *her* story.

But it's a good book – and so one must be wary and careful. Sober and plausible. At first.

April 30th [1958]
                                                                   Rocket House

Dear Mr Wyndham,

I want to thank you so much for your very kind letter – and to say how sorry
I am that I could not answer it before.

I have not been well – such cold! – and thought it would be wise to find
somewhere else to live.

Bude can be very bleak indeed – Glaring too – and this part of it is noisy.

However nothing is possible just now, it was a waste of time, and I'll think
no more of it – at present.

There is not much to say except to repeat how glad I am that you like the idea
of my book, and that Diana Athill likes it too and to thank you both.

It is in my head. I know how it can be done, a good deal is written though
not right yet – not what I want quite.

With a little luck it won't be so long, and I trust not disappointing.

I am vexed with myself for settling in Bude. There are no trees, and most of
the grass and flowers get torn up. Concrete inside and out is so trying. The part
we live in is a Deserted Tea Room – a strange atmosphere lingers. A Ballad of
the Sad Café? Not so good. However there is a huge black rock at the back and
I don't see what they can do to that. Very comforting but damp.

                                                                   Yours sincerely,
                                                                   Jean Rhys

November 17th [1958]
                                                                   Rocket House

Dear Mr Wyndham,

I am very sorry to hear that you are leaving the firm of Deutsch – pleased of
course that you will read my book, but sad all the same.

You have written so kindly, and that helped a lot when the usual doubts and
fears came along.

Yes, I am well again and have been working fairly steadily these last months
– I hope you will like what I have done – it ought to be finished by next March –
I wish I could say before Christmas but dare not.

Of course this idea – which seemed so easy that it would write itself (*idiotic* of
me not to be doubly cautious when I felt that!!) has turned out to be extremely
difficult.

Indeed it is a *demon* of a book – and it never leaves me. Sometimes I am sure
that it needs a demon to write it. Or a fraud. Well – I am not a fraud – and not
yet a demon. Sometimes I have great hopes. But no – not right. So start again.
It must of course be convincing – or no good at all. I do trust that something
final will be done. I've got over a few difficulties anyway. It ought to be
between forty or fifty thousand words.

I'll never forgive myself for talking about anything before the lovely word
End is written. Or for being so slow without being sure.

But one or two unforseen accidents did stop me.

I told you I would need a modicum of luck – remember? So please wish it – even so late in the day.

Yours sincerely

Jean Rhys

TO SELMA VAZ DIAS

January 10th [1959]

Rocket House

My dear Selma,

I have wanted to write to you since Christmas and A happy lovely and lucky New Year to you.

I have finished the first draft of Mrs Rochester.

The first draft you'll think. After nearly two years.

But it means a lot to me, and have only managed it because these last months I've raced ahead without looking back, re-reading or re-thinking and what I've done. Or it's fate.

There's a lot of cutting, joining up – all that patchwork – and one major difficulty to be solved.

But at least I've something definite to go on now the skeleton is there.

I won't tell you about the various worries – the worst being that the first year, when it was at the tips of my fingers, was spoilt. Nothing I could have foreseen or avoided – but enough to knock me flat for a time.

Then had to get back into the mood with the help of very bad drink.

One day drunk, two days hangover regular as clockwork.

I have talked about this thing too much, much too much, already – so that's enough.

Only please try to believe that unless it is quite right – as good as I can make it and as smooth and as *plausible* it will be useless – just another adaptation of "Jane Eyre". There have been umpteen thousand and sixty already.

That is my opinion and I can only stick to it, trusting in some kind saint and hoping that all will be well.

Have you cheered up? Please do. Your letter dated Oct 1st sounded so sad. But it was fine hearing from you and gave me some heart – badly needed for it is so terribly cold here and isolated.

I haven't got a radio you know, certainly no Idiot's Lantern – *Can you imagine my life??* I bought some Penguins at Christmas. One J. D. Salinger's "Catcher in the Rye". It made me laugh a lot. I liked it. Max not.

Are you having another holiday or are you in kindly England?

You remember me don't you? (One of the slow obstinate sort). Or has it gone a bit dim? Don't let it. Bless you and love. It will be done.

Jean

Jan 15th. This was started five days ago. It has been freezing and blowing like nothing I've ever felt. Max hasn't been very well and I seem to have spent my time going back and forth to Bude – about a mile away – half dead with cold. Never, *never* try N. Cornwall in winter – (Or South either) It's grim I tell you – daunting. The wind knocked down part of the cliff and our yard is full of stones rock and debris. However no one seems to care. This place is on the sea *and* the river. So gets the benefit of all the possible winds, N, NE, E, SE etc.

About that western wind when wilt thou blow. Not a sign of it. Though plenty of rain and hail small and large too.

V Affecly

Jean

Write to me sometime when you feel like it. It helps me to hang on. I nearly came to London last year. I was so stuck

TO SELMA VAZ DIAS

February 5th [1959]
Rocket House

[. . . . . .]

My dear Selma,

I was so glad to have your letter. (I haven't been very well for the cold here is not to be believed – the sort of cold that freezes your heart and marrow). However you helped me out of a black mood.

You wish to hear about Mrs Rochester? Well – the first draft is finished as I told you. The skeleton is there.

I have found it difficult to do. Perhaps because I was too anxious – or talked too much about it. Always a terrible mistake.

Please believe that I am going as quickly as I can and that I will stick here, in this abominable place till I have done it.

I wish I could tick faster. But I don't know how to and that is the truth.

It *is* life or death – you are right. But that thought does not do the trick at all. One must have blind faith – like walking on water and if that fails devil of a book or what have you. Sometimes I really do feel it would need a devil to write it well. I live in hope – Who knows? I may qualify. I must have been crazy myself when I thought it easy. Sometimes I long for an entirely new way of writing. New words, new everything – sometimes I am almost there. But no – it slides away.

Besides, the old ideas, clarity, unity and so on – I can't get away from them – they are *valid*.

So for her madness must be some sanity. Whose?? Rochester. One false start after another. Oh Selma I should never have talked about this till it was finished.

The Golden Rule. Never talk. Well here I am still anyway and two difficulties have been got over – One more river to cross.

What does really worry me like hell is that I have not made it clear enough that it is emerging as a book. I could not do a monologue of Mrs Rochester à la Charlotte Brontë.

But I see that you know that and your phrase "frozen assets" is exactly right. But you understand that she must be "placed". How when and where did it happen? How did she get there. That must be *clear* – Otherwise it would not do. Or I cannot do it. Sometimes a sentence makes it clear. Sometimes I have the sentence, and it vanishes.

Well my dear, all this is a bit boring. Forget it.

One thing I promise you that if I collapse or well *can't*, or vanish perhaps, I will send you or somebody will, all I have done.

I don't care what I look like and slop around (*very good sign!!*) in a horrible red dressing gown. I bet that "Woman in a Dressing Gown"[1] title was chipé. Or wasn't it? Anyway. Fair enough perhaps – and yet – Now I must eat some bread and cheese, have a bath and go to bed.

One stupid thing I did was to read "Jane Eyre" too much. Then I found it was creeping into my writing. A bad imitation – quite dreadful. All had to be scrapped.

I also read "Wuthering Heights". So magnificent in parts. But none of this probability nonsense.

Still a hurricane isn't *probable* is it? I'd never read it before.

I start with a dream too in Mrs R. but no ghosts – All the same my dream must stand for it is the only thing I'm sure of.

Well honey hope this crazy letter amuses you – and that you aren't sad now. Are you in Switzerland perhaps?

Did you like Italy? I only know Florence and Fiesole which I did so love. Not Florence. The other.

Love. All will be well for you.

Jean

The newspapers make me shiver and life too.

1. *Film (1958) written by Ted (later Lord) Willis: the title was original.*

TO MARYVONNE MOERMAN

May 4th 1959
Rocket House

[. . . . . .]

My dear Maryvonne,

I was so very glad to hear from you. I was wondering *where* you were, *how* you were and *why* I had no letter, when after all you are so near – comparatively speaking. But you see I'm as bad myself or worse, for I meant to answer at once and did not. Besides you have a lot else to do. I just moon around – That is a habit and it grows and grows and grows.

Well, now for pleasant things. It is lovely weather – all the flowers are coming out and bluebells outside the window mixed with those little white ones, they call "snow on the mountain" here. The sea matches the bluebells exactly today. There's a bitter cold wind though. The children are shrieking on the road, but I've got very cunning about curtains and how to fix them so that nobody can look in. (Max has just come in alas!! I say alas because I wanted terribly to be alone this afternoon. I never am you know, and I'm a recluse by nature.) Once I knew an American girl who used to say "If I could not be alone sometimes I'd go stark, raving mad". I understand that. As to Max, he hasn't been very well but OK again and sends love. Those awful gates have gone do you remember them? Those darned old things with iron bolts sticking out in all directions. They went after a battle royal with the woman in the next house who marched in here four times to tell me that they were leaning against *her* property, and would I take them off *my* property. When at last I got it through that the place was *not* my property that I hated the gates, etc. she was quite stunned. *No* property, Oh dear!!! Now there's a frosty silence. She threatened to dig up my stock (a purple flower very sweet scented) because she said that was on *her* property too – Hasn't done so yet, if she does I will place a terrible revenge on this property owner. What nonsense all this is.

About my book. It is done in the way that patchwork would be done if you had all the colours and all the pieces cut but not yet arranged to make a quilt.

No – it is not that I can't bear to let it go – tho' one often feels like that.

But you see this is *nothing to do with me*. It is imagination, and the time is 1840 or so, when really I wasn't alive so I can be detached.

I *know* it is a good idea, I know I can do it. But I do hesitate about *how* to do it. It must be just right or it will be no good. On the other hand if I delay much longer it will be no good either. I've been too long already.

I do not have perfect working conditions of course, sometimes it's almost there, I am stopped, and the thought goes. It does not come back either. But I'll stop too or I'll bore you as much as I bore unfortunate Max.

It can be done 3 ways. (1) Straight. Childhood, Marriage, Finale told in 1st person. Or it can be done (2) Man's point of view (3) Woman's ditto both 1st person. Or it can be told in the third person with the writer as the Almighty. Well that is hard for me. I prefer direct thoughts and actions.

I am doing (2). That is the end of that sermon – Amen. I am trying very hard please believe that. For many reasons.

I thought of writing three alternative Chapter I's and asking you which you liked best, but really my courage failed me – I've got the end. Not the start.

Well about your hair. Do not worry – for grey hair can be charming and no one will get up for you in the tram for a long v. *long* time you may be certain.

On the other hand colour rinses are very good now and can be done yourself. They wash out if you don't like them. If you try – remember to leave the front lighter than back. One grey or light lock is lovely. I *know* your hair is sacred. It has been so always. Aged two you became terribly angry with the 1st hairdresser you saw. He gave you some fizzy lemonade but you only cried louder. So you see you must be the judge yourself and I *know* it is sacred.

But listen I have struck an awfully good and inexpensive thing called *Vita Pointe*. It is a white cream. You use a little on the brush – brushing hair backwards *the wrong way*. Then when you brush it back again it is soft shining and easy to fix. *Try it.*

It even works on *my* hair which what with peroxide, henna, colour rinses and so on has had a hell of a lot to put up with. Too much poor thing. This stuff costs 3/6 here. If you can't get it in Amsterdam (but I bet you can) I will somehow send it. I'll write again for your birthday. Penguins will arrive also a handkerchief or something. So dull. I wish I could send a million dollars. A million dollars of Love.

Jean

Dearest Ruthie, So little space for so much love. Do you like spring? Please be happy.

Your loving
Grandmother

TO DIANA ATHILL

Monday May 25th [1959]
Rocket House

Dear Miss Athill,

I've been hoping for some time to write telling you that the M.S.S. of my novel – provisional title "Story of the First Mrs Rochester" was on its way to Andre Deutsch.

I can't be triumphant yet, but I've had news that may make some difference.

"Good Morning Midnight" is to be broadcast on Radio Bremen (Selma Vaz Dias' adaptation) and I've heard from a Hamburg publisher who is interested and may take the book.

His name:

Wolfgang Krüger Verlag
Hamburg Wellingbütter Weg 163

He asks for an option on my present book also.

It will be a shot in the arm for me if he does take it, the broadcast too of course, and may help me to solve the problem of existing which has been rather difficult.

(Not important I feel but *distracting*)

I have been writing letters all yesterday and all this morning, for I have no agent now, and am never sure that I'm saying the right thing. So please be patient with this one. And with me.

I feel that I ought to let you know how the novel is progressing. It is so much more ambitious and difficult than anything I've done yet that I don't think the time spent has been too long – A year and a half – for last winter I had to stop for a bit. If I've been too long then I can't let myself worry over it – Or panic which I do easily. Then I dry up!!

Mr Wyndham's letters were such an encouragement. I'm sorry he is not with your firm now but trust he will read the book.

I hope to come to London in the autumn, or I will write again more specifically.

Part II is done or nearly so. Part I (the why and wherefore) I'm struggling with. I have rewritten both several times but am not stale on it.

Yours sincerely,
Jean Rhys

May 27th [1959]
Rocket House

[. . . . . .]

My dear Selma,
I think you know how pleased I am about the Radio Bremen thing. I wish it much luck. What date? For I might be able to listen in. Don't understand German at all or hardly – after 2 years in Wien too!! – Still might gather something from the voice (voices?). Anyway I know Guten Morgen Mittelnacht now.

I am trying everywhere for a copy of G.M.M. – Martha Smith at Constable's of course, and some others. I have none of my books except "The Left Bank" and for some reason, poor old "Quartet" has also stuck with me. I never cared much to keep them around after they were finished – Sorry for that now. I meant to write you a long letter about Mrs R but it has all been said before. *I can do it.* But it is more difficult than anything else I've tried. Also circumstances haven't been always kind. Max thinks that without money and security nothing can be done. *I do not agree at all!* I know otherwise. All the same the time does come when a *little* money a *little* security a *modicum* of praise does help –

Well Part II is done or as good as. *"Day, and the slow approach of night."* Do you know who wrote that? I don't. Milton – sounds like. Anyway Part II is "the slow approach of night", in that awful room. As a lot was done with bottles at hand it must be put away and revised carefully when sober. I've got it though I think. Also Finale.

Am now struggling with Part I "Day" which though it's set in the West Indies I want clear, cold, factual. It's Mrs R's point of view – also the why and the wherefore.

All this has been said before. Also that if for any reason I fall down on it you can have what I've done. I've always told you that.

Naturally though I hope I won't fail.

Last winter so bitterly cold. Max was ill and moi aussi.

Now it is perfect. Sun and flowers everywhere. And not many people yet – *thank God* –

I've been sitting on the cliffs in the palish but lovely sunlight and am sleepy.

Sorry – writing paper gave out –

If all goes as I hope I'll be in London this autumn or if not me then Mrs R or a large part of her sad life.

My dear your house sounds so nice. I'd love to see it and hope to.

Do you give fine parties.

Vienna seems so far away like a dream – West Indies much nearer.

I expect it's awfully different now.

Such pretty clothes I think – Give it my respects with knobs on.

Much love and do let me know about date of broadcast. And so on.

> *Jean*

I've been working on Mrs R for year and a half. Not quite. Not long really. Delays and pauses not my fault exactly.

TO SELMA VAZ DIAS   *June 4th [1959]*
                                                       Rocket House

My dear Selma,

I expect you will be glad to know that I discovered a copy of G.M.M. after a frantic search and have posted it to Hamburg. Hoping – of course. The publisher told me that the Bremen broadcast will be for tomorrow at 7.45. I do wish it a lot of luck, though I doubt if I'll hear it.

Max's brother, Lt Colonel Alec Hamer[1], wishes so much to meet you. He is an awfully nice and kind man so trust it's all right to send your address and telephone number. I have told him that you are leaving for Vienna in a week or two but may be able to fit him in. I want so very much to see you, but daren't leave Mrs R just at this stage – Besides cash.

Alec knows something about my hopes and struggles – he thinks you have done wonders with G.M.M.

I feel it would be a good thing if you met. Do hope you can manage it.

> Yours with love
> *Jean*

1. *Frederick Alexander Hamer, Royal Marines (1885–1972).*

TO MARYVONNE MOERMAN   *Thursday 4th [June 1959]*
                                                       Rocket House

> I expect your house will be fine – how lovely to
> *have* a house. I bet you are very busy with it.

My dear Maryvonne,

Max has sent you a wire asking you to listen in, if you can, to the Bremen broadcast at 7.45 pm tomorrow.

We have no radio and though we could go to the house of an acquaintance it's a long way off – three miles, no bus and a *huge* taxi fare. So we decided to skip it, as after all I don't know German and it would be meaningless.

All the same I'm very curious to know *what* they've done to the thing. It is now apparently a play but I don't know who wrote it or anything about the matter at all, which is a bit odd. I heard the time from the Hamburg publisher and hope it's correct.

I have written to Selma Vaz Dias and have suggested that a friend should meet her and have a talk about matters.

You know even the B.B.C. broadcast was very much cut up (it had to be of course) but a radio play – well I don't see it – and fear it will be hashed about like anything. (But don't say I said so).

John's copy of "Good Morning Midnight" has just arrived – thanks. The sad thing is that I wrote around frantically all over the place and got Edward's. That has been posted to Hamburg. I will keep the one John sent and either send it back or let you have it if and when I see you.

You know how much I should like to (*like!!*). Edward also would be pleased I'm sure. But the chief, *the most important thing* is that yourself Ruthie and Job should have a happy holiday in the sun – with any money you have. That is why I don't insist more. Not because I don't long to see you. Edward's house is nice, but this place oh Lord it can be dreary – though better than when you saw it.

It's pleasant in the sun and lately it's been hot, so with great huffing and puffing I bought a cheap cotton dress. I put it on this morning, and *at once* the sun went in and a wind blew from the Arctic –

(Good morning midnight!)

So after shivering for two hours I've taken the dam thing off, though it isn't bad.

Well please if you can get Bremen tell me what you think of *"Gutten Morgen Mittelnach"*.

You know it is very funny but everybody wants to fool about with that book – One man asked if he could rewrite it "from the young man's point of view". However after some talk the idea was dropped.

Will you please thank John for letting me have it. I remember of course about the Dutch rights.

Love to everybody, kisses and hugs for you and Ruthie and as usual "Here's hoping"!

Yours with love
Jean

TO DIANA ATHILL   *[June] 11th 1959*
Rocket House

Dear Miss Athill,

Thank you for your letter. I thought that you might be away from the office, and I had marked mine personal.

Still, I was very glad when your sympathetic and understanding answer arrived.

I should not have been so sure that I would finish Mrs Rochester quickly – ought to know better by this time!

I'd been writing an autobiography, and imagined I could "lift" whole passages from it. This wasn't so at all. The time and the mood were quite different. There were other delays of course.

I will say no more until the MSS is finished – this autumn I trust. I do hope your firm will like it.

I'll be so pleased if GMM is published in Germany – it was posted about a week ago – and will be grateful and rather relieved if André Deutsch will negotiate with Wolfgang Kruger – provided he wants it – naturally. I'm keeping my fingers crossed and not hoping too much. But still, a bit. I understand and agree that it would be better if the whole thing were done together as you suggest.

I have no agent at present. Hughes Massie acted for me here, and Carol Hill in New York, but I've been out of touch with them for some time.

I hope that when I come to London this year I can discuss matters with André Deutsch. (If, and touch wood and etc) I'll be delighted to meet you. This is such a dull place and rather cold.

Apparently Radio Bremen made G.M.M. into a play with a large cast. Miss Vaz Dias says it was very well done. I would so like to see a copy of that script! I find it strange to think of myself toiling away to make the book as simple as possible, then, so long afterwards, somebody else toiling away *putting in* all the characters I so carefully *left out*.

When you see Mr Wyndham please thank him for his encouraging letters.

I have a book of short stories[1] written during the war and just afterwards.

Constable did not want short stories and I never offered them to anybody else.

They are "dated" of course and perhaps *too* carefully written. A bit lifeless maybe. Nevertheless, I think there might be an idea or two knocking about. Especially in the last which is called "In September, Petronella." Dated. But purposely.

I'll bring them along, and perhaps Mr Wyndham would glance through them and tell me what he thinks. If not a chore.

I hope I may say that I read your short story in the Observer[2] – The Return – and liked it very much.

It must be grand to win a prize.

Yours sincerely
Jean Rhys

1. *See note on page 40.*

2. *Diana Athill had won first prize in the* Observer *short story competition with "The Return".*

June 14th [1959]
Rocket House

My dear Selma,

Such a nice letter from you – I'm very glad you saw Alec. He wrote to me about your meeting, and added that he's been thinking about Mrs R as a radio play. The same thought occurred to me last winter when I was pretty well in despair – what with one thing and another. Easier in one way – the end perhaps more difficult – you will see. But this must not be a rambling and long talk.

First, then, I want to thank you for your invitation to Max and myself. The *kindest* thought. I can't tell you how tempted I was (and am) to accept it. This place can be a bit chill and bare (and so many glinting spectacles around – you know). It would be a lovely break. But, my dear, I cannot. I must stick with this thing now till it is done – finally finished. I *daren't* leave it – If I came to London now I'd seem a bewildered and distraught person. Very uneasy – with my duty left behind.

I said to somebody that the *first draft* was finished. The first draft only. So I suppose Alec thought the book.

My typewriter, such as it is, has faded out. I am getting another from Exeter on hire for nothing can be had in Bude the obscure. Max can help with first rough typing he says, then revision and cutting and so on, oh God! And then. . . .

I cannot imagine why I said that I could do this book quickly. Must have been crazier than usual. I've never done such a thing before, and after the last two years I will never do it again. Nor even talk of it. (I'm getting more and more superstitious by the way, and didn't write to you yesterday because it was the 13th!)

Now to put you wise about the book and publisher situation.

When Constable's sent fee for G.M.M. they reminded me that I was still under contract for another book. But really I was free, as I'd fired in those short stories. Then I had an offer from Francis Wyndham of André Deutsch to buy option. Not for much but something. So I accepted and left Constable's. Hope I did right.

The German publisher is much the same thing, except that he asked only to see a copy with view to publication and option on Mrs R. I sent book and ought to have his decision in a week or so. It's a maybe.

[. . . . . .]

I needn't say again that whatever contract I make (or don't make) radio rights are for you – if you want them. I think you'll like it. There I go again!

This superstition is awful. If I upset a drink am overjoyed (lucky). Next morning spider in bath. Unlucky. So it goes on! Soon I shall be counting pebbles.

I hope to be in London this autumn or if not the MSS – I did not hear Bremen broadcast and am so curious about play. I wish I could see script. Impossible? I suppose so.

Just one last thing before this long letter ends.

I have tried to persuade Max to go to London and rest for a week or so in your lovely house.

He hasn't been very well. I know it would do him good. However he says no – not yet. If I can persuade him to change his mind may I let you know? I'm sure you'll understand I've been worried about him, and oh my dear Bude is really a place to escape from sometimes. I know you leave on 26th. Have a good time and thank you for everything.   Love
                                                                               Jean.

TO FRANCIS WYNDHAM   *June [1959]*
                                                          Rocket House
Dear Mr Wyndham,

I will post the short stories to you tomorrow. As I've apologised already for the battered and not very well typed M.S.S. there's not much more to say except that I hope it won't be a chore reading them.

Looking at the book again I feel that most aren't real short stories at all – more like unfinished novels or parts of a novel.

"A Solid House" could be cut, "In September Petronella" expanded – I said I wouldn't give you my opinion and am doing so It's yours I want so much.

I've included two others[1]. I have no other copy but that does not matter. There is nothing to help me with the novel I'm doing now.

That is getting along, but sometimes the mechanics, like typing, hold me up and I fuss and worry about it. About typewriters and myself – it's very strange. They break down.

I hope you will like it and that I've got away with what I tried to do.

Thank you again. It was very kind of Miss Athill to mention the stories.
                                                          Yours sincerely
                                                          Jean Rhys

1. *"The Day They Burnt the Books" and "The Insect World".*

TO FRANCIS WYNDHAM   *July 8th, 1959*
                                                          Rocket House
Dear Mr Wyndham,

I am so pleased that you liked some of the stories – they are uneven – and it would be most kind of you to send a selection to John Lehmann, whichever you think best.

I'll be very happy if he takes one of course.

About *Petronella*:

Would it be possible to alter the name *Harmer* – make it say *Marston*? It was written long before my own name was Hamer! I should have done this myself before I sent it to you. Is Marston a good name for a painter? Will it do?

I have a thing about names – am sure they are very important indeed. But they can be elusive. The date is, of course, late July 1914. It's not filled in because I wanted to find out more about market day in Cirencester at that time (too fussy you see!). I am not certain if Norfolk people *do* say Fare you well, perhaps just farewell (the farmer).

No I never liked "Lotus" much – and "The Insect World" is not finished[1], did you notice? I couldn't get the final, well meant, remark that drove the poor girl frantic in the end – I was told the story was too long and so on. Gave up trying I fear.

About the hospital story[2]:

Could the present Mme Tavernier gives the girl (unfortunate as usual!) be altered. It ought to be the equivalent of three or four pounds – not five hundred francs.

Is all this very tiresome? I do apologise for not doing it myself. But I have noticed that wrong details can spoil a story.

At the read-through of "Good Morning Midnight" I asked them to alter the money mentioned to postwar present day values.

They forgot, or thought it didn't matter. Yet, when I heard the broadcast it seemed to me that the thousand franc note *jumped* out at one. All wrong.

I am pretty sure that most people notice details *without knowing it*. Anything false and bang goes the illusion and perhaps they don't know why – or care, naturally.

Or maybe I'm just dreadfully fussy and it slows me up – Still I *am* pretty sure.

The book is progressing – paragraph by paragraph. Now it's chapter by chapter. If only I can do it as I want and hope.

I wrote to you yesterday, then went straight on to working, and the letter got mixed up with the rest and I can't find it – So this is letter No. 2. It's a day late, and seems to have got longer.

I hope I've remembered everything, and haven't been tiresome or exacting. You have encouraged and cheered me up so much and I am very grateful.

Yours sincerely
Jean Rhys

1. *It was finished in 1973 and published in* The Sunday Times Magazine *in August of that year. The "final, well-meant remark" that drove the heroine frantic was "All right, old girl".*

2. *"Outside the Machine".*

September 14th [1959]
                                                                    Rocket House

> I *have* made it long. Don't bother to
> answer this. It's all self indulgence
> and can't be answered.

Dear Mr Wyndham,

This is the long letter – but I won't make it very long. How confused and tedious that would be! First I must tell you that I liked your article[1] very much indeed, and am longing for the printers strike delay to be over. Every letter you have written has helped and encouraged me and I can't thank you enough. I was pleased especially because you thought well of "Quartet" ("Postures" as it was called here). [. . . . . .] I think it is angry and uneven as you say, but it has some life and it wasn't an autobiography, as everyone here seemed to imagine though some of it was lived of course. On the contrary I was stuck for over a year because I could not see how to end it. I was about to give up in despair when I suddenly knew – and finished it fairly quickly – for me. (Already I was slow and over anxious you see. Not glib any more). I was astonished when so many people thought it an autobiography from page 1 onwards and told me it should never have been written. Well, I had to write it. Even in America it was supposed to be a roman à clef. Still I did make some money there and went back to Paris to write "Mackenzie".

Here now comes the real but condensed?? autobiography.

I think that I have had little success because I did not want it. Not in that way. Not really. Even now I cannot connect money or publicity with writing, though I adore money and need it badly, very. For me, these things are different – and opposed. Bitterly. I can only write for love as it were. I did once try to produce a short story for the Saturday Evening Post for I was advised to do this. Well I made it all glitter and de luxe and so on but in the end I *could not stop myself* from letting the sad, mousey companion steal all the jewels and the lover too. And *get away* with this antisocial act. I did leave the lovely mondaine with other jewels, and the second best lover. But still! It doesn't do. I tore up this thing on which I'd spent months of anxious care, plus research, and have never tried again.

When I say write for love I mean that there are two places for me. Paris (or what it was to me) and Dominica, a most lovely and melancholy place where I was born, not very attractive to tourists!

(I wonder what will happen to it now?)

Both these places or the thought of them make me want to write. After "Mackenzie" I married again and lived in London. Then the West Indies started knocking at my heart. So – "Voyage in the Dark". That (the knocking) has never stopped. "Midnight" was Paris revisited for the last time. The war killed it: and after the war was a bad time for me. I did those short stories – many got lost and some poetry. Mediocre – but what heaven to try.

When Selma at last persuaded the B.B.C. to give her version of "Midnight" a chance I thought the miracle had happened, and when I knew at once what

I wished to write – that was the 2nd miracle. – Your letter to me was the third.

The book has been written three times (not counting the first version a monologue for Selma. Not possible). At first the "I" was the Creole girl who became Mr Rochester's first wife. But she was obscure – her way of telling things, I mean – more obscure than I dare to be and all on one note. For she is mad. Then I tried her keeper Mrs Poole as the "I". The best idea technically for she saw much and heard more. It could be done.

But she wouldn't come to life, I wasn't even sure how she'd talk or think.

So now I have two "I"s, Mr Rochester and his first wife. I hoped to make him cold and factual as a contrast to the emotional creature he married for money.

I'm not very pleased at this solution though when I re-read Mr Rochester's version of his honeymoon it wasn't too bad. But it wants lifting up in parts – I must stress the romantic side of his character – Poor man.

I have done her death and hope it will go – I can't do more about that.

I've tried to make it move fast and have skipped years of course with a sentence or so.

It's plausible, but not smooth enough. Also because I tried to put in some of my love of the place where I was born (I shifted their honeymoon to Dominica) and some of my loathing of cruelty and hypocrisy all sorts of other characters have crept in.

Her "Da" or nurse, her pretty maid with whom Mr R has an affair. Naturally Obeah (touched on). It must all be smooth and a lot discarded I suppose. A pity. You see how excited I am about it. So forgive my incoherencies. My husband has been ill for over a year and for some weeks I've had to drop everything. He is much better and I can start again. Tomorrow perhaps.

As I've been so personal I must end by telling you that I am not a Scot at all[2]. My father was Welsh – very. My mother's family was Creole – what we call Creole. My great grandfather was a Scot. As far as I know I am white – but I have no country really now. I must rush to do all the things I have shamefully neglected, such as getting bread and so on. Endless – You can tear this up most certainly – And skip anything you find not legible, for really I should not have gone on and on. But it's been so nice for me – talking away and neglecting my duty.

I was going to write "Forgive me" but this morning someone wrote For God's sake don't be so meek.

Meek!!! When I long to slaughter for a week or more. All over the place.

Yours sincerely
Jean Rhys

Do you notice how often I've used the word "lovely". That's because I was thinking of my one true love.

---

1. Francis Wyndham had sent her a typescript of his introduction to "Till September, Petronella" which was shortly to appear in the London Magazine. *The editor, John*

Lehmann, also accepted "The Day They Burned the Books" and "Tigers Are Better Looking".

2. Francis Wyndham had repeated the Radio Times's *description of Jean as partly Welsh and partly Scottish.*

TO MARYVONNE MOERMAN   *September 22nd [1959]*
                                                           Rocket House

> I am trying to find a less wearying place.
> But it may be a job.
>   I sold a short story. Not
> published yet. Printers strike hold up.
> *What* luck.

My Dear Maryvonne,

I was so very glad to hear from you. Didn't answer at once because Max has been ill and I've been so worried and tired with the eternal walking into that fragrant spot Bude, and walking back. (Then ditto as I'd forgotten the most important buy!) So was in a *dazed* condition. Max is a great deal better – is really on the mend now, such a relief! –

He was taken ill the day I had my fee for the Bremen broadcast – So most of the fun was gone! But at any rate there was a bit of cash around for that particular emergency. Not much but something.

I am glad you went to Provence and will go again and believe me, you will be called "Mademoiselle" for a long long time yet – I'm delighted you were happy there.

I am glad too that you have your own balcony in Rotterdam. It is something – a great deal – an *enormous* lot.

As to the human race, yes they are devils – but poor devils most of them.

"The most horrible race of vermine that God Almighty ever allowed to infect? pollute? the earth" said Swift – or words to that effect. He poor man, was a genius and heaven help *them*, for no one else does. Or not much or for long.

Still one is left with all sorts of problems. How to explain away music, painting, poetry, courage, self sacrifice of *any* sort, flowers, gardens, good acting or writing. Grace or any beauty at all??

Well, maybe I'll know the answer to all this fairly soon. Or maybe there is no answer. And what does it matter? *Not to worry* – that is the great thing. Don't worry. Let it go like water running past you, and be as *serene* as you can.

I've had to drop my book just when another two months would have done it. I thought that would finish me.

So to encourage myself I'll write MAGNA VERITAS PREVALLI and stick it on the screen (*Great is truth it will prevail*). For I know that to write as well as I can is my truth and why I was born. Though the Lord knows I wish I hadn't been!

Besides, some of these poor human devils are *attractive*. What about that? Why does a rose smell sweet? And so on. It's endless –

It seems to me one is always up against this X – the unknown quantity – This *why?*

You are one of the attractive ones after all, and so I feel is Ruthie. I wish I could see her dance –

Tell her from me: This:

Sweet when you do dance, I wish you were a wave of the sea. That you might do nothing but that.

Mr Shakespeare wrote it of Perdita in the Winter's Tale – long ago.

Sheep not had a laugh lately. I expect Bude has – I have a new hair colour – not so negroid. But as it comes from Abroad expect it will be stopped soon by Them. Also I've got thinner. Praise be –

I don't mind about being laughed at any more. Isn't it funny? Probably I'm being hated instead. But if hate equals fear, Why?? I do often wish for a machine gun, but as I haven't got one – seems to me I'm pretty harmless. Well all this must lead to saying that the silver chain will be sent as soon as possible. For neck? And how long? Tell me in inches – You still don't tell me her birthday? Are you afraid I will steal her from all the other grannies??

Now I must stop this nonsense and go and warm up some horrible looking little pasties. Max likes them but what's inside I ask myself? Another unknown quantity. Better left unknown too.

M sends love and so do I as always. Sleep well, don't ever worry, Stay pretty and you will see. Special love to Ruthie of course.

Jean

Do you remember Tours? Of course not. Perhaps you do without knowing it. You were a sweetie pie baby and seemed to like the place in those days.

TO FRANCIS WYNDHAM   *Sunday 27th [September 1959]*
Rocket House

Dear Mr Wyndham,

My letter was incoherent, I'm afraid, and not at all fascinating – I expect it sounded phoney – But it wasn't.

Thank you for being so kind about it. I like being called Miss Rhys, and Mrs Hamer on the envelope makes it just right. It reaches me all right either way!

My husband has been ill for some time – over a year. But he is getting better now – though slowly.

I looked at this full of effort book a few days ago. It seemed a bit unreal after being away from it for some months. (No autobiography there. Or hardly) I realise that's what I have to guard against, and it's what I wanted in parts. I mean I've done as well as I can – sometimes and in parts.

In any case I must make it legible, which it isn't, send it to the typist, and see what happens. I am sorry to be such a slow starter.

I did not mean to be impertinent about Charlotte Brontë. I admire her greatly. Emily also. And I envy them both more than I can say.

Sometimes I have wondered if Miss Brontë does not *want* her book tampered with! This is the effect of N Cornwall which is rather a dour place. Superstition? – But so many things have got in my way. Never mind. It will be done.   Yours sincerely
Jean Rhys

This gigantic letter has just happened.

My dear Maryvonne,

I was so very glad to hear from you – I wondered if you were all right and getting used (though not too much, *never get used too much*) to Rotterdam. I seem to remember it, but so vaguely – perhaps I only dreamt it.

I have a theory that not nice places, I mean not lovable places are better in the winter.

The rain and fog hide them a bit. And the wind blows away old bones. For instance Manchester and all those Northern places are quite bearable in winter. It *never* stops drizzling, and there is always a fog or mist, so that warmth and a book indoors are heaven. Sort of. All this was long ago when I was young and tough. But apparently it's the same now.

Only worse.

Well here we are still on the damned "Cornish Riviera" (yes I *don't* think!) And sometimes I feel I'd prefer Manchester – for at least there is no pretence that it's the Riviera.

Gales and rain howl and batter at this wretched place. They batter at me too and I was knocked flat the other day. Indeed I nearly went into the bloody canal. But a fat man on a bicycle saved me.

However felt very rum for a day or two afterwards.

Nearly OK now.

I have decided that we *must* find somewhere else to live – Max is not very much better and I am certain that the real trouble is living in one room in beautiful Bude – (with me and book)

I carry on and swear at it, but he says nothing. Or hardly. That is worse – So am trying in all directions. My book is finished – at least there is a start, a middle and an end. Unfortunately it's not legible. No typist could make it out.

So a fair copy must be made – by hand. I don't have much clear time, now Max is ill. So it's going slowly.

Don't know if it's bad or good, and don't care – I've tried too hard and can't "see" it any more. So I only want to finish it – and must. And will.

I think I've sold a short story but I hear that the man who was "backing" the magazine has jumped out of a window[1]. (Not my story. Some million money scandal) – I have corrected the galley proofs, tho' don't believe I've done *that* the right way.

An old story – Not very exciting but I always meant to make it into a novel. It is called "Till September Petronella" and do hope the magazine doesn't disappear. Poor millionaire –

Do you know the really sad thing is that given the right surroundings I could earn my living and a bit over too –

You see – it is my only thing – All I can do. Nevertheless I can do it. Unfortunately – worry, Max being ill, and this damned place are not right at all at all. If I were rich I would give you such lovely presents and Ruthie too. A standing order for flowers every day, a fur coat (not mink though) and of course your house. Very attractive. A long list.

Many other things also. So now I'll talk about you and Ruthie –

The more love the better – I can guess that you protect her. *It is the best thing.* My joke about grannies was only a joke – a bit heavy I fear.

The more love the better. Once I told a rather shrewd and business like publisher that being soft hurt too much, that I intended to grow hard. He said "If you grow hard you will not be able to write. *You will lose your touch on the piano*" he said –

I was very surprised – as really he was supposed to be as flinty as a rock himself. But he was a clever man. And he was right.

Don't lose your touch and Ruthie at all costs must keep hers –

It is never wasted – loving. Never. For instance, when I was a child I had one person who loved me exclusively and really. My great aunt – whose name was Jane. I never returned this love (outwardly) and when I left for England I never wrote to her. Very naughty, as children are.

All the same I thought of her constantly more and more –

Now she is my favourite thought except you and Ruthie. She is very vivid for me. I can remember even her dresses and caps (She wore a lace cap).

All the *facts* in this book are stories she told me of her youth. When I'm awfully fed up and weary I think of her – and start damned book again.

So you see – it is not wasted – I expect my sentimentality is a bit boring. Besides I must make tea for Max.

Oh dear these bloody awful pots of tea and the washing up and the kitchen!! I did try about the kitchen but it is not a rewarding job, because the basic material is terrible. Now isn't it? Hand on heart isn't it?

"My dream kitchen"!! All the same *what* a dream. A kitchen!

Here I go then to my nightmare kitchen to make brown tea – The wind is starting to rage and howl again all ready to have another shot at blowing me into the canal tomorrow, which is shopping day.

Max sends his best love to you and so of course do I with special hugs and kisses. I'll write again for Christmas. I saw a silver chain the other day it had a meagre sort of look. However the girl swore that was the right thing. I'll get it.

Best love and a huge hug.

Jean

PS. One good thing, I've grown thin again. Count your blessings. Because really I hated being plump. I had a perm and the colour of my hair changed to white. Max was quite horrified. He said "Good God it's white!" I believe that's why he started being ill again. So as quickly as possible I'm changing it back to brown. As it gets browner he gets more cheerful. I quite agree that I'm *terrible* with white hair, but all the same I wish he didn't notice so much. This morning the first thing he said was "Your hair is getting back to its natural colour. Thank heaven."! "Natural"!! So I shook the bottle and put on some more natural brown.

I won't ever have it permed again. For this stuff can be washed and really it is a bit wearing – I envy auntie Jane her lace cap. But then she had a background to match.

Jean

Darling Ruthie,

Thank you for your charming letter. I loved hearing from you and will write you a long letter for Christmas. There are great winds here. Do you have them too? If you have don't let them blow you away but hang on tight, for good times will come for you.

Love and kisses

Grandmère

1. *Publication of* The London Magazine *was delayed by a printers' strike alone, and the rumour which somehow reached Jean of a millionaire's suicide was unfounded.*

TO FRANCIS WYNDHAM

December 2nd [1959]
Rocket House

[. . . . . .]

Dear Mr Wyndham,

The proofs of "Petronella" arrived from the London magazine last month. I corrected them – a word here and there and returned them. I do hope I've done this all right but am not used to galley proofs.

I very nearly asked you to help me, but have been fainthearted about writing to you, for I've assured you so often that my book is finished (nearly) and still no book! You may think it a myth, or that I've tackled something too difficult for me.

However – I've been reading over the generous things you said about my work, and that has given me courage. You said I could be trusted as a writer. Do believe that still, for it will help me enormously.

Yes, the book has been difficult, but circumstances have been difficult also (Such a relief to say this though very unorthodox).

My husband has been ill for nearly two years – seriously twice.

So I've been obliged to stop working for weeks at a time. Getting back the mood wasn't easy, and everything depended on the mood. This time. With this book.

He (Max) is better now I trust. He is such a very nice and kind person and told me this little rhyme. Verse?

> "They prosper who burn in the morning
> The letters they wrote overnight".

However I won't burn this one.

Now:

The book I said I would write *is* finished, that's to say it has a beginning a middle and an end. Part I II & III. All there.

But I'm not sure of it. Something is wrong – the start perhaps.

No one will like it probably anyhow. *I* look at it with horror believe me! And fear too.

But I will do it no matter what. For it fascinates me more than anything else I've ever tried to write and it is more elusive.

It's different. For instance I'm tormented with characters from heaven knows where. They don't fit in. They must be cut. I think. Yet there they are and alive too.

Well I expect you've heard all that before and can guess the rest.

And why I write a very incoherent and hasty letter. Or I trust so.

There's nothing to be done or said. Don't answer if you don't feel like it, don't think about it at all only wish me luck.

I'm pretty certain that if I could have real peace for say three months it would be finished.

That is difficult, but not impossible – Surely?

[. . . . . .]

Yours sincerely
Jean Rhys

I hope I did the proofs all right – have such a nagging idea that "delete" is not enough.

If I cannot do the book I will tell you so. But I can –though the real book will escape. As always.

TO SELMA VAZ DIAS

December 15th [1959]
Rocket House

My dear Selma,

I was so delighted to hear from you and your pretty lady cheered me up a lot.

I haven't been able to get into Bude for Christmas cards – it's such a way off and it's dark early now – but I've found some photographs of my island and here they are instead –

The haughty dame is *me* (pre war me) a bit ghostly in the sun but wishing you a lovely time for Christmas and a happy lucky New Year. Perhaps you will understand why I can't "forget Jerusalem" though my right hand has seemed so slow. *Why I am homesick.*

The fact is that Max has been ill – for six months seriously – so that over and over again I've had to drop everything. Nevertheless the book is done Part I II & III – all there. But it is bitty – a series of scenes – not a book. Three months and I can pull it together but I have not had three months (or three weeks) clear in Blasted Bude. We bought a horseshoe. It didn't do its stuff. I'd settle for some good obeah any day. I didn't see the use of speaking of this before, but now that he is so much better, and we are leaving the *horrible* place in a few weeks, I can unburden myself a bit.

I'm not sure if we've got the flat I hope for – it's in Devon – but as soon as I know our new address will let you have it of course. Good news will follow shortly I trust and think. One chance and I'll be home.

About the photographs – they're only photographs. No colour or distance. No sun. All the same . . . !

They were taken at "Hampstead" – that was the name of the estate lent to L.T.S. and myself when we were there ages ago it seems.

Good omen? That it's called Hampstead I mean. Most of the places there have French names.

Max too sends you all his best wishes for the New Year and his love.

As for me. I've just got to pack and move – Oh Lord! Then all will be well. You'll see – I've got a story in the London Magazine next month. Jan. John Lehmann.

Anyway I did proofs – "Petronella". Old stuff. Oh Selma *if I can do this book.* If I can have a little peace. Just for once.

Lots of luck and love for Christmas and New Year.
from
Jean
(*Max* also)

Part I and II against this background of sun and mountain and sea. Part III that beastly room in Thornfield House or whatever –

Martinique is called "the island one must return to". This is the island that escapes, and is often not liked much. An elusive place –

TO FRANCIS WYNDHAM
January 7th, 1960
Rocket House

Dear Mr Wyndham,

The London Magazine arrived this morning. I was delighted of course, and liked your article so much.

Max is a good deal better now thank you, and we are going from Bude to Perranporth. Probably. It's warmer there and not so tough.

As soon as I am sure of the new place I will let you know the address. It's near a hotel called "Cellar Cove" which sounds good to me because it suggests a drink. Unfortunately it's a teetotal hotel – so what to do with the bottles? I'm getting agitated about this. Now the book – I know that you understand and sympathize, but I'm angry with myself because I told the firm of André Deutsch that I'd be quick and have been slow.

I've had to stop working several times for weeks, so though it's all there (as it were) it's jerky. Not smooth. However I won't make excuses again. Boring.

Naturally, seeing Petronella has made me feel that I could finish it right away.

But I've got to pack, telephone, arrange, *move* in fact. I do so hate that. If only someone would give me a nice warm *safe* attic for a month or two or three you'd see how quick I'd be!

It will all be worth it if Max gets well – (I mean moving).

It is very kind of you to offer to look at what I've done, and yes, it might help a lot. When I write from the new place I will try to tell you just where I'm uncertain and why. I wish I could get the exact title – it would go from that I believe.

Yours sincerely
Jean Rhys

TO MARYVONNE MOERMAN

January 11th, 1960
Rocket House

> PS. I had my first fan mail letter this
> morning about the story. Very cheering.
> For it was from a publisher.

My Dear Maryvonne,

Did you get a greetings telegram for Christmas and New Year? I did send one, but like an idiot, put the number *200* instead of *48b*. I went back and corrected this at once, but they are very vague about whether it was actually delivered. Or not.

My dear I am having one devil of a time – as usual! Max has been very ill, though better now, and I've had to drop everything. I find it all a bit too much for me too, so we are definitely leaving beautiful Bude early in Feb. though I'm not quite sure yet where we will go to. It's getting awfully difficult to find anywhere now. The prices are quite *fantastic* in Cornwall. 20 guineas a week is quite usual in the summer –

Never mind. I will as usual manage somehow. And I don't want this to be a gloomy letter. It is too cold and dark for that. The best news is that I've had a story published in The London Magazine for Jan. (John Lehmann is the editor) and though I haven't had the cash yet it will be forthcoming I suppose. Not much but still! One of these days. Very welcome too! You will not like the story, I fear, it's an old one – though *not* as I've dated it 1914 – and *not* autobiography.

Still I'm trying to get hold of a copy to send you. Bude is an extraordinary place!

It's rather a good little magazine really.

You don't know what it feels like to be quite certain that if I had three months peace I would finish my book. It might change a lot in my life and other lives as well.

[. . . . . .]
Your loving
Jean

My darling Ruthie,

I was so very pleased to get your Christmas card. Which do you play? Violin or piano? Piano isn't it? I used to long ago – One night when I was about your age I played at a concert and was so nervous before I started. Then when I had finished without mishap I was very pleased. I can remember it now – the lights, and the people clapping and the palm trees, for this was of course in the West Indies. I do hope you aren't too cold in Holland. I imagine you skating in a fur cap and a little muff to keep your hands warm. But I expect that's imagination so I will add a bright red coat to make my picture complete.

I have to go and make an omelette now for lunch – not very substantial. This weather needs a big steak! I hope to send you a little present soon for New Year. Late but with all my love.
Hugs and big kiss from
Ooma

TO JOHN LEHMANN
January 17th [1960]
Rocket House

Dear Mr Lehmann,

I was so very pleased when Mr Wyndham told me of your interest in my stories, and that The London Magazine had taken "Petronella". A cheque for forty guineas reached me on the 15th – I thought you might like to know how much it will help me.

I am leaving Bude shortly and will let him know my new address when it is settled.
Yours sincerely
Jean Rhys

TO MARYVONNE MOERMAN
February 15th, 1960
Rocket House

My dear Maryvonne,

I was so pleased to get your letter. The story helped quite a lot (in cash I mean) and of course it cheered me up too. I didn't think it the best of the collection, but was delighted they liked *something*.

I always want to write you long letters too, but somehow don't – just think them busily and often. John is much in my thoughts also, and I'm always hoping to hear that he is better. It's rotten about the pain and the morphine –

You know of all the things I *might* say I will risk saying this: If I had never met John there would have been no books, no "aliveness" and above all, no you. I can't imagine what my life would have been at all at all – Useless and boring –

We hope to leave Bude on Saturday 20th.

The new address is:

> *The Chalet*
> *Cellar Cove Hotel*
> *Perranporth*
> *Cornwall.*

I am rushing about in my usual distracted way trying to collect and pack everything – including books and papers. It's strange that I spend my existence moving, and have never learned to pack calmly. Indeed I hate it more and more every time.

I do not quite know what is wrong with Max. He complained of giddiness, and had a bad fall not long after we came here – down those stone steps leading to the moor – remember?

These falls went on, then about nine months ago he fell badly (the same day I got some dough from the German broadcast).

He's been in bed nearly all this horrible winter but is getting on slowly now and has been out once.

The worst is that I had to drop the book – just when one more effort would have finished it. It seems feeble, but I get so God dam tired I can't think properly. However I'm hoping a lot from Perranporth.

Give my best love to Ruthie. I will write to her soon and send her the silver chain I hope (she probably has one already now!)

Tell her I have a pair of long pants too, one of those tapered horrors. When I climb on chairs I nearly topple over and swear like Jimmy oh. However they are warm that's one thing.

Love and kisses and a big hug

from
Jean

Max too sends love.

TO SELMA VAZ DIAS

February 24th [1960]
The Chalet, Cellar Cove Hotel
Perranporth, Cornwall

My dear Selma,

I've been having quite a time getting here. My abodes get stranger and stranger (this place is not so bad inside, but outside it looks like a very small horse box painted blue). Also my belongings become shabbier and shabbier – have to be held together with rope and even so fall apart. My dear I can't even begin to tell you all I want to – so won't try. [. . . . . .]

Yes – if heaven is kind and hell dozes off I can finish Mrs Rochester in three or four months.

I've been saying that for a long long time I fear – but please trust me – for that helps I am certain. (Quite certain of that much)

I have to fight against a horrible weariness, but there are ways and means of doing that – and I'm learning.

There are a series of minute rooms leading one into the other here. I've fixed one up anyway, and as Max is much better I can simply go underground – day after tomorrow. Tomorrow I must go to Perranporth and buy eats and drinks and find out this and that. (Tomorrow!)

I get so tired – but when we arrived the man at the hotel produced a bottle of Cyprus wine which everyone says is dreadful but I adored it and got unpacked on it too and a blissful sleep.

[. . . . . .]

That story John Lehmann took just about saved my life.

I was a bit down and out. All right now.

I would rather not discuss book – bad plan – but your part is finished because it was easier to do – It must be added to I think.

I am sorry you were disappointed at critics reaction – or lack of it. I do not care very much for myself. So few are helpful – and the others don't count. Still it is different for you I understand that.

Many people pretend they don't read their press cuttings, I really didn't for a long time – Ford's influence I suppose. Even now don't care much. I care for only one thing – to finish this book and my bitter disappointment is because I've been so long.

If I live it will be done. I do hope you had a fine time and a happy one.

Don't tell anyone I said so – But I don't love Cornwall. Or even like it. Oh God it can be grim and chapel and black. But the spring is nice. And here it comes!

Love from
Jean

[. . . . . .]

April 6th [1960]
Perranporth

Dear Mr Wyndham,

I was glad to get your letter this morning. Of course I am very gratified that Mr Grigson[1] wishes to include me in the survey he is editing.

I was born in Roseau Dominica August 1894. But I don't think about it much. (At present I must tell myself there is no time. Or I might be discouraged for I seem to have wasted some.) I had a letter from Mrs Norah

Smallwood, Chatto & Windus, about Petronella, and this book I'm toiling at now. It was kind of her to write, and I thanked her of course. You know – it delights me to be told that some people liked the story. Especially Mr Sansom[2], that goes without saying.

Gwenda David – 44 Well Street NW also wrote to me. She's the English agent for The Viking Press, and they want to have a look at "Good Morning Midnight". It might be worth trying – a slight chance – for that book never got to America – not even to Carol Hill, who was my agent in New York then.

There is a copy straying about at Constable's – not the file copy and I've been doing what I can to get hold of it – so difficult to find one. I haven't managed this yet, but I will write to Mr Sadleir – I expect it has vanished though.

Books do.

You cannot imagine how much I long to have a house, or a room or two, or a cave of my own.

Just now I feel like a displaced person and that is not a part I play well. Bad packing and bad management and that lost feeling for days and weeks afterwards –

I stayed at Rocket House as long as I could, but after Max's illness it became impossible.

This "chalet" is very small – minute – but sometimes it is quiet.

A cow looked in at the window yesterday. She had such a calm expression. It did help. Also there are a few trees. I hope we can stay here peacefully for a few months – long enough to smooth the book out. Do you know I wish I had the courage to write a really *mad* book. It would have been finished ages ago. But I have not. It is the sane orderly background I find so difficult in this case.

Even as it is, I have no idea whether you will like it – or anyone else. I want to go just one step higher. Step it up in part. Then it will be done and out of my hands.

It is very late, so I can't tell you again at length that this will happen. I mean it will be done.

It weighs on me that I am being so slow when I said I'd be quick, a crazy thing to be sure about anyway. Hubris?

The other day I wrote a short story as a holiday. It's called "*They thought it was jazz*" and is not typed. A bit of a crazy story. For fun.

I am so very grateful to you for such a lot, and please believe me, if I feel things are beyond me I will tell you so at once. But that, I trust, won't happen.

Yours sincerely
Jean Rhys

1. *The poet and critic Geoffrey Grigson had been so impressed by "Till September, Petronella" that he asked Francis Wyndham to contribute an entry on Jean Rhys to a survey he was editing for Rainbird, McLean Ltd called "World Literature 1900 to 1960".*

2. *The novelist and short story writer William Sansom had written to Francis Wyndham in excited enthusiasm over "Petronella".*

April 12th [1960]
Perranporth

> P.S. Do you know that "Petronella" was
> once a full length novel. Almost. I
> cut it and cut it. Was that right or
> wrong? Don't know.

Dear Mr Wyndham,

It would be so kind of you to lend your copy of "Good Morning Midnight" to the Viking Press.

I enclose Miss David's letters. Martha Smith told me that she'd try to find the one at Constable's, but as I've heard nothing it has probably disappeared – I'll write to them again though –

I do so agree that it would be an enormous help (in every way) if it were published in America, and – as they've asked for it – worth trying[1].

[. . . . . .]

I've never imagined that I'd have any popular success – and so I've never wanted it. This sounds all wrong, but is true.

Now, of course I'd be overjoyed – for all the bad reasons – such as no worries, a *real* hideaway to finish this new thing. And all the rest.

I probably don't deserve it. So late in the day.

The short story I wrote a few weeks ago is "not serious".

Still, I will get it typed and send it to you without working it over or revising it at all. If I once start that it's an endless affair.

What I'm really longing to do is to get your opinion on the novel – on a chapter here and there. I've hesitated about this. Am still hesitating –

For if I were to explain what is really holding me up, it might make me more confused, more uncertain.

Where to start? Who's to speak? What to cut? and so on. Please don't answer this part of my letter.

It will, I hope, come of itself.

What nonsense I am writing – for of course this is a thing that must come of itself.

Perranporth is one of those rainy places and the wind never stops.

Yours sincerely
Jean Rhys

1. *The Viking Press decided against publishing* Good Morning, Midnight, *however, and it did not appear in the USA until Harper & Row brought it out in 1970, when the success there of* Wide Sargasso Sea *three years before had led to a revival of interest in Jean's early work.*

May 31st [1960]
                                                                     Perranporth
Dear Mr Wyndham,

I was so glad to get your letter, and the good news about "Outside the Machine". Yes, I do know "Winter's Tales", I have the 1956 collection and like nearly all the stories very much indeed.

[. . . . . .]

I wrote to you some weeks ago about "Sargasso Sea" or *Wide Sargasso Sea* (that's the book's present title, as I think "Story of the First Mrs Rochester" gives away too much.)

However my own difficulties crept in and I did not send the letter. I've been hunting for somewhere to stay for a fortnight as someone else wants the chalet for that time and finding it impossible. Cornwall is full of people already – in July it will be worse.

Then I discovered that two bungalows are to be built in the next field and was in despair. Very noisy and no more peace.

I hope I'm on the track of something better and safer now. *At last*! I mean a place to live in. Three years is a long time to be uncertain and held up.

The book is done after a fashion but I'm not sure about it.

There are two I's – that is the trouble. In Part I she is I, in Part II (the longest) he speaks, in Part III she is "I" again. I've held it together with a dream (I hope) and indeed the whole of Part III must have the feeling of a dream. Well, I'm not satisfied with this. I'd prefer a long smooth story told by the girl – Afterwards of course the mad Mrs Rochester. I have tried and tried but cannot do it. I can only do it with two voices – as yet. But it is a break.

While I was house hunting I found a long short story about the West Indies as I knew the West Indies, but the final version seems to have got lost. So I fixed up the two first versions, and will get it properly typed, title "The Same Sun"? Price of Peace?

I've wanted for a long time to do a series of short stories – all about that period and setting – to be called "The Bishop and the Nun". That one is half written.

But all these plans must wait, of course, till I've finally dealt with Mrs Rochester – poor woman!

The story I wrote called *"They Thought it was Jazz"* is about Holloway Prison – So, all things considered, must not be taken too seriously.

It is supposed to be a Creole girl talking but still – .

I fear this is one of those unruly letters and I'm anxious to get the post.

I don't know how to *start* thanking you, but I do indeed feel so very grateful.

                                                        Yours sincerely
                                                        Jean Rhys

June 22nd [1960]
Perranporth

> *There is a spare bedroom.*
> If one of these days you can bear
> life on muted strings for a bit.

My dear Maryvonne,

This is to tell you our good news. Edward has bought a bungalow, is furnishing it with essentials, and will let it to us. So at last, *at last* we may have some peace and security. I can hardly believe it yet! I may even be able to finish my book – not too late I hope.

The bungalow is in Devon, right in the country, near a little village called *Cheriton Fitz Paine*. The nearest town is Exeter. Tiverton not far off. Something needs to be done to bath and so on, and we are still in Cornwall till July 21st – maybe a little longer while it's being fixed up.

I am so excited about it and a bit afraid I may wake up!

You know everything that is happening in Holland is happening here. They are pulling down all the lovely old houses not only in London. Everywhere. Then a dreadful rabbit hutch of flats or a battery hen factory appears.

Even so, it's getting more and more difficult to find any place to live in – I think it's worse here than in Holland, somehow. They are quite ruthless and seem to have a special hatred of trees and all things green – Also all beautiful houses.

How delighted I shall be to be out of the rat race I cannot tell you!

I don't think we could have gone on much longer without a catastrophe.

Max is not well enough to be pushed around any more, and I was getting despairing about book and not terribly well myself.

I have sold another short story to Macmillan's "Winter's Tales" and maybe two, but one is certain. It's a bit dreary, I fear, but what does that matter if they buy it?

Macmillan is a very good firm of course with a branch in New York.

So here's to more miracles! You know, I would like to send you a very short story and implore you to type it for me.

It is not (repeat *not*) autobiography, and not to be taken seriously. But the people here are terribly narrow minded and they gossip like crazy.

Really – this is true! I found it out in Bude I assure you. For them "I" is "I" and not a literary device. Every *word* is autobiography!

This thing is called *"They Thought it was Jazz"* and is quite short but I don't want to give it to a girl round here who is doing some stuff for me.

Perhaps you are on holiday or otherwise busy. Then don't bother. But if not, will post it by registered letter.

Mr Francis Wyndham wants to see it, and he has done such a lot for me. It's not much. I haven't worked on it a great deal.

Well, we may perhaps be saved after all! Not too soon either – and my gratitude is boundless for I was very worried.

Love and a *big* hug. Love to Ruthie too   *Jean*

Dear Mr Wyndham,

Thank you for letting me have the stories[1]. I'll send them along to Simon and Schuster and hope for the best. (But not hope too much.) They didn't do badly with "Quartet" – Postures over here – maybe there's a chance.

I'll change the title as you suggest, and put Petronella first.

I do hope you'll have a pleasant holiday.

I may ask your advice again about the order of the stories – which matters. But that won't be just yet, for I am packing – a job I hate so much and do worse every time.

I'm afraid the heaven of a permanent address is still round the corner, the builders have to do this and that it seems.

So, I will be here till *July 21st* and after that letters will be forwarded. I can hardly wait to get to the Devon place and security. *Will* I be glad!

The proofs of the "London" story got held up at the Bude Post Office for a month – I can't think why. Fortunately no corrections needed. I wonder if any others are knocking about there?

I do understand that the book "Sargasso Sea" is what is wanted. As soon as I am safe and sound I will work very hard and finish it. Not too late I hope.

I've done the two last stories (yesterday) and they're on their way to be properly typed.

Of course I am tremendously grateful to you. But I won't talk about it any more.   Sincerely yours
Jean Rhys

PS. I have just had a letter from Simon & Schuster, saying they are writing to you. I will let them know at once that I have the stories, and will post them in a few days or so to America.

July 15th. This is in answer to your letter of this morning. *Please* do not worry about the loss of "Tigers" (if it is lost). I haven't got a copy I'm afraid, but it does not matter so much. I though that it would lighten up the collection I'm sending to America. (A bit sombre perhaps.) But I've got another story very slight, though not gloomy, which may do instead.

I cannot remember much about "Tigers" – a letter, and a man called Sim – that's all. But if I try very hard it may come back – It must be *somewhere* and will probably turn up. I am a bit worried over the possibility that a cheque from the "London" for "The Day They Burned the Books" may have gone astray too, and I'd be so much obliged if I could know about that.

The Post Office at Bude aren't very forthcoming, and Rocket House is a dreadful place for letters. When I was there *numbers* used to arrive for previous tenants, and it was a chore sending them back. Once I had a long correspondence with a Cheltenham solicitor who just *wouldn't* believe that his client wasn't there. She had completely disappeared, and her relations were frantic.

Again please do not be concerned. I feel it is largely my fault. I ought to have copies of course and I ought to have a proper address. That I do hope won't be long! – The place is near Cheriton Fitz Paine and Exeter and when I get there I intend to *stay put* and never move again.

Meanwhile I will be here till *July 21st* and I am sure that the hotel will forward anything that arrives after that date. We will be in a rather horrid little room in Truro – all I could find – for a fortnight. Afterwards – it depends how soon the new place is ready.

Thank you for trying to place "Voyage" and "Midnight" with Penguins[2]. I do hope it comes off. I don't know the other people you mention but won't look at the lurid cover. I cannot imagine why somebody doesn't do a series like "Livre d'Aujourdhui". That was rather *large*, instead of short and thick. Plain orange paper and black lettering. Perhaps you know it? The print was good too and they did reprints of Colette's "Mitsou", Pierre MacOrlan[3] and so on, four francs fifty! They got snapped up at once. However, perhaps it wouldn't be the same here.

I enclose, to make you smile, a song I wrote last night for a joke!

I do hope it wasn't telepathy or something.

I would like to know about the "London" cheque, for I seem to be recklessly throwing away all I've got on this moving. Oh dear!

Sincerely yours
Jean Rhys

Song: *Stop Thief!*

> Who's stolen my blue bluebells?
> Who's stolen my flow-ers?
> Who got the roses that bloomed so late
> Who has my luvly flow-ers?
>
> Who's stolen the song I know
> Who's stolen my musick?
> Who's stolen my fresh mornings
> Who's stolen my sleep?[4]

1. *Maria Leiper of Simon and Schuster had written to Jean via the* London Magazine *asking to see her unpublished book of short stories.*

2. *Francis Wyndham was trying to get Penguins and another paperback firm, Ace Books, to reprint the early novels, but without success.*

3. *Pseudonym of Pierre Dumarchais, author of fantastic adventure stories dealing with pirates, the Foreign Legion, etc.*

4. *On February 2nd, 1960, Jean had written from Bude to Eliot Bliss: "This wasn't such a bad place when we came, though dilapidated. But unfortunately an enthusiastic gardener took the place next door. Her idea of a garden – to pull up every vestige of grass or flowers. Some of the Cornish flowers are very hardy and survive the winter. But she had them out root and branch.* Even the bluebells. We had a row over the bluebells *which she called "weeds". . . . Oh she's a devil. How glad I shall be to depart."*

July 21st [1960]
Perranporth

> This is a scatty letter – but I am a
> little tired. Stories will be sent and
> I wish you a very pleasant holiday.

Dear Mr Wyndham,

This is to let you know that we are not leaving the chalet after all. So the same address goes. At least – I do so trust that nobody will change their minds *again!*

With any luck we will stay put till the new Jerusalem and abode of peace is ready at the end of August. The builders are now working at it (I hope). For it's somebody else helping me.

I'm glad you liked song. I found out long ago that when very frustrated, it's better to write this foolishness than to collapse, weep, or break china. I've done *hundreds* in last four years. Don't worry, they'll all be torn up.

As I have a bit of a respite I can get the two stories (both finished in handwriting) in a tidy state and typed for you to see. It'll be very kind of you to tell me if good enough to fill a gap. About publicity angle – I just don't know. I've always hated personal publicity. (*Why Necessary?* Only the writing matters.)

Now, of course, though my life is still a bit rum – it would not interest anybody. Except that it's rather comic sometimes. For instance the words Dry Rot make me laugh like anything but I gather it's a tragic subject – very – Extremely so.

So I don't know. Could I be a *recluse*?? That is my great wish for the next few weeks – and why not for good?

I used to think that all writing should be anonymous. Was I so far wrong? A bit unfair perhaps, to past strivings.

About lurid covers. Do you know – so many people dislike them. Wouldn't a very vivid colour, and contrast lettering like the Livre de Demain [*Aujourdhui crossed out in original*] (you were quite right, but you see I've written it *again* – Perhaps I don't believe in tomorrow, or some complex). Well, and a different shape, and the series called – you know a title with "Tomorrow" – do as well? I expect the publicity people know – but I wonder! Can think of so many books "All Night at Mr Stanyhurst's"[1], "A Cargo of Parrots"[2] that would do splendidly.   Sincerely yours
Jean Rhys

1. *Novel by Hugh Edwards (1933). It was reissued in 1963.*

2. *Novel by R. H. Baptist (1937).*

July 23rd [1960]
Perranporth

Dear Mr Osborne,

Thank you for the cheque which arrived yesterday. I am sorry for mix up about my address.

Probably other letters sent to Bude haven't reached me, so I did not know when the "London" meant to publish the story.

I hoped to settle in Devon soon, and intended to write from there.

This plan has been delayed, I'm sad to say, and from now till the end of August I'll be here – at the Chalet.

As soon as I have a permanent address I will let you know, for if the MSS of "Tigers are Better Looking" turns up[2] at your office I would be glad to have it. (I ought to have a copy of course, it's entirely my fault!) It's probably at the Bude Post Office, or Rocket House and isn't very important anyway.

Still, if you do come across it and can post it, I'd be grateful.

Yours sincerely
Jean Rhys

1. *At that time editorial assistant on the* London Magazine.

2. *The missing story was eventually discovered in an obscure file in the* London Magazine *office and was published in October 1962.*

TO MARYVONNE MOERMAN

August 9th [1960]
Perranporth

I want to buy a tree – No beds of flowers.
A *Tree* and later on another. A wild dream
I suppose. On verra.

My dear Maryvonne,

I expect you thought me a bit of a phony when no M.S.S. turned up! No – not exactly correct.

This bungalow which Edward bought for us turned out to have something very wrong with the floor. DAMP! So, ever since I last wrote I've felt quite distracted, wondering what was the best thing to do, or what would happen. This whole place, the Chalet, which is very small, was full of half packed trunks and Max extremely pessimistic and *that* didn't help.

You know – optimists have their uses after all. I would love to meet one right now.

All will be well in the end. Edward has had in builders and so on and put it right. I simply shiver to think of the cost of this – so try not to think at all. The date of entry into the Ark is now *September 5th*. Touch wood and cross fingers –

Meanwhile I could not write – not even copying. I was a bit worried and dithering to be truthful.

However, now that I know just how things are, I can screw myself up to the big effort of moving. Then, I will (once established) *never* move again I hope. – I will try to have the story copied to send you. Also some poems.

The Ark sounds as if it will be very nice with a little garden. But the curtains are blue! However, Edward has fixed up all kinds of gadgets to keep it warm, so when you see that spare room perhaps you won't think the blue too cold.

Meanwhile I do wish yourself and Ruthie a lovely holiday and fine weather. Is she all right again? – I do so hope so. Be good, be happy and be careful of rainy days.

Your loving but still rather distracted

Ooma

Many kisses and hugs of course. Enjoy yourselves even on rainy days. Have some fun.

PART FIVE

Cheriton Fitz Paine

(1960–1963)

TO MARYVONNE MOERMAN

My dear Maryvonne,

Well – here we are – I like it so much – a rather tumble down cottage with a row of other cottages – which all seem to be empty. Inside there are all sorts of gadgets for hot water and keeping warm, and it is all clean and fresh. *No people* (or hardly!) about, and the most splendid trees and black and white cows, and green fields. Above all *Rain*. It has hardly stopped since we came! As the kitchen chimney leaks, it's quite a job mopping up. All the same I like it. I can imagine though, some people might find it dull – but me not. However I mean to make the inside very splendid, with red and gold things picked up for ten bob – or less – in junk shops. There are several in Crediton and Tiverton, our nearby towns. Lovely things like red velvet armchairs, and gilt candlesticks and old pictures. It is already very comfortable – but I will make it glitter a bit, for it can be dark in the rain. It needs *Red*. A lot.

There is a little pink and white room which I'll get ready for you. For you must come. And Ruthie too. I have a feeling she might like it here. As you can see I am very excited, for it's the first place I've had for so long. *For centuries*. I do think Edward has been kind. When this darned rain stops, as I suppose it must, unless this is Flood No. 2 – it will be fine and dandy and I do hope to finish book here.

I feel so much better – but Max, I can see, wants some cheering up. He does not dislike most people as I do. He *likes* people. Very odd! Meanwhile red and gilt must comfort him. You know – the cows here moo at me in a very disapproving way, and all the dogs bark like crazy.

I've always known dogs were cash conscious – but I didn't know cows were. It's probably surprise and they'll get used to me in time.

To tell the truth, I was darned glad to leave Cornwall. Perranporth in particular was really awful. Nothing but tourists and cars and portable radios, and boarding houses.

I must stop now and go to my lovely bath. There was no bath at the chalet. So it's a delightful thing to have one, a luxe.

I will write soon again but do let me have your news.

I just have this feeling Ruthie *might* like it for a bit. You too perhaps. Some time. Will you give her my best love and for you all the usual bear's hugs – and best love too.

Your loving
Jean

PS. I'm going to send along some typing if you have time. Did you have a holiday? Nice??

1. *Jean's new address was in fact 6 Land Boat Bungalows, Cheriton Fitz Paine, nr Crediton, Devon. It was the last (or first – the Post Office was to change its mind) bungalow in an isolated row of six. When the Hamers arrived in this village it was the custom to write it "FitzPaine" in one word. Nowadays it is usually written "Fitzpaine". Jean usually headed her letters with the version "Fitz Paine".*

October 6th [1960]
Cheriton Fitz Paine

[. . . . . .]

Dear Mr Wyndham,

Thank you for writing. I have given Macmillans this address and will let the "London" know too. It has rained ever since we came, and I've spent much time mopping up the kitchen chimney leak – but I still like it very much – indeed – if only we don't get flooded!

I will send one of those stories to be typed – there must be something wrong with the other, or the girl at Perranporth would not have made such nonsense of it. She was a bit silly, but all the same – it must be dull or long winded or something. I will look at it. "All Souls Day" is the title and I didn't think it so bad. It was called "The Price of Peace" but she told me there'd been a film Price of Peace. She asked to see one of my books but The Left Bank was the only one I had.

She said "Oh but didn't you know? 'Left Bank' is a new way of dressing." "It's taken a long time to get here" I said and she said "It's like 'Chelsea' – only more so. Don't you read books about fashion?"

No. I haven't a lot of time left. But enough I hope. I hope.

I have often wanted to tell you about the trying year in Cornwall.

My husband was very ill – so I could not work steadily. Just one of those things – too bad to be possible. So I pretended it was not so. However it did mean that what I wrote was "forced" – or done on drink. (Better but uneven.) The framework is done and much of it is the most I can do. Still it wants pulling together – naturally (I still long to do it rightly).

Max is so much better now and I'm happy about that. Besides I love it here, very green and a lot of cows and the most splendid trees. Hardly any people. Oh it is quite lovely. Outside it is shabby and tumbledown – nearly all our neighbours work on the land. (They get up *so* early!) Inside it is comfortable and full of gadgets (which *may* go wrong of course).

The only snag is the leak, and that I have to get up early too – to buy things at Tiverton or Crediton – Some days.

I hate that – am used to taking a long, thoughtful look at the day before I decide when.

I have written this sort of letter before and not sent it. I did not wish to be personal or boring.

But as I promised to finish the book in a year or eighteen months (a crazy thing to promise) it seems to me some explaining is necessary.

It may go better here.

[. . . . . .]

Sincerely yours
Jean Rhys

December 6th [1960]
                                                             Cheriton Fitz Paine

No I'll have the story typed first.
Such a bother reading a handwritten thing.

Dear Mr Wyndham,
   Thank you for sending the cutting from the Times. Lit. Supp[1]. No, I did not
see it – and was pleased.
   The river hasn't got to the doors of *Land* Boat Bungalows. Not yet anyway.
I hope it stays away, for I'm almost over a bad attack of cafard and once more
full of courage determination and optimism.
   I heard from Simon & Schuster – they don't want "Petronella", but Miss
Leiper who wrote very sympathetically suggests sending the collection to an
agent. She thinks it may have a chance. I've said yes of course. Carol Hill of
Hill & Peters used to act for me in New York but ages ago. It would be
splendid if I could sell one or two. It would complete my cure[2].
   I've finished the Holloway story long ago. It's "stylized patois" – how true!
– and I don't know if *that's* authentic for they speak (or spoke) French patois in
my island.
   Here are two pages. What do you think? Does it sound right? I've not read
any of the "West Indian" people. It's by ear and memory. Tear it up if you are
busy. I expect it's a waste of time, but I wanted to write it one evening and did.
   I had copies of Winters Tales no 6. May I send you one to say thank you?
Well I will anyway.
                                                             Yours sincerely
                                                               Jean Rhys
I've only just found out that this place is *Land* not *Long* and 6 not 1. The post
office doesn't mind but *Land* Boat very appropriate. It feels like a boat – water
all round. I do find myself in rum situations. Oh dear!

1. *A review of* Winter's Tales.

2. *None of the stories in the collection appeared in the USA until the publication there,*
by Harper & Row, of Tigers Are Better Looking, *in 1974.*

December 28th, 1960
                                                             Cheriton Fitz Paine

   I hope Ruthie is rested. Mightn't she
have some inherited talent for violin?
Maybe it's her thing.
      A happy and lucky New Year for you and
for Job.

My dear Maryvonne,

I had your letter on Christmas morning – so nice to see it – very much the nicest bit of a dull Christmas day. (If you notice, by the way, the address looks different but same old cottage. It does not matter to the post office, and I only found out correct no. and so on when the electricity bill arrived!) You would not *believe* how small this village is or how far away – it's scarcely a village, really more of a hamlet with one small general shop and some secretive cottages. Also a few larger houses. Even more secretive – One scarcely sees a human being. Perhaps they've all gone away for the winter but I doubt that! Even the pub is empty!

Now about this dull Christmas. No cards sent, or one single letter written.

About a week ago I dropped one of my fish (Remember those faithful but heavy glass fish I lug everywhere?) It fell on my foot the *idiotic* thing! It has quite stopped hurting, but I cannot walk much as I am anxious to get it well again. If I don't – we will be simply marooned with the bones of a chicken and I tin Oxtail soup. – Too bad.

My dear I think constantly of you and Ruthie, of all of you.

But I wanted to write good news when I did write, and since we came here I've felt like the patriarch Job. *Everything* has happened. Including bad floods – The river Exe is quite small but after a few months of rain it swells up and invades the entire valley. This happens once in every three or four years, but no one does anything about it.

Well, this was the year. As a matter of fact Cheriton Fitz Paine (romantic name for this rum place) escaped, as it's on higher ground, but Exeter, Crediton, Tiverton etc. and so on – all flooded not once but several times. No sooner did the unfortunate people dry their clothes and furniture and clear out some of the mud – than the water was on them again. It does seem extraordinary that they don't do *something*. They are awfully stingy people and say it would cost them too much. The floods cost more, but I suppose they forget. Talk about optimism! Here – only the bathroom is a wreck and the kitchen leaky. Otherwise OK.

It is nice inside – outside does take a bit of getting used to. But what doesn't?? So *damp*.

I grew rather sad for what with floods, walking in the dark and so on, I was tired. *Not my cup of tea* as they say. Needs some sugar! I will send you Winters Tales 6 as I have a story in it. So old and grey. I hate it. If only I could do my book. That is not grey but black with vivid colours here and there. I am constantly stopped and get frantic. This isn't at all the letter I want to write (It certainly isn't "a small word". As for that "something Lovely" – a flower perhaps?) but it must serve. You must fill in the gaps. My dream is to finish my book, get a face lift, and a bright red wig. Also a lovely fur coat. Underneath I will wear a purple dress and ropes of pearls. Or what do you say to rags? Then, in all my glory I will come and see you taking a large suite in posh hotel.

You can tell everyone I'm an eccentric acquaintance. I expect Ruthie would laugh and laugh.

Letter to her on back – I really meant to go to Crediton for cards and so on but that old fish put a stop to everything. Love to everybody special hugs and kisses for you.

All will be well. *Never fear.*

Jean

My Dear Ruthie,

This is to wish you a lovely and happy New Year. I hope all sorts of nice things will happen. I think a lot about you. Rest well during the holidays. I hope I'll be a more satisfactory Ooma one of these days – Meanwhile a big Hullo. Also Hi there!

And Love

TO FRANCIS WYNDHAM   *January 3rd [1961]*

[. . . . . .]

Dear Mr Wyndham,

Thank you for sending Sunday Times cutting[1]. What a nice New Year present, that review! –

It's already had some effect, for a friend[2] who gets annoyed about what he calls my "obsession" – that's to say two or three hours time *by myself* – has written a kind letter. "But," he says, "we don't speak the same language." Oh dear! Nobody understands how easily words can fly away, and not come back either.

As I know he takes "The Sunday Times" I'll leave the argument there.

I can't help feeling that all these stories about people working hard all day and producing a lot at night (*in kitchen*) are fairy stories. Not possible. Not now for me anyway. I hope to finish my story this week. I should not have started on it. But had to. I think and trust that grim obstinacy will be rewarded and that I'll have hours of peaceful writing this year. *No* fires, *no* sweeping, *no* cooking, *no* grocer or vegetable man. Hardly any.   Sincerely

Jean Rhys

It's quite a good kitchen.

1. The Sunday Times critic had chosen "Outside the Machine" for special praise in his review of Winter's Tales.

2. Her brother-in-law, Alec Hamer.

[. . . . . .]

My dear Selma,

I was so glad to hear from you – it made my day. I have had a kind of creeping 'flu – so needed some cheer. Yes, the Sunday Times thing did me a bit of good and I didn't know it had so much pull.

I'm delighted you had a prosperous year in 1960 – or partly so, and hope 1961 better still with lots of luck.

Please try not to be so sad. Can't you think that it is the price of feeling anything at all, or living, or acting or being yourself even – it's the shadow of light as it were, this black melancholy – or – the other way round.

I know it so well, my God, it goes everywhere with me – but almost despair my dear. Though never quite. Not yet anyway but I wonder sometimes how long I shall last.

The trouble is that most things that happen to me are so *unlikely*! My best friends (not so many) don't believe me. Unlikely, and a bit comic too as a rule.

This place, which I imagined would be a refuge, is a foretaste of hell at present – It has hardly stopped raining since we arrived, and I wish the bloody river Exe would make up its mind and wash this whole village and the damp fields and the cows right away and finish (Me with cows). Instead of that it oozes and drips away. (Drip drip into a blue plastic basin sitting in a dilapidated old arm chair. Poor thing, I must get it a cover for it looks indecent and pathetic. Pontings or Barkers. No cash but who cares?)

I will be seeing you this year if I survive the icicles in bathroom – I won't say more for I've said too much already in other letters. A grave mistake – about books. My fault. But really the floods aren't my fault, or Max's illness, or the damp making him worse when he was getting better, or perhaps other things. . . .

I deserted book for a short story called idiotically *Why?* Warum? is better.

That's finished – so on with the other. *"I hear voices"*[1] was my title – oh God why didn't I think of it?

I thought of *"Three voices"*[2] and dismissed it – wish I could get hold of that book.

There are *no* books here and drink difficult to get. Woe Woe.

Never mind I intend to spend my last penny on a spree soon.

Taxi to dashing Tiverton where Pernod, vodka, not bad vin rouge, *and* Penguins can be bought. I do miss books so much it's quite awful. However when the rain stops there will be flowers, and leaves on trees, cover on poor old arm chair – and other delights I trust –

Cambridge is a pleasant place. I should think Sasha Moorsom will like it – My dear I went to *school* there over a hundred years ago. Recollections a bit dim. Kings College Chapel *of course*, some bridge or other over Cam – and *falling off a bicycle.*

Am always falling off things – Oh and Ely Cathedral. So lovely I thought it.

I bet I wasn't wrong though a dreadful child I expect suspected by all (most unjustly) of being a Savage from the Cannibal Islands.

As a matter of fact I consider myself highly civilised – in some ways only I admit –

Lots of luck. Some time, when good news, will write – Spare a moment for news one of these days.   Affecly
                                                                                            Jean
P.S. Think yourself lucky. You would *perish* here. It's so dark and secretive and altogether wet. Not to be believed. As usual. Do you like your new house?

1. *Novel by Paul Ableman (1958)*

2. *Novel by Isobel English (1961)*

TO FRANCIS WYNDHAM   *March 20th [1961]*
                                                                              Cheriton Fitz Paine

                                    [. . . . . .]

Dear Mr Wyndham,

It was so nice to hear from you this morning. I was worried about the story – didn't think I'd managed it very well. The dialect was a difficulty – I'm not 100 per cent certain of it. So lapses and guesses.

Of course it varies from island to island and in mine is – or was – a French patois, not much help.

The word on page 17 is fouti and means "does not" in Trinidad. In patois – *dam extra plus* – that's how I've used it anyway.

"Country Coukie" or Cookie is "country cousin", someone not used to town ways. "Country Coukie comes to town" they say – mockingly. I wish I could have checked up a bit.

It will be splendid if the London like the story, and it's *such* a relief to know it's finished, and that you think it passable and possible.

I've started on the last stage of my book. I unpacked it this morning. The material is all there – more so than I thought – the *shape* isn't clear – not quite.

But if only I can be calm, and not get excited, or despairing, or any of those things it will come at last. I am quite well thank you and Max is better. This is a dull, peaceful place. If only it stays so!   Sincerely yours
                                                                              Jean Rhys

I can't thank you enough for getting that untidy MSS typed and for cheering me up.

May 23rd [1961]
                                                        Cheriton Fitz Paine

Dear Mr Wyndham,

Do you remember the "jazz" story – the one you so kindly sent on to the
"London"? Well, I heard from Mr Ross[1] (who said he liked it) and was
delighted of course.

But when I looked at it some days afterwards, it had a kind of a *jerky*
appearance – you know – in gasps – the first pages. So I tried to smooth it a bit
and sent it to a new and very obliging typist. She kept it for ages. Day before
yesterday I got it back, one copy, *all* retyped and very beautiful on lovely
paper. I have sent it on to Mr Ross. Is that all right? Or have I done something
too fussy?

I'm a bit uneasy about that story, although I tell myself it's OK if you think
so.

The truth is that I hate everything I write when it's finished, and cannot bear
to touch it. So probably that's what is wrong.

Still, I wish I'd gone over it with more care, and found a better title – "A
Sentimental Story" perhaps or "Jumping the Jail Gates".

For it is sentimental and I should not have tried to hide that.

Why, after all?

I do not feel quite like that about the black, coloured, white question either.
It's more complicated don't you think?

I am writing this after a fierce dispute about a clothes line made of *barbed wire*
just outside my sitting room window.

I can't imagine what they hung on it. Coats of mail I suppose. Very useful
too.

The horrible thing is gone, but I've made six enemies – at least.

There is also a perfectly terrible bed of old cabbages which I'm trying to root
up. My neighbours detest me because they think I'm putting on airs. Even the
cows shy at me – that's the worst. For *they know* who to shy at –

I mean to send this ridiculous letter for it has been such a relief.

If I can only finish my book I am now ready to lie down and die. But not
before – believe me. This would be exactly the right place if I could build a ten
foot wall all round. It would be lovely.

But there is no wall –   Sincerely yours
                                                          Jean Rhys

1. The poet Alan Ross had succeeded John Lehmann as editor of the London
Magazine *in April, 1961. "Let Them Call it Jazz" was published in February, 1962.*

June 6th [1961]
Cheriton Fitz Paine

Dear Mr Wyndham,

Thank you for your letter – it cheered me up a lot. I hope Mr Ross got the revised MSS safely, and I hope he approved of it. If not – I have that uneasy feeling still – would you please destroy it – though paper so lovely! I expect this is asking too much, and in that case I'll write to him myself. But I'm a bit at a loss, and the twenty first version bouncing back to Cheriton Fitz would be rather a trial. It is not important except for the bloody money. If he wants it cut I can do it, and with great pleasure. I have (stupidly) mislaid his letter.

It would be very helpful, and very kind too, if you'd look at one or two extracts from my book. I'm having these typed – long hand is an affliction I know.

A few days ago a friend wrote reproachfully "It was supposed to be finished last year". Well no – it was supposed to be finished *two years* ago. It is finished – in a way – the trouble being that I've had to stop several times – and for months.

Every time I have started again, but from a slightly different angle. So though I have a lot of words I have not a book. Not yet. I will. As if it mattered! Except, of course to me – more than I can say.

I've felt a bit tired lately, so I've been thinking what a lucky woman I am to have a refuge – for a while. This is a village to end all villages. There are nice people called *Greenslade* and *Gosling* and *Betty Stennyford* but there are some nasty ones too and the grape vine works. If I say dam everybody knows in half an hour! – They are really too respectable to live, also very muddled I think – I mean they never say either *yes* or *no*. Never. Because they haven't made up their minds and won't. One thing is certain – I ought not to have touched that barbed wire clothes line. – The answer isn't lies but silence. I do agree the English are very good at that. But what is behind the silence? Suppose – dreadful thought – there is Nothing – . Surely that isn't so?

While I was "resting" I decided never to fuss again. Not about *anything*. Yet here I am fuss, fuss, fuss.

Here is a poem about Cheriton Fitz – It stopped me from weeping. There are no hills or water nearby – and the sheep are cows. I have many short stories in my head complete with titles. It worries me that I can't find a title for book. I usually do – at once. It is too confused – Emancipation of slaves (so white black and coloured), Loneliness, madness, Common sense, Love of Money, Hypocrisy, Loveliness of my island. Poverty. I've gone at all these – Very confused. Confused voices –

Yet I feel I will do it – By that time I will be completely forgotten by everyone, and a good thing too. Sincerely yours
Jean Rhys

This outburst has helped me – but there won't be any more. I can be silent too, and behave nicely though *that's* a strain.

Titles matter to me –
Titles

        The Bishop and the nun (I want to do that one.)
        Pioneers, oh Pioneers – written
        The kind gentleman.
        All Souls.

        But these are unwanted short stories
        As for book I can only think of

        Marie Galante
        Sargasso Sea (The Wide) Crossing Across?
        The Image
        The? Question and the ? Answer ?

Nothing is what I want –
Is "All Souls" the best. *Perhaps.*
What a conceited and tiresome letter. It's "resting" does it. Or reproaches.

A field where sheep are feeding
        The silent field powdered with moonlight,
           And the low hills
        The low, meek unaspiring hills.
           And the tall trees
             The tall proud dark trees
                Leaning down to shallow water
                Looking into shallow water.

                                      J.R.
A bit like Hiawatha – not?
Still shallow water is right. Or is it deep water? "Shallow water" title but not
for book. Not mine anyway.

TO MARYVONNE MOERMAN   *September 17th [1961]*
                                        Cheriton Fitz Paine

                      [. . . . . .]

My Dear Maryvonne,
    I hope you had a good holiday and are not worrying about the old bomb. I
do not feel it will drop – except by accident. It sounds conceited, but I do feel
that human beings are *so* stupid that this may happen.
    I heard from John, which was a great joy and have answered him. Max is not
so well tonight so I must go and sit with him. He gets so down.
    There is a lovely red flower from the garden in the room – *such* a colour a
pinky-red. Not to be believed it is so beautiful.

I hope and hope all the time for even three weeks clear I could nearly finish my book. But three weeks peace is perhaps too much to ask. Hi-de-ho!

I *wish* people had not got rid of God – they seem to be getting along badly by themselves! All my love to you all. A big hug. Special howdy to Ruthie

from yr loving
MA

TO FRANCIS WYNDHAM

October 11th [1961]
Cheriton Fitz Paine

Dear Mr Wyndham,

Every week I have hoped to send you a chapter or more of that book – if you remember it – or me. *But*. Well, but –

My husband has been rather ill and I have been weary – just flat out tired – so make mistakes.

Last week end my brother-in-law, Alec Hamer, spent a few days with us, and as he has seen the MSS and heard some of it, it might be a good idea if he saw you I thought. He is nice and made us laugh – so unusual these days!

I hope you agree that it's a good thought – and not a tiresome one.

I haven't heard from the "London" so I suppose Mr Ross changed his mind about the story. I'm sorry of course, but understand it *might* sound phoney or too long or something. I did hear from Geoffrey Grigson's publishers Rainbird etc and signed a document about a few quotations.

I have not written to thank Mr Grigson – so you see I *have* been weary, but I will do so. It cheered me up a lot. Very much.

Alec thinks the mass of paper a muddle but I know how it goes. He does not understand my lack of method – but it's the way I work – Always.

I am not stale or disheartened only tired and that will pass –

Yours sincerely
Jean Rhys

No poems this time. Sorry about bloody money letter – I was tired. So stupid when you have been so kind, but I've been seeing a lot of the collective face that killed a thousand thoughts lately, and sometimes there is blue murder in my wicked heart.

TO FRANCIS WYNDHAM

October [1961]
Cheriton Fitz Paine

Next time I write an MSS will be be with my letter –
I trust.

I can arrange to cut it if Mr Ross wants
me to and if you feel *more* fuss not needed – well
it's probably so.

Dear Mr Wyndham,

I *was* pleased to hear from you, and it's grand news that the London still thinks of publishing – I'd given it up! *If* Mr Ross can pay me in advance it will be a help of course – and very cheering.

I enclose what I think should be the start of the story. As it is really about a girl who is hauled to jail not knowing why, and comes out of jail still bewildered – perhaps that note should be sounded at once. It's just a twist round of course and will mean deleting the same passage later on. I have a thing about the start of a story or a book. *Terribly* important to me. Perhaps. Certainly! I fuss about it. I have three starts to the novel, two really, I've scrapped one –

I will try to send you something very soon but it will be part of a jig saw puzzle remember. When the first part is typed I will send that. It's written but not legible.

I have written to Alec and asked him to ring you soon. I would be v glad if you met. 27 Cornwall Gardens sw7 will find him. FRO 1328.

Sincerely
Jean Rhys

I did not send this before, as I thought story was too long or unsatisfactory in some way.

> *They thought it was Jazz*
> Holloway Song?
> SELINA

I think "Selina"
a better title
than Jazz. Or not?

When they arrest me and take me to jail, I was living in the downstairs flat of a three-storey house, all tumble down and damp, pretty if you don't go too close. Red and blue flowers mix up with weeds in the garden, and there were five – six apple trees. The first drop and lie in the grass – so sour nobody want it.

I hear the place very old. It take up too much room, so it's going to be pulled down and destroyed. Meantime it make all the other houses that street look cheap trash – especially at night and I go there because I have trouble with my Notting Hill landlord when he want me to pay a month rent in advance. He tell me this on a bright Sunday morning in July after I *etc*

TO FRANCIS WYNDHAM   *October 17th [1961]*
                                     Cheriton Fitz Paine
Dear Mr Wyndham,

Of course you are quite right, I haven't a whole copy of the story – (in spite of my boast that I had fifteen or something!) only a quantity of bits and pieces. I thought of the other start going over it in my head (as I often do) but am pretty sure that if I reread it I would agree with what you say. So – no more of *that* idea.

[. . . . . .]

My husband's illness has strained me up rather, but I do feel that with a little will power and so on I'll be able to manage to fix the book up, write it legibly and sooner than you'd believe.

I've got some wonderful pep pills – unfortunately whenever I take one *something happens*.

Yesterday I was all set when a kind neighbour brought me masses of flowers. Instead of dumping them in the bath, I started arranging them. Fatal! All the pep had gone when I had finished trying to show them off. They looked very lovely but I felt finished. (But they *were* lovely)

Today, another pill, another neighbour who spent hours telling me about a TV writer who has settled in Cheriton Fitz and is going mad with worry because his play or whatever has stuck.

As he has a devoted wife who does all the chores, and *creeps* in with cups of coffee when he groans I could not pity him – (Gossip)

In case you don't meet Alec soon – My husband has been ill now for four years – all the same I have got the book done –

As to this cutting, starts, doubts and so on – well that began years and years ago in Paris and I will never lose it now (and I shall never be sure whether it was a good thing or not).

Good for me – but enough to drive everybody else crazy – I know.

"Petronella" started as a 50000 word novel – so did some of the other stories, the best part of Voyage in the Dark was cut. And so on.

But it will be done trust me. I will send the various Chapter I's and you will judge. I guess it'll go pretty quickly after that.   Sincerely yours
    Jean Rhys

TO FRANCIS WYNDHAM   *[1961]*
                                  Cheriton Fitz Paine

[. . . . . .]

Dear Mr Wyndham,

I heard from Alec this morning and am glad you met. I expect he talked a bit about my difficulties (and advantages). Peace etc. Though it's not as peaceful as all that. No, I never thought you were annoyed, but I did fear you were disappointed. For I am. That novel ought to have been finished long ago! But my husband's illness has slowed me up (and other obstacles) so I feel that excuses bore people. Perhaps I could have been more adroit but don't quite see how. Am not adroit!

Never mind. Endurance is needed now smoothing it out and so on. That is all. I've some wonderful pep pills – they may do the trick though I feel very rum, *extraordinary* next day if I take more than two. Drink *much* safer in my opinion. But no drink, or rarely.

I will post you a sample chapter tomorrow. Post Office shut today. That gives me this evening to look it over and add synopsis and remarks, or you will not know what it's all about. I'll make that short.

Part I is going to be typed by a Devon typist – very good I hear and used to strange thoughts but if she is busy or whatever I'll get it back and send it faults and all. You are so kind to bother about it – or me.

As to the title. It still worries me. I thought of *"I hear voices"* before it was grabbed. Also *"Dream"* which I hanker after still. They say the Sargasso Sea is full of eels but who cares? Another I want has bats. It's part of a set of Dominica poems which I wrote years ago – and *sold!* A Dutch magazine took them. *Poems again.*

> At sunset the hills are purple.
> Purple against red.
> One by one the bats fly.
> Blind Black Wings spread.

Purple against Red I thought. (Not Bats though I've got them in too. It is an odd sight.) But the colours are not right for this book. A colour? – "Le Rouge et le noir". Gone.

I took two pills yesterday, so this is next day. As perhaps you have guessed.

Now I will reread, but not I hope rewrite that chapter – explanations and so on.

It would help me of course, the "London" advance. But I know how difficult all that is, and not very wise perhaps.

So if you think not – then not. I have so much to thank you for already.

Yours sincerely

Jean Rhys

PS. I have a dread of seeing something not right in cold type. Can you understand?

I don't see any new books and know nothing of the new writers. The Crediton library is not good. Tiverton book shops are far away and expensive.

But I have a list of all I will get one of these days – then I'll be happy for ever and ever.

TO MARYVONNE MOERMAN

Saturday November 6th, 1961
Cheriton Fitz Paine

My dear Maryvonne,

I had your letter this morning, which seems years ago already. Yes, I feel very sad, but you are right. John did not like sadness, and it is useless to speak of it.

He counted for so much in my life. (I told him so when I wrote). Now there is you and Ruthie and that is nearly all. But that is a lot.

I have not been so well – nothing much and all right now, but it's cold and damp here and 'flu can hang on for days – or I would have answered your last letter long ago. If I do not write often it's because my life is a struggle, and it is my strong feeling to keep you away from that. I know how brave you are, but there have been great strains on you. I wish to bring hope and be of some use – that may happen. It's just a matter of stubborn work now for I still have some well wishers.

So my darling, as I will call you for this once, I send you my love and all my thoughts. I believe as you do – no one dies if they are remembered and I will always remember. I go one step on and say – No one dies.

I am very glad that John's wife is so nice – please remember me to her. She must be sad too –

I will write soon again – meanwhile here is a quotation I like. "But trust me, gentleman, I'll prove more true than those that have more cunning to be strange". It is from Romeo and Juliet. Well, trust me anyway.

Your loving mother

Jean

I do remember Kikimora[1] – it was sinister – even the word is. You were a bit afraid of it, I knew. But I did not know so much. Oh these fears – so many! Do not be sad. There is hope too. More than one believes. I will try and get a wire to you. Posts are erratic in this far away place.

1. *A cat belonging to Jean and Leslie in the 1930s, described by Jean in a story of that name collected in "Sleep It Off, Lady".*

TO MARYVONNE MOERMAN   *Thursday December 28th [1961]*

Cheriton Fitz Paine

My dear Maryvonne,

I was so glad to hear from you my dear. You must forgive me for a lousy letter instead of flowers or even Christmas cards. I have had 'flu rather badly, and as the nearest shops are miles away there was nothing to be done.

I am better now, or nearly, and Max, who has been in hospital for rest and a check up, is home again. I bought a bright red dress to celebrate – at Exeter – a cheap Christmas cracker dress, and, do you know although I've never worn it (as it is too cold) – the entire village knows.

I think they must be witches and warlocks. The dress is hanging in my wardrobe unseen and yet they gossip – "That Mrs Hamer bought a *red dress!*" So you will see the sort of place it is.

A bit sinister really – for it is very cold and it gets dark early. One meets dark figures in the road – and frost and ice are everywhere.

As you may know all the waterpipes are outside in England and any minute may burst. What can I do but stay calm and watch the flood?

The nearest plumber is miles away and would not leave his warm fire and turkey anyway!

I tried to chip away a bit of the ice but it is frozen solid all the way up! I mean to be a fatalist from now on. Perhaps I always have been really.

But you and Ruthie are different. Do not be sad honey – all will be well. It is nice in the spring and there is a spare room and I would so *love* to see you. Yes Edward often comes – if you can manage a visit I will talk it over with him, for I want it to be a real change and a not-so-bad time and that will be managed – Believe me –

Forgive a shaky letter for I'm not yet quite well, but though I have been very down about my book – as if it had no meaning – it has come to life again. (Hurray!) Also a Mrs Morris Brown who lives near by is going to type a bit for me, from dictation she says! It is so corrected and rewritten that no typist could make it out.

The title is

(Across the?) Wide Sargasso Sea. Not good?? and it is a romantic novel about the West Indies in 1840 – a bit difficult for me – Yet but for Max's long illness I could have done it – And will now. I will.

But it has been a bit tough really. If only I can – there will be a little cash.

My first dream is to see you both. My second to choose a suit when you are with me – for you're so good at clothes. You looked charming in Bude I thought.

Why don't you skate too?

Do not let anybody get you down *not ever. Never! Never.*

I can guess how you miss John – I can guess –

I will wait for more definite news about the spring. Meanwhile do not worry about Ruthie's mathematics and so on. What does it matter if she is a musician?

I have an awful pen-pencil and a muzzy head.

But all my love to you all. For you my best hug like a bear and for Ruthie a big kiss.

Happy New Year to Maryvonne Ruthie and Job.   from

Jean   Till soon.

[. . . . . .]

TO MARYVONNE MOERMAN   *March 4th [1962]*
                                              Cheriton Fitz Paine

My dear Maryvonne,

I was so glad to hear from you. It has been an *awful* winter from Siberia and still is as cold as ever. At Christmas (did I tell you) some tiles blew off the roof and the wind whistled through the place. I caught a bad chill which has been with me ever since – well, off and on. I wrote you a long description of my aches and pains so boring that I did not send it.

But though it's still cold it is not so wintry today – a few leaves and a bit of hope. It is so lovely to think that you may come over and I must tell you about this place. It is a small village very isolated – the bungalow is not bad *inside* and there is one tiny spare room – but outside is perhaps a bit dreary (less so when the flowers come out). So if you bring Ruthie perhaps the best idea would be for you to stay at *Crediton* which is only about a quarter of an hour (or less) away (by taxi and not expensive). There's a bus, but it runs in a haphazard way. Crediton not a bad country town.

You don't know how pleased I will be to see you and Ruthie with the long hair – *Pleased!!*

I feel I have been here for years, toiling away at my book – it's like pulling a cart up a very steep hill. Still I think I will do it. For one part is nearly finished and can be sent off. Then I'll know if it is any good –

Perhaps romantic novels of the 1840's are more difficult for me and God knows if I've managed it at all. Still I've sold another story that will be a bit more for what I call "my runaway money" –

I will not, or cannot, run away really. Still it's nice to know I could have one last wild dash for 2 weeks – or three. I have the most fantastic ideas about those three weeks.

Nothing happens and every day is the same and goes quickly. Still I feel I've been here for years and centuries. Even this winter dates from the dark ages.

Max is a bit better. He often talks of you and her violin and her dancing. It will be a great lift up for him to have you to look at.

Edward comes over sometimes – he too is tired of the cold. I am sure he would love to see you. He had a letter from Ruthie he said. He's got a car of course which is a blessing.

Well I won't talk about it any more now. But Crediton is not a bad area. It's close to Exeter and so on – and the Devon one thinks about.

I am very sleepy as you can guess by this erratic letter. I exist on pep pills the doctor gave me, and though they do give a bit of energy to start with, there's a sudden let down after some hours.

Goodnight then honey love to all of you and a big kiss and hug for you and for Ruthie too.

Let me know how plans work out. With more love

Jean

One nice thing here – the birds. I spend a lot of time giving them crumbs and they expect this meal now. The pretty little ones are very shy (yellow and blue black) so the sparrows grab everything while they hesitate and flutter about.

PS. The pub here *may* let rooms. I don't think so but I will ask. Crediton or Tiverton both boast hotels and things.

I have been reading a book about Indonesia called "The Net of Gold". It is so very unlike what you wrote me that it must be a complete fake.

Besides it is enormously long with dozens of characters all made of cardboard – the sort of book most people like and I detest. Still, I read it because it was about Indonesia.

[. . . . . .]

My dear Maryvonne,

I was delighted to get your letter. *Come Of course* and I'm longing to see you and Ellen. Well now – about sleeping arrangements. There is this tiny room with fairly comfortable bed for one. *But*, there is the sitting room. So if you bring your sleeping bag and mattress there is ample room for that.

You can decide when you come who will have what and just where.

One side of the sitting room can be cleared in the evening easily. It is not crowded with furniture and fairly pleasant. You know – this is a very cottagey cottage and small. I have grown to like it, but did have a few shocks at first. Edward has made it very nice inside, but let outside go hang, like they say wealthy Eastern people do. The gate especially is on its dam last legs (hinges) and a bit grim. However last time he came he *measured* it so I have hopes. In fine weather it can look awfully nice I think, but you know what weather is like here. One never knows! We had some lovely days in June though cold at night and I wished you were here. (That reminds me – I have very few blankets, so any rugs etc will be a blessing. I will also try to borrow a couple from E.)

I was a bit concerned about the camping idea because – remember how it *poured* in the punt and so on, when least expected?

I'll be sorry not to see Job – give him my love and it's for one of these days I do hope. England, at least Devon and Cornwall, can be beautiful sometimes, but oh my God the prices! Don't speak of them.

There is just one thing – Max, as you know, is not well and has not been well for a long time. He cheers up wonderfully sometimes and I know seeing you both will do that. But! Don't let that make you sad. Ever. I think you will rest here. When Max was in hospital I had a lovely rest.

Got up very early (*what* a change!) because the morning is the best. But he got bored and unhappy and wanted to come home, so my holiday was cut a bit short.

It is quite frankly dull or might be if you want excitement – "life on muted strings" as they say. But you may like it that way for a while and Exeter, Tiverton and Crediton are all within reach – Exeter with shops and cinemas – the other two for *junk* shops. I bought some old Victorian glass there for 6d *sixpence* a piece – just about my price. Perhaps it is hideous but it glitters in the sun (when any) and I like it. Max says he does too.

The junk shops may be fun and a happy hunting ground. As it is not touristy at Crediton you might spot a real bargain – who knows?

That is all I think except love and kisses and longing to see you – This is a rum place but certainly restful and there is quite a big garden, overlooked by neighbours on one side – but in the evenings mostly.

There's a huge bed all ready for flowers but I've not had much luck with seeds I planted. I wanted heaps of poppies – but no. Not one came up. I like to garden, I like the smell of earth and grass and if you do, or Ellen does – well that'll be fine too. Perhaps you have "green fingers" as they call it here. I haven't I think.

That's all for now as the BBC says except love again from

Jean

Saturday July 22nd [1962]
                                                       Cheriton Fitz Paine

Dear Mr Wyndham,

   [. . . . . .]

   I finished Part I yesterday – I had a free day for once – but cannot send it off till Tuesday as the village Post Office shuts on Mondays and I wish to register the envelope. I've a copy of the typescript, but not a clear copy of the rest – though I've written it often enough, God knows.

   I am glad to have the extra day – Won't make excuses about the MSS (state of) but do want it to be legible and clear. There are some notes attached to each chapter (3) difficulties and so on – *Short.*

   One thing I have never told you. I wrote this book before! – Different setting – same idea. (It was called "Le revenant" then). The MSS was lost when I was moving from somewhere to somewhere else and I wonder whether I haven't been trying to get back to what I did. (An impossible effort). Perhaps that has added to all the other difficulties.

   It was a sad affair, for a lot of stories disappeared too – and an unfinished novel "Wedding in the Carib Quarter".

   I tried to rewrite "Le Revenant" but could not – another title would have been found – however I discovered two chapters (in another suitcase) and have used them in this book. You will see perhaps.

   As for "Wedding in the Carib Quarter" it disappeared *completely.* I found some notes on it the other day, and they made no sense at all any more. A pity.

   I was a bit sad. But "Le Revenant" came to life *or back* again (in a way) when I met Selma and was talking to her.

   The first one was easier to do and perhaps more banal, but I was very excited about it and desperate when it got lost. All this was long ago. I was writing quickly then – far better circumstances.

   It is so kind of Alec to try to arrange a visit to London. I'd like to come very much and think it can be arranged in the autumn.

   Thank you for looking at MSS Part I, Part II unrevised, but typed will follow. It will be such a shot in the arm if you like it at all or even parts of it.

   I'm looking forward to London already – have been here such ages – and really it has rained most of the time. I am pretty certain I can fix it up (touch wood) and I will write to Alec this week.   Yours sincerely

Jean Rhys

August 22nd [1962]
Cheriton Fitz Paine

[. . . . . .]

Dear Mr Wyndham,

[. . . . . .]

I'm sending you Parts I and II of that heartbreaking novel – heartbreaking because I'm so near to getting it, yet – not quite. You'll find it confused perhaps, and certainly the handwriting is terrible for most of it was copied out late at night. Not my best time.

The typed (and heavily corrected) part is the most important – it's the story of an old West Indian house burned down by the negroes who hate the ex-slave owning family living there. The time 1839, the white Creole girl aged about 14 is the "I".

I did this fairly quickly so was optimistic. The trouble started when I realised that the place, the time, and the characters would be all quite unreal unless I "explained" them a bit. I've tried and tried and this is all I can do at present – for I'm pretty sure that if you "see" it with all its faults that'll be *such* a shot in the arm it will be done.

The first "start", marked with red pencil is more convincing but slower. I just don't know any more. I've numbered the pages from 1st start.

As the "fire" ends with girl being knocked on the head by her one time black pal, I must bring her to life again. This short chapter is not included. I will send it soon. I mean soon. The two other "chapters" carry her up to her unfortunate marriage.

They can be cut from Part I, they are sketched in.

Part II is typed and *unrevised*. Here the husband Mr Rochester?? takes on and describes his startling honeymoon. He decides that his wife is as mad as – well mad – and eventually hauls her off to England and locks her up. I've tried to make this more convincing than it is in "Jane Eyre".

In fact – well that'll come later – anyway she must die young, not old. She is not Jane Eyre's lunatic at all.

A lot that seems incredible is true, the obeah for example, the black girl's attack. I've stuck because it should have been a dream truth and I've tried to make it a realistic truth.

Anyway here it is and I'll stop about this dream book which has often been a nightmare to me. You bet.

[. . . . . .]   Sincerely yours and again thanks
                                            Jean Rhys

August or September [1962]

[. . . . . .]

Dear Mr Wyndham,

This is much too long of course. Everything or anything can be cut except the few things I've got right.

[. . . . . .]

Read it when you wish and have time. So kind of you. I have a copy of the typescript of Part II *Not the hand written bit* and can work on that and last two chapters of Part II.

Part III, the end, is short and will follow. Careless writing because I *must* get this off. Repeats sometimes I was "trying out". Part II hasn't been revised at all.

I shall be longing to hear if you think anything right in it. Perhaps you're away but if registered will surely get to you some time.   Sincerely
                                                                     Jean Rhys

P.S. Oh, "Jumby" is of course a corruption of zombie used in English islands and that's what I feel like!

TO FRANCIS WYNDHAM   *Wednesday September 12th [1962]*
                                       Cheriton Fitz Paine

> I also see all the faults and can correct
> some of these anyway I hope.
>   Part II bristles with the things.
> I nearly didn't send it. However you know
> the worst now!

Dear Mr Wyndham,

I can't tell you how much good your letter has done better than bottle after bottle of champagne. I "see" this long delayed book at last and will have the courage to finish it, I trust. Touch wood.

I won't thank you any more for I'm sure that you know how I feel – but will go straight on about *"Before I was set free"* – which is my name for it, whatever its other name may be.

The difficulty all along was this. I stuck, not at the end (as usual) but at the start. After about six toilsome efforts I only got a possible first chapter when I was writing it out (so badly) to send to you. Some of the "wrong" start must be inserted (I marked where with red pencil, but I remember anyway.) Like the death or poisoning of their only horse for that would isolate them completely. And so on – Part I will end of course as you suggest.

Part II is the real difficulty. I felt the man must tell the story of their "honeymoon". Not the girl.

While I was struggling with this, some people near by offered to type it.

What with my nervousness and reluctance and the awful noise of bookshelf making it did become a muddle. When they started suggesting this and that – I just ran away *(as usual!)* But it did get me down and it was some time before I could try again – I am awfully grateful tho' for it'll be easier to revise.

Here is what will help me most – if not too much trouble. I will handwrite the last two chapters of Part II and send them and I'll know then whether I've got it over at all.

This book should have been a dream – not a drama – I know. Still I want to make the drama *possible,* convincing.

The West Indies *had* a (melo?) dramatic quality. A lot that seems incredible could have happened. And did. Girls *were* married for their dots at that time, taken to England and no more heard of. Houses were burnt down by ex slaves, some servants *did* stick – especially children's nurses. I don't know if "obeah" still goes on. But it did. And voodoo certainly does – Also anonymous letters – and still come tragedies. I know of two cases. Only a few years ago. The boy involved shot himself, the girl just died (in two weeks and for no reason but sadness).

I can't imagine why I'm going on with all this. Forgive the rambling.

I am so glad that you liked "Interlude". It was one of the "bits" that was nearly right and could have been sent any time but I didn't think that would be a fair test. Its place, of course, is *after* the husband has had the anonymous letter, believes it and retires to brood over it without a word of explanation.

I know the letter must be short. Daniel speaks, Mr R listens when they meet.

The whole of Part II needs revising of course and can be cut by half. But to get back to questions.

Is the "Tea" episode too long in Part I? Could Mr R's contribution be a diary, a letter, or something written and dated long afterwards to exorcise a troublesome memory – the last I think.

Is my bit of "fine writing" at the start of Part II awful? I fear so. It can be cut with no loss. I wanted to alter the feeling completely.

The timing is wrong. I can fix it. Other things also. Please answer this whenever you wish or feel like it. I have a lot of writing to do and not so much time as you'd think. I do it at night now but look a bit haggard afterwards. Alec says Think of Dame Edith Sitwell and don't worry. But what cold comfort! Besides I'm not a Plantagenet (or is it Tudor?) and I loathe Henry VIII.

I will send along last two chapters of Part II. Then Part III which is madness and a dream and happiness in England. Then the book will be solidly *there* to be altered and pulled about afterwards.

This is what would help me most. Again, please answer this when you wish or when Part II's last chapters arrive, and thank you for so much.

Sincerely yours
Jean Rhys

14th
It should have been *all* a dream I know with start and finish present day. Or not?

[. . . . . .]

November 24th [1962]
                                                         Cheriton Fitz Paine

> *Please* don't trouble to send anything back. I have
> copies. Tear it up sooner.

Dear Mr Wyndham,

I've been away – trying to get rid of persistent 'flu. I did write to thank you for the typescript but, such a dismal letter. So tore it up.

This place can be very dark in November – dark and damp – and the doctor wants me to go to hospital for a while. I'll be made as good as new he says but I'm trying to stave that off. I hate hospitals – or imagine I do.

I've worried a lot about that book – it is so bad in parts, isn't it? It may come right quite suddenly though. At present it wants rethinking rewriting and all – especially Part II – *very* bad.

I wish I had not sent you something unfinished – better finish it first and hate it afterwards –

Poor thing! – I'm leaving it alone for a bit – but it does not leave me.

Meanwhile I've had some cheerful letters – a Budapest magazine wants the "Jazz" story – only there is such a lot of letter writing and "royalties in advance" and *taxes* here and there. Such taxes!! However it will be fine if it does get published – in Nagyvitag – which I spell wrong each time. Hungarian is an awful language – I remember – nobody can learn it or hardly. Nobody even *tried*. But everybody spoke French or English then. Harpers wrote about that story too. Nothing definite, and I did not answer – have not answered yet, I mean. It's disgraceful I know.

Mr Ross has asked me to do a piece about "Leaving School", one of a series. I said I would as quickly as possible and hope I can manage that. I swallow such quantities of bright red pills – but am still very tired. If I could *rest* in that hospital I'd love it. But no – that isn't the idea at all it seems.

Well now there was another letter from Chapman & Hall who would like to see the MSS when it's ready. I answered that I was under contract to Mr Deutsch but that if he did not care for the book – etc – I wonder if Mr Deutsch ever thinks of me except a stray curse or so but I think often about unearned advance. Unless I can do this book *a little* as I want to I don't want anybody (any publisher) to see it at all. I'd rather scrap it. Maybe the end redeems it.

[. . . . .]

This is written on *vodka* – I always knew it was a down the hatch drink – but as nasty as this is – no I don't remember that. (Meth probably.) I'm going to give myself a present of some Pernod and see what happens then. I do not want to send you Part III handwritten. So wearying. I *must* find a typist – I expect you are weary of that book anyway.   Sincerely yours

                                                         Jean Rhys

Alec has not been so well so I've had to postpone coming to London. I was looking forward to it, and I'm sorry.

March 23rd [1963]
Cheriton Fitz Paine

My Dear Maryvonne,

I was so glad to get your letter my dear – and am answering at once.

This has been a *horrible* month here – even the local people got depressed – and as they *like* rain and cold it shows the weather must have been something quite special – today there is a faint weak sun but *very* weak. Poor darling Ruthie! But tell her from me that to be nervous is a *good* sign. All the best ones are very nervous before hand. It is when one is not nervous that the trouble starts.

I've told her so myself in this enclosed letter.

But I'll tell you a true story. You know that years and years ago I was on the stage. Well in one show (London) there was a comedian, very popular, and very funny so I used to stand in the wings to watch him. It was Christmas and bitterly cold (*no* heating then) and he wore a football get up because his turn was a football skit. Well, that man used to sweat with nerves – every night! It *streamed* down his face and froze on the way nearly. Yet as soon as he bounced on the stage it was okay and no one would have guessed a thing.

That is what Ruthie will find, and it's a true story. Nearly everybody has stage fright.

I must rush out, post this and buy something to eat. The weather got me down a bit so I decided to hand write the final version of book. I get letters from London telling me to hurry up. No one will believe that I *can't* get a typist here, or indeed anything except bananas, ersatz coffee and so on. I tried Tiverton and Crediton too – no use. (They also seem to imagine I have a car! There's no bus even.)

I'm a bit afraid that I shall be so pleased to have a holiday from dear old Cheriton Fitz, that I'll dictate badly which will not do at all. So better finish first.

I hope that when I write next I'll have some good news for you.

The tax business is awful here too and not very fair I think.

On top of all else the electric people have gone on strike – Oh dear! and oh dam! –

Max was a little better when I saw him last and I've all sorts of plans. The primroses are trying to come out, but between the cold and the cat sitting on them are having a bad time. But they are very obstinate (like me). So I hope to have some. Also a few daffoldils.

My best love and a big hug also a kiss or so.

Jean

March 23rd
My Very Dear Ruthie,

This is to wish you luck. *Everybody* is nervous darling, and the better they are – the more nervous as a rule. It's just one of those things that can't be helped.

I *know* that you will play beautifully and I wish I could hear you!

But one day I will – I'm pretty sure of that.

I'd send you a lucky charm if I had one but I've only got a large old horseshoe very shabby and too heavy to post. You should see it!

So my love and best wishes instead. *Don't worry* – you'll be all right and more than all right.

Your loving
Ooma

Forget people – think only of the music.

TO FRANCIS WYNDHAM

Sunday [May 1963]
Cheriton Fitz Paine

[. . . . . .]

Dear Mr Wyndham,

Miss Athill's letter cheered me so much and I'm glad you gave her the MSS I managed to send you.

Part II and III are written. It is finished, tho it needs revision, but handwritten and barely legible – if that.

(I believe I know how to cut and fix up Part II which is not right at all and I'll tell you about that. Part III, the End, I will not alter much.) [. . . . . .] It is so tiresome and sounds very incapable and of course I ought to be able to type. *But you do not know Cheriton Fitz Paine or maybe you'd excuse me a bit.* I came here full of optimism (as usual) thinking it would be easy to find a typist, revise then send the MSS to you. But there are no typists, only flat fields and cows. Crediton is the same, so is Tiverton, both miles and miles away. Exeter bristles with difficulties. I say A typist, a stenographer, and they say At Cheriton Fitz Paine? Oh dear, such an out of the way place is it not? I got discouraged after a while.

Then Mrs Morris Brown who's only four miles off but uphill, offered to help me out. She typed the chapters I sent you. Then she went away, but if she's back I'll ask her if she'd be a good Samaritan again and maybe she will. There is not so much left to do.

I tried to copy out Part III anyway and send it to you, but I've not been well – and my handwriting was very odd.

I'm a lot better now and full of hope. And the MSS will arrive somehow *believe me.* If you blame me think hard about Cheriton Fitz. Alec calls it the Slough of Despond. Really it's not so bad. There's a lilac tree outside my window, but it does make one feel a bit vague and out of this world which I am anyway. (I don't mean out of this world in a nice way, I mean out of this world in a cowlike way. A cow with flu and bad dreams.)

Really I've been very worried. Much better now. The Buda Pest magazines wrote again. It seems that they went to the *British Embassy* to find out who I was and what.

I did laugh. All those blank astonished faces! But really isn't it a strange thing to do? I sent them something I cut out of the jacket of Winters Tales and hope they believe I exist, am harmless, and non political in the extreme.

But am not too hopeful. They sound so inquisitive and suspicious. I do wonder why? They wrote a lot last year.

You know so many people think I don't exist that sometimes I ask myself if I do. But that's just a 'flu hangover.

Thank you. It's so little to say but thank you. Now I'll write to Pond Cottage (Mrs Brown) and anyway my handwriting is not so shaky now is it?

Sincerely
Jean Rhys

May 23rd [1963]
Cheriton Fitz Paine

Dear Miss Athill,

Thank you so much for your understanding letter. I wish I could bundle all the rest up and send it to you – that could have been done ages ago. The trouble is that I do not think – indeed I'm quite sure, that any typist could make head or tail of it. It's written in two exercise books and what with jumping from page 3 to page 44 (last paragraph) then to exercise book No. 2 pages 6, 7 and 29, to say nothing of scraps of paper, well talk about exhausting – it would be *curseworthy* and impossible.

I can read it, or dictate it because I know how it goes, but I'm quite sure nobody else could.

I simply can't explain how it got so untidy. But it did. [. . . . . .] Now I am trying to get in touch with elusive Mrs Brown and if I can all will be well. She lives some way off (Mr Brown aussi of course) and they go away pretty often. Also I think (fear) I have shocked Mr Brown – that very tame love affair with the coloured girl.

He started pacing up and down, and banging doors and finally made a bookshelf – it was really a tense afternoon. Or maybe it all got on his nerves because *he's* writing a thing – about Jesus Christ (I gather). And you know
. . . .

Poor man! *I* know how he felt. But, after all he needn't have listened.

I may be all wrong of course. Anyway I will pocket any pride I have left and write to Mrs Brown *(now)* and ask her if she can finish the chapters that are left. [. . . . . .]

If she is away or anything I can only write in longhand and send it as I write. It will go quickly I hope for the awful frustration which has worn me to a frazzle is so much better since you wrote.

[. . . . . .]

Perhaps I ought to delete all that about Mr Brown who is a very nice man. Delete and forget. He made us endless cups of tea till that fatal afternoon and I think he's built a little garden house for himself which is splendid news (tea afterwards not during). [. . . . . .]

I do so feel that I am exhausting everybody. The only thing is that I've exhausted myself too – from rage to despair and back again. But so much better now and almost sensible. If I need any money I will tell you and thank you so much but a legible script essential I feel. Thanks again and you do cheer me up.

Sincerely
Jean Rhys

TO DIANA ATHILL
June 5th [1963]
Cheriton Fitz Paine

Dear Miss Athill,

What a very good idea – and it's so kind of you – and of Mrs Whitby[1]. The problem would be solved that way of course.

I'm seeing Mrs Brown tomorrow, and will find out how much time she can spare me. She's very nice really and so is her husband. I was only joking about him – not too cleverly I fear. But of course after the wretched winter they like leaving Cheriton Fitz quite often – and then there are friends visiting – and so on.

About this cottage – there is a small spare bedroom but it got a bit damaged during the deluge and I've not got around to putting it quite right yet. However I think I can make Mrs Whitby fairly comfortable for a few days. [. . . . . .]

I will write to you when I've talked to Mrs Brown. I am so much looking forward to seeing Mrs Whitby. It'll be so very cheering.

Yours sincerely
Jean Rhys

P.S. I forgot to say that if all goes well and the rest of the book is in type I shall want to revise it. (I'm sure you've guessed that.) It may seem confused and confusing but I'm pretty sure I can get it smooth – and fairly quickly.

Even Part II which is the least convincing – I feel.

It's very strange but the obeah which is quite authentic doesn't sound authentic. A girl of that age and of that time (later too) *would* rush off to her nurse for a love drink or spell of some sort – (Or easily might.) These drinks *do* make people or some people very sick and an Englishman might think it was an attempt to poison him – (Almost certainly would I should say.) Yet I have not made it sound true. Never mind I can fix it, and I'll tell you and Mr Wyndham how.

J.R.

1. *Esther Whitby, an editor at André Deutsch, had volunteered to help Jean put her material in order.*

June 18th [1963]
                                        Cheriton Fitz Paine

My dear Maryvonne,

I think it's time to let you know my news. As usual, some of it is good, some not so good. The publishers, André Deutsch have seen the typed part of my novel and are anxious to get the rest. They'll then give me an advance – as they like it.

One of the partners, Diana Athill, suggests sending down a stenographer – oh God if that could happen! Such a big leap forward! She will only stay three days and have it all done in shorthand.

The not so good news is that Max is again in hospital. He simply *hates* it there and wants to come home. (I saw him today and he's getting in an awful state.) I begged him not to go to hospital for I knew what would happen (it has happened three times after all!). I also told the doctor that I didn't approve at all. Useless!

So now I must think up some way of getting him back. Oh lord! *If only they'd let us alone.* Poor Max – they won't let him smoke, the nurses aren't very nice. He just lies there fretting. I did all I could to stop this, but the doctor (and Max) opposed me and what could I do? Now there's this *darned* situation!

I have often – these last weeks – thought of asking you to come over and decided that I did not want to mix you up with worrying. When and if you come – middle July, end July? August? September? I want it to be a holiday – not trouble.

I'm longing to see you. This stenographer, or editor, will only be here three days – about July 10th or so. How I hope and pray she will come.

We had a few fine days – everybody grumbled at the heat(!!) now it is rainy windy and cold again they're all delighted.

Not me though.

Give my love to Job and to Ruthie and *so* much for you. A big hug too. Don't sew too much – or if you do, make yourself a pretty dress and wear it to cheer me up for I'm darned tired sometimes. Anyway "And so to bed" –

                                        Yours always
                                        Jean also "Ooma"

June 24th [1963]
                                        Cheriton Fitz Paine

Selma my Dear,

What grand news and I'm so very glad. It's been an awful uphill business – you can't imagine! – I won't write a long letter but only say Yes *please* come. There is a pub here – Ring of Bells where they let rooms. I'll go there tomorrow. Anyhow something can be managed – for sure –

Above all *bring Frederick* (Alec). I'm writing to him about it by this post.
I'm awfully worried about Max. He has been hauled off by the doctor (a not

very trustworthy man) to a hospital in Tiverton – it was arranged when I was out and without my consent – and he is awfully unhappy there. No treatment. No smoking. He just lies there. He writes me every day – frantic letters asking me to get him out and I'm so worried I don't know what to do. Can't work or *think*. Selma if you could see him – it is pitiful – I burst into tears. There is something rotten about it, and judging by his letters he'll collapse altogether unless something isn't done to get him away soon.

I will write to Alec (Frederick) for really it is urgent. Very. Max has been to hospital four times and has never complained. There *must* be something dam wrong about this one –

Your letter and telegram were life savers believe me.

It's just the last hill to climb I hope, then all will be OK. He has been so brave all the time – A long long time isn't it? It's such a rotten shame. The matron and most of the nurses are dreadful he says and they are *beastly*. I saw how they treated him when I was there.

I am a bit battered too, but nothing that can't be put right. Thank you dear Selma

Love
Jean

[. . . . . .]

TO SELMA VAZ DIAS

Tuesday June 25th [1963]
Cheriton Fitz Paine

My dear Selma,

I've been cursing myself ever since I wrote that panicky letter. So stupid –

I went to visit Max today and found him much calmer. He's to see a doctor tomorrow who'll decide what is best – and there's a better atmosphere in the place. But why should I worry you with all this, just when you wired such good news?

It's happened often enough! Only a bit more difficult to bear this time. I also went to the Ring of Bells pub and yes they have rooms, but want to know some time in advance if one is to be reserved. Some days (or maybe two) that means – I should think. Cheriton Fitz is not bad when the sun shines – trees and grass in abundance all green and leafy, you might like it.

Tell Frederick that panic is over, though I'd like to see him *very much indeed* – and give him my love.

As I couldn't settle to work I've been weeding the flower bed, all weeds no flowers – hardly.

Also the cat is sitting on my lap – an adopted cat. She actually had the darned cheek to scratch my face a moment ago. Not a real scratch. She hates not being taken notice of – I do adore cats, but dare not have one in my unsettled existence. Have you ever read "La Chatte" (Colette)?

The worst of my situation is that it sounds a bit incredible, and the best that I haven't said much about it – or is that the stupidest?

223

If I were Ruthless – as they say *Be Ruthless* I'd long ago have insisted on six months to myself and dumped Max anywhere but I could not –

So it's dragged on and on – It'll be lovely seeing you and all will be right on the night.

I have the original version of the end of "Voyage". I had to cut it a good deal when I wrote it and was sad. Haven't looked at it for ages – and maybe they were right – but I was furious at the time.

So now that's the picture.

Love
Jean

There's an old shed here for your car, and a garage at the Ting a Ling. I have one bed – in the sitting room – the divan thing. Spare room was wrecked when the pipes burst last winter – another trying episode. Oh Lord!

Will I be glad to see a friendly face! It rains a lot, so be prepared for that.

TO DIANA ATHILL

Wednesday June 26th [1963]
Cheriton Fitz Paine

Dear Miss Athill,

I've been wondering if you are back from Harrogate. I used to know it ages ago. Also – did I post my last letter? (yes to that) or should I have left the dates to you? From July 3rd to 10th is bad, for I have to go to Exeter several times that week. After the tenth anything goes.

I do hope Mrs Whitby can come – she sounds so nice. Something like that is certainly my best way out or I shall be stuck for ever handwriting and revising.

Yes, of course I know that you are a writer. I have your story "Buried"[1] which I liked, but I've not seen the Observer one. So it's easy to tell you how much I agree – much of Part II reads like cliché. As I planned the book the girl told the story – then my husband was seriously ill, and when I got back to work it seemed better to tell it, Part II, from the man's point of view. I can fix it.

My husband's illness, for he never really recovered, has been the trouble.

Down here at Cheriton Fitz it's been very trying indeed, for they insist on snatching him to hospital, then sending him back and this does him no good at all. On the contrary. He is now at Tiverton hospital and sends frantic letters asking me to take him away. So I've been pretty worried. I shall never know whether it was wise, or extremely stupid, to say so little about all this.

Wise, I've thought for a long time. Now I'm not so sure.

Mr Wyndham knows a little of my difficulties (and has been so kind) though not a great deal. Other people's troubles are always boring and very *distant* somehow.

So enough of that – I will finish the book you may be quite sure. But I do feel that it must be done as well and *truly* as I can. Otherwise it will be unconvincing, second rate.

No I never think of possible readers, only a few people can help – indeed I, well, have very mixed feelings about an audience, so I try to blot them out, do my best, alone or nearly. I've sometimes thought Maybe they feel this withdrawal. If so it can't be helped, for that is how I've always felt.

Once, years ago I was on the stage. In the chorus. Well I *hated* the audience – and dreaded them too.

So much nicer in the back row I used to think, and panicked in front row.

I've had some news which may mean a let up on money worries, but till it comes off I won't speak of it.

If Mrs Whitby does come I can arrange matters. She'll be quite comfortable, and if the sun comes out may like Cheriton F. It's leafy green and secluded. I did not realise how secluded till I came.
Yours sincerely
Jean Rhys

1. *In the* London Magazine, *February 1961*.

(Typed original)
TO THE MATRON, BELMONT HOSPITAL
4th July 1963
Cheriton Fitz Paine

Dear Madam,
When I talked to you on Sunday I thought that you had my letter posted on Saturday which was stupid of me. I repeat that I am quite willing for Max to stay at the Belmont Hospital for another week, but at the end of that time I should be grateful if he could come home and I will see what I can do to take every care of him. If, after a week or so with me his condition is still serious I will at once inform you by telephone or letter that he may be returned to the care of the hospital.

I have thought the matter over very carefully and this is what I wish.

I do want to thank you for your kindness to him and to me and to my brother in law for saying that the bed will be kept open for him.

All being well I shall expect him on the 11th of July.
Yours very sincerely
Ella Hamer

TO DIANA ATHILL
July 7th [1963]
Cheriton Fitz Paine

[. . . . .]

Dear Miss Athill,
Selma left day before yesterday. (So did my brother-in-law who's been staying here in Cheriton Fitz.) It was fun seeing her again – and she came back

225

this afternoon, with a friend, to tape-record some West Indian songs for this "Voyage in the Dark" play she's working at now. She is such a dear and brings one to life wonderfully.

The 27th is my lucky number – (any multiple of three, so I imagine) and how kind of Mr Wyndham to arrange that lunch[1].

Thank you for the nice things you write about my books. It was fortunate for me starting at that particularly exciting time – and in Paris – don't you think?

Of course some people won't admit the spirit of the place (jealous!!), but everything is so much easier, they *must* admit that. All those little cheap hotels where, rent paid, one feels so safe and not noticed and nobody cares a hoot about anybody anyway. It is a free feeling. In London and England one has to pay a high price for privacy – how can you write without that?

But I must not meander as I'm anxious to post this letter tonight. When it's dark in Cheriton F it is very dark – post box some way off.

So now I'll go on to numbers again. I don't like 13 so can Mrs Whitby manage round about the 20th? I'll be so very grateful – such a help, and I can arrange everything – given a few days notice.

I'm looking forward to meeting her so much. The 20th will be better for me as I've been very rushed lately and not had time to get quite ready.

Nothing is settled about my husband – except that I cannot leave him in a place where he is unhappy. That is impossible – Besides I miss him.

I can manage. I have been silent too long it's true, for it has been very difficult, and I brooded and became downhearted because no one knew just what was happening.

I'd so much like a copy of your book. I've not got many here, so it will get read over and over again

Since I saw that tape recorder this afternoon I've been longing for one. It seems there is a small thing – not complicated, on the market now. I'll find out next time I go to Exeter.   Sincerely yours
                                                                        Jean Rhys

I am not tall, not very. *Or* thin – very. I expect I looked a bit Gothic when Selma saw me first because I was wearing an old red house coat which I loved and was faithful to for ages. Also it was an odd house and I was slightly absent minded (with reason I assure you). [. . . . . .]

1. *A meeting between Selma Vaz Dias, Diana Athill and Francis Wyndham, at which Selma gave a dramatic account of her first meeting with Jean, whom she described as tall and thin and Gothic.*

Selma my dear,

I wonder whether you are back in London yet – anyway this will reach you sometime.

Max arrived yesterday, and I've not had a moment since, for we've not got into our routine yet. When we do I'll have four or five hours a day free – *sans* pep pills, for he sleeps a lot. I know that on the surface taking him from the hospital is not wise – deep down it is. He was simply breaking his heart there, imagining they wouldn't ever let him go. If Frederick was shocked – so was I the first time I saw how worry had changed him. Once long ago Max saved me from smashing – and as you say, I've a good memory. (I have for all you've done too believe me) Besides I am fond of him.

If it is too much for me – lifting him about is the difficulty – I will move heaven and earth to find a friendlier less public place. But I think I can manage – and won't talk any more of it.

I hope the songs were some good. When you'd gone I remembered the best one (of course) something like the "Maladie d'amour maladie de la Jeunesse" which I used in Good Morning Midnight. Never mind – I expect you've enough to go on with.

Now about "Voyage in the Dark". I'm leaving it to you entirely. But in some ways I can be useful. So don't be bored if I give you a few tips, for I've been at it a hell of a time – a century it feels.

The first is obvious. *Everybody talks differently*. So to make dialogue truthful (and in some way truth gets over) one character's speech will sound wrong spoken by another.

(This is because you told me that you were making "Laurie" and "Maudie" into one person).

"Laurie" was what is now known as a call girl. I can't imagine why everybody seems to think all this originated with Christine Keeler and Mandy what's her name. How naive!! It's as old as Egypt and older.

Laurie then, is tough, worldly wise, a go getter, all there and so on. She is kind in a careless way and fond of Anna, up to a point, but is really concentrated on herself and her own affairs on making her life a success. Business first.

Maudie is a sheep – a nice sheep, but that's all.

She has had a sad love affair, longs to marry and be respectable, is not even envious. If she makes a shrewd remark it's by accident as it were. They are poles apart.

So when you are making the two into one, it must be *Laurie* who comes through. Not poor Maudie. As a rule and must be done carefully. You can I know.

I hope this has got over for if dialogue is important in a novel, then it must be still more important in a play.

Well honey I must stop. This has been written with the aid of whisky as you doubtless guess.

You did so cheer me up and I simply loved seeing you – oh Selma, it's been a long hard pull, but I've had a glimpse of something better than dreary heart breaking slog slog now. That means so much.

So I leave the music to you. I'm very excited about it. I will delve for the original Part IV – it's not so different perhaps but I was in a blazing fury at the time I remember.

I must just add that Max is not a rag doll or a symbol to me – He is Max. He is not the protector type – never was. For years I have given up hope of being protected – And lately (!!!)

But I see what you mean and meant, and in some ways and from some angles you are right.

But so, you see, am I. From my angle. Or I hope so.

Best and much luck and much love from

Jean

[. . . . . .]

My dear Selma,

    [. . . . . .]

I will not meddle with "Voyage" of course – I am certain that it's an awful mistake to talk about things before they are finished. I've never done it before this book and *never* will again. No, I won't talk of anything else either – to start with there's nobody to talk to! Max is, I think, much better (touch wood). Not so down and bewildered and despairing and neglected.

The only snag is that my plan of doing the chores and so on and *then* working – well has not worked at all!

I am so dead flat out tired that all the pep pills in the world couldn't do it.

At this moment my eyes are half shut! Also he is too heavy for me when he leans all his weight. Last night and again this morning there was nearly an almighty crash – and a broken back would be a sad end. All the same I am glad I insisted on having him here, for I've thought of several things to make him more comfortable and I do not agree that he has been very well looked after at the hospital. They are too busy I suppose to bother about one case. He may have to go back, for I *must* have a week or two before Mrs Whitby comes to help me with the rest of Mrs R – but if I can help it (and help it I will) he won't stay long there (I'm not mad about the Welfare State you know!).

Now my eyes are three quarter shut and no mistake.

It is grand finding a letter from you in the morning, it helps me for *hours* and I send you my very best love and good wishes and good luck honey. I do not feel so alone.

Jean

P.S. I hear that morning glory seeds chewed slowly, work wonders – so am trying to get some.

Must say I'm always willing to *try* new things – they act like mescalin (on dit). I don't believe it do you?

Francis Wyndham helped me type what's done and kept a copy. I asked him to. I expect he showed it to Miss Athill because they (André Deutsch) were getting restive. And with reason!! It's been a hell of a time. He (FW) has been most awfully kind to me and done such a lot.

[. . . . . .]

TO MARYVONNE MOERMAN   *July 15th [1963]*
                                              Cheriton Fitz Paine

I *may* be able to hire a tape recorder.

My hand is a bit tired from writing. Hope you can read this.
        André Deutsch is sending down a stenographer for 3 days on August 3rd.

My dear Maryvonne,

This can only be a short letter, though so much has happened. Max, you see, has had a stroke or rather several slight strokes. The first was at Bude, but at Perranporth he got much better. Then this last awful winter pulled him down again and some weeks (three I believe) ago he was very ill.

The doctor insisted on sending him to Tiverton hospital though I was dead against it. Hospitals are all right if you've broken a leg or if you can *pay*. Otherwise horribly drab and depressing and bad for someone like Max.

Sure enough he began at once writing to me asking me to take him home. Well I went and argued. No good. In the midst of this Selma Vaz Dias came down. She wants to make a play of "Voyage in the Dark". So did Max's brother Alec. Everyone – except Alec perhaps – was dead against my bringing him back. However I insisted and was – I believe – right. Already he talks and walks better and is more himself. A small reward for going against *everybody*. They said he'd get used to it. *One does not get used to feeling forsaken.*

He knows now that I am here and on his side, and that he is *not* foresaken. Even if he has to go back for a bit he will know I do not forsake people. Not ever. *I never have* and can't start now. Too late.

The only snag is that I'm not quite strong enough to bear his weight. It makes me a bit breathless and tired but I've a plan for that.

Selma is I fear rather vexed. She thinks I'm unreasonable. But I'll make her understand. If I do succeed in getting some cash it will be for you and Ruthie. I think I will.

So don't sew too much, don't count me out. I may surprise you.

I nearly wired for you – but I do *not* want you to be mixed up in all this hard hard work and arguments and so on. Absolutely *not*.

I think I can manage and I send you all, all of you, my love to you especially. I *may* turn up trumps and sooner than you think. from

Jean

Believe in me if you can

Tuesday July 23rd [1963]
                                                     Cheriton Fitz Paine

> I'll lay in some drinks and so on here you may
> be sure.

Dear Mrs Whitby,

It's good news that you can spare me three whole days. I'm looking forward to seeing you so much.

The Ring of Bells is in a state of chaos I hear, the owner has sold it and the new proprietor hasn't settled in yet.

So I've arranged for you to stay at the Rectory. Mr Woodard, the vicar, is a dear and his wife very kind indeed.

I thought that would be more comfortable (and more fun) for you than this small cottage, which can be dreary when it rains.

So when you get to Crediton will you go straight to the Rectory Cheriton Fitz, and Mr Woodard will bring you on here – it's not far – to fix up about Saturday.

We must have a drink some time at the Ring. I expect the bar is open. It's a picturesque place (so is the Rectory) and if the new patron is as nice as the other would make a perfect hideaway if ever you want one.

Till the 2nd then.

                                                     Yours sincerely
                                                     Jean Rhys

TO SELMA VAZ DIAS   *Wednesday [1963]*
                                                     Cheriton Fitz Paine

My dear Selma,

[. . . . .]

I will look forward to hearing from John Smith[1].

My poor Selma – do get over being sick – it is so wearing and all together horrid and worse than anything. I'm not sick thank God but tired to death for I've been sitting up to all hours getting the MSS ready for Mrs Whitby who arrives day after tomorrow. In a frenzy of tidying I tore up one chapter by mistake. So it must be somehow rewritten – *oh God!* – Imagine tidying at 4 a.m! idiotic.

I will send Voyage Part IV along as soon as I'm out of this muddle. It is so impossible to write if one is worried or distracted and don't I know it?

I've been searching for an answer to the problem for years as you know and haven't found it. It does not exist and that's a fact. Try as one may *it's not possible.*

No Max is not worse, but I thought it wouldn't be wise to look after him myself for the three days Mrs Whitby's here. But he wants to come back, and I think he ought to. Worry is worse than physical effort. Every time. And I miss him.

Look after yourself dear Selma, trust all your troubles are over when you get this.

Thanks for everything and my best love my very best –

I must stagger along to the shop for some food and so on now. One day I'll just collapse like they say worn out camels do. And that'll be finally that.

Meanwhile love,

Jean

1. *Of the literary agency Christy and Moore: Selma had suggested that he should become Jean's agent.*

TO ESTHER WHITBY   *Thursday 8th August [1963]*
                                        Cheriton Fitz Paine

[. . . . . .]

Dear Mrs Whitby,

This is to thank you for coming down – it will be heaven to work from a clean typed copy – instead of juggling with sundry scrawls – insertions appendix abc etc.

[. . . . . .]

I do hope you liked Cheriton Fitz and the Rectory. Mr Woodard is a dear and the real McCoy. He has so often come in for five minutes and cheered me up when I was at my last gasp – but I don't know the rest of the family very well. I don't go to church or jumble sales or do anything sociable and I've been given up as a bad job I fear.

Never mind – I'll go to a sale or something one of these days. And to church maybe tho I like it empty.

I am sorry you had to go off so quickly. Mr Greenslade[1] told me that he'd been rung up but they were both out. This place is a bit alarming – talk about Radio Cambon!!

The slightest whisper goes from one end of the village to the other – and it's a big shout at the finish.

[. . . . . .]

I do hope you'll visit Cheriton Fitz again one of these days. You'd like the Ring of Bells. Thank you again and I'm looking forward to finishing everything. Slept all yesterday and most of today and woke up with eyes normal. A great relief, as I thought a microbe or something had crept in when I was brushing that terrible old door mat outside.   Yours sincerely

Jean Rhys

1. *A neighbour who drove the Cheriton Fitz Paine taxi. He and his wife were to become increasingly important in Jean's life: he would take her to shop in Crediton, Tiverton and Exeter, and Mrs Greenslade would look in every day, bringing her a cooked lunch. Their daughter would sometimes shop for her, or bring her a book from the library in Exeter.*

TO DIANA ATHILL   *Friday August 16th [1963]*
                                                                Cheriton Fitz Paine

> It strikes me that I'm rather taking
> your interest for granted. I don't mean
> to do that. Again, read this when you
> want to read it.
>   Don't be alarmed at this long letter.
> It can be read a bit at a time. When you
> feel like it – and answered when you are
> in the mood to answer, and not too busy.
> No hurry.

Dear Miss Athill,

Thank you for your letter. I was very interested, for I'd noticed nearly all the "gaps" you write about myself, and got the inserts done, but it is better to know the glaring ones.

For instance I cannot have stressed the poverty and isolation of that family at Coulibri (round about 1834 – Emancipation time etc) enough. They would not be able to get to Spanish Town – far less to Grandbois which is in another island (Dominica of course, my island, though I don't want to be precise about that)

After her mother marries again (Maria) they might go there once or twice, and later on Aunt Cora falls in love with the place and goes (with Antoinette) for the hot months – June, July and August. (I have explained Aunt Cora's sudden appearance plausibly enough I think).

I wanted to look through the typescript before you saw it, but there wasn't time, and I've my copy to work on. If I'm still a bit uneasy, that's because I don't like anyone seeing unfinished work (indeed it's a great struggle to let anyone see it at all – finished or not!!) I know you'll understand this feeling, and how I rushed along regardless – only wanting to *get it down*. Thanks to Mrs Whitby's endurance it was got down, and I can't thank her (and you) enough.

But as you've seen the book unfinished I would like to explain the gaps and hesitations. I tried yesterday but it was such a long letter that I just gave up – This will be too if I don't watch out.

I started, ages ago, with a different idea, another *kind* of idea. The book began with a dream and ended with a dream (though I didn't get the last dream right for a long time). All the rest was to be a long monologue. Antoinette in her prison room remembers, loves, hates, raves, talks to imaginary people, hears imaginary voices answering and overhears meaningless conversations outside. The story, if any, to be implied, *never* told straight.

I was very excited about this, and did a lot of it. Then my husband's illness stopped me. He often got better (I hope, believe he will get better). Then relapsed. We moved twice and it was all rather a strain. (Francis Wyndham's letters and kindness helped me so much through this time.) When I did get back to the book (here) generally writing at night and I reread it I wasn't so sure.

I remembered the last part of "Voyage in the Dark" written like that – time and place abolished, past and present the same – and I had been almost satisfied. Then everybody said it was "confused and confusing – impossible to understand etc." and I had to cut and rewrite it (I still think I was right, and they were wrong, tho' it was long ago). Still I thought "if they fussed over one part of a book, nobody will get the hang of a whole book written that way at all" or "A mad girl speaking all the time is too much!" And anyway there was a lot left to be done and could I do it? I think I was tired. Anyway after a week or two I decided to write it again as a story, a romance, but keeping the dream feeling and working up to the madness (I hoped). That is why there are all those gaps and hesitations, for I used a lot of what I had done. But differently.

When the first part and some of the second were presentable I sent them to Mr Wyndham and his letter cheered me up a lot. But I did stick at Mr Rochester or whatever his name will be. Dreadful man, but I tried to be fair and all that, and give some *reason* for his acting like he did. So *that* led me into byways. Then Mr Wyndham showed the MSS to you and your letter also cheered me up and I could get on with it again. But it does explain the gaps, careless writing too long, not enough, and so on. Oh dear this is a serial story now, but I must hurry on and finish.

I *think* that Mr Wyndham, who only saw the MSS when it was conventionally done, felt that it should start calmly not too intensely and he was right now I look at it. So the first dream is a child's dream of being lost in a forest and someone, something, who hates her is there and she wakes up terrified but can be consoled by the familiar things protecting her.

Soon there is the fire and Coulibri gone and her mother vanished and her brother dead and Aunt Cora comes to the rescue and adopts her more or less, and Mr Mason rushes off to some other property in Trinidad or somewhere trying to forget the whole damned affair – And he does too. Yes, the second dream must be introduced. I did it, but I made Mr Mason too melodramatic. He'd visit her at the convent where she is a boarder, 17 or so, for Aunt Cora's health is not too good now, she's in England for a change of scenery. (There was a lot of coming and going at that time I know. There were big cabins I believe. Not too bad.) Mr Mason is just calm and kind and pleased about this lovely marriage he has arranged, for he's quite fond of the girl by now, and she'll live in England eventually with this nice young man and no more horrid West Indies. She is pleased too, on the surface, but that night she has the horrible dream again and now it is vivid and very frightening indeed. That is part I. Only to be tidied up I hope.

Part II is full of difficulties and always was, but I can manage most I trust. I have written of their week or so of peace, Daniel's first letter must be cut a lot and then his story told straight. Mr R goes to see him, but what with the heat (Massacre is on the coast) and Daniel's drawl and Mr R's bewilderment, there can be a few dots there perhaps, where Mr R loses the thread – or maybe dozes off. Anyway he comes away quite convinced that the man is telling the truth.

But I do not quite see how to get in Antoinette's visit to Christophine. Yet it must go in – too long for italics. I don't like "Antoinette speaking" it sounds like the telephone. There is a trick way perhaps. Like this –

The last line of Mr Rochester's part is something like "She rode under my window but she did not look up." Then there is a three line space. Then Antoinette. Indented [I saw him standing by the window. I did not look up. I rode straight on . . . and so on till the end and close brackets.] Then another space and you're back with Mr R on the verandah having a drink and thinking What on earth *now*? I don't know, perhaps I can find another way.

I can do the magistrate (retired) and his obeah story and I know where to put it in I think and what happens.

Part II has always been so much the worst and most difficult.

As to Part III, I *started* the whole thing with Mrs Poole's interview with the housekeeper once for I realised she'd be a key character if the book was told as a *story*. I did a chapter or two then felt she was not talking properly. I read Nellie Dean in "Wuthering Heights" but it did not help.

So decided to make the girl overhear the conversation and perhaps distort everything in her mad mind.

Hadn't it better be done like that? Cut a lot, twisted more? Perhaps Mrs Eff can say a few kind words. For Mrs Poole will talk wrongly *however* I do it! The important thing is to get her to say that the dismissed staff gossiped, that the whole county (Yorkshire) knows. But that they do not know the truth. Not about anything. How could they? Also that she's getting double money for the job.

I was going to call the book "False Legend" then – a bad title. But I'd quite convinced myself that something like that *did* happen, that Charlotte Brontë knew of the story and used it in the plot of Jane Eyre.

Maybe –

It is very late and this is the finish of this long letter – I do not quite know why it had to be so long.

I have to see a friend next week – then I can tidy up Part I and *that* will be done – Soon the rest I hope.

Yours sincerely
Jean Rhys

Sunday 25th [1963]
                                          Cheriton Fitz Paine

[. . . . . .]

My dear Selma,

It is as usual, late at night and I have not felt very well lately – indeed a real
black despair came over me today (Gloomy Sunday!) which is lifting a little
now. So if this letter rambles you must be patient.

Alec (Freddie) could not come down as you probably know by now – I was
disappointed and God can't this place be lonely! Rain Rain Rain all day and
every day. Never mind –

About the extract you want – I can, of course, let you have one (about the
right length I hope) but it is difficult to send one that will be the essence of the
book for all I have done has only got it every now and again and fleetingly.
Perhaps.

Still I can send something and you can see if you like it.

It is no longer called "Mrs Rochester" though it is *connected* with Mrs
Rochester and Jane Eyre. Also the last two parts need revision and inserts
which André Deutsch has not seen. In fact it is not yet a finished book though it
is finished in my head. At last and thank God.

[. . . . . .]

Will André Deutsch *want* the broadcast yet? But you know more about
publicity than I do. I know nothing – and you say you have spoken to Miss
Athill. As a matter of fact I *hate* publicity and the public – I hate to think of
them pawing at my book – Not understanding.

This of course is idiotic for I long too for it to be understood and read and so
on. A hell of a mix up is my poor mind. So that is the position and I will send
you the extract – the finished thing ought not to take long except for the eternal
problem of typing. I must get a tape recorder or I'm done.

Now about Voyage – I called it originally "Two Tunes" and it was
advertised in a trade paper as "Two Tunes". Then came this dispute about the
end and Michael Sadleir of Constables published it instead of Cape. By this
time I had changed the title to "Voyage in the Dark".

[. . . . . .]

About the theatre. The actual theatre we played at was the Kings
Hammersmith, so far as I remember, but I'm sure there was a place at
Holloway too. It's not important except that a music hall *wouldn't* do for a
musical comedy which travelled scenery costumes a large company,
conductor of orchestra and with George Edwardes, first violin, dancer
speciality and God knows what.

It was all so different, then. The pictures weren't much, it was all living
actors. Every Sunday companies big and small crisscrossed about. There were
the "straight" companies and "Sappho"[1] and so on, F. Benson Shakespeare[2] I
saw and the musical shows like "The Count of Luxembourg"[3] (I was in that).
It was awfully funny, they despised each other of course. But we saw each
other's shows for free and once I saw Sappho's lover pick her up to carry her off

to bed after a wild party in Paris (Eng) and the poor man staggered and fell because she was no light weight and talk about a laugh. The whole place shook.

I laughed too but I was awfully sorry for him. He was so thin.

Memories!

But the music hall "turns" travelled themselves I think. Not altogether as a company, never came across them somehow that I can remember. So a music hall wouldn't do – Not. Scenery and lights and so on I suppose – Better the Kings Hammersmith.

Well how I do run on. This is what happened to my story for the "London" which Mrs Whitby took on tape and John Smith has now. So I suppose he'll send it. Half of it! My voice sounded so prissy on her tape recorder – Dreadful. Perhaps it's turned him against me. I shouldn't wonder. It's not like that always is it?

So now my dear good night. I will try to send you the extracts next week but there are all those points to be considered. Title, André Deutsch etc.

Much love

Jean

1. Sapho, *dramatization of Alphonse Daudet's novel (1884), which had nothing to do with the poet.*

2. *Sir Frank Benson, Shakespearian actor-manager whose touring company was famous at the turn of the century.*

3. *Operetta by Franz Léhar.*

TO SELMA VAZ DIAS   *Friday 30th [1963]*
                                                                    Cheriton Fitz Paine

My dear Selma,

I am glad that "Voyage" or "Two Tunes" is finished. I found the original ending, looked at it and didn't think it would be much use to you. However if it'll help I'll post it to you, registered, tomorrow. Couldn't get out before. Felt ill.

I have never seen your play and have not a copy of the book. I put all I could into it long ago and now I'm with the other one. So it's difficult to make any suggestion – however tentative. (A tidier MSS has vanished, by the way).

All I can think of is *a voice speaking. Sometimes to music sometimes not – on a darkened stage.* (But so much would depend on what went before!) Or perhaps something quite different would be going on visually, a party, or as a background a dance? – a girl lying on a bed in one empty room? A dead girl? . . . Certainly a dying girl. Perhaps you will see no difference between the two versions and I agree that an abortion gone wrong is not a pretty sight and impossible on the stage or even in a book or radio. All the same I still think it

236

better – and more what I wanted. This girl is an innocent. Really without guile or slyness. Why should she live to be done in over and over again? . . . However it was long ago and there've been so many abortions since oh Lord! Plays, books galore (But never a true one.) The end? All I am sure of is that it needs a jump to catch it – a conventional ending would be *fatal*. Perhaps a voice speaking and a background of other voices, music, laughter perhaps. I don't know. Music (sometimes) and a voice speaking is all I can see hear or feel. The "smile please" is her first photograph being taken and the end is death. It might be done perhaps.

You may get a flash of *how*. But what went before matters a lot. For me it all ought to lead up to this final scene. More echoes perhaps – more voices remembered. Well assez. (Try cutting real life to the bone and concentrating on this final scene) Well I'll annoy you in a minute I expect.

Please return it to me when you've got what you want (if anything) for sentimental and other reasons.

The directions are for the printers of course. I've written in the confused paragraphs on opposite side. It might be something after all, but these flashes so hard to get, such agony waiting for them! You would not have the grim "bulldog" patience it takes. Or the time perhaps.

About Sargasso Sea or Mrs R question mark or whatever it's to be called.

It is difficult for me to show bits and pieces of a book when it is not finished and that book wants cuts, insertions and so on before it is a finished book. Then it will be away from me and I will not mind. I am (thank God!) indifferent when I've done my best. Like a cat mother when the kittens can look after themselves. Before that one is ready to scratch, claw and mew to defend the unfinished thing.

Still I can send one or two extracts though I'm doubtful if you (or the BBC) will make head or tail of them without a synopsis, which I'll send also.

It has been hell to write and most things have been against me – Max's illness a terrible blow. Still it's nearly over now (Then Hip Hip Hooray! I have a line to say)

If the BBC have any interest in me at all – apart from your influence – surely they'll understand how I feel? After trying so hard and so long.

Never mind. As it is you Selma who ask and advise it I'll send the "extracts" (doesn't that sound like Bovril?) Also a synopsis which is needed I think – I've said that before, and you can judge for yourself if they'll do and if they stand alone yet. Expect them some time next week.

Now I must get to work on part of a chapter which I *tore up* idiotically when preparing for Mrs Whitby. It was four in the morning and I thought I heard the mouse! – But that's no excuse – Luckily I think I can rewrite it or as near as makes no matter. It's important as this book is complicated and a bit like a patchwork.

I wish you and Voyage in the Dark all the luck there is. If you see nothing as I see it that does not matter at all. But I'd like it back when you've looked at it.

Yours very affectionately
Jean

A friend of mine in Paris (English) used to drink "To the torch and those who carry it on" with final whisky – Every night.

Doesn't it sound odd in London England 1963 and *very* odd in Cheriton Fitz. I'd like some whisky at this moment you bet. But not a drop. My dear this rain is enough to send the calmest round the bend. It *never* stops. Has not for weeks.

Well have fun with foreign pals.

JR

TO SELMA VAZ DIAS

Friday 6th [1963]
Cheriton Fitz Paine

My dear Selma,

I sent the version of "Voyage in the Dark" that you asked for a week ago. The post office was shut – it does shut at odd times – but I paid for registration and the man promised to send it off early Monday morning. I hope you got it all right and that it was some use. If not, I would like to have it back – for my own sentimental reasons.

I am, to speak the truth (I like truth) getting a bit worried about too many things. *Too worried!*

I have never seen "Voyage" as a play. I told you this at once. However you said you did and I said and still say Go ahead and much luck, for I don't care what happens to a *finished* thing. (Or not much.) I was a bit doubtful about its chances with the B.B.C. But after all I know so little about the B.B.C. If, in my opinion they often broadcast childish nonsense on "Home" or "Light" – well I may be wrong. It does seem to me that they scramble madly for "popularity" at one end and at the other there is this cursed snobbish hypocrite half lie – that is almost worse. But again, I don't know. I may miss all sorts of delightful things. But will you let me know what happens?

I heard from John Smith – a very kind and helpful letter. I am trying desperately to rewrite a mangled story (mangled by cutting and by the tape recorder) before I answer. It was ordered by the "London" months ago but they might still take it. After all, the few people who read the "London" are the sort who might like my stories, and they've certainly helped to keep me afloat all these dreadful years – for believe me it's been the worst time of my life (which as a rule hasn't been easy you bet).

At present I'm nearly off my head about Max. When Alec saw him he was *much* worse than he has ever been with me. He hates it there and who wouldn't?

So there he is, sent to this place by a penny in the slot doctor. (N.H.S. indeed!! A rotten set up) Growing worse and worse. And here *I* am quite alone and nearly in despair lest my own health should give way.

I intend to take drastic action and have Max back, for I would infinitely prefer physical toil to this terrible anxiety and loneliness.

Oh God how I hate penny in the slot thoughts and actions, and oh God what terrible harm they cause. If I live I will call my next and last book *There is no penny and no slot* and if you pinch that title or variations I'll climb up to your window and give you nightmares. (This is a joke.)

Anyway there is *no* penny for the slots. Not for writing or the black versus white question – the *lies* that are told – or for anything at all that matters. Only for lies. Yet everybody believes in the non existent penny and the invisible slot. So what to do?

Well ducks (or is it duck) there is a funny side to it too.

Yesterday I discovered for the first time that half the people in this village can't read or write. Also that they believe in black magic! Can you beat it? Not only that, but the woman next door says I am a witch! Well!!! What next? Especially as I have grave suspicions about *her*. She is too fat and healthy and hearty to be quite true, and why oh why did she borrow my books if she can't read?? Tell me that??? To learn spells??

Well I won't be gruesome any more. I do believe in writing my best and dam the rest. It's not my concern.

If I am afraid of trusting unfinished work to the BBC it's because they may not like it, and though I don't give a fico for that, it *may* take away a little of my strength – there's not so much left. However I'll send something next week (with synopsis) for you because you helped so very much and will understand what I'm getting at perhaps.   Yrs affectionately
                                                                                    Jean

PS Before thinking me round the bend imagine a life without drink or books or a friend to say "Onward" or a hairdo or a dentist. But never ceasing rain and wind and to cap it all this black eyed Susan next door saying I'm a witch!

I can of course get what I want (almost) by taking a taxi at about £1 a time to Exeter. Buses few and impossible. I'm doing this recklessly and who cares?

Seeing Max costs a quid a time too!

But that's the least of my worries. I really despise money and certainly it hates me!

So till we meet (when I'll be so repaired you won't know me) I am not bad at that –   Love
                                                                                    Jean

TO FRANCIS WYNDHAM   *September 6th [1963]*
                                                      Cheriton Fitz Paine

> I think that it is far more likely that
> *she's* casting spells on *me*.

Dear Mr Wyndham,

I am sorry not to have written before. If you knew the enormous *relief* I felt when I got your letter and was sure that you'd taken care of the typing inserts, cuts and so on – well – you would forgive me. Thank you many times.

It is so lovely not to be chivvied (or chivied) because that *distracts* me which is not necessary.

I've been working at a thing called "Leaving School and how I became a novelist" meant for the London. Mr Ross asked me to do it months ago. It was always too long or very dull.

But it would help if somebody wanted it.

Many troubles and only one bit of comic relief – if it is comic.

Cheriton Fitz has "pockets of black magic" so I'm told and a large fat healthy woman is saying I've cast a spell on one of her terrible children – I've never *seen* this child. It *is* comic, except of course that I've never really liked Cheriton F somehow – Also I can't think why she's always borrowed books as it seems she can't read. (That's rather sweet and I'm sure instinct is best.) But what about my instinct to distrust Cheriton Fitz and everything about it?

Or – Never mind.

I will try to finish Part I next week and send it to you. As quickly as I can.

Yours sincerely
Jean Rhys

The rector's wife told me about the magic (black). She said "Of course my husband got rid of it. *At once.*" I do trust he did. (How?) because for some reason it depresses me. I seem to have forgotten my obeah (I did know one thing) or would try an anti spell. What a ridiculous letter. I will write again more sensibly. I'm worried about a few things but that'll pass.

TO SELMA VAZ DIAS   *September 17th [1963]*
                                                     Cheriton Fitz Paine

PS. You know Maryvonne wrote "I'm afraid
of Cheriton Fitz!" Strange. Yes I do believe in
telepathy but hope that it hasn't been working lately.
        I had a wire that M. arrives today. So
I will not be alone for a bit.

My dear Selma,

I was so pleased to get your letter my dear, and I had started answering when all the rather horrible things that have been happening began. It's nothing to do with Max – who looked fairly well when I saw him last. It's to do with this place and people, both pretty fairly beastly. I wonder that you didn't guess when I argued so strongly that Max ought to be *here* and not in hospital how I felt. *This is not a place to be alone in.* It's not ghosts or darkness or even loneliness – it's the atmosphere of Cheriton Fitz, and its really unbelievable inhabitants. Some are nice yes but *so* few and *so* far away. If I tell you the reasons why things are trying well I expect you'd think I was right round the bend – better just leave it that (so far as I can make out) I'm disapproved or worse of because *I try to write*(!!!) Well I resent this deeply and bitterly – how deeply no one knows but myself – and of course it is doing me great great harm.

I would rather do any work, or bear any hardship than have these onslaughts on something so rooted in me. I do not know what to do – I did for one wild moment think of running away and for another of asking you to come. However I did see in time how crazy both these ideas were. I cannot run away yet. Not just now, and I would not really attempt to balls up your plans and hopes and daily life for me. On the contrary if you can do Voyage it might save me. (If not – well not.) I have sent for Maryvonne though what *she'll* make of it all God knows. Maybe I'll wire and stop her. I haven't made up my mind.

Now to take up where I left off. I *do* see that Sound Radio might be very new and exciting indeed but perhaps (I thought) the opportunity was missed. I see too that *it is still open.*

On the other hand I'm no judge.

We have moved four times – no five times since we left London. In one place the radio got Luxembourg and nothing else, in *three* there was *no* radio, here I can get Home with buzz, Light easily and Third late at night, Paris easily and so on. *Of course* I knew you were dealing with 3rd.

So you see – I *can't* judge (how I hate that word "judge" oh my God. *Who* can judge, yet everybody does.)

I won't say one word about Voyage (if you are still doing it) except this – It's after all an often related story. The difficult thing is the only worth while thing. The girl is *divided*, two people really. Or at any rate one foot on sea and one on land girl. She – but I won't go on as you must have seen what I hoped to do.

Now I come to think of it this *might* be easier on radio than in a novel. Her dream must be so vivid that you are left in doubt as to which is dream and which reality (And who knows?) In the end her dream takes her entirely so perhaps *that is* the reality. Well now honey don't get put off by this sermon. Or skip it. And much luck and I see all you say.

Now as to why I feel as if I'm in a nightmare.

(1) More than half the population think I am a *witch*! and that I do harm!!! For why? – Well because they cannot read or write! – *True*. So you see living as I do I *must* be a witch. (Mind you they only say straight out what many people think and do not say.)

While Max was with me they didn't attack openly. Now they are attacking. And how! I was not prepared for all this. So for the moment I'm a bit – well a bit . . . . Also I think my life *very* unenviable to outsiders. Yet I am envied and hated. Why? Dunno. It's *crazy* –

So I can only cheer myself with clichés like the great allies I have on hand – and who cares – and all the martyrs and all the ones who died, but meanwhile I *cannot* write. This is the first thing I have written since the troubles started. And am I exaggerating? Of course I am. Yet it's bad enough and as old Rochester says "It's a blow Jane it's a blow" – hatred always is.

I have three pals, the taxi man, the woman at the grocer shop (perhaps, in a way) and the Rector. But *not* his wife, so I expect those cosy chats will soon come to an end (women and Children first).

When I'm ok again I will try to keep going and fix all and so on.

If not – well not – Perhaps John Smith had better see me when not so wild and desolate and angry – I should have hidden myself better. [. . . . .]

I will write to everybody soon and to you about the whatever you call it from "Sargasso Sea" or "What the hell or Where's Jane?" thing.

I love seeing a letter on the faded mat. Don't forget that.　　Love

Jean

I'll be all right soon. When I was really down I did not write to anyone.

TO SELMA VAZ DIAS　　　　　　　　　　　　　　　*September 30th [1963]*
　　　　　　　　　　　　　　　　　　　　　　Cheriton Fitz Paine

My very dear Selma,

This is the third time I have tried to write to you. My daughter's name is Maryvonne not Yvonne[1]. She left day before yesterday and ever since I've been struggling with such loneliness and despair that it is useless to talk of it to anyone else. I really cannot bear the thought of another winter in this horrible place. It will kill me, and I'd prefer to die somewhere else. I think and think but every way out seems blocked. Meanwhile I cannot work or do anything but struggle (as I say) without result.

But you have, I know, your own difficulties so what's the use of three pages of lamentations? So boring. And so useless. And so cowardly (Perhaps).

John Smith did arrive here though he didn't find it easily and I liked him very much. He thinks, as I do, that I had better drop everything and finish the book. Then I will see that you'll have a copy of the M.S.S. and can use whatever passage you wish for the BBC if they are still interested. I'm very sorry not to do more. But, really I am not able. If you knew how I feel – but I don't wish that –

It seems impossible to collapse after years of effort. *So it is impossible.* A little would save me but it must be there. Dear Selma wish me well for I've tried long and hard.

If you think of a way out *however crazy* tell me. Sometimes at these moments it is the crazy thing that saves one. I know that well. But I am so tired. If you can imagine the crazy thing that would save tell me. All *I* can think of is to run away to Amsterdam, for I've enough cash to last for two or three months and a great longing to be with Maryvonne – to hear her voice and her laugh. Oh God the stupidity, the ugliness, the darkness, the loneliness and the cruelty of this *beastly* little place. This evil place.

Do you know I often take a taxi which I can't afford just to get away from it – to breathe again.

I tel¹ myself "Will you let them kill your book too?" – and feel nothing but the same dull hatred of the bloody set up. Well what's the good.

"And shall Trelawney die?" (He did I think by the way.)

　　　　　　　　"Rejoice all you that creep
　　　　　　　　For those who fly will perish."

Or words to that effect.

242

Forgive this crazy and selfish letter – the other two were worse I assure you.

I have always reacted against these fits of emptiness and nothingness. So this time I will too. Sooner or later. But my god I hope sooner not later. Or there will be nothing left of me – nothing at all.

My best love from *dark* Cheriton Fitz Paine.

Jean

I only heard a bit of your broadcast. The clock was haywire – so disappointed. Forgive that too. They believe in black magic here it seems. And in witches. And certainly in cruelty and stupidity.

They do. The parson's wife told me so! I was a bit taken aback I must say.

However she seemed quite calm about it. Her husband had almost done away with it she said. He'd prayed all over the shop. *Almost* is the word I think. He ought to say a prayer or two round here – I wish there was a Catholic priest around. I'd ask him to do *his* stuff. I'd believe in that more. Protestants are so lukewarm.

1. *Selma had written: "Please try to stop worrying and especially about others. I have been bewitched for years and fight bloody battles with my demon, they leave me exhausted and paralysed. Going through a particularly nasty bout right now.* Who is Maryanne? *I know that your daughter's name is Yvonne and Maryanne is a mystery to me. John Smith is coming to see you Thursday, he's nice and I'm sure will make you feel a lot better. He has no car and God knows how he'll manage, but he is determined. I shall be reading the morning story on Thursday next at 11 o'clock, not a very good story, but I do not choose them, am only chosen as the reader. Would like to think you were listening to me. Do let me know about Maryanne, I am intrigued! Oh dear, this is a sad time, still waiting for the miracle for all of us. Don't forget the Mrs Rochester excerpt, I still think Mrs Rochester the only title and I am sure I am right. . . ."*

TO FRANCIS WYNDHAM

October 11th [1963]
Cheriton Fitz Paine

[. . . . . .]

Dear Mr Wyndham,

[. . . . . .]

I will write to John Smith of Christy and Moore as you suggest and ask him to get in touch with Miss Athill – for I'm very excited and pleased about the new magazine[1]. It sounds so hopeful.

I am perhaps a bit worried about things in general and the rest of this long letter is an appendix (as it were) explaining why. If that's the word.

If you do not feel like reading it tear it up and just write "I've torn up appendix" for I'm sure that you will be better pleased if you didn't see it. But if you want to help me, read it. It is not personal. It's one of those heart cries.

I have told myself over and over again that impulsive letters do no good.

243

Only harm. If you agree tear it up. If not and I hope not remember that I've said nothing about myself for a long long time and a word might help.

Sincerely yours
Jean Rhys

Appendix or whatever

Last summer Selma Vaz Dias came down to see me. So did Alec. This was when I was trying to stop Max being sent to a hospital at Tiverton for I knew that he would hate it and that left alone I'd panic. At that time I was able to look after him – and work at night – After all I've done that for some time – I know what I can do and what I can't.

What I *can't* is to be left alone in a place like Cheriton Fitz which has to be seen to be believed. It is completely isolated yet not peaceful – full to the brim of very stupid gossip. Unkind too.

To get on with the story – you can (perhaps) imagine that what with worry and whisky nothing very sensible was arranged last summer. I gave in about Max (with reservations) and of course he is miserable and I am lonely, undecided, and near panic as I predicted.

Also I signed an agreement giving Selma the rights of TV and radio. I made it a condition though that I should have a look at what she did. The book in question was "Voyage in the Dark". She had written and wired about this before, and I understood that she was making it into a radio play. I don't see it as a play though I believe I could do so, and except a few random ideas, I could not help, but I was very pleased to do that much for her. She has been very kind to me, as you know, and I am fond of her. But, I think, she *forgets* – Also she thinks that writing is easy. I have told her that it is hard. Very hard. I have told her that it isn't a penny in the slot and I don't think she believes me.

There is no penny, no slot. Not thousands of pounds could work that slot if it existed. There is only trying to make something out of nothing, or what seems to be nothing. (Except of course disbelief in oneself and failure and emptiness. And above all waiting for the time when all that does not count).

(I did not tell her all this rubbish of course.) The agreement covered all my books but she has forgotten for the moment to send me a part of it and I was so worried in those days I don't quite remember. Oh yes. We were to share 50–50 if anything came off and if I died first I wanted my share to go to my daughter Maryvonne who lives in Holland.

I gave her the original MSS of the last part IV of Voyage which I think better than the version actually published. It needed cutting but not such drastic and careless cutting. However once I had given in I did not care any more – though I'd kept the MSS.

Well – Selma kindly persuaded John Smith of Christy & Moore to act as my agent – and he came to see me here. It was a short interview because his taxi couldn't find this place. (I don't wonder at that.) I gave him two or three short stories, not good ones, and I thought him kind and wanting to help. I hope you've got so far. It all sounds so confused. And was.

Selma also wanted me to send her a bit of this new novel for the 3rd BBC. I asked her if she could give me time [. . . . . .] but she was rather insistent that I must do it at once.

I showed John Smith the only "detached" thing, that obeah woman bit, and he skimmed through it and said "Selma could do this" then added that on the whole he'd advise finishing Part I first, especially as I've only one typed copy and can't risk losing it.

Another complication was that my daughter Maryvonne was visiting me when he came – She means a lot to me. She has such a clear, quick mind. It was heaven talking to her and seeing her after all the isolation and worse the stupidity. It was like light after a dark room alone and when she left (as she had to) I felt quite heartbroken.

So I wrote rather stupidly to Selma that I could not *bear* it any more and that I was quite seriously thinking of running away to Amsterdam and finishing my book there. It seems that she was annoyed at my letter for I said I couldn't send any extract or excerpt or whatever it's called, till Part I is finished in calm and I have not heard from her since. Perhaps she is away or busy. I don't know. But I know only too well that all this sounds as if *I* am finished. Not Part I.

But I do not think that is so. I think I have some reserves of strength. It is only outwardly that I'm a lightweight person.

But my mind goes round and round and I am still uncertain what I ought to do.

(1) I have given up the Amsterdam idea, getting a passport and so on so wearying and I am tired. Also when my money ran out – what? I have a little money but not much. About £100. Less.

(2) I can wire her to come back. Again no. I've sworn not to mix up her life, as mine has been clouded and mixed up. Besides she might not come, though I think she would – but her husband? He'd think me a hell of a nuisance.

(3) I can go to an expensive nursing home and "rest" for a week. It is not long enough to do any good. I don't believe in that solution and so expensive.

(4) I can stay here in the dark little cottage and say I must, I will till it works. As it must. Don't you think?

This letter is part of that – I felt I could not go on without talking to somebody even on paper. Telling someone how I felt.

It *has* helped me but do not think of it, dismiss it – Except I should like to know what is happening about Selma's play but don't wish to write again.

I should like to hear from John Smith for he has the letter from the Bureau International in BudaPest about my fee for the Jazz story which has been published in the September no. of the Hungarian magazine. Not much but a help.

Yes I would like a copy of "Voices"[2], for I have not heard from them at all. Again not much but a help especially to see it.

There is nothing more except to ask you not to leave this unanswered. A line will do.

I am not potty you know. My "sensible" brother who bought this awful place has already hauled me off to *two* specialists who both said I was quite sane but might break down under my present existence. So now he is convinced

245

and kind and suggests this "rest" solution. I do not think a week's rest would help and so expensive.

I will be all right. I must be. I wonder whether I'll post this?

So little would do the trick you know. But it has been so long and rather tough – and I am tired. Je suis Cassé.

1. Art and Literature *published in Paris and edited by John Ashbery, Anne Dunn, Rodrigo Moynihan and Sonia Orwell. There were twelve issues, from March 1964 to Spring 1967: Part One of* Wide Sargasso Sea *was to appear in the first.*

2. *A miscellany, edited by Robert Rubens and published by Michael Joseph, which included Jean's story "A Solid House".*

TO FRANCIS WYNDHAM

Wednesday 16 October [1963]
Cheriton Fitz Paine

Dear Mr Wyndham,

When I got your letter this morning I did not know whether I was glad or sorry. Glad because you are so very kind and generous and understanding, sorry because I'd set my heart on finishing that book first, and cracking up afterwards. And because –

However when I'd got into my mouse-haunted kitchen and made tea I knew that I was glad. Very glad. Not sorry. I have been strained up for so long that I could not decide anything at all. My mind went round in circles – but found no way out. Now there will be a way out. I think and hope, I can relax and plan.

I am seeing my brother tomorrow, he is very sensible and practical and will help all he can I'm sure.

I do not think that I will go to Amsterdam – at any rate not just now. Maryvonne is someone whom I've kept away from my mixed up existence and if I asked her to get me a flat and so on she might find it, in the end, a worry. For I am tired and would make demands on her whether I meant to or not. She has her own life and friends and *I* want to help *her* not the other way round.

I've managed (it's the only thing I *have* managed) to do this and can't *mustn't* change now. You know she has a sort of gaiety and living in the present nature, and I like that so much (I do wonder why seeing her was the final straw??) There was the witch business of course which was rather a surprise, and to tell the truth the mice are a trial, for I am terrified of mice.

I spend hours building up a barrier of wood and stones quite useless of course. Also there are alarming sounds from above where the hot water pipes are. (Things larger than mice?) But I pretend not to hear them. Altogether this is rather a nightmarish place and why it should have been chosen as a refuge I do *not* know. I did not choose it. (A slip up that was.)

Well I will try to arrange for my rest and while I'm away a kind woman here will brighten up this dingy cottage. She thinks she can get the mice away somehow.

You know I would have shot off long ago before things got so complicated, for I realised pretty quickly that Cheriton Fitz Paine and this place would need a lot of iron will power, but you see I am even more terrified of landladies (lords) that I am of mice or solitude. At least I was safe here and till quite lately, I could work.

I meant this to be a short letter thanking you – but how can I do that?

I will not even try. I will think that you have given me a lovely present[1] of a couple of weeks to rest and relax and then to straighten things out and to write again.

Such a lovely and grand present, just when I'd given up. (But I will not now.)

Of course one reason I cannot run away to some flat or house or some Amsterdam canal is this –

I can't leave Max alone and ill and unhappy – perhaps not to see him any more – I'd worry about it all the time. (A selfish feeling you see.)

On the contrary I want to fix it that he is a little happier. Perhaps if and when I think clearly it might be managed.

As soon as I have decided what to do (my brother says he knows two rest places) I will let you know.

A calm sensible *short* letter I hope. I'm going to read "Voices" now. I am not so dismal as I sound you know.
                                                              Yours sincerely
                                                              Jean Rhys
Thank you.

1. *Francis Wyndham had sent her a hundred pounds.*

TO MARYVONNE MOERMAN   *October 28th [1963]*
                                                 Cheriton Fitz Paine
My dear Maryvonne,

Thank you for the book and for writing my dear.

I did answer long ago, but in my letter I asked you to come over again and as I don't think that a fair thing to say I did not send what I wrote –

You know how cold, dreary and beastly this place is – and you have your own life to live.

The thing is that I've managed to get hold of some money, and I feel so rotten and ill and depressed that I'm afraid it will all be wasted if I stay here alone any more.

But I'll try not to let that happen – for I want you and Ellen to have half of it at least and all if I die.

It's not so much but worth saving. That was why I asked you to come for I can now pay your fare and something over.

But as I say I realise it's too much to ask. I missed you so much and I thought that perhaps if you could help me through this bad time it might be worth it for

I could make some more. Yes the sad thing is that I *could* make some more if I weren't so depressed and ill. I've worked so hard for this chance, it seems rather a shame to crack up now.

But when I think of this beastly place (and people) *It's not even healthy!* How could I ask you to leave your own home for such a really nasty place.

The papers have got hold of it now (Cheriton Fitz I mean) – they don't know the half of what goes on!

That my dear is why I didn't write.

Well honey I'll do my best to fight it out. I'm not sure if it would be wise to spend the winter here alone but I will let you know at once if I decide to go. And where.

I know how pleased you must be about Ruth Ellen. So am I. She has great talent I think. Give her my best love.

If I can fight down this panic it'll be all right and maybe I only feel ill because of the loneliness and panic fear of the winter here.

So I'll do my best. Meanwhile all my love and more too.

Don't bother about the underclothes. But *write to me.*

Jean

TO SELMA VAZ DIAS   *November 27th [1963]*
                                                   Cheriton Fitz Paine

My dear Selma,

You do not understand, Darling Selma. The worry and loneliness have been too much for me and *I am ill.* The doctor urges me to go to a nursing home in Crediton but up to now I've held out against this for I wanted to come to you – if only for a week or so.

Everything is in an awful muddle now and I still feel that I ought to come to London and sort it out.

Could you please let me know by return.

If I come on Monday or Tuesday next week how long can I stay? At what date is your flat let? I have the address of a London hotel but I doubt if they would sympathise with illness and I can't afford a London nursing home for long if at all.

I feel that a great deal of my illness and weakness is caused by loneliness and worry and that it would do me all the good in the world to see you.

I do not mean that I'm too sick to move or walk – only that I am sick at heart and almost incapable of action, even the walk to buy food.

To start with Max is terribly unhappy at that awful hospital (so called) and keeps imploring me to take him away – it's a *horrible* place, and I was right to protest against his going there. (No use.)

Also it is since I've been alone that all this gossip has started. Calling me "witch" is the *least* they say! Yet no one knows me. I've gone to the shop to buy food and twice to the Woodards – that is all.

The taxi driver and his wife are still friendly – I *think.* No one else.

I have always disliked and distrusted this village – but I did not know how beastly it could be. I did guess enough to dread being left alone tho' till quite lately I've not had the cash to move. Then there is Max, utterly wretched and hopeless.

All this wailing does no good at all – so I'll stop it.

I want desperately to see you and to clear matters up, so will you let me know if I come on Monday can you put me up for ten days or a fortnight? Or for how long? A week? If so I will come. Now I *must* see Max – first a long journey – and I must pack a bit. Everything I have will vanish otherwise. The sitting room window is easily opened from outside and a good deal has vanished already. They can see when I go out of course. Or very early in the morning they can get in – without any trouble at all.

It is in fact a devil of a situation. But I'll pull out the last strength I have for it is heartbreaking to fall and fail just when things might get better. For this book, which has cost me so much, too much, is nearly finished. Revision is needed that's all.

I do not think that I should have been left so alone and friendless and isolated in this place. Thank you dear Selma for caring to help. I will do my best.

My horrible mistake was coming here at all. I did not know how isolated I would be or how nasty the place was. Even getting food means a long walk – usually in a howling gale of wind and rain. Telephoning to London is impossible and even to Crediton difficult. The call box is automatic and usually out of order.

Indeed I'm really standing on the burning deck and most have fled! Never mind! Please answer this at once.

I'm not potty or even desperately ill. Just very lonely and sad and this has made me weak. But I'll make this last effort you may be certain.

Love
Jean

I think that seeing you will be better than champagne. It's getting to you . . . !!¹
But I will do it if I can for I am certain that loneliness is the cause of my despair. Loneliness! Solitary confinement is more like it.

1. *Jean never did get to Selma, who repeatedly put her off (see Jean's letter to Selma, March, 1964, page 257).*

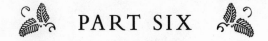

PART SIX

Wide Sargasso Sea

(1964–1966)

March 3rd [1964]
                                                    Cheriton Fitz Paine

[. . . . . .]

Dear Mr Wyndham,

I sent the corrected proofs, *one copy*, and additions to Sonia Orwell[1] last month – the 6th Feb – and was assured that they'd reach her in a day or two.

I hope she got them all right and didn't think the alterations tiresome. There were a few printers' errors.

I still have the other proof copy and am anxious to have it typed with additional paragraphs and corrections. It's very difficult to find anyone here, though I've tried – will it be a bother if I ask you to have it done for me? I expect it will, but I must risk that. It needs someone patient and accurate. I'd like *three* copies, and I can pay for this – largely or entirely thanks to you. It's clear, I trust, and I am sorry about the exercise book paper but I'd run out of typing paper and have to journey to Tiverton for that.

I could send it (Part I) to Miss Athill of course, but I'd so much like her to see it *finished*. Part II will be ready next week if all goes well. And the rest.

André Deutsch sent me a long list of questions which I answered as well as I could. As for people who might be interested I forgot Victor Van Vriesland. He wrote a preface to "Voyage in the Dark" when it was published in Holland – and Denmark I think. "Melodie en Mineur" was the title there and he reviewed my books very kindly. He's president of the International PEN now (if it's the same Victor Van Vriesland) and might remember me, though I did not know him personally and it's a long time ago.

I'm afraid the period photographs I sent must have been a bit startling – they were all I had. Anyway I'll get a present day version done when I come to London – or failing that in Exeter. They weren't flattering – one was an enlarged passport thing and I wonder how or why it got enlarged and covered with black specks too!

I feel that I've just about exhausted everybody's patience with delays and alterations, but, as I told Miss Athill I've always *known* that this book must be done as well as I could – (*no* margin of error) or it would be unconvincing. I reckon that I've spent about two and a half years on it. Working steadily I mean. Stopping so often was just bad luck – and I can only thank you for being so patient and helping me so much in spite of that. I'm grateful. Very.

                                                    Yours sincerely
                                                    Jean Rhys

I suppose it could be called "Gold Sargasso Sea" which would be colourful and appropriate? The Creole song I took the title from was written by a cousin of mine. She comes from St Lucia and has given up these artless songs now. She says she can only sell ersatz. I'm sorry – for she was going to do a Chanson Créole to end all Chansons for me. She said it would take years. Like my book.

I will write to Miss Athill about Victor Van Vriesland. I'm sure he'd help in any way he could. I am a bit out of touch with organisations and everything else.

I will post the proofs and additions registered (Part I) and I hope you won't think it all a great bother. When I can get to London, quite soon, I can manage the rest – and if anything has gone wrong do not tell me just now.

I'm getting along with the rest of the book fairly quickly and don't want to be discouraged. This place does that pretty well I assure you. When it is done as well as I can it will be out of my hands and I will not worry any more. I never do. Except perhaps that I ask too much of you. If you *saw* Cheriton Fitz in the winter you'd forgive me I think. Of all the remote and frowning places it frowns the most.

Yours sincerely
Jean Rhys

I hope it was all right keeping the second lot of proofs – such a temptation and I hope too that the first lot reached Mrs Orwell – and in time.

[. . . . . .]

1. *One of the four editors of* Art and Literature, *which published Part One of* Wide Sargasso Sea *in its first issue. Mrs Orwell was then living in Paris, but after her return to London a few years later she became one of Jean's closest friends, regularly visiting her in Devon, organizing and financing long holidays for her in London and elsewhere, and in fact completely transforming her life by her imaginative generosity and infectious vitality. She died in December 1980, outliving Jean by less than two years.*

TO FRANCIS WYNDHAM
March 7th 1964
Cheriton Fitz Paine

Dear Mr Wyndham,

I heard from Sonia Orwell day before yesterday, a kind letter. I answered at once. I'm sorry the corrections weren't in time, but of course it would be impossible to alter the set up of the magazine now. Not to be *thought* of! I repeated that as you'd looked at the extract, and she likes it I am satisfied, delighted and longing to see the first number.

I wish it all the luck there is. It's a good thing having the extra lot of proofs – very much easier to follow. I will have a look at the additions tomorrow (Sunday) then post everything to you – Part II ought to be ready next week, it's just a matter of copying out legibly. It will be such a relief knowing that they (Parts I and II) are safely typed, (No more additions. Delete perhaps) that I'm taking advantage of your kindness. Again!

I know that explaining makes the book more conventional – but I tried the other way and could not do it. In the end I had to tell the story straight – more or less – and keep the madness for the last act.

I've never read a long novel about a mad mind or an unusual mind or anybody's mind at all. Yet it is the only thing that matters and so difficult to get over without being dull.

Anna Kavan's stories I like, and I have her novel *Who Are You?* Very short but what a splendid title. If only I'd thought of it – but it would have been too late in any case. You know I understand how irritating all this is. Like Algernon in "The Importance of being Earnest" saying' *"I never knew anybody take so long to dress, and with such little result."* That's how it must seem.

My only excuse – I did have a bit of a raw deal over my first long novel. I sent the only copy from Paris *most* unwillingly, and never had it back to revise, never saw the proofs, and had to change the title at the last minute – don't know why to this day.

And *that* wasn't all either! Lots more.

I didn't care a hoot at the time [. . . . . .] but I think *now* that it has given me a delayed complex. About MSS not quite finished and cold print being so final and nothing to be done about it any more.

I have it badly about this book. It must be an awful nuisance for I do think that one's struggles to get the thing right ought to be private – not seen and if possible not known or even guessed. Certainly not.

As I can never thank you enough I won't even try.

Yours sincerely
Jean Rhys

There was a man in New York who liked Voyage in the Dark and (I was told) got it read (compulsory!!) in some girls' school which was a bit odd I thought, and not true perhaps. His name was Horace Something. Horace Gregory??[1] I could find out – if it matters. There was so much whisky about and it's all a bit hazy, and was in the 30's. Long ago.

1. Horace Gregory. See letter to Evelyn Scott, page 26.

TO FRANCIS WYNDHAM

Tuesday night [March 11th 1964]
Cheriton Fitz Paine

Dear Mr Wyndham,

I'm ashamed of this lot. Such *a lot*. But I can't face writing it all out again and I *must* get on with Part II which with any luck ought to be done this week. It's much easier.

I have two excuses. I would have revised it *first* if I'd known. I have forgotten the other but it's quite good too. Oh I remember. It looks vast in handwriting but will shrink when typed.

I hope it's clear but I wonder. "Aunt" Cora could easily be made a cousin or even friend but she must be explained for if she is rich and kind their loneliness and poverty wouldn't be so at all. I mean they would not be lonely or poor. It's a possible explanation.

The interview with the mad mother is also a "must". So is Mr Mason at the convent. I think Miss Athill noticed that gap. So did the magazine I hope. There is some mark just at that space.

I cannot say thanks as fussily as usual for it's very late.

But thank you I do say.   Yours sincerely
                                                            Jean Rhys

I will post this registered from Crediton perhaps where I've got to be tomorrow.

TO DIANA ATHILL   *March 27th 1964*
                                                         Cheriton Fitz Paine

Dear Miss Athill,

I was very glad to have your letter. Francis Wyndham told me that he had sent the proofs and corrections to you. Part II will follow – in two lots probably – for I'm most anxious to get it all finished – and clear. There's only one difficulty – in Part III and that can be overcome.

[. . . . . .]

I must come to London of course, next month I hope, and fix it all up. Shipshape. Book I mean. I'd have done so before but haven't been very well since Christmas. And after. So thought it wiser to stay and work in a familiar place – though not a loved place.

Cheriton Fitz Paine is – well it *is*, is *not*. You must miss Esther Whitby, though Latvia[1] sounds fascinating. I've often longed for Finland (lakes, forests and so on, and warm houses they say). But have finally settled on Rio. It would be so lovely *not understanding what anybody said* – and I haven't a word of Portuguese. I've always wondered why people want to – so much better not. Very peaceful I think.

Please keep the photographs as long as you wish – I came across them when hunting for a snapshot taken last summer – not too grim. But it had vanished, and others with it. I suppose I Put Them Away Carefully – always fatal. But where? There's not *much* room here and I hunted again yesterday. I'll have one done in Crediton. Someone gave me an address there – street house everything. Opposite the Post Office he said. So I went and was informed *No photographer in this street and never had been* – very Cheriton Fitz Painey that. However there is one in the High Street and he looks as if he's all out for truth (judging by his display) and doesn't know how elusive truth is. I had some lovely ones of my daughter Maryvonne taken when she was about sixteen.

An amateur – but he used light and shadow most beautifully. The Dutch can and do don't you think? The hair in full strong light, the face in shadow – pensive drooping – then splashes of light on a dark dress. *That's* vanished too!!

I sent the others for a joke – Dresses were pretty in Vienna – not chic but so pretty and one, which I hung on to through thick and thin started me on my literary career (I'm sure, say almost sure), I hope career will end happily after so long – a bit happily anyway.

I think one ought to keep a beloved dress, because it's like diamonds – for ever and will surely come round again – as you say. The way I tore along regardless – losing dresses, cigarette cases, furs, even rings all over the place – well "Now" is a judgement that's what! But I see the parson now and again. Also the next door cat – quite a darling, but she gets very offended if she can't have the arm chair. Cats do.

This letter mixes business and pleasure in an unholy way.

But there's not much left to say about book except to send it along. I know that those corrections look formidable. They won't in type. And *no more additions* to Part I, that's certain. Delete perhaps.

I've remembered all your advice and acted on it – very helpful. So was Mrs Whitby's clear typing.

I'm not mad keen on the title but all the others I think of like *"Solitaire"* which is the French for our Mountain Whistler, or "Before the Break of Day" or "Speak for me" aren't attractive or they are "used" or have the wrong number of letters (very superstitious about that). Yours sincerely

[. . . . . .]   *Jean Rhys*

1. *Esther Whitby was visiting relations in Estonia.*

TO SELMA VAZ DIAS   *[March 1964]*
                                                                    Cheriton Fitz Paine

          I got myself worked up a bit – don't worry.
          It will be a great gap if I can't think
          of you as a dear friend. But you must
          judge and feel that for yourself. In any
          case you'll have the MSS. Then perhaps
          you'll understand. Get well, be happy.
                                        Love from Jean.
          I hope to be in London 6th to 10th April
          – if well enough.

My dear Selma,

I've just had your letter which has left me feeling rather sad and puzzled, *amazed* rather, for it's only one of many brickbats hurled at me lately, some unexpected and those are the worst kind.

I have your telegrams and letters or some of them. Here are copies. Some words left out for brevity. The first came after I'd managed to borrow a suitcase and was on my way – so to speak.

" – just landed film . . . therefore advisable postpone your visit. Stay over Christmas. Letter follows. Love Selma." Then you wrote a short letter saying that there was a hitch over the film and that you felt ill and depressed. So I got ready for Christmas. *2nd wire* . . . Visit over Christmas ill advised. . . . Great upheavals, worries etc. Letter follows. Love Selma.

I was dreadfully sorry you were ill and told you so. There was an Irish friend coming to stay. Indefinitely, you said.

The letter of the 27th Feb. was: ". . . I sympathise with you about yr roof and workmen . . . it is impossible to get down to *anything*. (It is. J.R.) I am cured . . . ailments . . . have found two wonderful doctors . . . etc.

You are welcome to stay any time in my spare room . . . I would love to have you so make up your mind and let me know. The time is now auspicious. Love Selma."

[. . . . . .]

Dear Selma, nothing you write or feel or imagine you feel can change my affection and gratitude. Nothing at all. I wanted you to have the best of this book, not any old snippet. I still do. I wanted – but that would take too long to say. Part I is being typed (I hope) and am nearly ready with Part II, Part III is short *(Thank God)*. You will have a copy of the MSS.

I have made two big mistakes, the first was coming to this beastly isolated little place at all. Blindfold. It has nearly finished Max, and unless I am careful it will finish me. The trouble is that nobody will believe quite how isolated and difficult it is. There's no proper bus service and a fortune goes on taxis. So not even cheap.

The second mistake was not finishing the MSS first – no matter what and no matter who told me differently. Or how long it took. The golden rule is *Finish it first*. Then show it. Or trouble follows. I've known tragedy follow. Not everyone can stand the racket and it is a heart breaking business to have years of toil come to nothing or be hacked about into bits and pieces for hurry up's sake.

I've had no training as a journalist dear, I mean *dear* Selma, I cannot work to rule or to order. Not *won't* – *can't*, and any criticism or worry *before it's done* freezes me up and I'm unable to work at all. Afterwards – couldn't care less!

So I decided to finish the first two parts here. Horrible as it is and lonely – I can work in peace (when I've scrubbed the floor made the bed emptied the dust bin and so on.)

I have done it too – Self hypnotism I suppose. But I cannot type, and couldn't find a typist in this bloody utterly *bloody* hole, though I found a good one in Cornwall. So bits and pieces had to be sent off. This is hunting country – I often see them pass, and very nice too. I'm waiting for the Tally ho, and it won't be long. In fact it has started already! Books! Well no! not *books*! they say – *What next*!!

I spent all yesterday in tears and most of today on this letter. So it's time to work again which is all that matters in the end. I will finish this novel unless I get ill or something, be sure of that. Part II ought to be done in a week or two and the end firmly lodged so that I don't fluff it when dictating.

I hope I shall see you and *please* (though I'd love it) don't think you are bound to have me to stay. *Why?* I can stay at a hotel or something and still see you. If not, you will have the MSS as I promised.

I *seem* all sorts of foolish things but underneath it's fort comme la mort about some things.

Someone wrote to me that he'd seen some home-movies of Dominica, my home, and that it was ravishingly lovely. So it is. But it's rock too. Like the sentimental Judy I am I've stuck up a motto on the wall. *"Remember the rock from which thou wast hewn"*, a Cornish motto.

Doesn't all this sound balls? But it is not quite balls. Or corny either.

I must add a ps to this long gospel – I have been ill ever since Christmas – not coming to London then big let down though unavoidable I know.

Also I've forced myself to work – an effort. I do not remember what I wrote to you exactly, for what with illness, being alone, and worry over extract I felt distracted. I couldn't possibly have given any exact date or I'd have wired. Every day I thought I'll be OK tomorrow. But wasn't. The really brutal weather and some of the letters I had did not help. But this is a brutal place. I knew that at once – so no surprise really. Indeed I'm losing the power to be surprised. Also to write short letters. But, though you may have forgotten it, the only definite dates *were cancelled. By you. By wire.* With good reason I know.

However it does not matter much – Nothing matters much. Once you said "I do not like life." Perhaps you forget but I don't. Well I do not like life much either.

J.R.

TO DIANA ATHILL   *April 6th [1964]*
                                                        Cheriton Fitz Paine

[. . . . . .]

Dear Miss Athill,

Thank you for writing. Yes, I am rather worried (and puzzled too) about some things that have happened and continue to happen.

[. . . . . .]

It has just become a certainty that perhaps *no one troubles to read* my long hand-written letters – out of the Ark they must seem – and indeed this place *is* the Ark – with not very pleasant animals in it either.

So in that way misunderstandings arise and this better be a short letter (or short for me). What a hope!

What worries me the most is that I've been thrown off at a time – so long waited for – when I *saw* the book as a whole, and was working quickly and not too badly. (I was and have been afraid of that.) However the élan (though a bit tarnished) is still there. I will send Part II this month.

Do you think that it would be a good idea to send the proofs and corrections to some patient typewriting firm and ditto Part II? I don't know any, but they must exist – surely. Perhaps it *would* save trouble and more misunderstandings. I'd want three copies and would pay any typewriters fees.

Everyone seems to be so annoyed that I can't help feeling that something somewhere has gone wrong – *without my knowledge.*

Selma (Vaz Dias) has written quite angrily. She says that I have promised to come to London several times and not arrived. The truth is that I was ready to come – and packed – twice – when her invitations fell through, the first time because she had a film job, the second time because she was ill. (I have her wires).

The Christmas disappointment left me very sad and so on. This is a lonely place and not beautiful at all. Then out of the blue came this knowledge of how to finish and correct the book. That often happens to me (and to others also) and I was awfully anxious not to lose it – it's important not to. Especially after such a long and weary waiting.

However we will see. "Vous etes nègre?" "Oui mon général". "Alors – continuez mon enfant. Continuez."[1] I daresay he did and so will I.

[. . . . . .]

I can't come to London now for I'm not very well – and feel most strongly that finishing the book is first – that stands – whatever else crashes – a finished book.

I have worked off most of my sadness writing three poems – *one I like*. Could the typewriting firm do them too? Perhaps this has become a long epistle. Still please read it for I am now quite certain that most of my scrawls *are not* read – I wonder if anything is? I've seen these people at what they call "leafing through" (my second husband was a literary agent). It gave me the creeps, and still does. Also he told me he'd missed two good ones that way. So it is not even sensible.

[. . . . . .]

Yours sincerely
Jean Rhys

1. *It is Marshal MacMahon who is supposed to have said "Continuez, mon brave, continuez."*

TO FRANCIS WYNDHAM   *April 8th 1964*
Cheriton Fitz Paine

[. . . . . .]

Dear Mr Wyndham,

[. . . . . .]

It's been a bit difficult since Christmas – what between long long epistles from me which are unanswered. Are they *too* long I wonder? Is that the clue? (Mr Smith is often away I believe and everybody very busy.) Then of course several brickbats about not answering letters I've *never had* (Selma) and a wild search for a typist (those corrections and additions). But no typist, none. So I'm starting to feel a bit weak. However I have finished "Sargasso Sea" Part II. It was done at six this morning and I've not had much sleep but *that's* easily cured. The difficulty there is the half scrawl, half shorthand I use, which no one understands but myself – (No wonder either). There must be a way out of that and I'll find it. Exeter? London?

Part III is *(oh thank God!)* the shortest and easiest – I hope to do it this week.

I wrote three poems to cure myself of sadness, now I've the greatest difficulty stopping myself doing everything in poetry. I did hit on one phrase which may tie up with the title "wild sea of wrecks" or "that wild sea of weeds where I was wrecked". Or they. Poor Antoinette and poor Mr R.

I will write to Christy & Moore not adding "personal" and find out what is going on for there's another one, an Irish one (man I mean) who might answer. Also I may hear from Miss Athill. Not?

I have asked two or three times for a copy of my contract, but it's a long thing I know.

I was so pleased to have a copy of Art and Literature and am much enjoying it. I hope that's all right and will thank Mrs Orwell tomorrow. What a lovely preface you wrote for me and please whatever happens will you write another? But don't tell anybody how old I am for I think better not. Not??

I planned long ago to use Maryvonne (my girl) as a stand in but she refused flatly – aged then about six or seven.

She said "My father is an artist and has not one sou, my mother tries to be an artist and is always crying. Artist? Merci. *Non!* et NON!! et NON!!!" So you see *that* idea was no use.

Writing my poems I forgot the dust bins. There's an awful row due tomorrow when they come round. They can be *so* difficult.

I want one of them, poems, to be typed. Will you do it for me – please?

I keep thinking, if I am ill. Or something? They'd get torn up. I think it too about "That wild sea of wrecks and weeds" now it is so really nearly done (touch wood).   Yours sincerely
                                                                           Jean Rhys

TO FRANCIS WYNDHAM   *April 14th [1964]*
                                                Cheriton Fitz Paine

                         [. . . . . .]

Dear Mr Wyndham,
     [. . . . . .]
I am now so taken up with "Sargasso Sea" that I am proud to say that I've got "writer's cramp" – must be the only person in the world who has it – what with typists, tape recorders and so on. Isn't *that* something? I have to write carefully though – to be legible which slows me up (still more).

I am in touch with Miss Athill who wrote me the kindest of letters. There's a typewriting firm next door, she says, who can manage what I send – so that's *one* problem solved.

Now about the book – I was rather down with this and that, so flew to writing poems. This I've always done (aged 12 or 10 when I started). They are

261

strewn all over the places I've lived in – didn't keep many. I like some of them and can do them quickly.

Well I wrote four. The best, I think, is called "The Old Man's Home" but it's the one I enclose which gave me the clue to my book. (Please remember that what I write helps me – written clearly or not it helps. So don't be bored.) A struggle with my handwriting plus writer's cramp. Still – It is quite true that I've brooded over "Jane Eyre" for years.

The Brontë sisters had of course a touch of genius (or much more) especially Emily. So reading "Jane Eyre" one's swept along regardless. But *I*, reading it later, and often, was vexed at her portrait of the "paper tiger" lunatic, the all wrong creole scenes, and above all by the real cruelty of Mr Rochester. After all, he was a very wealthy man and there were many kinder ways of disposing of (or hiding) an unwanted wife – I heard the true story of one – and the man behaved very differently. (Another clue.)

Even when I knew I *had* to write the book – still it did not click into place – that is one reason (though only one) why I was so long. It didn't click. It wasn't there. However I tried.

Only when I wrote this poem – then it clicked – and all was there and always had been.

The first clue is Obeah which I assure you existed, and still does, in Haiti South America and of course in Africa – under different names. The others – sais pas. It was against the law in the "English" islands. The second clue was when Miss Athill suggested a few weeks of happiness for the unfortunate couple – before he gets disturbing letters. As soon as I wrote that bit I realised that he must have fallen for her – and violently too. The black people have or had a good word for it – "she *magic* with him" or "he *magic* with her". Because you see, that is what it is – magic, intoxication. Not "Love" at all. There is too the magic of the place, which is not all lovely beaches or smiling people – it can be a very disturbing kind of beauty. Many people have felt that and written about it too. So poor Mr R, being in this state gets this letter and is very unhappy indeed.

Now is the time for Obeah. The poor (she too) girl doesn't know *why* he's so suddenly left her in the lurch, so flies off to her nurse (presence explained) for a love drink. From the start it must be made clear that Christophine is "an obeah woman". When her, Antoinette's (rather confused) explanations fall flat, she slips him the love drink. *At once.* That is the only change to be made. It must be *at once*.

In obeah these drinks or sacrifices or whatever have this effect: The god himself enters the person who has drunk. Afterwards he (or she) faints, recovers, and remembers very little of what has happened (they say). I wouldn't know.

Not Mr R. He remembers *everything* including the fact that he has felt a bit uneasy in the early happy days and asked her to tell him what's wrong, promised to believe her, and stand by her, and she's always answered "Nothing is wrong." For, poor child, she is *afraid* to tell him, and cries if he insists.

So he strides into her bedroom, not himself, but angry love and that is what the poem is about.

Even when the love has gone the anger is still there and remains. (No obeah needed for that!) And remains.

Well this is now a long letter. Have you got so far? Continuez –

Mr Rochester tries hard not to be a tyrant. Back in Spanish Town he gives her a certain freedom, *tries* to be kindly if distant.

But now she is angry too. Like a hurricane. Like a Creole. For his second revenge – his affair with her maid (and next door) has hurt more than the first.

She uses her freedom to rush off and have an affair too – first with her pal Sandi – then with others. All coloured or black, which was, in those days, a *terrible* thing for a white girl to do. Not to be forgiven. The men did as they liked. The women – *never*.

So imagine Mr R's delight when he can haul her to England, lock her up in a cold dark room, deprive her of all she's used to – watch her growing mad. And so on – I think the governess and the house party rash. But I suppose he thought her *fini* by that time. Well, she wasn't –

I think there were several Antoinettes and Mr Rochesters. Indeed I am sure. Mine is *not* Miss Brontë's, though much suggested by "Jane Eyre". She is, to start with, young not old. She is still a girl when she fires the house and jumps to her death. And hates last. Mr R's name ought to be changed. Raworth? A Yorkshire name isn't it? The sound is right. In the poem (if it's that) Mr Rochester (or Raworth) consoles himself or justifies himself by saying that *his* Antoinette runs away after the "Obeah nights" and that the creature who comes back is not the one who ran away. I wish this had been thought of before – for that too is part of Obeah.

A Zombie is a dead person raised up by the Obeah woman, it's usually a woman I think, and a zombie can take the appearance of anyone. Or anything.

But I did not write it that way and I'm glad, for it would have been a bit creepy! And probably, certainly I think, beyond me.

Still, it's a thought – for anyone who writes those sort of stories.

No. Antoinette herself comes back but so changed that perhaps she *was* "lost Antoinette". I insist that she must be lovely, and certainly she was lost. "All in the romantic tradition".

As for what I've done – the time when "she magic for him". The letter – better and shorter. The interview with Daniel. That's all for Part II. The end when they leave for Spanish Town. Also most of the corrections and cuts and the *first chapter rewritten. Important* as it explains Christophine in Grandbois.

It's all a bit of a scrawl but I can do it and know it. It is done except Part III.

Yes I need a holiday, *short*, but I feel that perhaps I'd better get it straight here. I have solitude and privacy – both not so easy to get and there's rather a good tree to look at. I'm sure the neighbours think I'm potty but after all – they can hardly haul me off to the bin for scribble scribble scribble. Quite noiselessly. I really believe that if I had a typewriter they would, for I work late now. (They don't like books much.)

I must post this and the one to Miss Athill. So that is all for now and enough

too. The return to Spanish Town and Sandi have been *implied* not written
about directly. All along.   Sincerely yours
                                                                  Jean Rhys

Obeah Night

A night I seldom remember
    (If it can be helped)
The night I saw Love's dark face
    Was Love's dark face
"And cruel as he is"? I've never known that
    I tried my best you may be certain (whoever asks)
    My human best

If the next morning as I looked at what I'd done
(He was watching us mockingly, used to these games)
If I'd stared back at him
If I'd said
"I was a god myself last night
I've tamed and changed a wild girl"
Or taken my hurt darling in my arms
(Conquered at last. And silent. Mine)

Perhaps Love would have smiled then
    Shown us the way
Across that sea. They say it's strewn with wrecks
    And weed-infested
Few dare it, fewer still escape
But *we*, led by smiling Love
We could have sailed
    Reached a safe harbour
Found a sweet, brief heaven
    Lived our short lives

But I was both sick and sad
    (Night always ends)
She was a stranger
Wearing the mask of pain
Bearing the marks of pain –
I turned away – Traitor
Too sane to face my madness (or despair)
    Far, far too cold and sane

Then Love, relenting
Sent clouds and soft rain
Sent sun, light and shadow
    To show me again
Her young face waiting

Waiting for comfort and a gentler lover?
    (You'll not find him)
A kinder loving? *Love is not kind*
I would not look at her
(Once is enough)
Over my dead love
Over a sleeping girl
I drew a sheet
Cover the stains of tears
Cover the marks of blood
(You can say nothing
That I have not said a thousand times and one
Excepting this – That night was Something Else
I was Angry Love Himself
Blind fierce avenging Love – no other that night)

"It's too strong for Béké"
    The black woman said
Love, hate or jealousy
    Which had she seen?
She knew well – the *Devil*!
– What it could mean

How can I forget you Antoinette
    When the spring is here?
Where did you hide yourself

After that shameless, shameful night?
And why come back? Hating and hated?
Was it Love, Fear, Hoping?
Or (as always) Pain?
(*Did* you come back I wonder
Did I ever see you again?)

No. I'll lock that door
Forget it.–
The motto was "Locked Hearts I open
    I have the heavy key"
Written in black letters
Under a Royal Palm Tree
On a slave owner's gravestone
"Look! And look again, hypocrite" he says
    "Before *you* judge *me*"

I'm no damn slave owner
I have no slave
Didn't she (forgiven) betray me
Once more – and then again

Unrepentant – laughing?
I can soon show her
    Who hates the best
Always she answers me
    I will hate last

Lost, lovely Antoinette
How can I forget you
When the spring comes?
(Spring is cold and furtive here
There's a different rain)
Where did you hide yourself
After the obeah nights?
(*What* did you send instead?
    Hating and hated?)
Where did you go?
I'll never see you now
I'll never know
For you left me – my truest Love
Long ago

Edward Rochester or Raworth
Written in Spring 1842

TO DIANA ATHILL   *[April 1964]*
                                                         Cheriton Fitz Paine
My Dear Diana,
    One of my favourite names – (all ending in A I like). I cannot tell you how
much your letter cheered me. I've been a bit down since Christmas and lately
very tangled. The letters I write – trying to sort things out! Quite apart from
The Book (and here let me say that I'm very excited about your novel and
longing to see it but more of that later. *One thing at a time* I tell myself looking at
the muddle I'm in).
    Well first there's the laundry, and fierce notes about two sheets and a bath
towel. Well I've given that up. Then there's a nice woman in London who's
trying to sell me cut price cosmetics and *am* I willing to be made beautiful! But
her letters arrive half empty and when I say "Kindly *stick* envelopes" all I get is
Freezing Silence till the next lovely offer comes along. This time it's
Sandalwood things for a bath, or several, but *what* can I do when somebody
certainly opens these letters etc. on the way.
    (*Beauty*. It is marked on them and of course . . . .) So I'll have one more try,
"*Please use plain envelopes* when writing to the West Country" and if that's no
good – Give Up again.
    Also there are Birds in the Attic – at least, I'm told they are birds. All I can
say is – they don't *sound* like birds at all. There was a large hole in the roof and

266

the men who mended it told me "oh yes, birds up here". So I can only repeat they do not *sound* like birds, and anyway why aren't they asleep at 2 am? However I'll say no more about that alarming subject, or you'll think it's Bats in the Belfry. All my suit-cases etc. et al are there (y compris those snap shots I think) but nothing on earth would get me up to that attic as it's pitch dark and then – *Those Birds*. (If they *are* birds).

I tell myself Don't be silly but only plunge deeper into a sort of a kind of a *trance*. The book is finished but in such a scrawl, so must be done again, the bits and pieces I mean. I've got Mr Rochester nicely mixed up with Mr Heathcliff, have fallen in love with Antoinette and her legend. But as this is a serious subject I've dealt with it separately in a separate envelope – also the poem to "Lovely Lost Antoinette". Read it when you have time and want to – not before.

This is only to make you laugh (perhaps) and cheer myself up. Y compris et al and all – I would have written before but I hate the 13th. However there are so many spiders mice and so on that I'd better Give *that* Up too – being superstitious I mean. All the same . . . .

Bruges is now high up on my list of "places" after your letter, but was always there. My first friend (I mean copain) was born in Bruges, though living in Brussels, exiled of course in London, and I showed him some of my poems for I began writing them aged 12, having discovered that they are a cure for sadness and easily done – not like prose which can be a *terrible* worry to me. Well he told me about Bruges and that it was beautiful. He was writing a book about the Japanese theatre, No or Ko or something, which was afterwards published in Paris – but I never read it. His name was Camille, forget surname, and he got a job in the Belgian Congo bank (meanwhile) and won my heart completely when he said one day that he could easily grab the cash, and would I light out with him if he did. He was not serious – but what a darling man. He did cheer me up, and back me up too. I was very lonely then and young and kind of bewildered and he was a comfort I must say. How long ago it sounds – and is –

I've an idea that there are many lovely old towns still dreaming away and hidden away and that one's waiting for *me* – what a comforting idea too. (May I find it!!) Delft I liked, but too cold. I am utterly completely and for ever *Fed UP* with the country – soon I shall hate it as fiercely as any Mr Rochester hated any Antoinette.

I've only got a different *"slant"* on this book and I find that hints and so on of this "slant" are all over the place. It must have been in my mind – all the time.

The additions can be written and sent to you and typing firm – but the MSS is rather a snag. Some of it is all right, some must be cut, some twisted round. Only one copy. I know how it goes but I must certainly come to London and see to it. Or if not well enough for London, Exeter.

It will be done – God willing to be superstitious – And soon now.

I am sad I've been so long – but it was a difficult book and done under very difficult circumstances. Still I have it now (touch wood, cross fingers *and* spit). Over left shoulder. That's a stage one but you doubtless know it. (Gosh that was a thump from the attic!) An albatross must have got in – I'm the sort of person an albatross would like very much. I will post this tomorrow. The other day after.

There are four poems. One made me "see" the book, one is called "The Old Man's Home", one is about words.

One I send – because it's short.

Yours sincerely
Jean

I wish you so much luck with your novel.

After all – the poems are better sent together.

TO DIANA ATHILL *April 28th [1964]*
Cheriton Fitz Paine

> It's not "Stormy Weather" I'm thinking
> of now. It's "You'll take the high road
> And I'll take the low road
> But I'll be in Scotland before you."
> *Why?* Don't know.

Dear Diana,

I wrote you two long letters which I won't send for they are the same old song once again and what's the use?

I do not quite understand why, when *I* have told you that this book is finished (in my scrawl and a kind of shorthand I've invented) but finished (but for part III – short) you reply No *they* say it's unfinished. What *They*? and *Why*? However there are so many puzzling matters. So let's pass on. I think that in all the muddle two things stick out five miles.

The first one is that for several years (YEARS) I could not really work at this romantic novel (my first Romance) because my husband fell seriously ill not long after I started. Max is not a bundle of old rags to me – he is Max. (Nice too. Was. A stoic) But though torn in two I still worked and bluffed as well. At night. On pep pills. So at last the *Skeleton* was there. Then I got it typed with some difficulty you bet! *Got in one exit shot tho* at Madame Brown. Also *Monsieur B*, and so on –

When Max (who is a very important factor in all this), though he is, let's say, a *hidden* factor, disregarded, went into hospital I spent some bad weeks of loneliness and near despair. This is a lonely place.

Then I said *"Come On"* and *"Steady does it"* as my long dead PA said and started on Part II. Part I (a third of the book) was (I thought) finished – or nearly – additions corrections et al and in safe hands. But now I sometimes wonder – what *has* become of Part I and *needed* additions? *Don't* say it's lost stolen or strayed? "Or I shall weep. Then sleep Five fathoms deep. Nor ever rise" (quotation from Book).

I won't harrow you with my struggles. Damned old Part II!! Never mind –
Rot chucked out, Bits put in. Even spelling fixed up. Still it was (to me) dead as
a dead heart. Not all of course. So I remembered what I'd been told by one of
these old hat lot who after all *knew their job* and something about writing and
writers and all that Jazz and what one *feels* (which is also important). PUT IT
AWAY I was told. *Do Something Else.* So I did. Part II was put away and I
worked on four poems. [. . . . . .] Well, after second poem came what I call
the *Breakthrough* and I saw what was wrong and why it (the book) was dead. I'd
got the girl (less or more) but my Mr R was *all wrong*. Also a *heel*. First, he
coldly marries a girl for her dough, *then* he believes everything he's told about
her, finally he drags her to England, shuts her up in a cold dark room for *years*
and brings sweet little Janey to look at the result – this noble character! Noble!!
My God! As soon as I saw that it all came to life. It had always been there. . . .
Mr Rochester is *not* a heel. He is a fierce and violent (Heathcliff) man who
marries an alien creature, partly because his father arranges it, partly because he
has had a bad attack of fever, partly no doubt for *lovely* mun, but most of all
because he is *curious* about this girl – already half in love.

Then (this is good old Part II) they get to this lovely lonely magic place and
there is no "half" at all. My Mr Rochester as I see him becomes as fierce as
Heathcliff and as jealous as Othello. He is also a bit uneasy (not used to strong
magic at all). *Suspicious – (Why do I feel like this?)* (That you see is where I went
so wrong.) Well this is what I've done – as the letter is becoming a long letter
and tedious. Not much is *changed. A lot is written in and done. All done.*

I have tried to show this man being magicked by the place which is (or was) a
lovely, lost *and magic* place but, if you understand, a *violent* place. (Perhaps
there is violence in *all* magic and *all* beauty – but there – very strong) magicked
by the girl – the two are mixed up perhaps to bewildered English gent, Mr R,
certain that she's hiding something from him. And of course she *is*. Her mad
mother. (Not mad perhaps at all) So you see – when he gets this letter all blows
sky high. And so – I've fixed up the letter, written in his interview with Daniel
whom Mr R detests but believes. (Why) I could guess that too I think – because
he *wants* to – that's why. Also that awful bastard Daniel has persuaded him that
his wife is not only mad but plain *bad*. Sandi and others. So you see – poor Mr
Rochester – and poor lovely Antoinette too. She runs away to Christophine
but comes back for she also is now desperately in love. *(Of course!)* I have
written in a long interview with Christophine but the end of interview remains
as before – nearly. The last chapter when they leave I will send to you. It is part
"poetry" part prose. It *may* be fustian (I think not) but can be altered easily
enough to prose. *Not Now.* As I told you the *MSS* is not altered (much. *Some
wasn't too right you know).* The *slant* has been altered. It is not so tame – that's all.
Additions do it.

Oh yes I've cut out the vomiting and so on and made it that the "love" drink
on Obeah Night merely releases all the misery, jealousy and ferocity that has
been piling up in Mr R for so long. He pretends to think he's been poisoned –
that's only to pile up (again) everything he can against her and so excuse his
cruelty. He *justifies* it that way. (It's often done)

I do not think that it *justifies* him at all. I *do* think it *explains* him a bit. However (– So *cold* before he was). If when it is done you do not like it – then say so. No problem. All will be arranged. Cash etc.

But it's always *trust* or it'll go *bust*. This I got from a very wealthy man long ago, I've had a *rum* life! who (en passant) was explaining J P Morgan's intimate affairs. *Why?* That's gone. Me listening to all this not getting the point at all really. But he said "When you are dealing with *Big Money* you've *got* to trust the other chap sometimes – or the whole dam thing would collapse." Something like that. I've remembered enough to have "*Trust* or go *bust*" firmly fixed in my erratic head. Well Books can be Big too. Or small. Or nothing. (The writer doesn't matter at all – he is only the instrument. But . . . . he must not be smashed. Or *he* goes bust. Then no music if you smash the violin.)

Well please believe that I am doing my best. I have waited long for the Breakthrough trusting trusting it would come and it has now. I think. *No more slow painful stuff. Quick now. You will have it by summer.*

I heard from Christy & Moore this morning – thank you. *Beautiful* Dough.

Why do I love you so?

Indeed I feel a lot better already. A bit tired lately (said the crying child). I like *that* too.

But all this *write write all night* and food such a bore –

Not so-o good. Now comes the time to trust or I'll bust. Which is point no 2. That is the danger. *(I think not bust though)*

Mrs Whitby was and will be an enormous help. *So* nice. But give me a little time to fix up flat and my battered self. Also to get the stuff straight, and no fumbling. Or losing Bits. I will make it all shipshape & Bristol fashion. Meantime give her my best thanks past and to come. It's Stormy Weather here. But must stop sometime, surely.

> Yours what you will
> *Jean*

TO FRANCIS WYNDHAM
Thursday [1964]
Cheriton Fitz Paine

You see – I am not *used to being so* alone. *In the country too. Hateful* place!

Please read this *some time* – Please. Hope spelling right. I have a French-English Dictionary. Just discovered that some of the *English* words are spelt wrong(ly). Oh well!

270

Dear Mr Wyndham,

Thank you for typing the "poem". It's a bit "Hiawatha" isn't it? The swing I mean. But no matter. I will not trouble you with the others. Till typed. If ever. It is a strange thing that I can write mediocre "poetry" so easily, and labour so over prose. *Then* all traces of effort must be blotted out. Oh dear! Poor me!! If you knew!!! Now once and for all, I will finish *finish* with what I've to say about this book, which I have lived with for so long that now these people are real to me – far more real than anyone I meet. (*They* are not many. The parson is nice. One day he bought me some whisky. Oh my God! I've *never lived that down. He* could hide behind his Greek or whatever and the rectory and so on. I had nowhere to hide. I *did* think up keeping the radio on all day – balls and all. They understand that. My pin up boy is now – *Stalin*!! who machine-gunned these country characters like anything. Some are nice and I daresay all right. But a trifle puritanical perhaps. Which I don't like. And *hard* too.) Well – Continuez mon enfant. (That is *me* – l'enfant.)

I realise what I lose by cutting loose from Jane Eyre and Mr Rochester – Only too well. (Indeed *can* I?) Names? Dates?

But I believe and firmly too that there was more than one Antoinette. The West Indies was (were?) rich in those days *for* those days and there was no "married woman's property Act". The girls (very tiresome no doubt) would soon once in kind England be *Address Unknown*. So gossip. So a legend. If Charlotte Brontë took her horrible Bertha from this legend I have the right to take lost Antoinette. And, how to reconcile the two and fix dates I do not know – yet. But, I will. Another thing is this: –

I have a very great and deep admiration for the Brontë sisters (Though Charlotte did preachify sometimes). (And all the rest.) And often boring perhaps. (Me too!)

How then can *I* of all people, say she was wrong? Or that her Bertha is impossible? *Which she is.* Or get cheap publicity from her (often) splendid book?

She wrote: – Charlotte did:

"*This I know: The writer . . . owns something of which he is not always master . . . it will perhaps for years lie in subjection . . . then without warning of revolt there comes a time . . . when it sets to work. . . . You have little choice left but quiescent adoption (?) As for you, the* nominal *artist – your share is to work passively – under dictates you neither delivered nor could question – that would not be delivered at your prayer, nor changed at your caprice. If the result be attractive the World will praise you, who little deserve praise. If it be repulsive the World will blame you, who as little deserve blame.*"

So you see she *knew*. It is so. And it is so. (As for Emily – well less said about her the better. Hope Mr W S gave her a drink and a big kiss. In Valhalla.)

I will try – I have this book now. A lot is in poetry which I'll carefully turn into prose. Or perhaps not all prose. I too "little deserve praise or blame". (Sometimes) If I have been long – well it has been harder than you know. Or would believe perhaps.

I think you have been most generous to me, encouraged me when I'd nearly given up, helped me when I needed help. But a bit bored sometimes – Not? A bit impatient and *why doesn't this woman hurry up for God's sake? And why bother me* any more? Not??

Well it's all hard and lonely. And remember that *This* can force you to try to use others *almost* tho' not nearly as relentlessly as you are obliged to use yourself. But now comes the let up, and the breakthrough and no more asking for help from anyone – Or boring anybody. However understanding and merciful.

I will finish this book by myself and be passive and write what I am told to write. I don't care any more what happens to it – once written. If it swims and does not sink then I will ask you to write a preface. Please. For perhaps you can put into words what I cannot. After all I don't know many words so have to use them carefully. I *always* know what is wrong – it often takes me a *long* time to get it right. See? All the same . . . .

Last time I saw my pal (?) the parson [. . . . . .] he did not know the story of Bernadette of Lourdes. The beautiful Lady appeared to Bernadette – where? On the town's refuse dump – (Oh it's cleaned up nicely now I bet). The values are so different, you see and must be shown to be different. Never mind – he, the nice parson, knows Greek and so on and *did* get me *that whisky*, and it cheers me up to see him for I see nobody excepting the baker, milk girl etc.

I feel a bit of an automaton now, which is no doubt part of it. The only thing is I can't sleep so sit up to all hours. It's late now. I must get it all in for I'll write no more long letters. I have not the right to worry anybody any more.

Never say or think – "I wish I'd left this terrible creature alone." Really! . . . Because you see if I had not had this book, this hope – Of *What? Not dough* – these years would have been very tough. Too tough I think. Even for me. This is a very serious letter but I write jokey ones too. Fall a bit flat. But *I* laugh. I laughed over the *"Do you wish to be a Mental Giant? Easy Terms. Fill up Enclosed Form"* that circular for days. I *can't* learn that in England business is no joke. No joking either. . . . Oh dear – does so remind me of "You know me? I was the one who laughed at your one line. Heard every word. Come on cheer up and have a drink." *(I long and long for that).* [. . . . . .]

I have no telephone and the village one (automatic) has (thank God) *Out of Order* on it and never will have anything else. Even the post box is miles away and I go to it singing in the rain. I do *not* think! Only my book matters. *Nothing but that.* Well last long letter, my hand and seal on it.

Yours sincerely and gratefully
Jean Rhys

I will not crack. Sometimes I can write. In my twenties fashion. *And After too.*
How about
"There comes a time" for title
The *poem* ties up with "Sargasso Sea"
but with very little in the book. It's not important.
Yet.

I will send everything to Miss Athill. Even though I've heard nothing about

Part I. Or additions. I expect it's in the dust bin – Or lost. Oh Well! Bon Dieu!

Don't you think I am being penalised rather heavily because I can't rattle away on a typewriter? And live in this impossible place? Perhaps not – I don't know.

I will finish my lament for Antoinette (and many others). Then I will ask Alec to come down though he doesn't care for Cheriton Fitz (*Who would?*) I will rest a little then come to lovely kind London. For the money you sent is there to be used for that.

Nothing but that.

Merci and thank you for so much.

Very much.

J.R.

I have not been very well since Christmas – (*years* ago) or I'd have come to London – the sensible thing. But better be well I think – much better. Don't you?

I'll be OK. *And sensible too.* When my book is finished.

It is not a "sensible' book. Nor can I be "sensible" when writing it. But I'm not round the bend. Only trusting perhaps.

> This is not another poem. Don't worry.
> But please read it – my letter.

> I know very well that
> my worry doesn't matter to anyone
> Not much. And quite right too.
> But it's so nearly done now, this
> book
> And I *think* it is worth saving. Now. At last –

As for the others

Well – I do not know. I suppose it'll be all fixed up. Some time. Or no time.

It seems very long to wait – for a typed letter –

Talk about "Years are so long" (Victorian ballad)

> *Days* can be too long –
> (And damaging in the end)
> But *I* am *okay* – or will be. Soon – You'll see.

> Oh listen in Obeah nights   (I do not think
>   It's not   Mr Rochester would hurt
> Too strong for Bébé   a baby. But one never
>   but   knows.)
> Too strong for Béké

Béké, Buckra, now ofay or something

> Words for "white people."   New York (Was)

There is a *lovely* song (Trinidad I think)

"Glory dead when white man come.
Glory dead Glory dead.
Glory dead when Buckra come
Glory dead Glory dead.

I said No poem
That's a good one – don't you think?
All I know of it though

My awful handwriting. *Sorry*.
If I write carefully – it's so *slow*.

May 7th [1964]
                                              Cheriton Fitz Paine

It's very good for work (except for
mice – they do alarm me). So OK. Please
– my whisky story is only a joke, too bad
a joke. So forget it.

Dear Mr Wyndham,
Thank you for sending the "poem"[1] – not quite right yet, is it? I will put it
away and fix it up sometime – I've been working very hard at passionate Mr
Rochester, sitting up to all hours (I heard a cuckoo one morning – so realised it
was morning not night any more). I've nearly finished now and am glad, as
that man is making me very *thin*. The weeds are growing and growing and
soon I'll be really hidden away – For keeps.
    Seriously – I am anxious to know what you think of him – that is one reason
I'm bothering you – the other is that it's perhaps difficult to dictate something
which one isn't sure of – an experiment.
    I'm afraid it won't be a wonderful book(!) – it ought to have been just a
romantic novel – but my boat has been capsized (upset I mean) so many times
(and I've had to start again) that I'm not quite in control of it now. *It's* in
control of *me*. But still – in control enough. I have always meant to make the
first two parts *possible* – if not probable (to English people) and I've still got
hold of that.
    All the rest *is* written (unfortunately legible to me only) though nobody
believes it – and as soon as I've posted this lot to you I will write to Diana Athill
about getting it typed. In her last letter she said that it was becoming an
"unfinished book" to some people – oh dear who? whom? I do hope you
reassured her. It worried me for a bit – then got into boat again – Volga
boatmen had a fine time compared with me. One of these days I'll write a *short*
letter – but what with one thing and another – you just talk away on paper. I
had a very nice letter from Sonia Orwell. I told her about the weeds, and
difficulty of borrowing a sheep to eat them. It's quite impossible to get sheep

away from each other, and I can't manage a *flock*! Mrs Orwell also told me there had been some nice notices. I haven't seen them – but no matter – the two (or one) you sent, of course. I'm glad about the New Yorker – used to like it – and hope Carol Hill (Mrs Brandt) still has the MSS. Those stories seem very far away now – excepting Petronella which saved me.

I shocked the village (talking about salvation) because one afternoon or evening, the parson said "*What* can I do for you?" I said *whisky* and he went to the pub for it. Hadn't got his car – so the Watchers saw him. It took me quite a time to realise why coldness had become deep freeze – and I suppose it was a – tactless? thing to do! Never mind – he has promised to pray for me and they can't stop that. I did so like him too – never mind again.

I simply *cannot* understand why so many people imagine that I'm a bit of rather battered ivy waving around – looking for any old oak to cling to, because I'm really a Savage Individualist. Still have the letter – "Dear Jean, You are a *savage individualist* so do not realise etc." I am too. A very expensive thing to be I assure you. All the same – I am that – I *think* and hope. Also pray.

If you knew what an odd life I lead here you'd forgive my letters. Sometimes I can't believe it myself.

To feel quite *dazed* about things and people is a strange feeling. If someone knocked on this door I believe I'd say "Dr Livingstone I presume"? or "Hullo Man Friday!"

I've got the end of the poem and here it is. After all other people must like doing them.

I read Scott Fitzgerald's "Tender is the night" and didn't love it somehow – but liked

> Won't you wait
> Mister Fate ? Tender is the night

so much that I'll try again – if I can.

I'll send Mr Rochester along (Mr Rochester I presume?) and please tell me exactly what you think. I'll be really grateful. As I am anyway –

Yours sincerely
Jean Rhys

> And if I've got him mixed up
> With Rudolf
> And Marie
> Or guess they played the same trick
> The exit trick, the best trick
> The oh so hard, so easy trick –
> (Gone away. Gone away)
> Of course that was Tokayer
>   or Tokay
> Nothing to do with me (for once)
>   Nothing at all (you'd say)

J.R.

I *did* see an acrobat fall just like that. They *said* because he was working too near the ground. Very dangerous (they *said*)

As for the Tokayer, I'll find out some time – Yes I spelt Marie Vetsera wrong –

1. Not *"Obeah Night"* but another, longer poem called *"The Easy Trick"*; mingling the description of the death of a young acrobat during a performance in a music-hall in Vienna with references to the double suicide of Archduke Rudolph of Austria and Marie Vetsera at Mayerling.

TO FRANCIS WYNDHAM   *[May 14th 1964]*
                                                                    Cheriton Fitz Paine
Dear Mr Wyndham,
    Your letter cheered me up so much. I have finished with Mr Rochester – or I hope so. The problem now is – shall I send him along tidy or untidy. Probably untidy with corrections and so on visible – for that would be much quicker.
    I could write a very long letter about this book (I have I suppose) – not even asking myself *have I said this before?* Haunting question. I probably have, and all day long I've been trying to remember the words of Jean Harlow's song – a thirties song, called "Everything's been done before."¹ I like it very much and sing it a lot – to my words – as the only other line of the original that's stuck is "But it's new to me – it's new to me". (I can tell right away that unless I pull myself together this won't get posted.)
    Last night I sat up very late – another bad habit – and got what I thought four or five lines right, fixed inevitable and not to be changed and as they were the last lines of part II I was pleased – because four lines right can mean a lot. Well – this morning I woke up to this song and the words "Madame Bovary" and realised at once that these lines were not the *words* but the *situation* at the end of Madame Bovary, her death. Well (again) as I have not read that novel for years I find it odd – and have thought and thought about it and finally decided. No it was not Mme Bovary, it was me – I wonder though. Thoughts are strange and books too. Very.
    And that brings me to what I wanted to tell you – or rather myself – (Now I'm Le Bateau Ivre as well as the Volga boatman but always a boat for some reason and in stormy weather too).
    I do not think it's a jinx or being lazy (certainly not *that*) or not caring – the trouble has been that in long novels – facts are very comforting to me. Of course they are always distorted, twisted, changed and so on. But all the same they are there. When I was despairing I could say *this happened*. So I could manage Part I because I *did* go to a convent. (I was 16 when I came to England, not a child really.) The place I have called Coulibri *existed*, and still does. It is now owned by a Syrian called Ayoub Dib (I'm not making this up – it's true). He is very fond of champagne it seems – and so am I. So I only grudge it a very little. I like all Eastern people too – count Syrians Eastern – and how I wish I

could have been one of these people who could just sit behind a screen and write poems or songs but otherwise protected. I'd have been very happy I think and not minded anything else. *Much* better than Cheriton Fitz and being such a storm tossed boat. *Well there's Part I explained.* The end was also possible because I *am* in England and can all too easily imagine being mad. (So can you I guess, by now.) It's a bit risky perhaps imagining madness, but risks have to be taken. It was this Part II which was so impossibly difficult. I had no facts at all. Or rather I had one – the place. Again a real place. It was a small "estate" my father bought. "Coulibri" was, for Dominica, an "old" estate – about 178-something (I rather think before that too) on sea level very fertile and so on. It had that feeling too of that time. The place my father bought was way up – mountains, forest – oh incredibly beautiful but *wild* – I do not like writing about places much. Still – a great effort and I could be back there, remember – *be* there. The characters though had to be imagined – not one real fact. Not one. No dialogue. Nothing. So what with my stormy private life – (no "stormy" isn't the word. More like one wave after another knocking me against rocks – you see am sticking to being a boat.)

(Do you know

"Oh mon Dieu
La mer est si grande
Ma barque est si petite"?)

Well – it seemed so hopeless – so plodding. Then you see I got right away from it and wrote what I call poetry and suddenly saw that I must lift the whole thing out of real life into – well *on* to a different plane. If it seemed melodramatic – then so much the worse. I remember so well strangers saying that Dominica was "theatrical" "mysterious" and so on. It *is dark* Dominica. Or was.

(I thought them very odd for I knew nothing else – then –)

Then I got this idea of making the last chapter partly "poetry" – partly prose – songs, anything and that is what I am sending to you. It is not finished or polished up at all. I may not have done it. If not – well – I wonder if I can do it any other way – now. I could I suppose shift the songs to the mad Part III and leave the man – whatever or whoever he is – down to earth.

Anyway it would be fun to do a whole *book* like that wouldn't it? I rather think somebody some time will. I do not mind criticism at all. Here was America calling – about "Midnight" 1939. "Dear Miss Rhys, I am sorry. Your novel is one behind the eight ball." England: "This is not a novel but a case history" or something like that. I am, as you see, still alive – though I must say I was a bit worried about the end myself. It was sent off while I was asleep – and the argument was still going on when Michael Sadleir rang up to say he liked it – so I didn't worry about it any more. I let it go. I wonder if I will post this?

I have to go to Crediton tomorrow but I'll post it, the MSS, this week end with corrections visible I'm afraid.

But legible I hope.

There is no great hurry for it. When you feel like looking at it – not before. There is a lot of other work.

I wonder too if I am terribly excited about something that has been done ages ago –

James Joyce tried to make sound I know like Anna Livia Plurabelle – but this is of course lighter, different – a musical comedy compared to grand opera.

Oh listen! I was in a *musical comedy* not a pantomime – all those years ago. A Viennese one too. As I stuck touring without perishing of cold must be deathless. *Two years* of it before I was ill and all the rest.

Oh I do hope *not* deathless.

Sincerely yours
Jean Rhys

I was going to tear this up as I tear up a lot that I write! "Not good enough" or "boring". But have decided to post it.

The MSS will reach you early next week.

I call it the MSS! I am already getting into a panic – so it'll probably be revised and watered down. J.R.

1. *Written by Harold Adamson, Edward H. Knopf and Jack King, this song was featured in Jean Harlow's film* Reckless *(1935)*.

TO FRANCIS WYNDHAM

Thursday 21st [May 1964]
Cheriton Fitz Paine

Dear Mr Wyndham,

Here (at last) is all I was so anxious for you to see. The red exercise books are the *last* chapter of Part II. The ruled paper is not the start, but nearly so, of Part II. (The first two chapters will stay as they were in the MSS with minor changes –) I can see already that Mr R's poetry will have to be cut or turned into prose I *think*. It's all only a *sketch* as it were, some important lines and clues have been left out. But you said Send it as it is so I'm doing just that.

Yesterday I heard from Christy & Moore about the other two books[1] – thank you for sending them – I will correct the printers errors and one or two (or 3) slips of mine. It will not take long – a day.

But I have such a *haunt* that they may publish the *skeleton* as my finished book. It's a ridiculous haunt I know, but it has happened twice to me – the last time was that extract which you saved. So it's a possible calamity. Not, I am sure, with Miss Athill and I'll write to her.

I think I'll take a few days rest now for I am a little tired. All "hurry up" letters send me into such a panic. They are no use for me – I can't do anything for two days after I get one. I know, of course, that though *I* think I am moving a mountain, *everyone else* thinks "*Why* doesn't she hurry up with that old feather duster?" – All the same – It isn't needed now. I wrote you a long letter yesterday which I won't send – it's full of quotations. But one I will repeat.

O mon bien! O mon beau!

Fanfare atroce où je ne trébuche point. . . . Well that is not true. I trébuche all the time. But *fanfare atroce* does ring all the bells. If ever I write again that will be the title (though *how* to translate it!) and as no fiction and no long and desperate effort trying to make something out of nothing it will be quick.

I could not get Dominica. Perhaps that can only be got (by me) sidelong, sideways – a throw away line as it were. If at all.

I put a red line near the bit I'll cut or rewrite. All wrong and not so. The solitaire has only one note – and *which way* is more like a cuckoo – two notes.

I am glad Diana likes them for so do I. But the Solitaire (the mountain whistler) is very wild and lovely and do hope there are some left – and not all trapped or something. You only hear them *high up*.

Well the Rimbaud quotation[2] ends:

"Nous avons foi au poison. Nous savons donner notre vie tout entière tous les jours."

That is the sort of thing I hang on my kitchen wall to cheer me up.

What I send is only a *sketch* at least the ruled paper is.

It is what was asked for and runs on to the letter which spoils this odd romance. Really it is done or nearly. *Why* am I writing all this? when it is so late 3 am –

I will have it all fixed up by summer. I did say *late* summer but nobody took any notice. Unless of course I die first. Here is another quotation.

> Then am I
> A happy fly
> If I live
> Or if I die

And another
   "One more effort gallant horse."
(I bet you don't know where that comes from.) Thank you for all you have done for me.
                                                                Yours sincerely
                                                                     Jean Rhys
I am posting the "experiment" in another envelope. Read it when you feel like doing so.

1. *André Deutsch was planning to republish* Voyage in the Dark *and* Good Morning, Midnight.

2. *From* Matinée d'Ivresse.

May 24th [1964]
                                                                Cheriton Fitz Paine
Dear Diana,
      [. . . . . .]
   I have corrected the two novels Christy & Moore asked for – the revisions in "Voyage in the Dark" are small but important – making it a better book – for

now 1964. For the other, its mostly printers errors (two bad ones) and too many dots. . . .

Though sometimes perhaps dots . . . are useful instead of saying "What crap!" Or *what* a lie! – Or even – Poor me! –

I struck a book yesterday written about the nineteen twenties in Montparnasse. Not an Englishman. Very good. Very. Especially as he stressed something that no one here realises at all. The "Paris" all these people write about, Henry Miller, even Hemingway etc was not "Paris" at all – it was "America in Paris" or "England in Paris". The real Paris had nothing to do with that lot – As soon as the tourists came the *real* Montparnos packed up and left. Here is an extract, "They're nice aren't they? These so called artists with dollars and pounds sterling at the back of them all the time! As immoral as they dare . . . and when they return to their own countries it's always on the back of Paris they put everything they have done. Considering that no Parisians will have anything to do with them. . . ."

That is quite true. And if I saw something of the other Paris – it's only left me with a great longing which I'll never satisfy again.

You see – I have never liked England or most English people much – or let's say I am terrified of them. They are a bit terrifying don't you think? I suppose not. It's a matter of "coping".

But really when I think of well-washed Stella[1] hovering about Ford, polishing him up to meet visiting Anglo Saxons and *now* what happens? Years and years afterwards, all the British papers saying he never cleaned his teeth! I find it a bit sad. He'd have been so hurt – and really not true. It's this awful mixture of being *very* naive and being *very* spiteful – *they* are I mean – that makes me such a coward. So *unterglubstammilch*. I've just made that word up. Isn't it fine?

Anyhow this book has woken me up as some books do. So I'm determined not be killed by loneliness whatever way I die –

You said you read my letters.

Here's hoping
Jean

1. *Stella Bowen, the Australian painter with whom Ford Madox Ford was living when Jean knew him.*

TO FRANCIS WYNDHAM   *Wednesday 27th [May 1964]*
                                              Cheriton Fitz Paine

[. . . . . .]

Dear Mr Wyndham,
    Thank you for the very kind letter and I am glad that you like what I sent, though a bit nervous that it's been handed over to Deutsch (Miss Athill). She

may not have time for reading before she leaves on the 2nd, and three weeks is so long to wait. (That can be done of course) but supposing it gets *lost* meantime? I have no copy.

[. . . . . .]

As to what I wrote – The book *as a whole* must be considered and if Mr X's poems get in the way then I will scrap them or turn them into prose.

As to this strange love affair. Well I have the death wish myself and always have had, so can write about it. As to what *he* thinks – it's guessing. I do not know and can't do it the usual way – by dialogue because I'm uncertain about *that*. Indeed all through the dialogue has been a stumbling block. I can remember. I *can* record speech. But I was not listening in 1840. Well it'll go I think – for I do not believe it was so different, and one can always scrap. I feel that I have failed in one important link. I want the man to fall in love with the *place* however unwillingly – the girl becomes a symbol of the elusive place. But not (he thinks) elusive. Well that's enough of that – I will get it, if at all, sideways and throwaway –

Now what's the next thing. Except of course, Why the effort to make a run of the mill "romantic novel" into something else. Because I could not help it. It walked in on me.

All I can do now is to get it all tidy for a typist. I will do that. I'm starting tomorrow. It's done.

Meanwhile I'd like to tell you about a book I read which helped me[1] when I was very down. It is by a man who was a poet manqué and who knew me well – I would like to send it to you for I think that however unflattering his idea of me, it would show you that for a long time, for years, I escaped from an exclusively Anglo Saxon influence and have never returned to it.

Of course *why* I was thought a doll when I was young by *everyone*, even by him, I do not know. Now of course I am no longer a doll, but a kind of a ghost. Never to be taken very seriously anyway. It's just like that and one of those things. And who cares?

Last night I bought some whisky and drank a lot. Then I thought I'd try to write a calypso – A real calypso is not thought out. It's done on the spot – Words and music. The audience judges who's best. At least that's how it *was*. So I gave myself a little time and had a whisky and wrote this. I meant to call it *Montparnasse 1925*. But enough has been said about *that* and a few (?) lies too [. . . . . .] One day if I live I'll write "Fanfare atroce" though more atroce than fanfare. Especially now. Never mind. Thank you again a thousand times.

Sincerely yours
Jean Rhys

Calypso 1964

I dreamt about Judas
   Last night, last night
I dreamt about Judas
   Kissing

I dreamt about trees
Last night, last night
I dreamt about trees
Watching

I dreamt about God
Long night, lost night
I dreamt about God
Weeping

Oh I dreamt about Jesus and I dreamt about Judas
And I dreamt about trees
Watching
I dreamt about Jesus and I dreamt about Judas
Weeping

J.R.

Whisky Song (I got the tune too)
"Another allegory Mrs Jansen?"
from *Good Morning Midnight*

1. Barred by Edward de Nève (a pen-name used by Jean's first husband, Jean Lenglet). This novel covered the same set of events as that described in Quartet, *but from the point of view of the young husband who loses his wife while he is in prison. Jean translated it from the French and worked hard to find a publisher for it, eventually placing it with Desmond Harmsworth in 1932.*

TO FRANCIS WYNDHAM
Friday [June 5th 1964]
Cheriton Fitz Paine

Dear Mr Wyndham,

I am sending the book I spoke of – not, as the writer says very gay but interesting perhaps. It's rather battered.

[. . . . . .]

As you'll see the writer of this book thinks of me as without will power, unable to fight, languid, indolent, a kind of a shadow. Yet I wonder very much – I wonder – if that's all – I wonder. I'm sending it because he was brave gentle and a poet. And would not have minded.

I got to know the Santé and Fresnes very well – what odd places I half understood! In any case he influenced me greatly and for keeps. (It's strange that he didn't know it, or I show it). Far more than anyone else ever has done, or will do. Anyway I'm for the second time rescuing his forgotten book. So please read it. This place is more dreadful and damaging too, than any prison to me. Don't like the "feeling" of it. Not one bit. It's not regular. Never mind!

I do feel that everything I care for is being threatened. (Such big battalions too.) And I fight back so feebly. All the same I will not desert. I'm "regular". You'll know the meaning of that if you read "Barred". I can't think of any jokes today.   Yours sincerely
                                                                          Jean Rhys
The book is, like mine on the same subject, partly fiction, very partly.

I think mine is more true to facts – his to the spirit. (Perhaps again?) The Santé and Fresnes fact.

Oh dear c'est une vaste blague but goes on too long altogether. After all brevity is etc, and whatever orders things (*I* think Satan in person) does so love a long long drawn out bit of fun.

                                                                               J.R.

Saturday 19th [June 1964]
                                                                     Cheriton Fitz Paine

> I am sending this because I am a bit
> sad and lost feeling, and wanted someone
> to talk to on paper. Being able to
> write to you even untidily helps me a
> lot for I have been rather sad. Please
> believe that.

Dear Mr Wyndham,
    I am glad you liked "Barred" though it is a grim book in parts – I do not quite know why I looked at it after years, or why I sent it to you. An "accident" like so many other things. Like my translating it – for I did, and it's oddly comforting that you saw something of my writing in it for I tried to follow the book itself closely, though it had to be cut and arranged a bit. – Confusing. Not anything about the Santé and Fresnes, but what happened afterwards.

    I went to see Maryvonne who was then at a convent in Weerden. (This happened after our divorce and I'd married again.) I found him – the writer of the book – very unhappy. He'd finished this very long and, yes, auto-biographical mostly, novel in French, but made no attempt to publish it. So I took the MSS back to London and worked at it with rage, fury and devotion. Desmond Harmsworth published it.

    I'm afraid I did leave out some of his bitter remarks about me but left some in. (The same went for the nice ones). "The Sidi" in the "Left Bank" was a story he told me about the Santé but it was of course his experience and his life.

    It was a very little thing to do and it did help a bit I think, for "Barred" did fairly well in Holland and Scandinavia and then he got on to an Amsterdam paper.

No I don't *think* he influenced my writing, but he influenced me tremendously which is the same thing. So of course did Paris and my life there with him.

I'm afraid I can't write about it coherently so won't try.

I was such a hunted haunted creature when I left London long ago and I became almost alive and self confident for a time. Well. Self confident! Alive! Nearly.

Anyway I'll tell you what happened to "Jan". We often met, and once when he was very ill in Italy he asked me to come to him and I went. One evening at Fiesole, when he had recovered, was a lovely evening. We talked about Maryvonne mostly. She was in Holland when the Germans arrived and they both joined the Resistance (of course). She was about sixteen then – but helped him with an Underground paper. When they were caught (or betrayed) she was sent to prison. He was to be shot but it was a concentration camp instead. Of course others were involved, two were shot. Maryvonne was released after a few months in prison. They thought her too young to be dangerous, I suppose. They were wrong – for she got in touch with the Resistance people at once and was very useful for she is cool, a good bluffer, and an "Aryan". An attractive one I think which helped too. I knew nothing of what had happened, for though I tried every way I couldn't get a letter through. I heard once indirectly that she was safe – that was in 1942. Then nothing – till the end of the war. "Jan" survived the concentration camp but his health was badly damaged. However he went to Warsaw on some Dutch Government thing and married again. Happily. Then I believe to Moscow. When his health broke down completely he lived in Amsterdam. He wrote to me a few days before he died and asked me among other things, never to give up writing. (About 2 years ago that was.)

Please do not think of this as a sad story for it isn't quite for me. Leaving London was a great gain. I cannot imagine what would have become of me if I hadn't – or rather can. Besides it alarms me.

It was *such* an escape! – and to such a new, but in an unexplainable way – a *known* world – a déjà vu world when I did. Nearly all my memories of those years are alive – many are happy and exciting. I loved Vienna and Buda Pest.

I think that "Jan's" Polish wife was kind and sweet, and Maryvonne loved him very much. So did he her. So he was not lonely or deserted.

As for Maryvonne's adventures as a "gun-girl" and her narrow escapes, she has never spoken of them – till last time she was here when she said casually . . . "When I got into the cell I saw . . . " She talked for a long time, stopping sometimes to sing "West Side Story" songs. I know that Resistance stories are old hat, but not perhaps the dead pan, almost joking way she told hers. Such fantastic bravery some of these Resistance people had. So many died.

If I were one hundredth part as cool and calm – and day in day out steady – *cynically hopelessly* brave. *What* wouldn't I give! –

I've been in a very blue mood lately for though I still can make wild leaps at difficulties there are awful pits of despair. I'm *not* day in day out steady and that is needed.

284

Is this book any good? *Have* I got anything of that far away time. A vanished time? Does André Deutsch like it at all? Does anybody? – Do you? I mean *sans blague*? Does Diana Athill?

I don't think the last MSS I sent you was much good but some sentences may bridge a gap.

Well I am slowly climbing out of the despair – so I must sweep the kitchen. It looks like Fagin's den now. Oh dear! I mean it looks gruesome – A bit.

But you know Cheriton Fitz is rather gruesome in its way – in spite of lovely weather.

I'm going to get a gramophone and Edith Piaf's records. Also some others. Ella Fitzgerald I like. Some others – yes – then I will *Cheer Up* – I think, and make one last frantic effort.

Then if I am still alive I'd like to write one book with no hopes. But no despair. A real one.

Oh yes, to finish Maryvonne's story. They worked in pairs. She married the man she worked with and they went to Indonesia for a long time. – He is nice.

Yours sincerely
Jean Rhys

[. . . . . .]

TO MARYVONNE MOERMAN

July 28th [1964]
Belvedere Clinic, Exe Vale Hospital
Exminster, Devon

My Dear Maryvonne,

I think that Edward has written to you[1] my dear. Well – I've been feeling rather rotten for some time, but am a good deal better now.

So – if it will mean a great disturbance of your plans do not worry to come.

On the other hand it *might* be a very good thing if you could manage it, even for a week or two. I can stand expense of your journey. [. . . . . .] So – *it will help if you come – but if too much upset of plans – Don't.* Better write Edward your decision. I'll be all right!

Enclosed an answer to a sweet letter I had from Ruthie. She gave me her address on back of envelope but I can't quite make it out.

All my love
Jean

July 28th [1964]

Darling Ruthie,

Thank you for your lovely letter. It made me think of the sun, wine, France, and all nice things. I'm so glad too that you are good at English and quite good (I bet) in French. *You don't know what a help it'll be later on.* Even if it's a mix up at first, it gets sorted out.

Listen – if you want a tan and no freckles why not try sun oil. "Ambre Solaire" is best but there are others for sensitive skins. Sun-Tan Cool Tan and so on. I must say I love a brown skin – if it can be got.

285

I couldn't quite read your address so am sending this to Maryvonne.
I haven't been very well but am getting fine again.
A big hug and three kisses from

Ooma Jean

PS. You must make up a name for me but let it be a NICE one.

1. *Jean's brother, Colonel Rees Williams, also wrote to Diana Athill on July 28th, 1964: "My sister has been going downhill for some time and it was becoming increasingly obvious that she was in no state to continue to live alone, yet she would agree to nothing I suggested. A very sad but inevitable happening, I'm afraid. . . . I saw her on Wednesday last, the day she was admitted to hospital, and again yesterday. Already much improved and calmer and the doctor and nursing staff most helpful. But I'm afraid it is early days yet to say what the eventual outcome will be. . . . I don't know what the chances of getting Sargasso Sea finished to my sister's liking are likely to be. But let's hope. . . ."*

TO DIANA ATHILL

September 2nd [1964]
Cheriton Fitz Paine

Dear Diana,

[. . . . . .]

Yes, I've decided to come to London and break the Cheriton Fitz spell. It'll certainly be an Event for me – last time I was there to see Selma just before her broadcast – all that time ago. The BBC got me – us – a terrible hotel just off the Strand – nothing I pick could be worse.

My brother-in-law told me of a good one in Onslow Gardens but his letter has vanished. I'll write to him if he's available, or stick a pin in the Sunday papers advertisements.

I used to know Primrose Hill very well. I lived near there "after I came back to England" that watershed of my existence, and during the blitz too.

They wanted me to stay longer at the clinic, and I found this cottage incredibly small and dark when I got back. However I've got used to it. Isn't it alarming how quickly one gets used to things? And people? And – or – lack of people? Of course I like a small dark room to write in, but it's wise to break away for a bit perhaps.

When I remember how light heartedly I began this book! – I thought it would be easy – my God! Quite apart from illness, moves, catastrophes and ructions galore there's the effort to make an unlikely story seem possible and inevitable and right.

Part II has, of course, been the worst – pity me out on a limb without one fact, one line of dialogue – not a clue. Only the place which is or was really romantic, mysterious and beautiful – (But I failed to get that across).

So nothing but whisky to help and now it's time for another shot and another effort.

I hope you'll never get stuck in a book (I think not!) for it's like lifting a too heavy weight. N'importe. .

Yours
Jean

Saturday 21st [November 1964]
Nightingale Ward[1]
St Mary Abbots
Kensington

TO MARYVONNE MOERMAN

My dear Maryvonne,
   I can't write very well yet as you see, but this is to send my love and to tell you my new address. It is

> Surrey Hills Clinic,
> Tupwood Lane,
> Caterham,
> Surrey

a convalescent home where I can stay for two or three weeks. Afterwards I don't know but I will write. I still feel very weak.
   I loved seeing you though I was too ill to say so. I thought you looked well and "very pretty" – as Lily would say in spite of your cold. But I am glad that has gone.
   Lots of love and luck to everyone.

Yours always
Jean

1. *During the night after her arrival in London Jean suffered a serious heart attack and was admitted to hospital, where she had to remain for almost a month. Two months in nursing homes followed, at first in Surrey, then in Exeter. For the rest of her life her heart condition was controlled by medication.*

TO DIANA ATHILL

December [1964]
Surrey Hills Clinic

[. . . . . .]

My dear Diana,
   It was very nice to hear from you. I guessed that you were busy – and then Christmas! I will be leaving here quite soon, on the 5th Jan. I think and am not looking forward to the journey but it's just a bad moment to pass. My address will be 19 Morton Road, Exmouth. Though not for long I hope. I think it would be better to go to Cheriton as soon as I can. A good deal of the *corrected* Part II is there already and some more stuff that I meant to send. It's difficult to get at.

Do *not*, if you can help it, get the MSS set in galleys, they are a bit difficult to work from – and the corrections are extensive. I know how very long I've been, but things have got me down, then just as I saw daylight *this* happened!

I am certainly better than I was, and will be well enough to finish the book as I should wish. Or I'll try. I've always known that it wasn't right yet, and if you have time to read it through carefully I'm certain you will see what I mean.

I admit that some of the changes I meant may not be necessary. One gets fussy and I'll try to do it as quickly as possible you may be sure of that. I wish I could have talked to you about it, but I was too ill at the hospital and this place is crowded, noisy and very difficult to get at, I believe.

I feel as if I'd been ill for months – well I have. However I'm able to walk about and so on, rather groggily, and am able to think about things. I always was. You were so very kind – what a bother I must have been.

I do hope 1965 will be a very lucky year for you.

And for me!

Love
Jean

February 21st 1965
TO DIANA ATHILL   Caroline Nursing Home
                                                      Exmouth, Devon
My dear Diana,

I was glad to hear from you. When you wrote to the Surrey Hills place in December last year I answered at once. Then I tried again. Finally asked Mr Smith to telephone. As I had no reply from *him* I decided to wait for news, though I was very worried.

It's a relief that the book is not in galleys and I'll do my best to get all revisions done by the end of April. That gives me six or seven weeks and I'll let you if I fail then go ahead. I think the most helpful thing now would be to get a typescript of Part II done as quickly as possible. As there is some money in hand perhaps you could do this for me. It would be very kind of you.

[. . . . . .]

I should like to have had May as well as March and April. There used to be an autumn list and a Christmas one, but I suppose it all takes longer than I thought. I mean I'd imagined a short step between galleys and print!

Don't despair of me or of my book please. I do understand what you mean, and it is a great temptation to let it slide. But I feel I could improve it, it means a lot to me, and it's my responsibility too. Indeed it really is my responsibility.

I am going to Cheriton early in March. No, I haven't anyone to spoil me, and the doctor and my brother (of course) are very pessimistic – which isn't cheerful. But I think I'll be all right. I haven't much choice, for I'm not really as good as new, so can't look for a place myself.

Those I hear of are very unsuitable. Exmouth is a rum place and antipatica I feel.

I fear that my wretched illness has caused delay and trouble. I knew it would be so – that was the reason of my "emotion" in the awful hospital. I was too weak to argue.

However I'll keep as well as I can, and do revisions by end of April if I can have Part II in type. Please let me have a few lines about this.

Yours
Jean

[. . . . .]

February 24th [1965]
Caroline Nursing Home

Dear Selma,

I am still here and feeling dreadfully upset and worried about many things that are happening. As soon as I can get a bit calmer I will write to you.

I had a letter from Mr Smith about an agreement with you. I will sign it[1].

I should not have come down to Exmouth it was an awful mistake. But so many things that I do are awful mistakes I feel! I'm feeling horribly friendless and under the weather – I do hope I can get some courage from somewhere and be able to go on.

Yours as always
Jean

I will return to Cheriton early next week.

1. *When Selma visited Jean in Devon in July, 1963, she asked her to sign a paper about the broadcasting rights of* Voyage in the Dark, Good Morning, Midnight *and the novel which Selma called* The First Mrs Rochester. *Jean (who later said that she was rather drunk at the time and thought the whole thing a joke) did so. What she had actually signed was an agreement giving Selma fifty per cent of all proceeds from any film, stage, television and radio adaptations of any work by Jean, anywhere in the world, to last until the works came out of copyright, and also granting Selma sole artistic control of such adaptations (which would probably have meant that Selma would insist on doing the adaptations and on playing the leading roles). Selma had now got the agent John Smith to prepare a more formal document stipulating the same terms. He asked Jean if she really wanted to sign it, and apparently she felt bound to do so. Later, when she had finished* Wide Sargasso Sea *and it was about to be published, Jean understood the implications of the agreement, and her anxiety about these, and her feeling that Selma had tricked her, clouded any pleasure she may have had from the success of the book. Repeated attempts were made by Jean's publishers to persuade Selma to cancel, or at least to modify, this agreement, but she remained obdurate and legal advice taken on Jean's behalf confirmed that the document signed by Jean had the binding force of a contract. Diana Athill asked the distinguished theatrical agent, Margaret Ramsay, to intervene, because she was an old friend of Selma's as well as having been her agent; and she, by her tact and firmness, was able to persuade Selma to waive the clause giving her complete artistic control and to reduce her share from fifty per cent to thirty-three and a*

third. This final agreement is still in force, and a large proportion of the posthumous earnings, which Jean was so anxious should go to Maryvonne, goes instead to Selma's heirs. Margaret Ramsay acted for Jean from that time onwards in all matters concerning film, theatre, television and radio rights.

TO MARYVONNE MOERMAN   *February 25th [1965]*
                                              Caroline Nursing Home

My dear Maryvonne,
     I was so pleased to hear from you. No I did not think it strange of you not to come – at all. I knew that it would be difficult. But I have been several weeks at this nursing home, and it has been terribly expensive – I daren't think how much. (The place Edward found was too crowded, three people to one room. So I came here.) I would very much rather have given the money – nearly £200 – to you. I thought that if you thought of being with me for three weeks as a job, a chore, you might find it worth while. But I do understand the difficulties, and that you didn't think you could leave Ruthie and Job. There is no news except a new murder every day. Life is so expensive that it is not possible to breathe without paying, but there is nothing to be done about that. My illness has lasted for so long, and I'm so tired of hospitals and nursing homes that I can't feel very gay. I can only just keep going, but that is nearly at an end. I am returning to Cheriton Fitz next Monday. It has many drawbacks but one great advantage. I am *free* there – and I've always had "Give me Liberty or give me Death" as my slogan. In nursing homes one isn't free at all, and as for hospitals . . . !! There was a Dutch girl at the London hospital and every time I wrote you or had a letter she'd say, "Who do you know in my country?" She was rather nice.
     Yes I heard from Selma yesterday, she wants to do a bit of my book on the BBC, so I must spur myself to arrange it.
     I'm worried over that book. My illness came at the very *worst* time of course. Still, I hope you can come over in the summer and cheer me up and I will try to be gay. You are right. It is the small things that count. They make one enjoy life (Or not!) Perhaps a better time is coming after such a long bad one. I wish I could see the suits you are making – but perhaps I will some time.
     Much love to all especially to you.

                                                         Jean

TO DIANA ATHILL   *March 24th [1965]*
                                              Chilton Fitz Paine

My dear Diana,
     Yes I got the typescript all right and your letter.
     I feel a lot more calm about things now, though still a bit puzzled about the

best thing to do. I came here because I thought it, with all its drawbacks, a good place to work in. But the weather has been terrible, gales rain fog just about everything. Today is a little better but still a gale blowing, and an impatient woman waiting to post this letter. That is the worst part of this illness one's horrible dependence on other people! But the doctor assures me that I shall be well again so I've got to believe him.

She's just come in again and reminded me that she's waiting so all I wanted to say must be wrapped up in thank you, and I will do what I wanted I hope, though I have to struggle against what seems a lot.

I will write again when things are more peaceful and I send you my love. Yesterday I had to go to Exeter, and the streets and people have left me bewildered. I feel that I've been ill for years not months! It will be famous to be well again.

Jean

I will do my best and all that you hope may happen. I re-read your book the other day. It was lying on the table and the farmer's wife who sometimes cooks for me remarked on the title. You know it made me feel a lot less lonely, thank you for writing it.

TO MARYVONNE MOERMAN   *August 4th [1965]*
                                                      Cheriton Fitz Paine
My dear Maryvonne,
    I was so glad to get your letter and hear your news. I would have asked you for Ruthie's address in Cambridge for I'd have loved to see her. But it's awfully dull here and not very comfortable. I thought it might make her sad. It's not so comfortable as before.
    "And yet" you must be thinking "you asked me to come."
    Yes I did ask you as one cries Help! when one is drowning. I am very lonely, bewildered and unhappy. I thought that to talk things over with a friend who understood, would help a lot. I do not think I ought to stay here. Edward's wife is very ill and I can't trouble him too much. Besides he does not understand. But perhaps it was a very selfish thought, for it is dreary here and rains from morning till night. Still, if you can *do* come even for a few days for I am too unhappy to write which is perhaps the worst thing that has happened, worse even than my illness which gets better but slowly. Very.
    I read a lot, and yes, I should like "A Moveable Feast" awfully for I am a Hemingway fan. I knew him by sight, tho not personally, but I liked what I saw. I remember, at a dance, watching him and thinking that he danced as if he were gay and loved life.
    You know you write English awfully well and I can't tell you how I love your letters.

Mine are, I'm afraid, not too grand. I do not feel gay but rather frightened. Not "rather" either.

It's as if for the time being, my courage has gone, and how do I know when it will come back.

So very hesitatingly I say *please* if you can come. If not write to me for I don't feel so bad then. I know and can guess all the difficulties though!

I hope Ruthie liked Cambridge and had a day or two's good weather.

I was there long ago when I first came to England.   Your loving
                                                                                    Jean
P.S. You used to write poetry. Do you remember?

TO MARYVONNE MOERMAN   *September 15th [1965]*
                                                                       Cheriton Fitz Paine
My dear Maryvonne,

I was glad to have your letter this morning, and would be even more glad to see you. You can help me very much indeed, but it is all too long and complicated to explain in this letter. I am quite alone here it is like a nightmare, so I will not talk about it. I've been here by myself since March and am now au bout.

I know that you cannot stay longer than a fortnight, but it will mean a lot to me.

If it wasn't very urgent I would not bother you. So when you get this come if you can and I did enjoy the Hemingway but it wasn't very truthful I think. Everyone sees people differently. However he says at the start that it may be read as fiction! Anyway it was very interesting and thank you.

It is not quite so cold today. I wish you were here so much and send my love and best wishes to all. Especially to you I send my love and I hope that you will understand and come soon if it's possible,   from yours with love
                                                                                    Jean
I know quite well that it may be difficult and seems a great deal to ask. I'm glad about the French.

TO MARYVONNE MOERMAN   *November 9th [1965]*
                                                                       Cheriton Fitz Paine
My dear Maryvonne,

I'm so sorry that you've hurt your back – is it quite well again – and have you central heating for the winter on its way? (I think you said you hadn't.) It has been pouring with rain all day, and I've just remembered that I left my umbrella in the taxi so I must break off and go and fetch it before it starts again –

Have got it! No adventures except a large yellow dog sitting in the middle of the road growling and barking at everyone who tries to pass.

These huge dogs are a special Cheriton Fitz Paine breed I think, and I can't say I like them! But it is an unpopular opinion.

About three or four weeks ago the doctor started me on a new treatment – did I tell you? Life is far less of a nightmare but I still find it awfully difficult to concentrate on my book, simply stage fright I expect. I ought to see Miss Athill but am too wobbly to go up to London, do so dread another collapse. Stage fright again!

Such a funny existence here. I go to bed at *eight* p.m. Can you imagine it? But by that time it's been dark for *hours*. So I take a shot of whisky (which is too expensive really) and pretend it's bedtime. Then at three or four am I'm broad awake. So I toss and turn a bit, then get up, still in the dark, and go into the kitchen for tea. It is, funnily enough, the best part of the day. I drink cup after cup, and smoke one cigarette after another, and watch the light, if any, appear at last.

It is the one nice thing about this place. I can prowl around at these strange hours and nobody is disturbed. I think a lot about you and try to imagine your house (red staircase nice) and one day I had a brain wave. Don't laugh at it. Why don't you start a "boutique"? They are springing up all over the place in London – sometimes, on not much capital they say, and I'm sure they have not half your talent and taste. Then Ruthie could be your partner. *Think about it.* I know it is awful hard work but awfully interesting too. Then when you can somehow meet me I will be a client. Please make me what I call my *last dress*. I should so love it and know just how I want it. By the way I simply hate these *very* short skirts they are trying to force on the world. Most women will look so awful in them! They were pretty short in the twenties but not like that! By "they" I mean the London group.

Well what other news have I for you. I force myself out for a walk every day and could meet these awful Cheriton dogs, and strings of cows ambling along. Cows have a most inquisitive way of looking at you. Will you wish me luck and the courage to finish my book and I will wish you luck with your "boutique". Do not turn down the idea without thinking it over. Then you will make me my last dress and first pretty one for a long long time. With love and hugs and my love to all,

Jean

TO MARYVONNE MOERMAN *Monday [November 1965]*
Cheriton Fitz Paine

My dear Maryvonne,

I was awfully pleased to hear from you so soon. About the French I always think that the most important thing is to learn to speak it, next to read it (or perhaps the other way round) and Grammar comes last. But I'm awfully bad at languages. After all I was two years in Vienna and Buda Pest – all I learned was "Vas kostes?" "Vie gates?" and spatzien and those are spelt wrong! I learned "spatzien" because a little maid we had called Dini, used to take me by the arm saying spatzien and walk me up and down. French it was mostly "argot".

And that stuck. But I can read it fairly easily.

And about the boutique well I suppose Rotterdam isn't a good place and the rules and regulations apply to Amsterdam as well. (There are plenty of snags about Socialism here too I can tell you!)

Do you know what I did long long ago, before I ever met John[1]. I joined up with another girl who could make hats and we had a corner of an establishment, a dress shop, in Bond Street and there we sold hats. She made them, I sold them. We had a tiny room upstairs and a bell rang whenever a customer came for hats. Well my dear I made a rotten saleswoman as you can imagine – I was always trying to sell hats that were becoming, instead of expensive hats and the effort didn't last long. Still it was a sort of forerunner of the boutique I suppose.

I don't know how Dawn made the arrangement (Dawn was the other girl's name) but she was a very business like person and she managed it somehow.

I have stupidly caught cold and a bit of 'flu. I had meant to go to Exeter tomorrow but perhaps ought not to. But Cheriton is a dreadful place. There are no shops and nothing to be had. And a wind like a knife that never stops.

I must go now to the doctors.

All my love. Will write for Christmas.

Jean

1. *Jean Lenglet, Maryvonne's father.*

TO FRANCIS WYNDHAM   *January 28th [1966]*
                                            Cheriton Fitz Paine
Dear Mr Wyndham,

I hope Miss Hughes[1] has got in touch with you. Her address is 60 Charrington Street NW1. I don't think she has copies of all the stories. Art & Literature have bought three more and there is one in this month's magazine[2]. She also took "Postures" – but hasn't got Mackenzie.

Mr Smith seemed to despair of them, so it seemed all right to say OK. The situation is a bit complicated though, so I must write to him this week-end and explain.

Some weeks ago I had a letter from a Mr Mizener[3] of Cornell University. He asked if I had any letters from Ford, as Cornell would buy them if I had. (He is writing a life of F.M.F.) Of course I had nothing to sell. He also wanted to know about the translation of Perversité.

I did that ages ago and when it appeared my agent wrote to ask about it, for I hadn't been told that I was "ghosting". It was Covici the publisher's fault, and

I know Ford did his best to put things right. Then the book was banned and I heard no more about it. Mr Mizener said that a lot of ink had been spilled, which surprised me, for several people knew I was doing it at the time. I wasn't very pleased with the translation for it had to be done in a hurry and there was a good deal of slang.

Mr Mizener read "Postures" and "Mackenzie" in the British Museum, and said he thought he could sell them as paperbacks in America.

I believe he's gone back to America now. I gave John Smith's address as my agent so you see it is a bit complicated, however I daresay it will sort itself out.

I must post this before it gets too dark.   Sincerely yours
                                                                  Jean Rhys

1. Olwyn Hughes (sister of the poet Ted Hughes) had visited Jean earlier in the month and Jean had asked her to act as agent for The Left Bank, Postures/Quartet, After Leaving Mr Mackenzie *and all her uncollected short stories. John Smith of Christy & Moore remained the agent for* Voyage in the Dark, Good Morning, Midnight *and the as yet unpublished* Wide Sargasso Sea. *Jean's situation regarding her agents was to grow increasingly complicated until 1975, when Anthony Sheil became the sole agent for all her books.*

2. "I Spy a Stranger"; Art and Literature *had also bought "The Sound of the River", "The Lotus" and "Temps Perdi".*

3. Arthur Mizener's biography of Ford Madox Ford, The Saddest Story, *was published in 1971.*

TO DIANA ATHILL   *February 15th [1966]*
                                                                  Cheriton Fitz Paine

My dear Diana,

This morning I had a letter from the Royal Literary Fund. They sent me a cheque for £300, and will give me this yearly for five years.

I feel as if not a peach[1], but a rock, had banged me on the head – quite dazed – so this letter's going to be rather incoherent.

I'm so used to wondering what on earth's going to happen to me in a few months time that I haven't quite taken it in really. However doubtless I will tomorrow.

What I have taken in is that you did your very best for me and so did Mr Deutsch they say.

Will you thank him for me, and many many thanks to you.

I expect you can guess how I feel, for though one can get accustomed to anxiety, it's not an awfully good thing. I mean it's *there* all the time, and cramps one considerably in the end.

So thank you Diana, and will you thank Mr Deutsch for me. I won't bother him with a letter.

Now I want to talk about the book for a while. I am working on the last bit – the end.

Sometimes I have to force myself but I do force myself.

I have this idea that all difficulties can be solved, and all put right by *cutting* – in fact I nearly wrote to you and suggested cutting all Part III, ending it in Jamaica and calling it Prelude to Thornton House or Thornfield or whatever. But that won't do.

So I will struggle on and try to make it as convincing as possible.

I can see it all up to a point. I mean a man *might* come to England with a crazy wife. He *might* leave her in charge of a housekeeper and a nurse and dash away to Europe. She *might* be treated far more harshly than he knows and so get madder and madder. He *might* funk seeing her when he returns. But really, to give a house party in the same house – I can't believe that. But then I've never believed in Charlotte's lunatic, that's why I wrote this book and really what a *devil* it's been.

Don't take all this too seriously. I do feel a bit light headed as I told you.

I hope to send you Part III by the end of this month. When you send me the typescript I'll go through the whole book. There's an addition in Part I, some deletes in Part II but No additions and No chapters.

Then it will be really ready as it should have been from the first of course.

Yours
Jean

The answer is delete house party. Well I will as far as possible.

It's got quite dark while I've been writing this so can't post it till tomorrow.

1. *This is a reference to a description in Diana Athill's autobiographical book of a glorious surprise being like a beautiful great peach falling out of a tree and hitting one on the head.*

TO DIANA ATHILL   *Sunday 20th [1966]*
                                                      Cheriton Fitz Paine
My dear Diana,

(I want very much to write to you but this is the only paper I have today).

I am very delighted about what has happened of course. I wonder *what* made Hamish Hamilton think of me[1] after so long – I suppose I'll never know. I've written to tell him how pleased and grateful I am [. . . . . .]

I wish it had happened before, instead of after, my crack up but that's asking too much of "Dominica luck" which is supposed to be very uncertain to say the least of it.

Now about my book. I have finished it and will post the last part to be typed early next week – if you let me have one copy I'll put the whole thing together.

Please read this some time, though I always imagine you very busy.

I came to England between sixteen and seventeen, a very impressionable age and Jane Eyre was one of the books I read then.

Of course Charlotte Brontë makes her own world, of course she convinces you, and that makes the poor Creole lunatic all the more dreadful. I remember being quite shocked, and when I re-read it rather annoyed. "That's only one side – the English side" sort of thing.

(I think too that Charlotte had a "thing" about the West Indies being rather sinister places – because in another of her books "Villette" she drowns the hero, Professor Somebody, on the voyage to Guadeloupe, another very alien place – according to her.)

Perhaps most people had this idea then, and perhaps in a way they were right. Even now white West Indians can be a bit trying – a bit very (not only white ones) but not quite so awful surely. They have a side and a point of view.

Well years and *years* afterwards the idea came to me to write this book.

I started off quite lightheartedly thinking I could do it easily, but I soon found out that it was going to be a *devil*, partly because I haven't much imagination really. I do like a basis of fact. I went on – sometimes blindly.

Part I was not too hard, but by Part II I'd quite abandoned the idea of "Jane Eyre".

There were many unfortunate marriages at that time and before – West Indian planters and merchants were wealthy before sugar crashed – and their daughters were very good matches.

Some of the owners stayed in England and managed their estates through agents, but some didn't. Perhaps you know all this.

Well this was the story of one arranged marriage, with the bridegroom young, *unwilling*, rather suspicious and ready to believe the worst, not liking the semi tropics at all, and the bride poor bride very romantic, with some French or Spanish blood, perhaps with the seeds of madness, at any rate hysteria. The most seriously wrong thing with Part II is that I've made the obeah woman, the nurse, too articulate. I thought of cutting it a bit, I will if you like, but after all no one will notice. Besides there's no reason why one particular negro woman shouldn't be articulate enough, especially as she's spent most of her life in a white household.

So I only borrowed the name Antoinette – (I carefully haven't named the man at all) and the idea of her seeming a bit mad – to an Englishman.

Of course with Part III, I'm right back with the plot of Jane Eyre, leaving out Jane! I didn't know how else to end it. I didn't even know how to explain their entirely changed life, England not the West Indies, quite mad instead of a bit strange. I thought the best way out was to do it at once through Grace Poole. It *could* be done by putting it in the third person but perhaps that would lose something. I rather shiver at the idea of doing it *again*, but I will if you tell me that it would gain a lot in clarity. By it I mean Part III.

It wouldn't take long – it's casting about trying this way and that – takes the time. And the worry.

I mean all the action to take place between 1834 and 1845 say. *Quick*. My Antoinette marries very young, and when she is brought to England and shut up isn't much over twenty. Her confinement doesn't last long. She burns the house and kills herself (bravo!) very soon. I think she would become first a legend, then a monster, quickly. Charlotte may or may not have heard the legend but that is guesswork and impertinent because really I don't know. Now I must end this monstrous letter which please read when you're in the mood.

Yrs
Jean

Thank you Diana.

1. *It was Hamish Hamilton who had sponsored the application, made by André Deutsch and Diana Athill on behalf of Jean, for an award from the Royal Literary Fund.*

February 25th [1966]
Cheriton Fitz Paine

[. . . . . .]

My dear Olwyn,

[. . . . . .]

The situation about Selma is complicated as I told you.

She "discovered" "Good morning midnight" in a second hand bookshop, adapted it for the Third, and got in touch with me by advertising. Everything else – the book, some of the stories and so on followed. So when she was down here two or three years, more I think, ago she asked me to give her radio and television rights for (as I understood) "Midnight" and "Voyage". I said yes of course. I thought it only a joke really, but later on John Smith asked me to sign a more formal paper and I did so.

I don't remember about film rights but it may be so. She didn't seem at all interested in the stories, or my two first books – "Postures" and "Mackenzie" but started to do an adaptation of "Voyage in the Dark" (I did tell her it would be difficult). She wrote about it for a bit then must have dropped it for I heard no more.

In October 1964 I thought I'd better find out what was going on, and went up to London. However it wasn't a lucky journey for I got this damned heart thing in a day or two, and landed up in hospital. Selma came to see me there, but we didn't discuss "affairs" at all, I felt too rotten.

After this and that I found myself up here again last March (1965). I was very weak and had a *monumental* cafard.

I don't like to think of that time for I couldn't write and was pretty lonely and unhappy. I didn't hear from anyone either.

In October last I was able to work again and have managed to finish the book. I sent off the last part to be typed yesterday. There are still the proofs to be done which I dread for I am not used to them.

Selma is an actress and I thought that as I hadn't heard from her at all for well over a year, she'd given up all idea of adapting my books but still I did sign that paper. I promised to let her have an extract from book.

Please Olwyn if you can, do not give up the idea of the B.B.C. and stories. I think you can work it if anyone can. [. . . . .] I'd be quite willing to share any profits with her, Selma (and you needless to say) or perhaps *she* could read the stories?

She isn't very well and is worried about a play called "Sister George"[1].

I will finish Leaving School and Mr Ramage[2]. A bit sentimental perhaps, and the West Indies as they *were* sound unreal, but I can't help that. Can only write about them as I knew them – minus tourists.

I think it *might* be possible to sell a story to the New Yorker. They reviewed the first part of the new book in "Art and Literature" favourably I believe, though I didn't see the review. The trouble is they are all *too long*. "Petronella" is the best I think, but what an awkward length!

I'm all right – a touch of that old cafard sometimes, but nothing like the perfectly awful time between March and October last year which I wouldn't live again for millions.

There's a watery sun today after days and days and days of wind and rain. That wind oh dear it does shrivel one up.

I know there are a lot of snowdrops out for someone gave me a bunch, and there are two or three crocus(es) in my wild garden. Brave things! What enormous letters I write these days.

Yours
Jean

I've had a bit of luck with the Royal Literary Fund so am not so poverty stricken. I'd like to make this place a bit less gloomy, the trouble is *who* in Cheriton Fitz will do it.

I'll write to Selma tomorrow.

1. Selma had taken the part of Madame Xenia in Frank Marcus's The Killing of Sister George *when it opened at the Bristol Old Vic in April 1965. She was dropped from the cast before it reached London a year later, where it had a long and successful run.*

2. "Leaving School", which had been commissioned by Alan Ross for a London Magazine *series on this theme in November, 1962, eventually became "Overture and Beginners Please", published in* Sleep It Off, Lady *in 1976. "My Dear Darling Mr Ramage" was published in the London* Times *in June, 1969, and again in* Sleep It Off, Lady *as "Pioneers, Oh, Pioneers".*

TO SELMA VAZ DIAS   *March 3rd 1966*
                                                    Cheriton Fitz Paine
My dear Selma,

I am sorry and rather worried not to hear from you. I suppose you are busy or perhaps not well.

Please believe that I will send the extract and Part I along to you as soon as I have them myself and I do hope they'll be what you want. I simply *dare* not send the only copy I have.

I hope too that you will see (or write or phone) Miss Hughes.

I certainly understood that you weren't interested either in my stories or my first two books, and if the BBC take a story it will mean a great deal to me – I'm sure you understand that, for I sold a story and a radio play to radio Budapest through the "London" and you knew of that. I am quite willing to share any cash I may get with you, but if *no one* can handle my work, and you *do* not the situation will remain stagnant for good. That mustn't be for everybody's sake.

I will write to John Smith about the matter.

I am (as usual perhaps) in a terribly anxious position. Max is very ill indeed and yesterday I had an urgent phone call from the hospital. I wasn't well enough to go there this morning so am awaiting news. I went yesterday.

I think I will be seeing Alec. Perhaps if he could talk to you it would be a good thing.

I feel buried alive down here, everything moves with great slowness and I don't know what is happening.

I keep a tight hold of myself or I'd crack completely – again.

I do need all my friends, or even acquaintances, terribly badly, and am desperate about Max.   Yours as always
                                                                              Jean

TO MARYVONNE MOERMAN   *Monday March 4th [1966]*
                                                          Cheriton Fitz Paine

My dear Maryvonne,

So at last you are coming – I am so glad – you don't know!

There is only one thing worries me – it is a so bitterly cold.

Today is really awful and I am shivering as I write – the east wind is blowing through this ramshackle cottage like a tiger – no like a knife. So dress *very* warmly, bring all the warm things you can – as if you were going to the North Pole. A rug if you have it tho' I'm getting all the blankets I can. If it gets warmer suddenly, we can always buy something else.

But really it is *frightful* now. It will be so lovely to talk and give you my news (also hear yours) that I can hardly believe it.

I want to post this at once so that you are sure to get it.

Mr Greenslade will meet the one o'clock train, and I will be there too perhaps. Best love my very dear and to Ruth Ellen and everyone.
                                                                              Jean

TO DIANA ATHILL   *March 7th [1966]*
                                                      Cheriton Fitz Paine
My dear Diana,
    Alec Hamer who has been staying here has written to you I know.
    My husband who has been in hospital is very ill indeed now. He is not
conscious and does not know anyone.
    It is awfully difficult for me to write letters at present but I do want you to
know that I want to use any strength I have left to really finish Sargasso Sea.
    I have Part II. I will *delete* some lines. Two or three *additions* are needed to
Part I. Part III I sent to you (registered). Selma tells me you have it – I was
getting anxious. Could I have a copy?
    I am terribly sad, lonely and anxious but I do want to finish that book.
                                                                    Yrs
                                                                    Jean
I hoped for a respite so this has made me despair – almost.

TO DIANA ATHILL   *Wednesday March 9th [1966]*
                                                      Cheriton Fitz Paine
My dear Diana,
    Thank you for your letter. I don't know what else to say. Max died
unconscious, and this morning very early we went to the Exeter crematorium.
    A sunny day, a *cold* sun, and a lot of flowers but it made no sense to me.
    I feel that I've been walking a tight rope for a long, long time and have finally
fallen off. I can't believe that I am so alone, and that there is no Max.
    I've dreamt several times that I was going to have a baby – then I woke with
relief.
    Finally I dreamt that I was looking at the baby in a cradle – such a puny weak
thing.
    So the book must be finished, and that must be what I think about it really. I
don't dream about it any more.
    I am sorry for a sad letter and I send you my love.
                                                                    Jean

It's so *cold*

INDEX

GENERAL INDEX

Page numbers in *italic* type refer to the notes or the Introduction. When a subject is mentioned in the text and an accompanying note, only the text reference has been indexed; if the subject is referred to obscurely in the text, and is identified in the note, the letter "n." and the note number have been added in brackets after the page reference. (The notes themselves have been indexed only when they introduce new material.) The biographical details and publishing history on pp. 13–16 have not been indexed. A figure 2 in brackets after a page reference (without the letter "n.") means that the subject is referred to in two separate letters, or two notes, on the page. JR stands for Jean Rhys.

INDEX OF CORRESPONDENTS

References to Jean Rhys's correspondents in the text of the letters or in the editorial notes will be found in the General Index.